10 0136389 8

KT-233-010

Working Fam

Working Families:

Age, Gender, and Daily Survival in Industrializing Montreal

Bettina Bradbury

NOTTINGHAM UNIVERSITY LIBRARY

Toronto Oxford New York
Oxford University Press

Oxford University Press, 70 Wynford Drive, Don Mills, Ontario M3C 1J9

Oxford New York
Athens Auckland Bangkok Bombay
Calcutta Cape Town Dar es Salaam Delhi
Florence Hong Kong Istanbul Karachi
Kuala Lumpur Madras Madrid Melbourne
Mexico City Nairobi Paris Singapore
Taipei Tokyo Toronto

and associated companies in
Berlin Ibadan

Oxford is a trademark of Oxford University Press

Canadian Cataloguing in Publication Data

Bradbury, Bettina, 1949-
    Working families: age, gender, and daily survival in
industrializing Montreal

(The Canadian social history series)
Includes bibliographical references and index.
ISBN 0-19-541211-7

1. Working class - Quebec (Province) - Montreal - History -
19th century. 2. Montreal (Quebec) - Social conditions.
3. Family - Quebec (Province) - Montreal - History - 19th
century. I. Title. II. Series.

HN110.M6B48 1996   305.5'62'0971428   C96-930053-0

100136 3898

Cover image: Work: "You complain, my poor husband, of your ten hours of labour. Yet
I have been working for fourteen hours, and I have not yet finished my day." *L'Opinion
publique.* 2 novembre 1871. (National Archives of Canada, C129851)

This book has been published with the help of a grant from the Social Science
Federation of Canada, using funds provided by the Social Sciences and Humanities
Research Council of Canada.

Copyright © 1993 Bettina Bradbury

2 3 4 5   99 98 97 96

This book is printed on permanent (acid-free) paper ∞ .

Printed in Canada by Webcom

Contents

List of Figures

List of Tables

8

In memory of John Bradbury (1942-1988)

Acknowledgements

Family and work interact in most of our lives and in varying degrees at different moments of those lives. This book is about a period when, for the growing working class of cities like Montreal, the nature of the interaction between family and work was in the process of changing. The history and progress of this book have been closely tied to the unfolding of my own life, of the life cycle of my family, and of my ideas and the state of the literature over the years since it began as a doctoral dissertation at Concordia University.

The evolution of my work has been punctuated by family events, both happy and tragic, that have slowed down its progress. In ways I could never have anticipated and would never have wished, my own experiences followed the structure I had set out for the book, which proceeds from marriage, through an examination of the work roles of husbands, wives, and children, to an examination of how people managed in crises like the death of a husband or wife. I had been married for seven years when I began the research. The first paper I wrote based on that research was presented when I was pregnant with my first daughter, Anna. Emily was born before I managed to complete the thesis. It was further slowed down by the fact that my husband, John, had organized to have a year's sabbatical in New Zealand so we could be near our families there. It was completed in 1984.

Transformation of the thesis into a book went slowly, too, at first because of the energy required to learn to teach in French at Université de Montréal. Then John got stomach cancer, had a series of operations, went in and out of hospital, and came home to die. We were able to get through those months in large part because of the help of my mother, Elespie Prior, who came from New Zealand and helped with the washing, ironing, cleaning, and child care, freeing me to spend time with John. My neighbours helped perpetually by taking care of Anna and

11

Emily, giving them at least four homes on Oxford Avenue and proving that community continues to flourish in late twentieth-century cities. My thanks go to family members, neighbours, and friends who got us through those months. The book is dedicated to John, who wanted to see it finished, believed in what I was doing, and was proud when my work was well received.

Many other colleagues have contributed to the shape and content of the book over the years. Bob Galois taught both John and me the importance of a class-based analysis, a lesson we only learned by consuming many late-night beers in Vancouver pubs. At roughly the same time a women's reading group that included Lee Seymour, Suzanne McKenzie, and Susan Williams introduced me for the first time to feminist theory. In the years since then numerous women friends and colleagues have sharpened my awareness of feminist theory and provided support in a variety of ways. I think particularly of Veronica Strong-Boag, Marta Danylewycz, Frances Early, Joy Parr, and Andrée Lévesque. My thanks also to Ron Rudin, Katy Bindon, Jean-Claude Robert, Bill Hubbard, and Joy Parr for comments on the thesis version of the manuscript. Brian Young, Alan Stewart, Greg Kealey, Dominique Marshall, and Craig Heron have commented on various more recent versions, giving me hard criticism when necessary and the encouragement to continue. My graduate students have each in their own way provided stimulation, feedback, and encouragement, for which I thank them. Kathryn Harvey shared her feminism and material from the judicial archives, both of which have improved this manuscript. Special thanks to Yves Otis for doing all the graphs and the map. Errors of fact, unacceptable interpretations, and any other problems with the book remain my responsibility.

While doing this research I have benefited greatly from research grants received from both the Social Sciences and Humanities Research Council and the Fonds pour la formation de chercheurs et l'aide à la recherche, initially as a doctoral student and more recently for my work on widows, some of which is integrated into the final chapter. I am grateful for this support.

Introduction

Politics has its time. It is sometimes as important as social questions, but usually, and for the most of humanity, "What shall we eat?
What will we drink? How shall we be clothed?" are the questions
that take precedence over "how and by whom are we governed?"[1]

Families with more than one wage-earner are not a new phenomenon
today, whatever newspaper and journal articles, government reports,
or sociological literature dealing with the growing importance of married women's labour force participation might suggest.[2] Over one hundred years ago, when factories were just beginning to replace small
artisanal workshops in Canadian cities, workers' families invariably
included more than one earner at some point. Three and even more
wage-earners were not unusual. François Lusignan, a fifty-year-old
carpenter, for example, was the head of a dual-income family when the
census enumerator called at his house in Saint Jacques ward in the eastern part of Montreal in 1871. His twenty-year-old daughter Albina was
working as a seamstress. Ten years later eight members of François's
household reported having a job. Three daughters, aged seventeen to
twenty-seven, were seamstresses, a twenty-one-year-old son was a
painter, and a fifteen-year-old son was an apprentice painter. A female
relative and a female boarder who were living with the Lusignans also
both reported working by the day.[3] Only François's fifty-seven-year-
old wife, Elmire-Marie, reported no formal employment in either 1871
or 1881. Her work, largely invisible to the census-taker, was also crucial to the family's standard of living, especially in the years before any
children reached working age. Wives who managed and stretched the
wages of other family members, shopped with care, scrimped on their
own nourishment so that others would eat better, or took in boarders or
even a whole extra family to stretch the rent were performing work that

13

was vital to daily survival and to the reproduction of the working class. So, too, was the work of young boys selling newspapers, scrounging for firewood, or going daily from house to house gathering a herd of cows to take to pasture. Or of girls who stayed home from school or did not seek waged labour in order to look after younger siblings or a sick parent.

This book examines continuities and changes in the ways working-class men and women fed, clothed, and sheltered themselves and their families in the years between 1861 and 1891 when Montreal first became an industrial city. It addresses an old question. What was the impact of the industrial revolution on the family?[4] To answer the question, I argue, it is necessary to consider the work and roles of all family members, not just in the workplace but in their homes and on the streets. If we are to understand fully the significance of economic change, to grasp the wider ripple effects of the accumulation of capital, the re-organization of work, and the concentration of production in our history, we must look beyond the economy, narrowly defined, and beyond the factory and workshop. Working-class survival during the period of competitive capitalism depended as much on the unpaid or informal labour of women and children as it did on wages. Struggles and strategies originating in the household were as important to standards of living as those of workers on the job.

The combination of wage labour with a multitude of diverse other forms of work, revenue-generating and money-saving strategies, ensured the survival of working-class families in nineteenth-century Montreal. What was different then from today was that children, rather than wives, were the usual secondary wage-earners. These offspring, as in the case of the Lusignan family, were more often in their late teens or early twenties, rather than being young children, whose exploitation in factories has traditionally captured the attention of historians of the industrial revolution. Younger children's contributions were less visible and less formal. The other major difference from today was the absence of state support for the sick, unemployed, or needy. Families and individuals too poor to get by alone turned to neighbours, kin, and church-run charities for short- and long-term help, often forging dense webs of mutual aid, obligation, and interdependence within local communities.

To examine how the expansion of industrial capitalism in Montreal changed the bases of daily survival within working-class families I draw on concepts, methods, and approaches developed within working-class, family, and feminist historiography. Working-class historians in Canada have sought to understand the transformations of this period by focusing largely on the workplace. In so doing they have greatly enriched and changed our knowledge of the processes of industrial growth and of workers' reactions to it.[5] By going past the factory gates to other aspects of working-class culture, they have begun to broaden our knowledge of the working-class past, to unravel the complex, dialectical relationship between tradition and innovation in the shaping of class culture.[6] However, because such historians have looked mostly at skilled workers and at institutions related to their crafts, the role of other family members in working-class culture and survival are still too often neglected. Little Canadian working-class history explicitly bridges the fields of family, women's, and labour history.[7] Historians who have attempted to estimate the standards of living of Canadian workers have seldom completely ignored working women and children. Yet they tend to base their estimates on the wage of male workers alone, making no systematic attempt to incorporate consideration of the informal and unpaid work performed by other family members.[8] In a period when wage labour was not solidly entrenched and when the availability of work was irregular, it is essential to take other ways of making ends meet into account. By integrating consideration of women, other non-wage-earners, the family, and reproduction into this examination of daily survival, I hope to contribute to a history of the "totality of the working class"[9] and to a better understanding of the nature of the nineteenth-century urban economy.

Historians and sociologists who have studied the history of the family have placed most emphasis on how the growth of industry has modified family structures and demographic patterns.[10] Too often, early histories of the family presented the institution simply as a residential unit whose main interest lay in its structure, particularly in the question of whether the nuclear family was a product of industrialization.[11] In many ways, however, debates about the relative importance of nuclear or extended families diverted attention away from other important processes, strategies, and phenomena that are essential to understanding how families coped during periods of major economic transformation. This does not mean that structures are not important. The structure of families tells us much about people's daily lives. By showing who lived with whom they offer one indicator of the role of kin as a source of help in times of trouble, as a pre-welfare state social security system.[12] I examine family structures here, not primarily seeking long-term change over the years between the 1860s and the end of the century, but rather endeavouring to see what can be learned about how couples and women managing alone used their living spaces.

The most useful concept family historians have developed to understand how men, women, and children ensured their daily survival is the idea of the family economy. Its origins lie in sociological studies of family structures, work patterns, budgets, and standards of living in the nineteenth and early twentieth centuries.[13] More recently, historians have been able to show the patterns of wage labour of different family members by using computers to analyse the jobs reported in the decennial manuscript censuses.[14] However, until feminists began to examine the role of women in the family economy, historians using this approach tended to treat families as units collectively devising strategies of survival, inheritance, or property transmission that were presumed to be equally beneficial to all members.[15] Their approach stressed co-operation and the complementarity of roles. While the division of work by sex might be mentioned, gender was seldom a serious consideration.[16] Furthermore, historians only too often limited their consideration of the work of family members to the paid, formal labour that was reported in the censuses.

The work of feminist historians shows that women's work roles and patterns of reproduction are best understood within the framework of the family economy.[17] Such scholarship also demonstrates that the family is a particularly complex social institution. Working-class families were at one and the same time basic units of survival, solidarity, and support and a locus and source of tension, conflict, and inequality between the sexes.[18] Individuals were bound together by bonds of kinship, marriage, and cultural tradition, by their past history, and often by present circumstances and economic need. Yet families also contained individuals of different ages and sexes, with unequal power and legal rights within the family.[19] Their different economic potential and legal rights in the wider economy and society constrained and shaped their roles within the family and conditioned the social relations between generations and between the sexes. Interdependence generated different forms of dependence for men and women, parents and children.[20] To unravel and understand the sexual division of labour within the family and the complementary yet unequal nature of the roles of men, women, and children within working-class families is one of the major goals of this book. It is central to its organization.

The first two chapters present the economic, social, and legal contexts within which working-class Montrealers laboured and lived. Chapter 1 examines the emergence of Montreal as Canada's major industrial city. It introduces the two wards, Sainte Anne and Saint Jacques, chosen to examine working-class families. Chapter 2 looks at the legal framework of family life, demographic patterns, and family and household structures. Then, because family responsibilities and roles, deriving largely from people's sex and age, conditioned their positions in the family economy and in the wider society, the following chapters take apart the family economy. Chapter 3 looks at the earning power of male family heads, while Chapters 4 and 5 examine the work of children and of wives and mothers. The focus moves from the wider economy and its formal labour markets, which were crucial for men's work, toward the less visible and informal work worlds of children and women. Finally, Chapter 6 considers how women who had no husband at home, either because he had died or deserted them, sought to manage their lives and families.

To begin to understand the contours of the family economy of Montreal's wage-earners the book addresses a series of simple questions. Which family members worked for wages and how much could they earn? What kinds of work did other family members do? What other ways did they have of making ends meet? And, how do the answers to these questions change in Montreal between the 1860s and the 1890s?

To ask simple questions does not guarantee that simple answers will be found. Historians' ability to describe the past is initially constrained, frustrated, and shaped by the sources created in the past, and further by the number of those sources that have survived to the present. Increasingly, however, historians are demonstrating that a re-reading of traditional sources and a determined and sustained search for new ones can reshape our vision of the past. Biographies, institutional records, newspapers, the acts found in notarial archives, criminal and civil trials, and government investigations all offer snapshots of aspects of family life and of the work of men, women, and children. Such sources are drawn upon selectively in the book to provide details and to suggest interpretations. For working-class families, the information that can be gleaned from such sources constitutes only too often fragments of a jigsaw puzzle whose total picture is more difficult to grasp. They show us families in trouble more often than in comfort and in times of sorrow more often than of joy. Without them, however, the figures that one can calculate from more quantitative sources remain skeletal, without context and meaning.

In the absence of a solid body of qualitative descriptions in which people talked about their own family life I turned, like other historians seeking to understand the past of ordinary people, to the records that individuals generated unwittingly, perhaps at times unwillingly, as members of an organized nation-state. The most important of these, here, are the manuscript forms of the censuses, the schedules upon which, just as today, families or enumerators answered a series of questions about diverse details of their occupations, backgrounds, and family situations. The manuscript census offers several major advantages for the study of the family economy. First, censuses exist for the most important years of Montreal's consolidation as an industrial city, having been taken every ten years between 1861 and 1891.[21] Second, the censuses tell us which family members were living together and give some indication of the formal jobs they held. Families are treated as residential units, so that it is easy to see which women took in boarders and, sometimes, which families were sharing space to minimize rental costs.[22] In addition, the Canadian censuses of 1861 and 1871 allow us to identify families keeping pigs, cows, or other animals and sometimes listed garden produce and home production of textiles and other goods. Furthermore, by identifying owners of workshops and factories, these censuses make it possible to distinguish among artisans, employers, and wage labourers.[23] This residential focus is not without dangers. It can lead too easily to a neglect of fundamental social and economic ties with family members residing elsewhere and of links between the family and other institutions.[24] However, it offers major advantages over apprenticeship contracts, marriage contracts, other notarial deeds, parish registers, judicial records, or evaluation roles, all vital sources for answering other important questions about the family, but less useful for seizing the contours of the family economy.

Balanced against the major advantages that censuses offer for the study of the family wage economy are some of the drawbacks of the source. Censuses show us families at one point in time, at one moment in the evolution of their life cycle. To understand fully the dynamics of family development, it is best to follow their unfolding over time. We need to see what happened to family members who left the residential unit temporarily or permanently, to see how often people moved and into what kinds of housing, to find out whether their children were apprenticed or left home to seek work elsewhere, and to know when they married. Ideally, we could trace what education children received and what material goods or property they inherited.

While such careful reconstruction of the evolution of families might be possible in small parishes or rural communities, it is easier said than done in a large city. A longitudinal picture can be achieved, however, by linking families between censuses. I have done this for a few families, but most often the patterns that emerge represent those families randomly chosen for each census date. Layers of complexity are added to the individual histories by combining details from other sources, by confronting one source with another.[25] For selected families I have complemented the census information by finding out about people's addresses and movements within the city in the city directories, by determining the value of their property in the city's evaluation roles, and by searching for the births, deaths, and marriages of family members in parish registers. This was done systematically for families apparently sharing space to try to determine both the relationship of the individuals to each other and the boundaries of rental units, as well as for those traced between several censuses.

The book shares with other investigations of families in the past, then, a methodology relying partly on computer analysis of the manuscript censuses.[26] It is based on a random sample of households in the Montreal wards of Sainte Anne and Saint Jacques in 1861, 1871, 1881, and 1891. This resulted in a total sample from the four censuses of just under 15,000 individuals living in approximately 3,000 families.[27] Historians have traditionally been rather wary of sampling techniques. Carefully used, however, a sample, particularly a random sample, offers the only way to analyse large populations.[28] In this period Montreal's population increased from 90,323 in 1861 to 182,695 in 1891. No single researcher could hope to examine the total population. Resources, time, and faith in the representivity of sampling dictated an approach that would focus on specific areas of the city and use carefully drawn samples to make even these smaller areas manageable.

The two wards sampled, Sainte Anne and Saint Jacques, were chosen because both were largely working-class and because together they allow examination of French-Canadian, Irish, English, and Scottish families, the groups that made up the majority of the city's population. Located at the western extreme of the city and bounded to the south by the St. Lawrence River and to the north by the largely wealthy residential suburb of Saint Antoine, Sainte Anne was the heart of Montreal's industrial development. The Lachine Canal, which cut through the middle of the ward, was the major source of water power for the city's early factories. The Grand Trunk Railway's workshops, which employed hundreds of workers by the 1870s, took up acres of land in Point Saint Charles, in the southeastern part of the ward. Saint Jacques ward was part of the increasingly Francophone east end of Montreal. It had few major factories within its boundaries. Production there remained on a small scale throughout this period, taking place largely in artisans' homes and small workshops. Yet in both wards the majority of the inhabitants depended on wages. While the people of Sainte Anne could find work in a wide variety of workshops, factories, and construction projects along the Canal, around the port, and in the Grand Trunk yards all within the ward, those of Saint Jacques could walk fairly easily to the tobacco and other factories of Sainte Marie ward, just to the east, or work at home on the sewing put out by capitalists in the shoemaking and garment trades. Work in the older parts of the city centre was between a half-mile and a mile away. Sainte Anne remained predominantly working-class throughout the period, while in Saint Jacques a growing number of professionals moved in as the century progressed, thus reshaping the class structure of the ward.

The different characteristics of production in the two wards therefore afford the possibility of determining how the structure of local labour markets influence family work decisions. At the same time, the

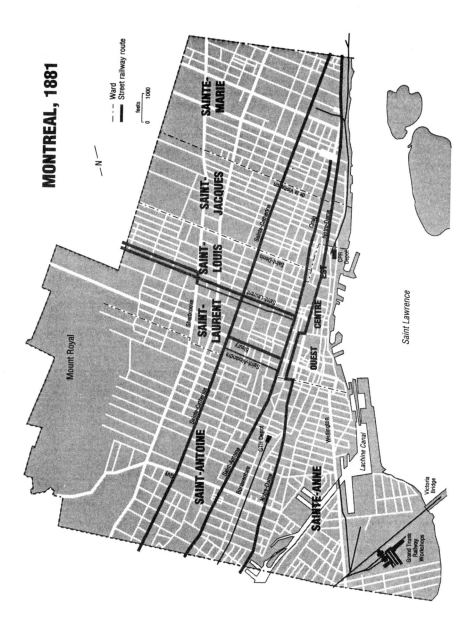

MONTREAL, 1881

- - - Ward
━━━ Street railway route

feets
0   1000

—N—

SAINTE-MARIE

SAINT-JACQUES

SAINT-LOUIS

SAINT-LAURENT

SAINT-ANTOINE

SAINTE-ANNE

OUEST

CENTRE

EST

Mount Royal

Saint Lawrence

Lachine Canal

de la Visitation

Sainte-Catherine

Dieu

Notre-Dame

Saint-Denis

CPR Depot

Saint-Laurent

Sherbrooke

Saint-Alexandre

Bleury

Sainte-Catherine

Saint-Antoine

GTR Depot

Bonaventure

Notre-Dame

Wellington

Victoria Bridge

Grand Trunk Railway Workshops

very different origins of the people of the two wards offer a chance to examine variations in the family economy related to people's 'ethnic and religious backgrounds or cultural traditions. In their contrasts as well as their similarities, the wards symbolize the complexities of the transformations under way and provide a portrait of Montreal's emerging working class and of the roles of men, women, and children within it. Their ingenuity, persistence, and struggles in a period that offered both new opportunities and major challenges bear witness to the flexibility of the family as an institution. The challenges these families faced highlight the dangers of dependency that men and women both confronted in new and particular ways.

1

The Economic, Geographic, and Social Context of Montreal Working-Class Life

Half French and half English – a diversity in manners and dress as well as in creeds – institutions drawn from the coutume de Paris and the Parliament of Westminster. . . . nunneries next door to Manchester warehouses . . . priests in long black dresses and Scotch Presbyterreans – cabmen in frieze jackets fresh from Ireland, and native market carters in coloured sashes and night caps – in short, a complication of incongruities; the old and new world jumbled together, and then assorted according to some odd device in social economics. Such is Montreal.[1]

By the mid-nineteenth century Montreal was the largest, wealthiest, most vibrant city of British North America, the tenth largest city in all of North America.[2] Characterized, like other nineteenth-century cities, by a jumble of contrasts, contradictions, and inequalities, Montreal was special because of its own particular place in the North American and Canadian economy and because of the patterns of settlement, conquest, and development that had shaped its social, political, and cultural heritage. Visitors were struck by the incongruities and dichotomies that seemed to typify and divide the city. Like William Chambers, quoted above, they invariably noted the linguistic divisions between French and English and the religious differences between Catholics and Protestants. Increasingly toward the end of the century, they also commented on divisions between the wealthy and the poor. Lucy Isabella Bird, who visited in the late 1850s, was among those who were struck by the difference between this long-established commercial centre and rougher, newer American cities.

It was a most curious and startling change from the wooden erections, wide streets, and the impression of novelty which pervaded everything I had seen in the New World, to the old stone edifices, lofty houses, narrow streets, and tin roofs of the city of Montreal. There are iron windows and long dead walls; there are narrow thoroughfares, crowded with strangely dressed habitants and long processions of priests. . . . On all sides a jargon of Irish, English and French is to be heard.[3]

From the 1850s on, the more perceptive visitors saw not only the mixture of old and new but the growing importance of industry as a new motor force in the urban economy.[4] By the 1850s it was said that Montreal "might fairly lay claim to the character of a manufacturing as well as of a commercial city." By the 1880s Montrealers were proudly labelling their city the "Workshop of Canada."[5] Once the focal point of the fur trade, the heart of the commercial empire of the St. Lawrence, and long the major port for the imports and exports linking the British North American colonies to their metropolis and home of the wealthy merchant elite, Montreal had always been an important production centre. Some of the wealthiest families, such as the beer-making Molsons, were involved in various combinations of trade, banking, and the fabrication of goods.[6] Like other cities and villages of North America, Montreal had always had a small group of artisan shoemakers, coopers, bakers, and tailors who produced some of the goods used locally.[7]

Between the 1820s and 1850s local artisans in some trades had been slowly accumulating sufficient capital to re-organize production, to take on extra workers, and to produce a large stock of goods to sell.[8] Americans, Scots, English, and Irish immigrants joined them, drawing on capital or knowledge garnered elsewhere to set up small factories.

Mid-century Montreal offered many advantages to such enterprising industrialists. The Board of Trade had ensured that the port was accessible by dredging the channel in Lake Saint Peter to ease the passage upstream from Quebec City. The quays and docks were solid structures, impressing even Charles Dickens when he visited in the 1840s. More importantly, in the late 1840s a small but eager group of entrepreneurs had pushed the government to complete a plan to lease industrial sites along the newly enlarged Lachine Canal. The redevelopment of the Lachine Canal provided water power for industry – making possible a rapid acceleration and diversification of industry.[9] In 1860 the Grand Trunk Railway Company opened the impressive Victoria Bridge that linked Montreal to the South Shore and hence to the railways of the United States, giving the city a winter port at Portland, Maine. Stretching east to Rivière du Loup and westward to Toronto and beyond, the Grand Trunk consecrated Montreal's central position at the hub of a rail and water transportation network that could provide manufacturers with raw materials, imported machinery, and immigrants seeking work, as well as access to Upper Canadian, Maritime,

American, and "even overseas markets."[10] In the port and on the river the mixture of sailing and steam-powered ships signalled the importance of transatlantic exchange and the co-existence of old and new motor forces on water as on land.[11]

From Artisanal to Factory Production

The shift from workshop to factory production involved much more than the substitution of wage labour for a master-apprenticeship relationship, and more, too, than the possibility of teaching only part of a skill as labour processes were divided up. The emergence of industrial capitalism precipitated a gradual reshuffling of the distribution of responsibility for the daily reproduction of workers away from the owners of the means of production to the families of the workers. This re-adjustment lay behind the growing physical separation of productive and domestic labour and contributed to the expansion of the proportion of workers "free" to sell their labour power where they wished, but dependent on wages to survive.

Transformations in two of Montreal's most important sectors in the first half of the nineteenth century, shoemaking and dressmaking, serve to underline this changed relationship between families and the economy. As late as 1830, most production of shoes, indeed, most production in the leather trades in and around Montreal, apparently occurred within a workshop peopled by the master, one or two apprentices or his sons, and sometimes a journeyman. Historian Joanne Burgess argues that in these trades the craft household remained the fundamental unit of production. Each apprentice continued to reside with his master and his master's family; all of his basic needs were met by his adoptive household. Thus, the master agreed to provide bedding, heating, food, sometimes clothing, and less frequently lighting for the apprentices. Usually the workshop was part of the master's house, most commonly a separate room or apartment. Sometimes it was adjacent to the store where customers were served. Occasionally the workshop was housed in a garret.[12]

When, as was usual in apprenticeship contracts, a master shoemaker agreed both to teach a trade and to provide for the food, clothing, and lodging of an apprentice, he was in effect contracting in part for work that his wife would perform. Any increase in the number of apprentices hired concurrently would put more strain on that domestic labour than on the productive work. The decision of some masters to pay a clothing allowance rather than provide wearing apparel may have been an attempt to free up female family members for other tasks. This practice may well have been more common initially among masters who were widowed.[13] When the parents of the apprentice agreed to provide clothing, either they had to purchase it, or women in their family had to produce it. The significance of this shuffling around of domestic responsibilities is highlighted in one case cited by Joanne Burgess where a father agreed to provide his two sons with clothing as long as "his daughter Eliza did not marry or die in the interval."[14]

When women were both the producers of goods and the hirers of apprentices who were responsible for their care, the weight of domestic labour was particularly heavy. It was probably precisely because of this double workload that Montreal's major dressmakers seem to have ceased housing their apprentices long before master shoemakers did. These women entrepreneurs effectively passed the onus of daily reproduction back to the parents, specifying more and more often in the hiring contracts of the 1820s that they would not provide room and board. While this solution to the burden of domestic labour made sense, it raised a host of new problems that had to be addressed. No longer able to control the time at which their workers woke or breakfasted, these mistresses began to specify carefully not only the hours of work required but also that it was the parents' responsibility to see that their daughters should arrive on time. Dressmakers hiring larger numbers of girls and young women stopped housing their apprentices, yet they still avoided paying a wage. In tailoring, and increasingly over these decades in the other trades that hired males, various forms of payment replaced some of the domestic services of the master's wife. Gradually a daily wage came to replace the multitude of professional and domestic services that master craftsmen and their wives had provided for their apprentices.[15]

Reproduction – the education, training, daily care, and paternalist protection that had been an essential part of the contract between master and apprentice – was removed from the responsibility of the employer and placed on the shoulders of the workers. The decline in apprenticeship combined with large-scale immigration and unskilled employment in construction to expand the portion of the population earning a wage. Wage-earners were individually responsible for their reproduction. Daily wages were meant to cover the costs of housing, meals, and clothing. Yet workers did not have the time to shop, clean house, and perform the other tasks necessary for daily replenishment. This was the task of wives and mothers. Domestic labour was not new to women. What was new was that a growing proportion of wives in cities like Montreal largely depended on wages earned by others to perform that work.

Factories did not suddenly eliminate artisanal production. Widespread wage labour did not eliminate apprenticeships in all trades.

Rather, a mixture of artisanal workshops, small manufactories, and large factories characterized Montreal's industrial structure by the 1860s and 1870s. Some of the new factories were impressive complexes of brick buildings spreading over whole city blocks. They offered visible proof, hard architectural, material evidence, that Montreal's industrial revolution was well under way. Chunky, almost phallic, factory chimneys began to thrust up above the roofs of houses, stores, and workplaces, challenging the hegemony of the graceful church spires, the former skyscrapers of the church-rich, pre-industrial city.

Canada's "modern industry," one writer has argued, "was born on the banks of the Lachine Canal."[16] It cut south and east across Sainte Anne ward from the small village of Lachine to the west, dividing Point Saint Charles from the northern and eastern sections of the ward that blended into the central city core, and joined the St. Lawrence River just east of the southern tip of King Street, where earlier in the century windmills still stood. The water power of the Canal, harnessed by enterprising entrepeneurs, attracted the greatest density of early industries in Montreal and made Sainte Anne the city's most industrial ward.[17] The flour mills, iron foundries, nail and spike factories, cotton and wool mills, and woodworking establishments that stretched along the sides of the canal were estimated to employ some 2,000 men, women, and children in the mid-1850s.[18]

Over the following decades of the nineteenth century large factories came to dominate the landscape of much of Sainte Anne ward, often pushing out housing or crowding in around it, filling up odd spaces and city blocks that in other parts of the city would have rapidly been used for housing. In 1861 Sainte Anne had at least seventeen factories employing more than fifty people each and accounting for nearly 70 per cent of the ward's industrial work force. A decade later six establishments reported over 100 workers, while eleven employed more than fifty. The diverse operations of the Grand Trunk Railway in Pointe Saint Charles employed over 1,200 workers. Foundries, engine and machine works, one cotton mill, and shirt and clothing factories were the other major employers. Most of these large workplaces used steam or water power, often both.

From the 1860s on, capitalists using only steam power in their workshops and factories spread out into the older residential parts of Sainte Anne and onto the streets leading to the Canal and the port. In the 1860s William Rodden's foundry, the largest in the city, covered about an acre of land on William Street and turned out a diverse array of miscellaneous machines, stoves, and iron furniture.[19] Such foundries and other similar establishments using extensive machinery and steam or water power captured the imagination of visitors and residents alike, evoking descriptions full of praise and wonder. Factories, steam-driven machinery, and artisans whose skills were being downgraded constitute the core of popular and academic descriptions of the emergence of industrial capitalism. The reality was more complex and untidy. In smaller workshops, scattered throughout the city, production continued to be the domain of a master and several apprentices. Construction work on canals, railroads, and housing remained relatively unchanged, and even in the large factories only some workers faced the degradation of their skills.[20]

Nor did all those involved in production work on machines. The speed and contours of change varied dramatically from sector to sector, from craft to craft. The growth of industry eliminated some traditional forms of production, led to an increase in others, and often multiplied the amount of work that had to be done by hand, opening up segments of the labour process to women and children. Dramatic variations in the capital invested in land, buildings and machinery, or tools, as well as in the numbers of employees and wages paid, continued to characterize the industrial structure. Small specialized production units were as much a part of the industrial revolution as the large factories that dominated landscapes and imaginations alike. Their growth resulted in part from increased specialization, for example, the creation of separate bakery and confectionery establishments, previously "carried on under the same management."[21] In Sainte Anne ward, such small, often artisanal workplaces co-existed with factories. Coopers and blacksmiths continued to run their own small workshops despite the fact that most large foundries and factories had coopering and blacksmithing departments. The very presence of a few large, heavily capitalized, and mechanized flour and sugar processing plants seems to have spurred the opening of small baking and confectionery establishments in the neighbourhood.

While Sainte Anne ward represents the heart of industrializing Montreal, the nature of production in the more residential ward of Saint Jacques serves to underline the continuing importance of smaller workplaces and the unevenness of the development process. In Saint Jacques no manufacturing workplace reported over fifty workers in 1861 and only three did so in 1871. One-third of Sainte Anne establishments used water or steam power in 1871, but only 5 per cent did so in Saint Jacques. William McDonald's tobacco factory dominated local employment opportunities with 550 workers that year. Over half of them were women and children. The only other major employers located within the ward in 1871 were two tanneries, those of Camirant and Blondin and of Donovan and Moran, with eighty-three and fifty-three men, women, and children respectively.[22] Metal-working in Saint Jacques took place only in numerous small blacksmiths' shops and in a few tinsmiths' workshops, where tin boxes and roofing were made. These men employed only one to five people.

Most of the production that occurred in workplaces within the boundaries of Saint Jacques ward appears to have remained artisanal until 1871, the last date it can be determined from the manuscript censuses. Fully two-thirds of productive establishments that year reported under five workers. A small workshop, with between one and four employees, often the craftsman, an apprentice, and members of the family, remained the most common enterprise. The crafts that predominated were in construction and woodworking, especially carpenters' and joiners' shops; food-processing, including bakers and butchers with small stalls at the local markets; and shoemaking and dressmaking.

The one large tobacco factory and the importance of sewing and shoemaking in Saint Jacques ward meant that more jobs were available for women and children than in Sainte Anne. One-third of the workers reported by local employers in 1871 were women and girls. The heavy, capital-intensive industries that predominated in Sainte Anne ward, in contrast, offered more employment opportunities to males than females throughout the second half of the nineteenth century. Females represented only 20 per cent of workers reported by its manufacturers in 1861 and a mere 13 per cent a decade later. This characteristic of the local market would influence family work strategies and women's patterns of labour.

The economic structure that emerged in Montreal was complex, quite different from many of the smaller North American mill towns or cities that historians have studied where one or two specific sectors or large companies dominated the economy.[23] In Canada, only Toronto rivalled Montreal for the depth of its industrial base.[24] Six broad sectors employed over three-quarters of the people working in production in Montreal over this period. Diverse types of metal-working, machine-making, and transportation-related production absorbed around one-quarter of the city's manufacturing work force across the period. During the 1870s and 1880s the two other major sectors, clothing and shoemaking, mushroomed. The numbers of workers reported in leather-working and boot and shoemaking establishments jumped dramatically from 1,500 in 1861 to over 6,500 in 1871 and 1881 before declining rapidly. In 1861 only 500 workers were officially enumerated in the clothing trades, though hundreds more women sewed, either in small seamstress shops or at home as part of the putting-out system. Their numbers rose to nearly 5,000 women and girls and around 1,700 men in the city's 513 establishments listed in 1891. Numbers employed in the fourth major sector, tobacco work and cigarmaking, expanded more slowly, from around 1,000 in 1871 to the nearly 3,000 men, women, and children reported by the owners of the thirty-five establishments existing in 1891. A similar total was reported in food-processing in 1891. This sector, so important in producing food and drink both for the local population and for elsewhere, consistently produced the most value across these years.[25]

In most of these leading sectors Montreal was the major Canadian producer. In 1863 the Board of Trade announced proudly that Montreal manufacturers produced three-quarters of the boots and shoes manufactured in Canada, drawing on immense quantities of leather from tanneries in the vicinity and from all parts of the country. Ten years later, Montreal was said to produce about four-fifths of the cigars manufactured in Canada.[26]

Numerous printing and publishing establishments made up the final major sector, producing newspapers, pamphlets, city directories, and the profusion of other reading materials consumed by the literate population of this growing metropolis. A wide variety of producers of luxury goods of all kinds, and of daily basics ranging from cutlery to coffins, gave depth to the industrial structure of Montreal, widening further the types of work opportunities that the city offered. By 1891 the census listed over 130 different types of industrial enterprises.

Labour Markets and the Sexual Division of Labour

The different involvement of men, women, and children in industrial production and in these major sectors of production highlights the continuities and modifications that the growth of industry made to the sexual division of labour within industry over the period. In artisanal production women's contribution had been largely hidden except when a widow took over her husband's craft following his death. With the exception of dressmaking and domestic service, few women had been hired specifically as apprentices or workers by Montreal's craftsmen in the early nineteenth century. Wives and children performed both productive and domestic labour, but this is seldom visible in most of the records generated at the time.

New divisions of labour in specific sectors opened up wage-earning possibilities in manufacturing to women and children. A total of 7,309 women and girls were reported as working in Montreal's industrial establishments in 1871. They constituted 34 per cent of the industrial workers. A decade later females comprised 37 per cent of the manufacturing work force of 32,132. As factory labour was further transformed, eliminating the necessity for some of the hand labour that women performed, and as more work opened up for women outside production, the proportion decreased. By 1891 under 30 per cent of industrial workers were women. Within the boundaries of Montreal the absolute numbers of female workers reported by employers in production dropped from 11,681 to 10,263 between 1881 and 1891, as changes in industry and the opening up of different areas of the economy began to reshape the female labour market.[27]

Women were both sought after and hired by the city's industrial capitalists, so that the chances of finding work were greater than in towns where heavy manufacturing predominated but fewer than in the mill towns of England or New England or in shoemaking centres where manufacturers assumed that females and families made ideal workers.[28] Available jobs were varied, yet women were largely concentrated within specific sectors and in particular departments of industries. Their work was fundamental in the clothing trades and shoemaking, negligible in others. Industries based on traditional or new male skills, such as metal transformation, boat and railroad-related construction, and the housing construction trades remained bastions of male employment. So, too, were the majority of traditionally masculine crafts: cabinetmaking, coopering, blacksmith establishments, and carriage-making.

In the sewing trades, which by 1881 reported more workers than any other industrial sector, women and children constituted 70 to 80 per cent of the reported work force across the period. Male craftsmen became less important as more and more types of clothing for farmers and soldiers, in particular, began to be mass-produced by female workers.[29] In tailoring shops where males had traditionally worked as both masters and apprentices, females constituted 64 per cent of reported workers by 1891. Other branches of these trades were close to exclusively female. In 1891 women and girls made up 98 per cent of those working in the city's 250 dressmaking and millinery establishments and a similar proportion in the five corset-making factories.

In shoemaking, one of the most sexually mixed trades of the city, female employment appears to have decreased from over 40 to around 30 per cent across the period, in part, perhaps as in sewing, because the putting out of work hid large numbers of predominantly female workers. More probably, the growing concentration of production within factories, the limitation of women to specific departments, and the emergence of male unions combined with technological changes to reduce the proportions of women hired.[30] In the early years of factory production in the tobacco-processing and cigarmaking sector, girls and boys under sixteen made up over 40 per cent of the labour force, while women constituted a further 25 per cent. Over the 1871-91 period, as the work of such youngsters in factories became less and less common, females aged sixteen and over largely replaced younger children.

Women did not predominate in all sectors of the economy that duplicated or replaced domestic labour in the home. In food production females made up only a quarter of workers reported by the city's employers in 1891, although the proportions varied dramatically between trades. Baking and meat curing, like work in large breweries and flour and grist mills, remained male preserves. In confectionery, pickle-making, and vinegar-making establishments, in contrast, men and women were employed in roughly equal numbers. The only areas of food production where women predominated were in small enterprises producing baking powder and flavouring extract.

Women and children clearly occupied specific niches in the industrial labour markets of Montreal, and the jobs available in different parts of the city varied. There was nothing inherent to the process of industrial growth itself that determined that some jobs should be viewed as male and others as female and remunerated accordingly. Workers' struggles, employers' decisions, and local family income needs all played a role in fashioning local divisions of labour, in determining the proportions of men, women, and children employed. The division of labour that preceded and accompanied the transition from artisanal to factory production made possible, but not necessary, the employment of large numbers of women and children. The growth of industry had the potential to eliminate differences of age and sex in the marketplace. In general, it did not do so. Changed but limited work opportunities for women were one result of the expansion of industry. Equality in the labour market was not.

Average annual wages paid out in the leading Montreal sectors declined as the proportion of females employed increased, underlining the different costs of male and female workers to employers. In 1891, for example, the average annual wage paid in railway-related production firms was $454. No women were employed. In baking, which was largely male, an average of $409 was paid out to each worker compared to $277 in confectionery-making, where around 40 per cent of workers were women. Within the clothing trades average wages varied directly with the proportion of women involved, dropping from just under $300 for furriers and hatters to $270 in tailoring establishments, and down to $173 in dressmaking and millinery.[31]

In shoemaking and dressmaking, the availability of French-Canadian workers, reputed to work for low wages, had influenced some employers to locate in Montreal. "Nowhere" were people more "intelligent, docile and giving less trouble to their employees than in Lower Canada," the Montreal General Railroad Celebration Committee had suggested to prospective manufacturers in 1856. A further advantage was that "the manufacturing population can be drawn from the immediate vicinity of the city . . . and hands can be obtained to work in the factories at reasonable rates."[32] On some counts they proved to be wrong. French Canadians, like other workers, did organize, demonstrate, and fight to improve their work conditions.[33] Certainly, however, the presence of this local labour supply, apparently more willing to work for lower wages than the people of Ontario or the United States, was seen as important by employers in several of the leading areas of employment in Saint Jacques ward, especially shoemaking and sewing. Shoe manufacturer George Boivin suggested in 1876 that labour in Montreal was cheaper than in Upper Canada but cost more than in Quebec City. Cotton manufacturer Mr. Nye believed labour was "cheaper by from 25 to 30 per cent." A decade later another shoe manufacturer, M.C. Mullarky, attributed the success of the Quebec City and Montreal shoe industries over those in other provinces to the "cheap labour" upon which they could draw.[34]

Many of these "cheap" workers were women and children. In 1874 Montreal clothier Mr. Muir explained at the hearings of the Select Committee on the Manufacturing Interests of the Dominion that his workers were predominantly French-Canadian women. "You have a surplus population in Montreal which enables you to get cheap labour?" he was asked. "Yes," he replied, "in fact it makes my heart ache to have the women come crying for work."

Q. Then, your labour is very cheap?
A. Yes; too cheap.
Q. I fancy that from the surplus in Montreal you get labour cheaper than you could in any other part of the country?
A. We think so . . .

Two years later, Mullarky reported that there were "more than sufficient" of the women and children who made up his cheap labour force.[35]

This perception of Quebec as a place where wages were lower than elsewhere was important in the expansion of industries relying largely on female labour, and specifically on French-Canadian workers. This was true for the shoemaking and sewing industries within Montreal, and for the cotton mills of Hochelaga, on the city's eastern boundary, and elsewhere in the province.[36] "You know," Muir explained, "that Irish women . . . if they come to this country and do not get the wages, will emigrate. The French women do not emigrate, and therefore we have that class of labour in the Province of Quebec."[37]

French-Canadian women were not alone in working for minimal wages. Few women earned as much as a male day labourer, and most women's patterns of work and possibilities of work were different from those of men or boys. Only occasionally did men and women perform the same tasks. Few trades that had traditionally been male crafts were opened up to women. Labour markets were gendered. A sexual division of labour characterized both industrial work and employment in other sectors.

Even when men and women worked in the same industry, women performed specific jobs, usually different from males in both content and remuneration. As work processes were cut down into their component parts, the more labour-intensive processes tended to fall to women. In a city type foundry, for example, a complex machine cast type "so rapidly that 200 small type could be cast in a minute." However, a small "jet" remained on the type. These were broken off by young boys. Then,

> the type is next given over to a number of girls, who sit around a circular stone table. These young women rapidly pick up a type each and rub it upon the table . . . to smooth the surface. Their dexterity . . . is astonishing.

Or, in Lyman's chemical plant, where most of the workers were men, and where water-powered machinery operated powerful presses and complicated cutting systems, women were "kept constantly employed in the washing of bottles." Similarly, in De Witt's Buckskin Glove Factory on the Lachine Canal a machine cut out the pieces for the thumb and fingers. "In an adjacent room a number of young women, operating on sewing machines stitched them together with great rapidity."[38]

The classic example of how women's work fitted into specific parts of changing labour processes is the sewing industry. In a growing section of the clothing trades over this period, the cloth was cut in factories. Mr. Muir, the employer whose heart was aching because of the women crying for work, explained in 1874 that his factory had a "15 horsepower engine running three machines" with fifty needles each, "and a knife which cuts cloth by steam." Four male cutters could "do the work of from twelve to fifteen." The next stage was carried out by women working in their homes.[39]

Most women worked in sectors or at tasks that were of little interest to men. They were paid as women, at rates that assumed they were all secondary earners in the family. Only rarely did they actually replace men in jobs in production. John Beatty, the virulently anti-union foreman of the composing room at *The Witness,* reported in 1888 that they had hired women as strikebreakers fifteen or sixteen years earlier and had no labour troubles since then. Divisions of labour by sex were less clear in the printing industry than in most other sectors, perhaps because Montreal printers had not succeeded in controlling hiring.[40] Women competed with men as compositors in some shops. Employers paid them at lower rates than men, thus producing their papers at a lower cost. On the other hand, most employers were convinced that women could not work as fast or as hard as men. In combined book-binding and printing establishments girls were employed feeding machines and sewing and folding blank account books.[41]

Outside industry the lines between men's and women's work were equally solid. The growth of industry did not eliminate the jobs that had traditionally been performed by women. Indeed, the number working as domestics, washerwomen, midwives, or cooks expanded over these years, both with the growth in the number of professional and bour-geois families who were desperate to find good servants and with the shift toward hiring women rather than men for domestic work. In 1861 there were 2,770 female and 544 male servants listed in the census. By 1881, numbers had increased much more rapidly than the population. There were nearly 6,000 female but only around 650 male domestics. Service remained the leading sector of employment for women, despite the growth of opportunities in production.[42] And, as the pro-portion employed in manufacturing declined, a growing number of women were beginning to work in offices, replacing male clerks as the beginnings of the administrative revolution increased the amount of paper work performed in both industry and commerce.[43]

The different history of industrial development in Sainte Anne and Saint Jacques meant that those seeking work in and around the two wards faced employment opportunities in different sectors and dispar-ate kinds of workplaces. The possibilities for men, single women, mar-ried women, and widows were not the same. The sectors in which indi-viduals reported working in Sainte Anne and Saint Jacques wards when the decennial censuses were taken underline the difference between men's and women's areas of employment and the importance of local labour markets (Table 1.1). Until 1891 over half the widows, married women, and girls in Saint Jacques ward who listed a job sewed for a living, whereas in Sainte Anne the proportion hovered around one-third. Most of these women in Saint Jacques appear to have worked in their homes on material put out from factories and work-shops. In Sainte Anne, in contrast, some worked at home and some in the shirt and collar factories located nearby. A few owned their own small workshops, employing one or two helpers, or simply hung a sign at their door to attract occasional customers.[44] As wealthy profession-als and entrepreneurs moved into some Saint Jacques neighbourhoods, they offered more work opportunities to women as domestics, washer-women, and cooks. By 1891 one-third of that ward's female workers were employed as domestics, compared to less than a tenth in Sainte Anne. The greater variety of jobs available in Sainte Anne ward is indi-cated by the fact that in 1871 women in the sample population reported thirty-eight different kinds of work, twice the number of Saint Jacques women. Sainte Anne men reported a total of 122 different job titles compared to ninety-two in Saint Jacques.

The Expansion of the Working-Class and the Changing Rhythms of Daily Life

The need for wages to survive dominated the daily lives of the men, women, and children who made up the expanding working class in parts of mid- to late nineteenth-century Montreal such as Saint Jacques and Sainte Anne. Wage labour took many forms during this period, including piecework, work on contracts, and subcontracting. Yet, whatever the particular configuration of the wage relationship, a growing proportion of the city's population was subject both to the new possibilities and to the new dependencies it implied. Men and women did not experience either the possibilities or the dependencies in the same way.

The number of workers reported by industrial capitalists and artisans mushroomed between 1861 and 1891 from 6,500 to 36,000. This was an increase of 554 per cent, in a period in which the city's population expanded by only 102 per cent, from 90,323 to 182,695. Had each of these workers been the sole supporter of a family of five they would have been supporting just over one-third of the total population in 1861. By 1891 virtually every man, woman, and child in the city would have been dependent on wages earned in some branch of industrial production. Clearly this was not the case. Employers hired not only the heads of families but also their sons and daughters and less often their wives, as well as people who had no families. And, as we shall see in subsequent chapters, these secondary family earners constituted a growing proportion of the labour force over these years.

By 1871 the working class constituted the majority of the population of the city. In Sainte Anne about four-fifths of household heads appeared to be dependent on wages between 1861 and 1881. In 1891 when the question was more explicitly asked in the census, 90 per cent in Sainte Anne and nearly 80 per cent in Saint Jacques were listed as wage-earners. Among Sainte Anne's non-working-class residents were some factory owners and a sprinkling of clerks, professionals, and other white-collar or service workers. And there were the artisans who ran their own bakeries, butcher shops, or blacksmith shops. Together these groups never constituted much more than a fifth of family heads. In the 1860s some manufacturers reported living close to their factories. Increasingly, however, the wealthier industrial capitalists and merchants would have scorned life among factories, noise, and pollution. Nor would they, or their wives, have relished life too close to the ubiquitous taverns, staggering drunkards, leaking sewers, outside toilets, and roaming gangs of boys, wandering pigs, and other animals that characterized daily life in Sainte Anne.

In the more residential ward of Saint Jacques lived both a sizeable working-class population and many of the city's leading French-Canadian merchants, industrialists, politicians, and professionals. Its small workshops did not stand out much from commercial outlets or homes. Only William McDonald's tobacco factory compared to those of Saint Anne, and by the 1880s it had moved east into Hochelaga.[45] The largest, most impressive buildings were not factories, but such church institutions as the convent, orphanage, and school of the Sisters of Providence, which filled up much of the block between Saint Denis, Sainte Catherine, Saint Hubert, and Ontario streets adjacent to the Saint Jacques cathedral. There the working class decreased steadily across the period from around three-quarters of all families in 1861 to three-fifths in 1891 (Table 1.2). While it continued to be home to a considerable number of respectable skilled workers, the proportion of labourers, carters, and other unskilled workers shrank as the number of wealthier families increased. Clustered together in their grey, stone houses on prestigious streets like St. Denis, Sherbrooke, and St. Hubert and other major thoroughfares the merchants, doctors, lawyers, and clerks formed an important bourgeois and petit-bourgeois component within this predominantly working-class suburb. Such family heads supported their dependants on salaries, fees for services, or profits. Salaries might be low, as in the case of clerks, but they were not usually as irregular as wages, nor was the work as uncertain. Profits and service fees might also prove precarious, but they demanded a different capital and family work commitment from wage-earning, the focus of the families being studied here.

Yet, both remained predominantly working-class wards. The majority of the families in Sainte Anne and Saint Jacques needed wages to survive. The work they could find was conditioned by the particular opportunities of the areas in which they lived, the distance they could afford to travel, their own skills, and the general economic conjuncture. Employment possibilities for the people of Saint Jacques were not necessarily limited to their own ward, for the factories in nearby Sainte Marie were easily accessible, even by foot, to those in the eastern section. Construction work could be found throughout the city, and sewing could be done at home.

Wage labour, for a growing proportion of these workers, meant either having to be at work at a specific time each day or, as in the case of day labourers, having to seek work again and again over the weeks and months. For artisans used to exercising some control over their work rhythms, for any apprentices who had been housed and fed in their master's house, or for ex-farmers whose work had been dictated by the forces of nature and the rhythms of the seasons, this was a new experience both because it involved working somewhere else than at home and because of the different concept of time involved.[46] Employers in the 1870s and 1880s speeded up the process of learning punctuality and new rhythms by locking the factory gates at the time work was supposed to begin. Latecomers could not enter until the gates were re-opened at lunch time. No pay was given for the time lost. For workers who failed to appear, existing master and servant laws, whose origin lay in the pre-industrial period, could be invoked. Several workers testifying to the Royal Commission on the Relations of Labour and Capital in the late 1880s described how an employee could still find "himself liable to a sentence of imprisonment for absenting himself without permission." Despite legislation passed in 1877 that decriminalized breaches of employment contracts, Montreal lawyers giving testimony in 1888 made it clear that almost any wage-earner could be fined, imprisoned, or both for leaving work without due notice.[47]

The increasing separation of home and work and the coercion to arrive at work on time changed the rhythms of daily life and translated into different patterns of street use. Most workers walked to their jobs, seeking housing that made the journey to work and home again possible. As a result the streets filled up well before six each morning with men, boys, and young women, the proportions of each depending on the work available in the neighbourhood. Six days a week, from homes throughout the city, thousands of workers took to rickety, rat-eaten, wooden sidewalks, brick pavements, or dilapidated flagstone footpaths, spilling over into the streets and converging on the major thoroughfares that led to the city's largest factories.[48] Ten, eleven, or even twelve hours later, at dusk and at times well after dark, hundreds of work-weary men, women, and children, released in waves, again trudged the streets, now heading for home. This filling up of streets at predictable and increasingly standardized times was the precursor of today's traffic jams. It was a new phenomenon, a product both of the growing spatial separation of home and work and of the formalization of work hours that accompanied the spread of waged labour in large workplaces.

The rhythms of formal wage labour set the workers' experiences apart from other members of their family. For those new to such work this was an ordeal that assaulted their body rhythms and unravelled old links between daily work and family life. Responsibility for ensuring that the wage-earners in a family were awake, fed, and ready to leave on time no doubt fell usually to wives and mothers who arose even earlier to prepare some kind of breakfast. For the majority, who did not seek permanent formal employment, their work day passed differently, too. When the wage-earners had departed, women and children took to the streets, heading for the market, exchanging goods and services, seeking household supplies from passing pedlars and hucksters, gossiping, arguing, or at times fighting. Throughout the day, the gender configurations of street use changed and shifted, reflecting the roles that men and women played in the economy and in the family. Such divisions by gender were never absolute. Unemployed males, like the gangs of "idle" youths, could be seen at all times of day. At lunch time some workers returned home or scurried out of factory or workshop to seek a quick and cheap meal. These images point, however, to what Christine Stansell has graphically portrayed for early nineteenth-century New York. The city that women inhabited was not the same as that of men.[49] Nor was the city that children experienced the same as that of their parents. Living in the same homes and neighbourhoods as their male relatives, walking the same streets, women's role in the family and in the economy made their experience of the emergence of industrial capitalism different.

On the streets new sights, smells, sounds, and urban textures mingled with old to herald the complexity and extent of changes begun, beginning, and to come. In mid-nineteenth-century Montreal, people and animals intermingled in a way unimaginable today. Cows grazed in backyards and green spaces and on street verges. Pigs scrounged in courtyards and alleys, and poultry could be heard and seen throughout the city. Carters and their horses transported their wares from railways and docks to the factories, warehouses, and shops of the city. Horses were the motor power for Montreal's street railway system, which expanded over the decades between the 1860s and 1880s without ever offering rides at a price that ordinary workingmen could afford. Horses pulled passengers over some 471,229 miles in 1867, over 550,000 six years later, leaving immeasurable tons of manure on the city's streets in the years before electrification in 1892.[50] Distinctive smells of industrial pollution mingled with the older city smells, the stink of decaying animal carcasses, the smell of animal and human excrement, and the dank odour of oozing, decomposing drains to testify that for all the senses both continuity and change characterized the period.

A visitor, S.P. Day, found the "bustle and din of industry were unceasing in the streets" in the mid-1860s.[51] Inside one nail and spike factory the noise was so loud that he lost his "hearing for some minutes, owing to the deafening clamour of the heavy cutting machines – fully a dozen of them being simultaneously in operation."[52] From the 1850s on the rattling, whistling, and screeching of brakes of the growing number of trains converging on Montreal set up new dissonances, as the expanding network of railroads linked the city to hinterlands in the

West and East as well as southward to the United States. Such new sounds recomposed the symphony of the streets, merging and competing with the older score of clacking horses' hooves, street vendors' cries, and the sounds of construction work.

Immigration, Population Growth, and the Ethnic Geography of the City

Onto these streets, by railway, steamship, stagecoach, carriage, horse, or foot came migrants from rural areas of Quebec and immigrants from the British Isles and Europe. Their impact, combined with births to families already living in the city, boosted the size of Montreal's population by 280 per cent between 1851 and 1891, fuelling the expansion of the working class and creating a work force that was regularly larger than the supply of available jobs. The most dramatic increase occurred in the years preceding the 1861 census. In ten years, the population swelled from 56,715 to 90,323. The Board of Trade could proudly announce that Montreal had become the tenth largest city in North America.[53] Over subsequent decades fluctuations in the economy and the relatively greater attraction of employment opportunities in the New England states put a brake on such rapid expansion. The population increased by 19 per cent between 1861 and 1871, when it reached 107,225, then by about 30 per cent over each the two following decades, reaching 140,247 in 1881, then 182,695 in 1891.

From the 1830s on, whole families as well as non-inheriting sons and daughters had left the over-exploited, under-capitalized farms of rural Quebec seeking work in the cities of New England and Lower Canada. Between 1851 and 1861 more and more chose to migrate to Montreal. By 1865, the city in which Anglophones had dominated numerically for several decades had become predominantly French-Canadian in number, thought not in economic power.[54] From 48 per cent of the total population in 1861, French Canadians increased to 53 per cent in 1871, remaining at around 55 per cent over the following decades. From the plain of Montreal and surrounding counties, families came seeking new possibilities or the survival that the land and rural life no longer seemed to offer. From smaller cities and villages of Quebec came artisans with skills they could sell in the changing labour market of Montreal.[55] And when in 1873 the Great Depression hit American cotton mill towns, peopled in large part by French-Canadian immigrants, several thousand families headed back north to Montreal hoping to find there the jobs that were no longer available in the States.[56]

Ever since the Conquest the ships arriving in Montreal during the spring and summer months had brought some immigrants from

England, Scotland, and Ireland. Many stayed a few days in the city, then moved on to seek land or work elsewhere in the colonies; many were lured on by the opportunities believed to predominate south of the border. Some remained, carving out futures for themselves in the trade, commerce, crafts, and day labour of Montreal. Successive waves of Irish Protestants and Catholics, first in the 1820s, more dramatically in the decade of the famine, contributed most to the reshaping of Montreal's social, class, and ethnic structure that would continue over subsequent decades.[57]

Within the city as a whole the Irish swelled the working-class component of the population and became the largest non-French-speaking group. In 1861, 16 per cent of all Montreal residents had been born in Ireland. A decade later, when people were asked about their origins as well as their birthplace, fully one-quarter of the population was of Irish origin. Gradually their relative importance declined as new waves of immigrants from England and Scotland reshaped the Anglophone population of the city.[58]

Most of the Irish Catholics who stayed in Montreal settled only a short distance from where they had disembarked. Griffintown, in the heart of Sainte Anne ward, just to the west of the docks, housed one-third of Montreal's Irish population. In this "teeming Irish centre" on a Saturday night in the 1860s:

> the old market was alive with an active crowd laying in the week's supply of greens and the meat for Sunday's dinner. And up and down both sides of the street were the gas lit shops all hives of trade, and at every corner on the west side stood in groups the men of Griffintown, all after their week's work, now clean, and dressed in their good clothes, but, withall, not to be trusted to keep the peace if a redcoat or a sailor brushed against them. . . .[59]

Ex-tenant farmers and rural labourers joined their wealthier fellow ex-patriots, forming a body of workers that could be drawn on for large construction works, casual labour around the port, and early industry. The "week's work" of the majority of male Irish Catholics continued to be found throughout these years in the unskilled jobs that abounded in good times on the wharves, around the port, with the Grand Trunk Railway, and in the factories. Their very visibility led H. Clare Pentland to argue that these Irish constituted Canada's earliest proletariat.[60] It is now clear that Montreal's emerging proletariat included French Canadians and English and Scottish immigrants as well as the Irish.[61]

In-migrating French Canadians, immigrant Irish, and immigrant workers from elsewhere in the British Isles merged in the city with more settled compatriots. Their decisions about where to live created a complex ethnic tapestry of settlement in the changing city. Balancing the visibility of the Irish in much of Sainte Anne in the west was the growing concentration of French Canadians in the eastern wards. In Sainte Marie and Saint Jacques they rapidly filled up the rows of duplexes thrown up by small-scale speculators and contractors with little regard either for city building codes or for basic sanitary measures. These parts of town, geographer Raoul Blanchard argues, became agglomerations of proletarians, bursting with children and subject to the vicissitudes of epidemics, fires, and floods.[62]

The linguistic geography of Montreal hardened over these years. The eastern city became predominantly French-Canadian, the western parts a mixture of people of French-Canadian, English, Irish, and Scottish origin. Population changes in Saint Jacques mirrored those of the eastern city (Figure 1.1). Between 1861 and 1891 its population increased by almost 150 per cent, from 13,104 to 32,393; over the 1861-71 decade its population grew at nearly double the rate of the city as a whole before gradually slowing down. Population densities rose to the highest in the city – from 150 people per acre in 1877 to 168 in 1884. In the poorer parts of the ward, houses were crammed as close together as possible, constructed on the narrowest of city lots. Since the early decades of the century Saint Jacques had housed a significant kernel of Protestant Irish, English, and Scots. In 1861 non-French Canadians made up more than one-third of the population. They were concentrated largely in business and the professions. Over the period of study this non-Francophone group faded into relative insignificance in the face of the sheer size of the increase in the numbers of French Canadians, from just under 9,000 in 1861 to 22,000 two decades later, when they made up 87 per cent of all residents.

In Sainte Anne, in contrast, the residential population grew slowly, from 16,200 people in 1861 to 23,003 in 1891, always increasing at a rate well below that of the city as a whole. There, empty spaces were filled not by houses but by large industrial establishments. Rising land values for industrial land limited the possibilities of housing construction and of home-ownership as a working-class option.[63] Sainte Anne's population was the most mixed of any city ward in this period. The numbers of Irish origin nearly doubled between 1861 and 1871 but hardly increased after that. The pattern among the English and the Scots was similar. The majority of non-French-Canadian residents were at least second-generation immigrants by 1871. In 1881 only 16 per cent of the residents of Sainte Anne had been born in Ireland, while nearly 50 per cent were of Irish origin. Similarly, 8 per cent of the population had been born in England or Scotland, but 22 per cent were of English or Scottish origin. Older heads of families predominated

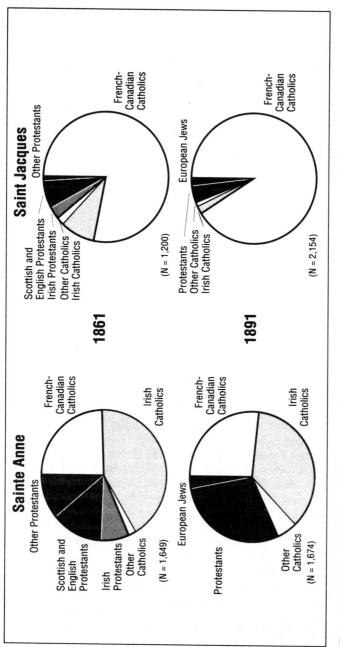

Figure 1.1 Major Religious/Ethnic Groups, Sainte Anne and Saint Jacques, 1861 and 1891

among the immigrants. Younger couples and most children were of the second generation. By 1891 a new wave of Protestant immigrants from England had boosted the Anglophone population of the ward, while growing numbers of Catholic Newfoundlanders added to the Catholic population. Also, although there had been few Jewish families in these wards in the 1860s and 1870s, by 1891 2-3 per cent of residents in each ward were Jewish, largely recent arrivals from Europe (Figure 1.1).

Major concentrations of French Canadians also settled in Sainte Anne ward, attracted by the greater variety of jobs available within its boundaries and stretching up the hill into the lower sections of Saint Antoine ward to the north. Moulders, many of whose family histories could be traced back to the Saint Maurice forges, resided together in street blocks, not too far from the foundries and factories that valued the skills they had to offer.[64] Carpenters, joiners, and other skilled workers, as well as labourers, penetrated certain streets in Pointe Saint Charles and in the northern section of the ward, forming French-speaking ribbons and pockets along the once Irish-dominated streets. In 1861 there had been only 3,323 French Canadians living within the ward's boundaries. By 1881, with 5,849 people, they constituted nearly 30 per cent of the ward's population.

The different generations of French Canadians, Irish, English, and Scots who made up the majority of the population of these wards and the city as a whole brought with them diverse work skills and histories of wage labour. Combining with pre-conceptions held by employers about the skills and desirability of specific groups, these produced a distinct but changing ethnic division of labour within the city's labour markets. In Sainte Anne the Irish dominated unskilled day labour throughout the period. French-Canadian males in the two wards were more concentrated than other groups in construction, carting, and shoemaking. Protestants from the British Isles were overrepresented among those working for the railways and in those areas of metalworking and factory production that drew on skills that many had probably practised before leaving Great Britain. Ethnic clusterings added a further layer of complexity to labour markets already divided by age and gender. French-Canadian Catholics, Irish Catholics, Protestants from the British Isles, and their descendants clustered in somewhat different trades and sectors of the economy and dominated different fractions of the working class. That working class as a whole was predominantly Catholic, while most though not all of the larger, modern factories were owned by Anglophone Protestants. Religion, ethnic traditions, and class solidarities collided, competed, and at times complemented each other as individuals and families adjusted to the challenges of survival on fluctuating and inadequate wages.

Institutions, Ideologies, and Daily Life

The predominance of French Canadians and Irish in the city meant that Catholics consistently comprised the major religious group, representing in 1891, as they had in 1861, around three-quarters of all residents. Bishops and priests were powerful influences in state policies and in the daily life of much of the population. The religious and the secular were hardly separable in this metropolis that had until recently been the seigneury of the Sulpician priests, men who proved quite capable of transforming themselves from feudal landlords to capitalist real estate agents and investors over the early decades of the nineteenth century.[65] Imperialist and ascendant, the Catholic Church increased the numbers of its personnel dramatically over these years as Bishop Ignace Bourget oversaw the formation of a complex structure of male and female orders and associated institutions designed to ensure hegemony in an increasingly secular and dangerously Protestant city.[66] Schools, orphanages, homes for the sick, the aged, and for young women seeking work as domestics or shelter from the dangers of the streets, soup kitchens, dispensaries, and branches of the Saint Vincent de Paul Society were only a few of the network of social institutions run by diverse religious communities and lay people to assist the city's Catholic residents. Protestant groups working alone and together built an even more complex grid of similar institutions for their poor and needy.[67]

Working with families was at the heart of Bishop Bourget's vision of how to maintain and increase control over the Catholics of the city. Their numbers doubled from 65,896 in 1861 to 134,142 in 1891. Sisters, priests, and brothers were to educate and to care for the growing number of poor in the city. By visiting the poor and the sick, Bourget argued that lay and religious workers would be able not only to bring relief to those in need, but might also succeed in instilling peace in households, correcting vice, suppressing scandals, and encouraging love of work among parents as well as participation in the sacraments. He further hoped that once the city was carved up into smaller parishes after 1865 his priests would be able to intervene directly with families, calming internal dissensions, bringing together alienated spouses, encouraging rebellious children to obey their parents, and pushing negligent parents to raise their offspring well.[68]

Religion was in daily evidence and important in many citizens' lives, yet priests and ministers had trouble overseeing their flocks from day to day. Despite the goal of Protestant and Catholic churches and middle-class reformers to fashion more conforming, less unruly congregations, profanity remained part of popular expression, vice part of many lives. Cases of bigamy, prostitution, wife-beating, and other forms of assault were frequent in the city's courts. Almsgiving was widespread, but so, on occasion, was alms taking. Witness two somewhat imaginative criminals who dressed up in priests' robes, somehow armed themselves with the official certificate of a priest who had left for New Orleans, and managed to convince the public that they were legitimate collectors for the wounded in France.[69]

Montreal's institutions were not only church-based. As the re-organization of work increased the distance between worker and employer, oppositions between the interests of workers and capitalists hardened. Each was increasingly likely to create its own organizations to better control the conditions of work or accumulation. In the 1850s and 1860s Montreal engineers, shoemakers, carpenters, typographers, and other skilled workers had organized their own unions or affiliated with international ones. They fought to preserve control within their crafts or to improve pay or work conditions. "Strikes were becoming epidemic among skilled mechanics," reported the *Montreal Gazette* in 1861.[70] In the same year that Canada was being forged as a nation, Montreal workers united in a brief burst of collaboration that transcended craft boundaries to express their needs as wage-earners within the emerging industrial-capitalist economy. Médéric Lanctôt, an iconoclastic liberal lawyer who had fought ferociously against Confederation, brought together skilled craftsmen from at least twenty-six different unions as well as some unorganized workers into la Grande Association. He argued that capitalists and workers should combine to eliminate the misery and disorder that he saw as a product of the growth of industry. The only way he saw that this could be done was to force industrial capitalists, by law, to share their profits with the workers. Otherwise they would exploit the workers, even let them die of hunger, and would combine with other capitalists to create monopolies. Preaching against strikes, la Grande Association nevertheless supported several. A co-operative shop was organized to make cheaper food available to workers.[71]

La Grande Association evaporated after a year. In subsequent years workers in diverse industries united again to express their demands, their needs, and their identity as workers. In 1872 Montreal workers expressed their solidarity with their Ontario counterparts in the fight for a nine-hour work day. The Ligue ouvrière de Montréal was founded in March. It assembled delegates of at least twenty-three industrial establishments to attempt to negotiate a nine-hour day in Montreal workplaces by the first of July. By June, workers at the vast Grand Trunk works and in other Montreal industries were being promised a fifty-four-hour work week. Some strikes had been successful. The employers, however, were equally conscious of their interests and determined to unite to combat such worker initiatives. They organized their own committee to fight the movement and locked out and black-listed strikers. By August the movement had disintegrated. A few workers retained their nine-hour work days; others found their hours increased back to sixty a week.[72] Unorganized and unskilled workers continued to work for up to twelve hours a day, untouched by this essentially craft-based movement.

Any gains temporarily won in 1872 were dismantled as the Great Depression took hold after 1873. Unemployment, short time, and wage cuts "put workers in a position where they had to fight for basic survival; other battles were postponed."[73] Then, the economy picked up in the late 1870s as the tariff protection of the National Policy induced capitalists in some sectors to invest in new industry or to expand production, Montreal workers again began to organize and to seek to changes in capital-labour relationships. Craft unions were re-invigorated in Montreal as in other Canadian cities, and thousands of men and women, many from jobs that had never been organized, banded together in locals of the Knights of Labor. The first Montreal locals were formed in the early 1880s. By 1887 there were some twenty-nine assemblies with several thousand members. Numbers dropped for a while following Bishop Taschereau's promise to ex-communicate Catholic Knights, but involvement picked up rapidly even before the Pope reversed the decision.[74] By 1894, when the order was declining in many parts of North America, Montreal boasted over thirty locals. Unlike most unions during this period, the Knights accepted women members and argued for equal pay for equal work. Drawing in English-speaking and French-speaking members initially in the same assemblies and after 1886 in separate ones, this ritualistic, secret society sought to assert the honour and value of workingmen and women and to instill pride in themselves as well as a sense of being members of the working class.[75] The Knights left their legacy in factory acts passed to eliminate some of the worst abuses of employers, in the idea of uniting beyond craft and regional boundaries, as well as in the creation of the Royal Commission set up by the Prime Minister, Sir John A. Macdonald, to examine questions surrounding relations between labour and capital.

Organizations of manufacturers wielded greater power than those of the workers. They were increasingly able to influence governments to pass policies furthering their interests, to unite against striking workers, and to prevent what they saw as ruinous competition within their own trades. A combination of stove-makers had fixed the price of stoves by the 1880s. Members of the coal exchange set the price of coal.[76] Grocers were organizing to control the prices at which goods should be sold.[77] And, like the workers, Montreal manufacturers arranged organizations grouping members within the same industry and joined with capitalists from other cities to express their interests to government. Throughout the 1870s the Montreal Industrial Association joined with other manufacturers' associations throughout the country to push for higher tariffs.[78] While their particular goals varied and conflicted at times, the existence of such associations and combinations underlines the hardening of the difference between employers and their workers that occurred over this period.

Formal institutions run by the churches, by unions, or by organized groups were important in some people's lives. For much of the working class the texture of daily life revolved more around the sociabilities built up within families, between neighbours and friends, on the streets, or in taverns and shops. Montreal's streets buzzed with activity until the early hours of the morning. Shops were open as late as ten at night. In working-class neighbourhoods some family members and neighbours stayed up together late, drinking and carousing. When someone was in need they stepped in and provided money, food, and support. Many neighbours could not avoid sharing in each other's joys and sorrows. Walls were thin, and quarrels spilled out onto the streets. Entertainment was free at the courthouse, where real-life stories dealing with anything from insulting language to murder attracted crowds who only too often frustrated judges with their noisy participation.[79]

Between the 1860s and early 1890s the collage of contrasts and incongruities that had characterized the earlier period was reworked as industrial capitalists, land speculators, builders, and reformers imposed a new order. Lines became clearer and more fixed in the city that emerged, and class divisions became more concrete than they had been in the early 1860s. The testimony of workers to the Royal Commission on the Relations of Labour and Capital, held in Montreal early in 1888, made clear the antagonisms of many workplaces. Geographical segregation of the residential areas of the working class from the rest of the population was firmly established. Working families became more and more dependent on wages, as other ways of complementing the family wage by raising animals or keeping gardens were rendered either illegal or impractical. Visitors to Montreal commented less on the differences between French and English, more on its industry and on industrial conflict or on the apparent weariness and poverty of the workers.[80]

In the process of industrial transformation that accelerated untidily and unevenly in Montreal between the 1860s and 1890s, the working class had expanded and consolidated. That working class was not homogeneous. It was as mixed, as characterized by elements of continuity and of change, as the forces that created it. Different cultural backgrounds and languages, diverse experience with industrial labour and organization, and major discrepancies in wages divided up the working class into a patchwork of sub-groups and fractions within which males and females played distinctive parts. Local labour markets offered different opportunities and work possibilities to men, women, and children. Their roles within the family economy varied accordingly.

Overriding these differences were two shared factors. First, the family was the most important institution of working-class life. Families remained work units, in which all members had specific responsibilities and tasks that ensured survival from day to day as well as from generation to generation. Second, for skilled, unskilled, and those in between, wages were the dominating factor, the major but seldom the only source of survival in these "family wage economies."[81]

2

Marriage, Families, and Households

The Legal Framework of
Marriage and the Family in Quebec

"Marriage is no uneven game. It is a tie," suggested the *Montreal Daily Witness* in December, 1879.[1] The legal structure, economic possibilities, and roles of men and women in nineteenth-century Quebec all suggest the opposite. Marriage created an unequal legal partnership sanctioned and perpetuated by the unequal alternatives and possibilities that the wider society and economy offered. Women over the age of twenty-one gave up whatever rights they had been exercising over property, in the courts, and in much of daily life. Marriage rendered a woman legally incapable in most public spheres, the judicial equivalent of minors and idiots. On marrying, a man became the legal and economic head of his family, the "seigneur" of property held in common and of the family. Regardless of his position in life it was his duty to provide shelter, protection, and the necessities of life according to his means.[2] Among the dwindling number of Montreal couples signing a marriage contract during this period, this obligation was often indicated explicitly. The future husband agreed to "provide alone for the expenses and costs of the household, the linens and personal clothing of the future wife will be provided by him according to their circumstances."[3] It was the husband's right to choose where to live and in what dwelling. His wife was legally bound to follow. The man had sole legal rights over the correction of his children. They had to seek his permission to leave home before the age of majority or to marry. A wife could not appear in court without her husband's permission.[4] Husbands could expect their wives to submit to them at all times, and in principal, at least, their legal and economic subordination ensured that most would do so.[5]

Relations between spouses and family members were framed by the same law for all classes. In Quebec, the *Coutume de Paris* governed civil law and spelled out in detail the legal and property rights of husband and wife. Centuries-old assumptions about gender relations were hardly changed when jurists reviewed them in the 1860s and formalized the Civil Code. Indeed, they remained largely the same until well into the twentieth century.[6] Yet while the patriarchal assumptions of the law transcended class boundaries, they worked out differently for propertied and non-propertied women. So did daily work and roles and relations within marriage. In the abstract, the legal structures may have seemed rigid and unbending. In practice, as people lived, worked, and sorted out their relationships in a city and society in transformation, they carved out new areas of practice within or despite the structures of the law, just as they modified their demographic behaviour and adjusted their family strategies.[7]

Quebec's Civil Code, like legal systems in most other parts of Canada, North America, and Europe, directly and unequivocally articulated the patriarchal basis of marriage and family relations, severely limiting women's legal right to act as independent agents.[8] The man was to protect his wife; the wife was to obey her husband. Her subordination was presented explicitly in legal texts as the counterpoint to the protection that he offered, a logical consequence of the fact that marriage made the man the legal guardian or tutor of his wife. This did not mean, one Quebec lawyer argued quite sincerely in his 1899 doctoral dissertation, that women disappeared during marriage. Not at all. Rather, she "slept" for as long as she had an administrator of herself and her goods at her side![9]

Wives might slumber rather than sleep by taking advantage of provisions in Quebec's civil law that allowed men and women to specify in their marriage contracts that the wife would control her own property. This was done increasingly over the century by propertied families but was rare within the working class. The only other way in which women could officially circumnavigate their legal incapacity was by identifying themselves as public merchants or traders. Such women were free to operate without their husbands' consent "respecting the acts and expenses of their trade."[10]

Such legal capacity was the exception, however, limited to those married separate as to property and to public traders, yet constrained even for them.[11] Clauses concerning property, perhaps even trade, impinged little on the daily life of poorer working-class men and women, who seldom possessed real property. For them, marriage and family life thus posed different challenges, demanded different strategies, and created different kinds of relationships and dependencies.

Unlike in the period of New France or after the Conquest in some rural areas of Lower Canada, few ordinary Montreal couples bothered to make a formal marriage contract in this period.[12] Without a marriage contract specifying otherwise, working-class couples who married in the province fell under the regime of community of property. Under this marital regime each partner held an equal share in most kinds of property acquired by either party during the marriage. The wife could not, however, control or administer her part of this until the marriage was dissolved by the death of her husband. In the day-to-day functioning of the couple the husband had the right to control common property and could "sell, alienate or mortgage them and make use of and dispose of them . . . at his pleasure and will." A wife could not sell, alienate, or mortgage even her own "estates without the authority and express consent of the husband." Such authorization was also necessary to acquire property, to receive donations, to make contracts, or to set up a business. Without it such acts were null and void. [13] Nor was the husband's power limited to control of real property. Under this regime, the wife had no legal right to control the wages she earned. [14]

Wages entered into the community property, administered by the man. Like men in English Canada and the U.S. at the beginning of this period, most Quebec husbands could legally spend their wives' wages or claim them as their own. [15] The common law, which formed the basis of marriage law in the U.S., England, and English Canada, put women in an even more insidious position than those in Quebec. Not only had they no right to contract, but, as historian Amy Dru Stanley has pointed out for American women, their very labour belonged to their husbands. She points out that the wage system of labour posed fundamental challenges to the "time honoured assumptions of marriage law. At the heart of the contradiction lay the wife's title to her wages, a right that the wage contract pre-supposed, but the marriage contract denied." The spreading wage system and the legal conventions of marriage law were thus in tension, creating a potentially more significant barrier to independence for working-class women than the property provisions that American feminists were attacking at the time and that were soon to be revised in England, Ontario, and the United States. [16]

As long as relations between a husband and wife were reasonably amicable, it is unlikely that this aspect of the law caused major problems for working-class wives. In Montreal, the majority earned only occasionally and usually in small amounts. Their day-to-day work included managing family budgets based on the wages of others. This gave them effective if not legal power over much of the family purse, a responsibility that was explicitly recognized in the jurisprudence. Court cases acknowledged the right of wives to contract debts for household purposes. [17] However, when a husband's vindictiveness, inability to earn, or desire for drink led him to claim his legal right, such women were crudely reminded of the rank that they shared legally with imbeciles and minors. [18] When Anne Simpson's carter husband spent all his earnings on drink she supported the family by doing washing and running a small shop. He not only expected his meals on the table and turned up regularly to eat them, but also stole from her pocketbook and threatened her life when she tried to stop him.[19] The law did not sanction the threats. It did give him the right to her money. Counterbalancing this right was his primary responsibility to provide for his wife and children with his earnings. Anne, obviously a woman of many resources, took her husband to court for failing to provide her with the necessities of life.[20]

The Unmarried

Marriage, then, was a complex institution that seemed to offer more advantages to men than to women. Yet, for women of the working class in particular, the alternatives only too often involved prolonged economic and social dependency or poverty. Women were much more likely to remain single than men, less because of conscious choice than as a result of demographic and economic inequalities. In Montreal as a whole only one in ten men never married across this whole period compared to up to one in five women. In a city that attracted women seeking jobs, the excitement of the streets, or life in a religious order, there were always over 113 females of marriageable age for every 100 men. Most men married for the simple reason that they needed a woman to run their household. Yet, when they found themselves in parts of the city where sex ratios were more equally balanced, or where men predominated, as in Sainte Anne ward at the end of the century, they were less likely to find a spouse.

Fluctuations in the economy delayed marriage for some, made it unlikely for others. Following the Great Depression that struck Quebec in 1874, the cohort of women who were already in their thirties and still single were unlikely to marry. Within Sainte Anne and Saint Jacques wards, single French-Canadian women were hit especially hard. When the census had been taken in 1871 three-quarters of French-Canadian girls aged twenty-five to twenty-nine were already married. Ten years later, after eight years of depression, almost all of the remaining one-quarter of this same cohort, now aged thirty-five to thirty-nine, were still single. In the city as a whole, 20 per cent of women aged 41-61 were single. Once the depression lifted most seem to have been too old to find a spouse, and the majority remained single.

Pressure to remain at home and contribute to the family economy was perhaps a further reason why some women never married. The need of aging parents, widows, and widowers for their daughters' help with domestic labour and caring, or for help with sewing for the putting-out industry, may have delayed marriage for some of the French-Canadian daughters of Saint Jacques ward, where rates of celibacy were generally higher than in Sainte Anne.

Other women, always a minority, may simply have managed to build an independent life free of men, avoiding some of the disadvantages of marriage. Studies may well show that this was more common outside than within the working class. Such apparently high rates of non-marriage, with up to one in five women but only one in ten men remaining single, are not particularly high compared with patterns in Europe. They fit well within the broad contours of the pattern of increasingly universal marriage that constituted part of the demographic transition in Europe and that has generally been associated with industrialization and urban growth. And they are similar to the situation in Ontario at the same time.[21]

The unequal sex ratios underline the importance of single women in Montreal's population and the need to study this largely ignored group.[22] Whether unmarried or widowed, deserted by their spouses, or separated by migration, propertyless single people faced special and particular challenges. The very different problems that living outside a family posed require that the unmarried be studied separately. The focus in this book on families should not blind the reader to their existence.

Patterns of Marriage

For the majority of women without property, finding a husband with a skill that could be sold in the marketplace was the most usual way of ensuring their own support in a society and labour market that assumed female dependency. Few could live on the wages that a woman could earn. Most could not expect aging, poorly paid parents to support them all their lives, whatever the pressures exercised to keep them at home contributing either their wages or domestic labour. Only the Church and life as a nun offered comparable or even superior economic security, depending on the order chosen. For those with a calling or a preference for a life of chastity, becoming a nun also offered the possibility of gaining a profession.[23] But for women who fell in love, were attracted to men, or were more interested in sex than chastity, marriage must have seemed more attractive.

For men who no longer wished to live with their parents, whose parents had died, or who had no relatives in the city, a wife offered major advantages over the costs and possible loneliness of lodging or staying in a boarding house. The amount of domestic labour necessary simply to feed, clothe, and look after a worker made living alone pretty well impossible for male workers, who could be away from home from five in the morning to eight or nine at night. Hence, lack of ability and practice at fending for themselves, strongly ingrained ideas about who should do housework, and a variety of other individual and societal factors meant that most men sought a wife.

Men and women might meet prospective spouses in the neighbourhood, among friends or relatives, or in the workplace. Most working-class young people chose their own spouses. Parents without property had little leverage with which to prevent a son's or daughter's marriage. For the family of origin, a daughter's departure may at times have been welcomed because she made a good match or as one less mouth to feed. Or it may have represented the loss of a wage-earner or valuable domestic helper and thus constituted a source of tension and friction in the family. In either case, if the girl had lived at home before marrying, as more and more appear to have done, her marriage reshaped the family economy that she had left as well as heralding the founding of a new one.

Historians in Canada have only recently begun to study how working-class men and women met, courted, and married during the nineteenth century.[24] Friendships, contacts, or shared customs dating back before arrival in Montreal were often important for immigrants and in-migrants. Irish immigrants not only married fellow Irish, but often married those from their county of origin in Ireland.[25] Migrants from the North Shore of the St. Lawrence were quite likely to marry someone from the same parish or zone.[26] And most people married spouses of similar ethnic and class background to themselves.[27] Even in Sainte Anne, the city ward that offered the most opportunity for encountering those of different backgrounds, over four-fifths of couples were of the same origin. Language and culture combined to keep English, Scots, and Irish apart from French Canadians, despite the religion shared by the two latter groups. In 1871, for instance, only 8 per cent of French Canadians did not have a French-Canadian spouse. Over three-quarters of Irish partners were both Irish, with a significant minority (13 per cent) married to Englishmen or women. Some of these had met and married while working in England en route to Montreal.[28] With fewer compatriots in these wards, the Scots and English were more likely to take a spouse of a different origin.

Evidence from the turn of the century suggests that the marriage at the church was a fairly private affair, often involving only a few family members, invariably performed without much ceremony on weekday mornings, often before the work day began.[29] Here, apparently, was a quiet family celebration, the founding of a family economy in the presence of a priest or minister and one or two relatives. Among migrants from the North Shore of the St. Lawrence who married after their move to Montreal, fully 80 per cent chose kin as witnesses at their weddings.[30] Whereas middle-class marriages were witnessed by a vast array of friends and kin, most working-class couples' unions were witnessed by no more than two relations, usually the father of whichever spouse came from the Montreal area and one other relative.[31]

Most Montrealers married, formed families, and lived within families. Few married after reaching forty. Yet, the ages at which they married fluctuated over this period as the economic conjuncture, the changing reality of life on wages, and the transformations occurring within some jobs interacted with older patterns and traditions of marriage. Continuity and change mingled in a complex dialectical fashion. The patterns of marriage among the men and women of Sainte Anne and Saint Jacques wards demonstrate the interrelationship among marriage, conjuncture, class position, and cultural tradition, supporting Elinor Accampo's argument that "wage labour in an industrial context . . . did not promote earlier marriages as it had among proto-industrial workers" in Europe. Average age at first marriage in the industrial period, she argues, suggests that couples "faced more complex if not more difficult social, economic, and cultural conditions than did their proto-industrial predecessors."[32]

For Canada as a whole the age at marriage appears to have risen across the nineteenth century.[33] No such clear trend is evident among the people of these wards. In this relatively brief period of demographic time we see only short-term adjustments, reflecting the diversity of factors influencing the personal choices of the people making up the marrying population. Women consistently married younger than men; people of all ethnic origins and occupations tended to marry earlier in the more prosperous years preceding the censuses of 1871 and 1891 than prior to those of either 1861 or 1881, when times were bad. The men of Sainte Anne and Saint Jacques wards married, on the average, at around 26.5 years of age across the period. Women's average marriage age varied more, fluctuating noticeably with the economy. From around twenty-four in 1861, the average age dropped to twenty-two in 1871, rose to over twenty-five in 1881 as marriage was delayed, then fell again to around twenty-four at the end of the century. Like most averages, these must be treated with caution. Not only are they based on relatively small numbers, but they also hide a diversity of patterns related to ethnic background and class position that need to be unravelled if we are to understand the interplay among occupation, ethnicity, and marriage patterns.

French-Canadian and Irish Catholics, Montreal's two major ethnic groups, had opposite cultural practices regarding marriage age and the

proportions marrying. Marriage among French Canadians had traditionally been early in comparison with most European populations, as
was typical in societies where land was available and where inheritance traditions did not constitute a brake on marriage.[34] In Ireland, in
contrast, subdivision of the land, expropriations, and general poverty
had led to the postponement of marriage for many and a single life for
growing numbers in the early nineteenth century. By the 1840s males
in Ireland were marrying at a mean age of almost twenty-nine, women
at nearly twenty-six.[35]

These different cultural traditions seem to have been duplicated initially in these two Montreal wards, then modified somewhat over the
second half of the century. In 1861, French-Canadian males married on
the average at twenty-five, Irish men at 27.5.[36] A decade later the differential was similar. The differences are clearest within the group aged
25-29. In 1871 nearly three-quarters of French-Canadian men in this
age group were already married, yet only a little more than a third of
Irish men were. Among women the pattern is similar, but because
women married earlier it is clearer among those aged 20-24. Around
half the French-Canadian women in this cohort were married across
the whole period, compared to between a third and a fifth of Irish
women. The depression of the 1870s led both French-Canadian and
Irish men and women to delay marriage and to a temporary conver-
gence of their marriage patterns, most noticeable among men. In 1891,
however, Irish women and men were again marrying later than were
French Canadians or the English and Scots.

Economic reality and cultural tradition were so interwoven among
these populations, characterized at the most general level by an ethnic
division of labour, that disentangling their relative influence is complex. In its broadest configurations the behaviour of the Irish and
French Canadians conformed to that found in other North American
cities.[37] The timing of marriage among the English and the Scots contrasts with the two largely Catholic ethnic groups. In 1861, English-
speaking Protestants, the majority of whom were better-paid skilled
workers, married later than all others, with an average marriage age of
nearly thirty for the men and almost twenty-six for the women. Until
the 1880s, however, the average age dropped steadily as the proportions married before age thirty increased. Men of these origins do not
appear to have married later in the years leading up to 1881, perhaps
because the depression did not hit them as hard as other groups. In
1891, however, the average age shot up again to over thirty, possibly a
result of new waves of immigrants joining the marriage cohorts.[38]

The different experiences of the three major ethnic groups reflect
something more than cultural and religious tradition. The interaction

between cultural traditions and the exigencies that derived from the workplace and from the wider economic conjuncture must be understood.[39] Outside the working class, men in Montreal, as elsewhere, tended to marry later. The difference was greatest in 1861, when non-working-class males married at an average age of twenty-nine compared to around twenty-five for working men. Throughout the period, men in non-working-class occupations were usually less likely to marry before the age of twenty-five than were working-class males (Table 2.1).

Within the working class, marriage patterns were complex, reflecting the ever-changing uncertainties facing men in different trades, but showing clearly that economic ability to set up a family was an important component of the decision to marry. In the years preceding the Great Depression, men in skilled work in particular, but also those in the trades undergoing most rapid transformation, the "injured trades," appear to have found sufficient work to marry fairly young. In the relatively prosperous period captured by the census of 1871 over 40 per cent of the skilled and over 60 per cent of those in the injured trades were married by the age of twenty-four, around 70 and 90 per cent respectively by age twenty-nine. This compares with under 25 per cent of the unskilled aged 20-24 in 1871 (Table 2.1). How much this early marriage was a product of decisions made in good times becomes clear on looking at the figures for 1881. Seven to eight years of major depression had levelled wage-earning discrepancies in much of the working class and modified differences within the working class as well as between workers and non-workers. The behaviour of the unskilled changed relatively little, as befits this predominantly Irish group whose timing of marriage had consistently been governed both by cultural tradition and by the uncertainties that accompanied day labour. The skilled and those in the injured trades, in contrast, ceased marrying early until the economy picked up. In 1881 under 30 per cent of skilled males aged 20-24 were married, compared to over 40 per cent a decade earlier; only 15 per cent of men the same age working in the injured trades were married, compared to over two-thirds a decade earlier.

These Montreal marriage patterns serve as an indicator of economic transition and crisis, of the interaction between cultural norms and economic realities. Behind a general stability in the average age at marriage for all the men of Saint Anne and Saint Jacques wards lay disparate demographic regimes the logic of whose workings is embedded in complex and often contradictory individual responses to the transformations of the period. Men with different jobs made different decisions about when to marry, reducing but not eradicating differences apparently based on ethnic tradition.

Child-bearing and the Decline in Family Size

When whole cohorts of men and women choose to marry earlier or later than previous cohorts, short-term fluctuations in fertility result. It is not possible to measure how fertility rates responded to these modifications of marriage patterns or related to differences between ethnic groups or fractions of the working class without a full-scale reconstitution of the population of the city. Some idea of the numbers of surviving children living at home, which is essential to understanding the family economy, can, however, be determined from the censuses.

The numbers of young children who were living with the couples of these two wards when the censuses were taken only tell us how many of their offspring had survived and not been given up to relatives, strangers, or institutions. Nevertheless, the patterns in the numbers of youngsters at home between the 1860s and 1890s do suggest that there was a real decline in the number of children born across this period. This supports demographers' suggestions that changes in fertility occurred earlier in Montreal than elsewhere in the province.[40] Furthermore, although there are some real differences in people's behaviour that relate to their origin, religion, and class position, the decline appears to have been common to all age groups, nationalities, and occupations.

Demographers and historians without the documents or the time necessary to reconstitute whole populations have calculated the number of children under five as a ratio of the number of women of child-bearing age to measure changing fertility patterns. Such a measure has the advantage of being easy to calculate. The disadvantage is that it cannot account for differences in the patterns of infant mortality or of age structure between ethnic or class groups. With this disadvantage in mind, it is worth using for the families of Sainte Anne and Saint Jacques because it not only gives some indication of fertility change, but also indicates how many young children married women had to care for as part of their domestic labour and daily life. Two major trends are clear in the child-woman ratios set out in Table 2.2. First, there was a general decline across the period, which accelerated in the years leading up to the census of 1891. In 1861 there were 1,100 children under five for every thousand married woman aged 20-49, or 1.1 under-fives for each woman. By 1891 there were only 840. Second, women in all ethnic and religious groups were likely to have fewer children in 1891 than in 1861. The decline was greatest among English, Irish, and Scottish Protestant women, most erratic and smallest among Irish Catholics, and steady among French-Canadian mothers. This decline is slow in the decades between 1861 and 1881 when compared with those recorded elsewhere in North America. However, by 1891 it constitutes what appears to be a major and significant trend.[41]

These child-woman ratios also puncture several myths about the size of families among different ethnic groups. In 1861 there were exactly the same number of children under five living with Irish mothers as with French-Canadian mothers. In 1871 and 1891 Irish mothers had more young children, partly because infant mortality hit French-Canadian families much harder than the Irish and other groups. These explanations do not change the fact that the number of children in their households was remarkably similar. And, despite infant mortality, both Irish and French-Canadian women had more young children than did their compatriots in American cities that have been studied in the same period.[42] The ratios also show that, early in the period, contrary to common belief and despite their later marriage age, Protestant families had more young children than did Catholic ones. In both 1861 and 1881, English, Irish, and Scottish Protestant mothers had more living youngsters than the other groups. But these mothers appear to have limited births more decisively by the end of the century than did Catholic women[43] (Table 2.2).

As infant mortality did not increase over this period, the fall in the numbers of young children at home must reflect a real fertility decline. That this decline was not simply the result of the later age at which women were marrying but of men and women exercising some form of control within marriage is suggested by the age-distribution of mothers reporting the birth of a child in 1861. This is the only year in which the census asked whether women had given birth. The proportion of married women of all cultural backgrounds who reported giving birth declined steadily from over 50 per cent of that minority within the working class who married before the age of twenty to 38 per cent of those aged 20-29 and under 25 per cent of those aged 30-34. The decline in births among women over the age of twenty-nine is greater than would be expected were no form of birth control exercised.[44] Patterns varied among ethnic groups, with each group most likely to have babies in the years following their average age at marriage (Figure 2.1). Thus, for French-Canadian women who married at an average age of twenty-four in 1861, the most fertile married years were between twenty-five and twenty-nine years old. For the Irish, the years between twenty and twenty-nine were the most fertile, while births among English and Scottish women peaked later, largely concentrated between the ages of twenty-five and thirty-five.

Several factors, all of which merit more detailed investigation than can be given here, could explain this fall in births. Some women were consciously attempting to control births once they had borne several

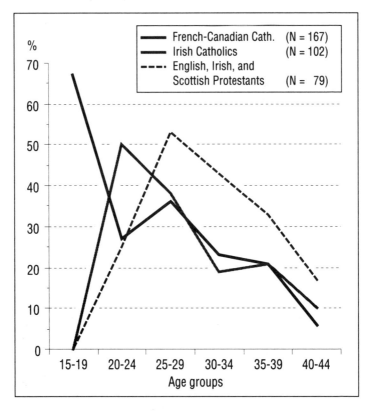

Figure 2.1   Proportion of Women Reporting a Birth in 1861;
French-Canadian Catholics, Irish Catholics, and English, Irish, and
Scottish Protestants

children, either by agreeing on a method with their husband, or turning to commercially available "remedies" or traditional folk methods
of avoiding conception. Others were able to increase the time between
conceptions by prolonging breast-feeding. Abortion, infanticide, and
desertion of newborns all occurred in Montreal during this period,
though measuring their frequency poses major problems.[45] Yet, in a
city where approximately one in three children failed to reach the age
of five in the 1860s and where, well into the twentieth century, almost
one in four were dying before age one, only the most desperate
women needed to abandon their offspring in order to control family
size.[46] Equally difficult to measure are the effects of long-term

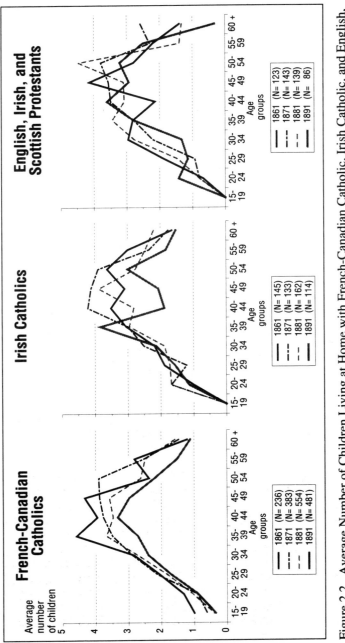

Figure 2.2 Average Number of Children Living at Home with French-Canadian Catholic, Irish Catholic, and English, Irish, or Scottish Protestant Women, 1861-91

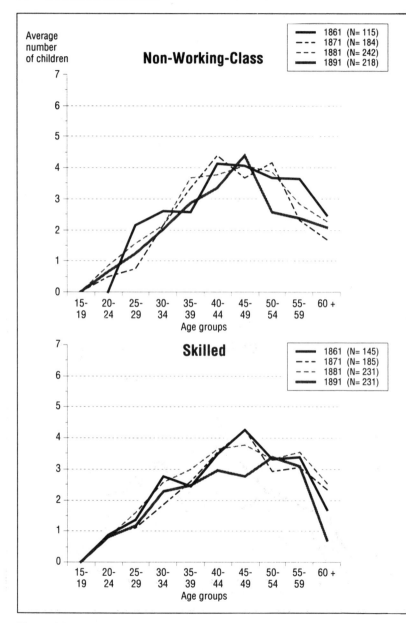

Figure 2.3 Average Number of Children Living at Home with Men in Different Class Positions, 1861-91

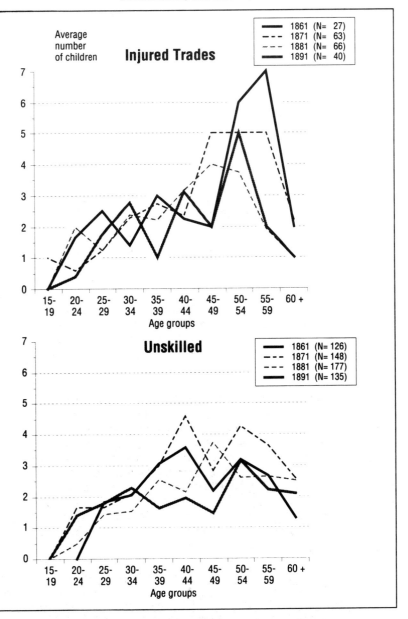

malnourishment, fatigue, and illness that could well have hindered either conception or the ability to carry a fetus to term among large numbers of women in the poorest fractions of the working class.[47]

Some of the methods of controlling family size may have enabled English-speaking women to limit their number of children. Irish-Catholic and French-Canadian women practising anything but abstinence transgressed Church teaching, which forbad contraception, condemned books dealing with sexuality in marriage, and actively encouraged women to do their duty and have children.[48]

Family size declined in part as a result of forces outside people's control but also as a result of conscious decisions. Smaller families made sense in the context of dependence on wage labour and of transformations in work and fluctuations in earning possibilities. Most men and women became parents shortly after marriage and the number of surviving children increased steadily as they aged. For couples of all backgrounds and occupations in 1861 the average number at home peaked at over four children when the husband was in his forties, then fell off gradually. There were still an average of nearly two and a half children in the household when fathers were sixty and over. By 1891, the average number of children in the home was lower at all ages, peaking at just over three when men were in their late forties and early fifties, then falling off to one by their sixties. Averages here give an idea of general trends, hiding the particularities in the responses of men and women with different backgrounds and ethnic and religious traditions or those who faced different economic challenges (Figures 2.2 and 2.3).

During the 1860s and 1870s French-Canadian and Irish males had over one child to support when they were in their twenties. Lower infant mortality meant that Irish-Catholic men averaged three children at home in their late thirties, compared to under three among French Canadians despite their earlier age at marriage. Families were largest for both these groups in 1861 among men aged 40-44. This contrasts with families headed by Protestant males, which because of their later marriage age were larger when men were in their late forties and early fifties. Men and women of all ages and origins had fewer children living with them in the 1880s and 1890s than at mid-century. There was a shift, too, in the age at which couples had the largest number of children at home. Family size peaked for couples of all origins when the men were about five years older in the later decades, hinting at the growing importance of keeping youngsters at home where their earnings could contribute to the family budget.

The similarities among these broad ethnic-religious groupings are greater than the differences. Despite divergent traditions and patterns of marriage, families of all origins in these Montreal wards ended up with quite similar patterns of family size over their life cycles. French-Canadian women may have given birth to more children. In these wards they did not have more who survived and remained living with their parents. Nor were large families concentrated among them. The average number of children living at home at peak moments of the family life cycle declined from around four to nearer three in all groups, and a similar proportion of each group continued to have large families. In this, French Canadians were little different from other groups. Among mothers aged 40-44, around one in five of all origins and religious practices had six or more children at home in 1891. All groups were somewhat less likely to have over six children at home in the 1880s and 1890s than earlier (Table 2.3).

Over these years ethnic differences decreased at the same time as those between fractions of the working class appear to have increased, underlining the divergent impact of industrial transformation and economic depression within the working class. In 1861 non-working-class families averaged more children than did those of workers. By 1891 the situation had changed. Non-working-class families were somewhat smaller, probably as a result of exercising some form of birth control[49] (Figure 2.3). When the family head was aged 40-44, usually the point at which families were largest, the non-working-class family averaged 4.13 children at home in 1861 and more in 1871. By 1891, however, men at this age had only 3.34 co-resident offspring. Within the working class the number of surviving children varied with men's occupations and across their life cycles and changed over time, although a decline was general to all groups. Men in skilled jobs generally averaged more children than the unskilled and managed to keep them home longer. They were the only group within the working class that seems to have conceived and succeeded in supporting and rearing more children over most of this period, despite the problems that they, too, faced during the depression. Theirs is the only group that shows no decline in the average number of children at home between 1861 and 1881. Earlier marriages in the good years preceding 1871 had lengthened their wives' chances of conceiving, and the more adequate food and decent housing that their salaries generally permitted no doubt helped their infants' chances of survival. It seems likely, too, that in whatever decisions children made about leaving or staying at home once they reached maturity, the greater comfort such a home could offer over that of an unskilled worker, or the greater power that an earning skilled father could exercise, may have induced more of their sons and daughters to remain with their parents prior to marriage. By 1891, however, skilled workers, like all other fractions of the working class, were having smaller families on the average.

The experience of these skilled workers diverged increasingly from that of the unskilled and those in injured trades. In 1861 both skilled and unskilled men aged 40-44 averaged approximately 3.5 children at home, but by 1881 the skilled averaged 3.6 and the unskilled only 2.1. Various factors closely tied to the precarious economic situation of these groups combine to explain these declines. Most had married late in the decade preceding 1881 because of the depression, thus eliminating some of the most fertile child-bearing years. They also included some of the groups most hit by infant mortality.[50] In addition, they were the groups least likely to be able to convince their earning children to remain at home, given the minimal standard of living they could offer.[51]

These various measures of the numbers of children living in families of different origins and headed by men in diverse kinds of occupations offer us glimpses, first, of an overall fertility decline in the province's major city and, second, of the complex relationship among position within the working class, marriage age, and family size.[52] Economic fluctuations and major transformations in the economy and in men's workplaces were permeating the inner rhythms of family life, influencing differently the behaviour of the skilled, the unskilled, and those in trades undergoing the most rapid transformations. The effects of the "feeling of depression" that shoemakers reported when their employers introduced some kinds of machinery into their craft clearly stretched beyond the workplace and into the home.[53] Men and women rethought old customs about marriage and family size. They adjusted the age at which they would marry, perhaps even the number of children they would have to fit the ever-changing realities of wage labour in a period of major upheaval. The working-class men and women making these decisions did not simply continue traditional patterns of family formation. Nor did they hopelessly or helplessly do "themselves in by producing more children than they could afford to support and keeping themselves bound to a precarious standard of living."[54] Instead, for reasons that were very different from those of the middle classes, they attempted to adjust to the situation within the parameters of their knowledge and abilities.

Family, Kin, and Residential Arrangements

As children were born and grew older families' space and income needs changed. The diversity and flexibility apparent in decisions about when to marry and in patterns of family size are clear, too, in the ways in which people adjusted and re-adjusted their living arrangements in response to the growth of families, income levels, economic fluctuations, and the needs of family and kin. Among the people of Sainte Anne and Saint Jacques wards, family and household structures varied between those headed by men and by women, they diverged with men's class position, and they changed over families' life cycles. At each census date, the majority of residential groupings were what Peter Laslett and his colleagues define as a simple family – either a couple with or without children or a lone parent with children. Around 85 per cent of male-headed families fell into this category across the period, while between 60 and 70 per cent of female-headed families did. Women were consistently more likely to be living either on their own, with siblings, or with other relatives than were men. They predominated among the heads of lone-parent families (see Table 6.1). What can these structures tell us about the role that kin played, or about working people's ideas regarding whom they should live with? How much does the way in which families and households were defined by census-takers influence the patterns?

Perhaps the question that sociologists initially asked, about whether families became increasingly nuclear with industrialization, should be rephrased. If we ask instead about when in time, among those in what occupations, and at what points in their lives did people live with kin other than their immediate family, we will better understand family structures. Montreal families headed by a man were less likely to include kin in the immediate residential unit in the 1890s than they had in the earlier period of industrialization. In 1861 nearly one in five male-headed families of Sainte Anne and Saint Jacques wards were extended to include relatives. The proportion dropped steadily, to under one in ten by 1891. This decline occurred among non-working-class and working-class families alike and at all stages of the family life cycle (Figure 2.4). Families in Saint Jacques had been more likely to be extended in 1861 than those living in Sainte Anne. By 1891 patterns in each ward were similar.

Between 1861 and 1891 personal preferences, fluctuating financial resources, and changes in housing stock combined to generate a certain geographical distancing of kin that appears to parallel what was occurring in other North American cities.[55] House-sharing or taking in kin continued to occur at some point in the lives of the poorer members of the working class, but over most of their life cycle the residential unit was the couple or a widowed spouse and their children.

People were not rejecting their kin. They appear simply to have been somewhat less likely to live with them. Sharing housing might provide needed support in the short term, yet it could also contribute to overcrowding and unwanted interference in family matters. Kin were not less important. Relatives offered essential help in critical life situations. They constituted the major source of social security and assistance in coping with uncertainty and personal crises such as unemployment, childbirth, illness, and death.[56] This was especially true among the working class. Kin in Montreal lived on the same streets, in the same courtyards, or in rear houses behind their brothers, aunts, and uncles. The duplexes and triplexes that came to characterize working-class housing over these years offered the ideal solution to family autonomy and family support. Whereas about one in five families lived in the same building as relatives in 1861, by 1891 over one-third of the families of Sainte Anne and Saint Jacques wards were living either in the same apartment or in the same building as kin.

In the early period of Montreal's industrialization, living with parents or siblings was not uncommon during the initial stages of the working-class family life cycle. In 1861 nearly one-quarter of couples lived with a relative, usually in the short period between their marriage and the birth of their first child. Over two-fifths did so when they had only one small child. Most lived either with the parents or with the siblings of one spouse. Couples whose children were older and required more space were much more likely to live alone until most children had left home. By the 1880s and 1890s this pattern of living with kin was no longer apparent. But couples were more likely to live in the same duplex or triplex as relatives at those stages of their life cycle when they were most likely to need help – as a young married couple before and after the birth of their first baby; over the years when all the children were under eleven and needed more care; then again as an elderly couple with grown children (Figure 2.4).

Which relatives were taken into the family depended on a subtle interaction between the needs of the host family, the needs of the relatives, and the life-cycle stage of each. In 1861 newlyweds and those with one young baby were most likely to live with their parents or with siblings. By 1881 the most common form of extension was that of taking in parents, predominantly widowed mothers of the husband or wife, or married children with or without offspring of their own. The rest were some combination of these forms of family extension.

Residential arrangements give us glimpses of the kinds of mutual aid that family members could provide for each other and of the proximity of kinfolk beyond the nuclear family. Sometimes arrangements were temporary responses to a moment of crisis, to unemployment, or to the arrival of newcomers in the city.[57] Taking in a widowed parent was usually more permanent. Yet, most couples attempted to live alone as their children aged and took up more space, despite the increased cost of feeding and clothing them. This becomes clear both in following particular families over their life cycles and in examining the structures of all families at different life-cycle stages. Stone-cutter Joseph Cérat, for example, was married to Philomene Laberge in 1856 in a ceremony witnessed by Joseph's older brother Edouard. There is no evidence of where or with whom they lived immediately following their

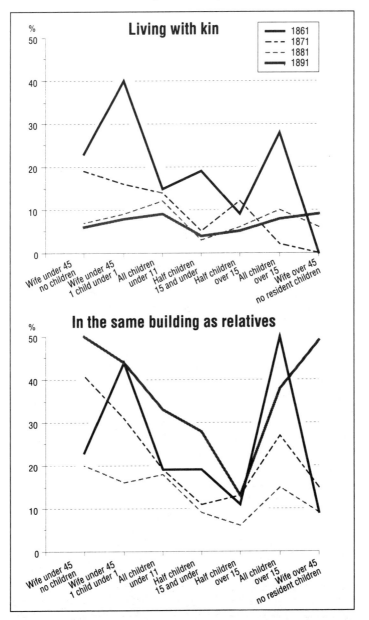

Figure 2.4 Percentage of Working-Class Families Living with Kin or in the Same Building as Relatives at Different Life-Cycle Stages, 1861-91

marriage, but five years later Joseph was recorded as head of an extended family that included brother Edouard, now with a wife, Sophie, the young children of both couples, and the Cérat grandparents. They were living in a two-storey wooden house in Saint Jacques ward. Whether this household sharing was in response to some crisis in one of their lives or to the general shortage of housing cannot be determined. It was not a permanent situation. Ten years later each brother headed his own household. They remained, however, within several houses of each other on Jacques Cartier Street. Twenty years later, Joseph was still heading a nuclear family, while his sons, now stone-cutters like their father, approached marriage age.[58]

Co-residence and living in close proximity often followed each other. Stays with relatives could be long term or fleeting. They might last a few days, weeks, or months after a newcomer's arrival in town, after the marriage of a young couple or the birth of a baby, or throughout a lengthier crisis period. On census day in April, 1881, for example, twenty-nine-year-old shoemaker Augustin Martineau and his wife Marie, their three-year-old child, and Augustin's parents were all living with his brother, Zephir, a carter, in a house at the rear of 164 Montcalm Street. A few months later the young couple had moved one or two blocks up the street to rent a dwelling by themselves. They remained there at least a year, still close enough to their relatives to get help minding the child, if necessary, and to exchange other forms of support.[59]

As these examples suggest, sharing a residence with kin was more widespread among French Canadians, particularly in Saint Jacques ward, than among the Irish or English. Housing shortages in eastern Montreal, the in-migration of large numbers of relatives and family members, and a tradition of family support combined to make more kin available both for assistance in times of crisis and as a source of orientation for newcomers to the city.[60] Kin for the Irish, English, and English Canadians of Sainte Anne and Saint Jacques would be drawn from a smaller pool of siblings, grandparents, and cousins.

Housing Conditions, Households, and the Question of Sharing Space

The geographical reshuffling that accompanied the expansion of industry, land purchase, speculation, housing construction, and population growth in Montreal created new residential patterns, a new class segregation in the city. Housing available to Montreal's working-class families changed over this period. Vast areas were redeveloped following the major fires of the 1850s.[61] Duplexes and triplexes sprouted in the fields of the northern and eastern parts of the city, pushing Montreal's populated boundaries toward small villages outside its limits. Empty spaces were filled as small builders, speculators, and individuals seeking retirement security reshaped the geography of the city and the housing market.[62]

Four features of Montreal housing are important to better understand the living places of working-class men and women. First, the polarization between bourgeois and working-class housing increased over this period and the possibility of working-class families owning a home within the city boundaries diminished. Second, new housing types, and in particular duplexes and triplexes, came to characterize most working-class areas. Third, the sanitary state of most old and much new housing for the working classes was deplorable. Finally, overcrowding and doubling up with other families remained a reality for a certain proportion of the poorer families of the city in part because of their financial problems, in part because construction of housing stock did not keep up with population growth.

"Whether building materials, roof types or basements are used as measuring sticks, the city's housing stock appeared to be polarized," concludes David Hanna after an examination of housing construction in Montreal between Confederation and the 1880s. The houses of the wealthy inhabitants of Saint Antoine ward, which stretched up the hillside above Sainte Anne, were in stark contrast to the "working-class reality" of the area of Sainte Anne that reformer and shoe manufacturer Herbert Ames would later dub "The City Below the Hill."[63] Within specific areas of Saint Jacques the luxurious, four-floor duplexes of French-Canadian bourgeois and professional families, with their raised basements and mansard roofs, constituted niches of affluence standing apart from the eastern section of the ward and western Sainte Marie, where whole districts of duplexes and the "quintessential Montreal fourplex gained strongest foothold."[64]

Housing was much more complex than the concept of polarization implies. The very way in which small builders and speculators alike constructed duplexes created differentiation within the buildings themselves. Thus the typical working-class Montreal housing was a two-and-a-half-storey duplex with no basement. The top unit, comprising one and a half floors, commanded a higher rent and was usually occupied by skilled workers, artisans, or small local businessmen, while the lower apartment was quite small and more likely to be rented by a labourer, shoemaker, or others attracted by the lower rent. Some older housing in areas like Sainte Anne remained single family, and, on some of the streets around the Grand Trunk Railway, working-class men built their own tiny, one-storey homes. Increasingly, however, such little houses were submerged in a dense townscape of multi-family housing.[65]

The growing differentiation of the nature of housing was accompanied by an increase in the difference between working-class and bourgeois and professional patterns of homeownership. Whereas in the 1840s around 32 per cent of all Montreal families had owned their own home, by 1881 only 15 per cent did. Montreal had become a city of tenants to a degree unmatched in other Canadian cities. Doctors, merchants, and a few other bourgeois and professional groups were more likely to own at the end of the period than at the beginning. Those in crafts undergoing major transformation, in contrast, were much less likely to do so. In 1847 half the city's coopers had owned homes. By 1881 only 11 per cent of the men in this trade and 7 per cent of tanners and shoemakers were homeowners. Carpenters and other workers in the construction trades are an exception to this trend. They often used their skills to build duplexes, then lived in one apartment themselves and rented out the other.[66] As a general rule, homeownership increased in those parts of town with the highest assessed rental values but decreased at the lower levels.

Changes in the earning and saving power of artisans and craftsmen that accompanied the transformation of their crafts and the emergence of industrial production combined over this period with the higher land values to remove the possibility of homeownership within the city from a growing proportion of the working class. Those making home-ownership a priority who were not tied to the city for work reasons could move outside the city boundaries to growing villages such as Saint Henri, where buying real estate remained a possibility. There, at least up until the 1870s, some families could save up and buy land before they had too many children and living costs drained all income.[67]

The duplexes and triplexes that were built after the ferocious fires of the 1850s replaced detached houses and obliterated their gardens. Historian John Cooper explains that this

> was also the plan adopted in building the railway workers' houses in Pointe St. Charles. They were constructed in terraces, the fronts set flush with the street line, and having scarcely more space in the rear than was required for privies, and the community well and wash "house."[68]

The duplexes, triplexes, and fourplexes constructed over the following decades became the typical working-class housing, lending a distinctiveness to the city's streets that remains today, and allowing the nurturing of kin networks. The renewal of Montreal's housing stock that followed the fires did not respond adequately to the demand for housing or to the need for improved living conditions. Working-class housing was generally constructed hastily and flimsily either by small builders who cut corners to complete construction with minimal capital or by major speculators interested only in profit.[69] A perennial, permanent housing crisis accompanied the growth of the city.[70] In Saint Jacques, where whole blocks were rapidly filled with fourplexes in one or two years, the population density shot up rapidly to the highest rate in the city, although never to rates comparable with the tenement houses of such cities as New York. Houses were crammed as close together as possible. Fire regulations were evaded in Saint Jacques at a rate unrivalled elsewhere in the city.[71]

Rapid settlement, poor construction, and population growth stretched housing and inadequate sanitary systems beyond what they could bear, exacerbating health problems that pre-dated industrial expansion.[72] Across the century Montreal registered higher mortality rates than any other British North American city. Dr. Philip Carpenter argued in the late 1850s that rates were eight to nine per thousand higher than in Boston or Quebec City, twenty per thousand higher than in the cities in the West. Despite the appointment of a health officer in the 1870s and the creation of a Health Department in the following decade, Montreal citizens retained "their unenviable distinction as the dwellers in the city of wealth and death" throughout the nineteenth century, even into the twentieth.[73]

Within this city, where life was so tenuous for French-Canadian babies in particular, Saint Jacques ward consistently registered the highest death rates. Municipal records placed rates at between thirty-five and thirty-nine per 1,000 during the 1870s and at around thirty in the following decade. "In certain unhealthy and overcrowded courts mortality rose to 40, 50, 60 and 70 per 1,000." In a swampy area in the southeastern corner of Saint Jacques stretching across into Sainte Marie ward, the largest proportion of deaths in the city was reported.[74]

Throughout this period, doctors and health officials identified unsanitary housing as the root of the health problems and high rates of illness and mortality that plagued Montrealers. As early as the 1850s Dr. Carpenter had argued that the City Council should take more responsibility for the sanitary state of Montreal housing:

> It is the duty of this council to see that the wages of death are no longer wrung from the hard won earnings of the poor, but that all who undertake to let homes shall be compelled to put them and their surroundings into a condition favourable to health.[75]

A decade later he was still linking the "principal causes of the death rate" to "the condition of the dwellings." Workers from the Montreal Diet Dispensary, a non-sectarian Protestant group formed to visit the poor and sick, came to the same conclusion. They added a welcome understanding of the problems of wage dependence. The root of the trouble, they suggested, was to be found in "bad housing, bad feeding and bad employment conditions."[76] By the 1870s doctors were blaming either mothers who did not breast-feed their children for the infant deaths that contributed most to the high mortality rates or the population in general for their ignorance or resignation.[77]

The city's health committee also believed that much of the illness, disease, and death in the city was a direct result of housing conditions. Their reports point repeatedly and explicitly to the problem of damp, overcrowded, unsanitary houses. Blame was placed squarely on landlords who did not bother to build on dry ground and neglected to provide proper drainage or on proprietors who refused to clean up homes that had been flooded following the spring break-up of the river ice. Such homes, they pointed out, were "generally occupied by poor families who are unable to remedy such defects."[78]

When the Royal Commission on the Relations of Labour and Capital took evidence in Montreal in 1888, the descriptions of the state of working-class housing focused on the worst cases, the "nests of contagion," the "rows of houses, rickety, propped up facing dirty sheds and germ breeding closets," in many of which sickness reigned "supreme." In most working-class housing, there were no facilities for bathing, and toilets were privy pits in the backyards. Journalist Arthur Short described a rear yard on Ottawa Street in Sainte Anne ward where eight families were paying four dollars a month in the lower apartments, slightly more in those above. In front of the houses in the yard were twelve outhouses, serving both these occupants and the families on the cross street, McCord. Some fifteen cases of diphtheria had recently spread among these families.[79] Shortly after the Commission's visit, the city began a "vigorous campaign" against privy pits. They encouraged the use of water closets but abolished the meagre total of 136 privies. Ten were in Sainte Anne and twenty in Saint Jacques.[80] When "water closet Ames" meticulously examined parts of Sainte Anne a few years later, 70 to 80 per cent of dwellings in the southern parts of the ward around the Lachine Canal and more than half the homes in the area he studied still relied on "that insanitary abomination, the out-of-door-pit-in-the-ground privy."[81]

Not all working-class families lived in such terrible housing. Different levels of rent roughly reflected the quality, age, and size of housing available. Families settled into specific street segments, upstairs or downstairs apartments, and sections of the city according to their ability to pay. Only specific groups within the working class – the unskilled, those in precarious, highly seasonal jobs, those who were frequently sick or who used up their money on drink – were concentrated in the worst, lowest rental housing. And those who were able, changed dwellings as soon as a better job, more regular work, or a child reaching working age gave them the means to do so.

Overcrowding and house- or apartment-sharing were another feature of the Montreal housing market that doctors and sanitary officials identified as a leading cause of the spread of illness and of child and adult deaths.[82] "Doubling up," subletting rooms to other families, or renting one or two rooms from landlords who had divided up their dwellings would certainly have been one way to reduce rental costs, the one major fixed and rigid expense in the working-class budget. Furthermore, if such sharing was leading to major overcrowding, it would indicate both a potential source of disease and a significant level of misery among the Montreal working class at this period. Thus, it is important to try to assess just how widespread the phenomenon was, whether it was an important working-class survival strategy, and to examine briefly the arguments that historians have made about it.

Qualitative evidence from the 1870s and 1880s suggests that house-sharing as well as overcrowding existed and that among certain fractions of the working class it was widespread. When Montreal physician Dr. Dougless Decrow described "two to three" families of day labourers occupying three- to four-room houses, he clearly meant they were sharing a dwelling intended for a single family. Whole families, he explained to the 1888 Royal Commission, slept in a single bedroom, sharing cooking facilities. Furthermore, he believed, this kind of "doubling up" was "getting to be the rule with the poorer classes of people," who would rent a "large house . . . well knowing at the time they took the house that they would have to relet the rest of it" because of the "poverty of the family."[83] Five years earlier a reporter for the *Montreal Daily Star* had highlighted the overcrowding of families in parts of Saint Laurent and Saint Jacques wards. In the buildings that he visited, families were limited to a room each. Yet another seeker-out of poverty and squalor, the anonymous author of *Montreal By Gaslight,* described the very worst cases in a Sainte Anne hotel that had been transformed into a "low lodging house." He reported that "within its four walls and upon its four stories lived at one time no less than twenty-eight families. In the direst of poverty, in abject want, without air, with no appliances for health and decency, in dirt and filth appalling, over one hundred and ten human beings herded like rats in a pit, barely existing from day to day."[84]

Sensational, muckraking journalism like this has to be read with extreme caution. Some of Montreal's poor did live in conditions of abject poverty, as in most cities in North America and Europe. Injuries, disease, alcoholism, even sheer bad luck made dire poverty a life-long state for some. For others, it was a temporary period that would be overcome by determination, persistence, good health, and good luck. This fraction of the people, unable to work for a variety of personal, structural, and societal reasons, constituted a group set apart from most of the working class.[85] They should not be seen as typical.

Yet other less sensational evidence does point to crowding and doubling up as phenomena that were not limited to the city's outcast poor. Scattered complaints from city officials, especially assessors, who felt they were not usually informed about "how many families are under one roof" or of subtenanting arrangements, hint at strategies deployed that might or might not appear in leases, evaluation roles, or the censuses.[86] Evidence in court trials was consistently given by people who boarded, either as families or as individuals, with the plaintiff or the defendant.

It is difficult to determine just how widespread or common either subletting by tenants or subdividing by landlords was.[87] Montreal's multi-family dwellings were constructed with one outside door leading into two or more separate apartments. (The spiral staircases that lend character to triplexes today came later.) This meant that strict application of the census definition of a household inflated the apparent rates of sharing compared to cities where single-family dwellings predominated. Enumerators were instructed to count a separate house "whenever the entrance from the outside is separate, and there is no direct and constant communication in the inside to make it one."[88] As a result, they often enumerated a duplex or triplex as if two or three families were sharing one living unit, rather than each renting their own apartment.[89] When I initially uncritically accepted the census definition and reported that in 1871 up to 30 per cent of French-Canadian families in Saint Jacques were sharing housing with non-related families, that percentage included some families simply dwelling in duplexes or triplexes.[90] Similarly, Darroch and Ornstein's assertion, that in "the urban areas of Quebec and Nova Scotia nearly one quarter of all households had two or more families or marital units," is based on a lack of investigation into how the enumerators applied the census instructions to the specific types of housing stock predominating in the different Canadian regions.[91]

Gilles Lauzon has meticulously reconstructed families' residential strategies using the census, enumeration roles, and leases in a new working-class suburb, Saint Augustin Village, located in Saint Henri, to the west of Montreal's border. He concludes that few lodgings there were shared and suggests that in Montreal, too, the sharing of lodgings by unrelated families would have been an extremely marginal phenomenon, concentrated only in certain specific sectors of the city.[92] This critique is important. Some caution should be exercised, however, before extrapolating from behaviour in newly constructed areas out-side the city to Montreal. Many families went to such outer communi-ties precisely because housing was cheaper to purchase or to rent. They were thus a population with specific goals and with less need to save on rental costs.

A similar reconstruction of patterns in one small block of Labelle Street in Saint Jacques ward, where sharing appeared widespread, underlines the importance of Lauzon's arguments, but also the differ-ences between older inner-city areas and outer suburbs.[93] The mixed nature of housing on the street and the discrepancies between what appears in different city directories, assessment rolls, the census, and on maps highlight the difficulty of unambiguously identifying cases of household-sharing, or of ruling them out. On the eastern side of Labelle Street, between Dorchester and the Convent of the Sisters of Provi-dence, for instance, the census enumerator listed a total of forty-eight families living in twenty-four households. The walk north up the street from Dorchester led past a cluster of single-family homes of mer-chants, traders, and white-collar workers, some employing servants and each assessed at around $100 annual rent. Rapidly, the nature of the street changed and lot sizes became much more erratic, with mixtures of duplexes, front and rear housing, brick, stone, and frame construc-tions creating a residential patchwork, matched only by the diversity of the occupants and their high levels of mobility. Widows lived upstairs, labourers down. Carpenters and masons were to be found on the street front, labourers in the rear houses behind. The street was a veritable jumble of families whose heads and members listed a range of occupa-tions, and whose annual rent assessments varied from $24 to $100.[94]

The census-taker generally equated street address with household, even listing as one dwelling unit separate buildings constructed on the front and back of the same lot. Close inspection of these forty-eight census families living in twenty-four households suggests that dou-bling up within residential units occurred unquestionably in only four cases, but was possible in several others. This involved eight families, suggesting that rates of sharing were definitely lower than any simple application of the census categories would suggest. However, even taking the most conservative count of the phenomenon, house-sharing did occur among at least eight of the forty-eight families, or one in six. Using a similar methodology, France Gagnon found that one in five families who had migrated from the North Shore to parts of Saint Jacques and Saint Louis wards prior to the 1861 census were sharing with unrelated families. Almost as many again were in some form of extended family.[95]

Most Montreal working-class families did not share their living space with relatives or other families. Yet many did so at one point over their life cycle, and some of these situations are captured in each census. Such sharing sometimes involved real overcrowding. Most often it occurred when families were small and when the situation offered benefits to one family or the other. Sharing rent was only the most obvious advantage. Extra care for a pregnant mother or her newborn baby, for young children, for an aging, widowed parent, and initial integration to the city all constituted reasons for temporary co-habitation. Household and family structures were modified with a frequency that paralleled an equally important characteristic of housing, the extreme geographical mobility of working-class families. People moved frequently, often within a very small area of the city, adjusting their housing to ever-changing levels of income and to the expansion and contraction of their families.

Not all Montrealers married, had children, and lived within families. Women were less likely to do so than men. Most did, however, and it is their experiences that are studied here. Marriage represented the beginning of a relationship between husband and wife that in most cases continued until it was broken by the death of one partner. The inequality and complementarity of that relationship were spelled out explicitly in sections of the Civil Code that assigned responsibility for support of the family and interaction with legal, economic, and social institutions to the man and stripped women of such rights upon marriage. Little in the law had changed since pre-industrial times. What had changed was the nature of the society and economy within which spouses related and with which they interacted. Between the 1860s and the 1890s the growing formalization of wage labour, the expansion of the working class, and the destruction of artisanal production changed the material basis of marriage and family life. In response to the material reality of wage-dependence, to the economic fluctuations that characterized the world and local economies, and to the particular nature of their own work experience, working-class men and women adjusted older patterns of marriage and child-bearing.

The logic behind the timing of marriage for all groups lay increasingly in the expansions and contractions of the economy. Large numbers of children represented a major drain on the minimal and fluctuating wages of much of the working class until they reached an age at which the childrens' earnings could complement those of their father. Some working-class families consciously controlled the number of their children, not from any abstract desire to emulate bourgeois practice but because it made sense as one way of controlling their standard of living. In this city where illness and death were ever present, others lost child after child to the diseases that hit in the first year of life or failed to conceive or to carry pregnancies to term.

The birth of successive children changed the housing needs of families and posed major challenges to the intricate balancing of wages against expenses that dominated working-class family economies. Most working-class families managed to maintain their own households, but often in housing that was unhealthy, cramped, and inadequate. In times of crisis or difficulty, kin and neighbours opened up their homes to each other, shared space, or took in relatives and boarders so that family and household structures differed over family life cycles and between different groups. Patterns of marriage, childbirth, and housing varied within the working class in part because of cultural tradition, but increasingly as a result of the different earning power of the skilled, the unskilled, and those in such trades as shoemaking that were undergoing rapid transformation.

3

Men's Wages and the Cost of Living

Once married, a man was expected to support his wife with the necessities of life according to his position and means. This was no empty legal responsibility. Not doing so ranked equally with keeping a concubine in the family house, ill treatment, and grievous abuse as a legitimate cause for requesting "separation of bed and board," the closest state to divorce recognized in Quebec.[1] Wives could and did take their husbands to court for failure to provide for them and for their children, although their chances of winning, and of receiving some form of support, were not good.[2] Providing was a legal responsibility, but much more. Both male and female conceptions of masculinity were rooted, in complex and changing ways, in the work they did and in their ability to provide. "Why do not you act as a man; when you work why don't you give me a dollar?" Marie Cyr was overheard to yell at her husband, Israel Beaume, as their relationship soured.[3] She eventually took him to court for failing to provide.

Within working-class families men's superior earning power made their wages indispensable. They set the parameters of a family's standard of living. Yet those wages were often insufficient. The conditions of wage payment, the fluctuating availability of work, and the prevalence of disease meant that many husbands and fathers faced periods when providing for a family on their wage alone was impossible, when even the superior earning power of skilled workers was easily eroded.

All families dependent on wages were constantly having to balance incoming revenues against the costs of living. Neither were stable, nor wholly predictable. Wages varied not only between trades but over the seasons, with cyclical fluctuations in the economy and as as a result of the transformations occurring in many Montreal workplaces. Costs changed, too, both with the seasons and with the economic conditions.

Expenses increased rapidly as children were born, appetites increased, and larger living spaces were required. Unexpected illness in the family could at any time involve additional expenditures or, when it hit the wage-earners, a break in earning power.

Consistent evidence of wages paid, weeks worked, the incidence of disease, and the costs of food, housing, fuel, and clothing are sketchy for Montreal, as they are for most other Canadian cities during this period.[4] By piecing together the fragments that do exist, however, it is possible to delineate in general terms what was required to survive and to identify which, if any, families could best do so on a male wage alone and, hence, which would be most likely to need additional income – from children and/or working wives or from money raised in other ways. Families headed by women faced difficulties of a totally different order because of their inequality in the marketplace and in society. Their situation merits separate consideration.

Work and Wages for Men in the Leading Occupations of Sainte Anne and Saint Jacques Wards

The growing diversity of Montreal industry created a great variety of jobs for men. In Sainte Anne and Saint Jacques wards, working-class men listed fifty-three and thirty-four different job titles respectively in 1861, eighty-seven and sixty-seven by 1891. These jobs fell into four major groups – the unskilled; those in trades like shoemaking that were undergoing especially rapid transformation, which, following Clyde Griffen, I have called the "injured trades";[5] the skilled; and those, such as carters, who were involved in the variety of jobs involving transportation or communications within the city (Table 3.1). The latter group is not dealt with in detail here because it is extremely difficult to determine which men were independent entrepreneurs and which were wage-earners. The proportion working in these trades increased slowly but steadily in Sainte Anne with all the work provided by the docks, canal, and factories, but declined in Saint Jacques as it increasingly became a residential area.

Most of these workers received a wage for their daily labours. Yet, in this period of transition, the forms and timing of payment, indeed, the very nature of the contracts between employer and employee, were as varied as the industries within which people worked. Wage labour was in the process of becoming the dominant form of hiring but co-existed with other forms. In the earlier years apprenticeship was still important in some Montreal trades.[6] By the 1880s employers frequently contorted traditional forms of apprenticeship. Children were hired and paid as apprentices but seldom learned more than a small fraction of the trade, thus providing the employer with several years of

particularly cheap labour. Foremen and journeymen were still sometimes hired by formal contract before a notary. Here again, employers
could use an old form of hiring to new ends. In the 1870s, for example,
several employers stipulated that journeymen coopers or shoemakers
should not associate themselves "with any body of men or become a
member of any society which shall or may prove detrimental to the
interest" of the master's business. More positively, employers might
also guarantee that the journeyman would be paid "every Thursday" or
"on Monday of every fortnight," a major advantage at a time when
irregular payment of wages constituted a serious problem for many
families.[7]

In other trades skilled workers themselves subcontracted out part of
the work. Montreal moulders, for example, pushed by their employers
to increase production, seem to have relied much more heavily on less
skilled helpers than did their Toronto counterparts. These "berkshires,"
as the moulders called them, appear to have been hired by the moulders
themselves, despite their antagonism to the berkshire system.[8] Montreal shoemakers went on strike in 1869 largely to get rid of the system
of subcontracting within their industry that was allowing a few skilled
workers to hire other men at minimal rates.[9] Similar subcontracting
occurred in cigarmaking, in the needle trades, and quite probably in
other sectors. And such skilled workers as carpenters and painters
could alternate between wage labour in factories or workshops and
work on contract at a predetermined price for private individuals or
small employers.[10] The predominance of piecework in Montreal printing establishments, foundries, dressmaking, and other establishments
further highlights the variety of ways in which wages were earned.

Nineteenth-century job titles, whether labourer, shoemaker, or
blacksmith, thus hid a diversity of hiring situations. Wages cited for
any specific period reflect the experience of some workers but never
all, oversimplifying the complexity of a situation in flux. Determining
the level of wages earned or attempting to evaluate the standard of living is, therefore, complicated in part by the very nature of the transformations under way in the city's workplaces. Such an attempt is compounded because costs of living and the standard of living should not
be equated in a period when so many goods and services were procured
without cash. Only some elements of a complex and changing reality
are captured when a male's wages and the market price of goods are
considered. To begin to understand the working-class family economy,
however, it is essential to seek typical wages for the leading jobs and
compare them with the cost of living. Only then is the need for additional family workers and for other survival strategies within the working class clear.

Unskilled Workers

The unskilled made up around one-third of Sainte Anne family heads from 1861 on (see Table 1.2). In Saint Jacques, such casual workers declined dramatically from around one in five family heads in 1861 to under one in ten in 1891. Labourers dominated unskilled employment in each ward.

One in three of Sainte Anne male family heads were labourers between 1861 and 1881, one in four in 1891. Roughly half that proportion of husbands in Saint Jacques also made their living performing repetitive factory work or heavy physical labour on construction sites, at the railways, on the port, or in the myriad other situations around the city where casual labour was frequently or sporadically required. Insecurity characterized most of these men's labouring jobs. Employment might last for a few days or weeks, but it was seldom long term. Labouring work shrank each winter as the port closed and construction ground to a halt. Such jobs were the first to disappear when economic depressions froze capital in labour-employing sectors.

For labourers, seasonal and cyclical variations in rates paralleled fluctuations in the availability of work. A dollar a day was the usual wage, but wages on a variety of sites employing day labourers ranged from seventy-five cents to an occasional peak of $1.50, as in the summer of 1882 when construction of the Canadian Pacific Railway, enlarging the Lachine Canal, and other public works around Montreal created a demand for unskilled labour that "generally could not be satisfied."[11] Winter and economic downswings invariably punctured such periods of relative prosperity, quickly using up any extra money earned and pushing wage rates back down to a dollar or less.

Labourers' wages were so low that there was no flexibility in their family budgets. Invariably they responded dramatically and quickly to any threats of wage cuts. Little wonder that historian Bryan Palmer found that their conflicts were most often "to secure wages and to gain an immediate and tangible end," rather than to secure a measure of autonomy or control.[12] More than a thousand predominantly Irish day labourers on the Lachine Canal, for instance, went on strike in 1877 for a dollar a day after some contractors tried to reduce their wages from a promised winter wage of ninety cents to eighty cents. The "rate of wages is not high," their petition to the government argued, "and in many cases is not more than sufficient for the immediate and daily necessities of the labourer."[13] Moreover, some contractors were paying only once a month, "and in store or due bills and not in cash."[14] Men like Charles Egan, a Sainte Anne resident and one of the 121 strikers who signed a petition to the government, could not afford a long strike. Aged thirty-seven, this Ireland-born labourer had no children at home to earn while he was on strike, and his forty-year-old wife had no formal job.[15] In other families, such as the McHughs, where at least four family members appear to have been involved in the strike, the possibility of additional family earnings seems to have been slight.[16] With little chance of having made savings to live on at such times and with no union or strike fund to support them, such labourers could not sustain a long strike. After eight days, including Christmas, "they returned to the canal at the old wages." [17]

The Injured Trades

Men working in trades undergoing rapid transformation were more common in Saint Jacques, where the expansion of the local shoemaking industry in particular led to an increase in the proportion of family heads in this category until 1891. Shoemakers were the largest group in these injured trades. They headed around one in ten families in Saint Jacques in 1871 and 1881, only one in fifty in Sainte Anne. In 1861 and 1871 only labourers and carpenters were more numerous than shoemakers among the family heads of Saint Jacques ward. By 1881, shoemaker was the second most commonly held male job in Saint Jacques after labourer. In Sainte Anne the number of workers in this trade declined as work conditions deteriorated and as producers located their workshops and factories further east in the city, nearer the bulk of their French-Canadian workers. Cigarmaking, the city's other most obviously injured trade in this period, was also concentrated in the eastern part of Montreal, particularly around the huge factory of William McDonald, which he opened initially within Saint Jacques ward, then moved eastward into Sainte Marie ward in the 1880s.

Both the shoemaking and cigarmaking trades had once been the domain of highly skilled workers, trained to fabricate shoes or cigars from beginning to end. Starting in the 1840s and 1850s, accelerating in the 1860s and 1870s, masters and employers in both trades began hiring more workers, dividing up the work into more specialized tasks, and introducing new tools and machines. By the 1880s in shoemaking and cigarmaking, as in clothing, the use of machines had revolutionized some parts of the production process. Yet these remained labour-intensive industries. Hand labour and skilled work remained essential in other tasks. Within both trades complex new divisions of labour, methods of payment, and work relationships were organized to increase productivity and save on labour costs.[18] In William McDonald's tobacco factory the man at the head of each work bench was responsible for hiring, overseeing, and paying those working with him.[19] In sewing and shoemaking, men, women, and children working at home constituted an important but unknown proportion of the labour force. Subcontracting and putting-out saved on overhead rental or property costs, on machinery, and above all on labour costs. It had the added advantage of keeping workers isolated from each other so that they were unlikely to organize. During the 1860s employers in shoemaking introduced a series of new machines that made it more practical to concentrate most production within factories and led to a gradual decline in the number of women workers in the industry. Yet the machinery in no way constituted an integrated system. Hand work and machine labour continued, as did some homework, both in the city and in surrounding rural areas.[20] In 1888 "lots of men and women" were reported to "repair to the factories, with small vans, and take a load of boots and shoes, all cut," home to finish in "private houses" in rooms where eight, ten, or more hands might work.[21]

By the later decades of the nineteenth century the title "shoemaker" hid a spectrum of occupations and workplaces. Within Saint Jacques ward in 1871 the census returns indicate that there were fourteen shoe-makers' workshops. The majority of these involved single artisans working alone or with one or two assistants making all kinds of shoes and usually doing repairs. Here were skilled craftsmen who probably worked pretty well as their predecessors had. One manufactory that reported employing eleven workers also gave "work to be done outside the establishment." The largest shoemaking establishment in that ward reported only forty-eight workers. Altogether, establishments within the ward reported a total of only 110 workers, whereas between 600 and 700 residents called themselves shoemakers.[22] Most must have worked in the large and increasingly complex factories located else-where in Montreal or at home. Certainly by the 1880s some such fac-tories were employing over 300 hands inside, perhaps more outside. They were large, impressive places where men and women usually worked on separate floors at different tasks and using different types of machines.[23]

At that period shoemakers explained that "as a general rule, all the men working in factories, especially the large factories, are able to do only one kind of work . . . set a heel, or sew a sole, or set the uppers, because to-day perfected machinery has replaced handwork." Tasks that had once required years of learning were performed by machinery and by unskilled workers, including women and children. "Outside of . . . lasters," a shoe manufacturer explained, "in our business skilled workers are not required . . . most of our work that skilled men would be desired for is done by machinery." In the late 1880s, lasters and cutters earned a healthy $12 a week or $2 a day compared to the meagre $7 to $9 that other shoe workers could earn on wages in the factory.[24] Lasters, leather cutters, and, later, machinists came to constitute an elite within this increasingly differentiated work force. By the end of the century they were represented by their own small craft unions.[25]

While low wages and fluctuating work opportunities characterized the earning experience of the largest group of male workers, the labourers, throughout the period, the degradation of the craft in shoemaking led to a steady fall in the average wages earned by workers in most branches between the 1860s and 1890s. As early as 1869, striking shoemakers claimed that their wages had fallen by a third in the previous five years while the cost of living had increased. Those justifying joining the Knights of Saint Crispin argued that their masters no longer gave them sufficient to feed themselves and their families.[26] In 1888 the shoemakers giving evidence to the Royal Commission all agreed that wages had fallen a further 15 to 20 per cent.[27] They argued that supporting a family was more and more difficult, leading to a "considerable feeling of depression" among men in the trade. Increasingly, employers hired younger men, women, children, and those complementing others' wages rather than supporting their own family. Workers complained of the use of young people, who as "soon as they get a chance of increasing their wages by taking the place of a mechanic, or even of a man who had a family to work for, they do so."[28]

In cigarmaking, the process was similar. Initially, the introduction of moulds allowed a redivision of labour within the workplace that enabled young children to do many of the tasks previously performed by skilled craftsmen.[29] In M. Fortier's Montreal tobacco factory, made infamous in 1888 by publication of testimony about the draconian punishments he meted out to children, six machines were said to turn out an average of 25,000 bunches in a day, the equivalent of the manual labour of twenty-five swift hands. In the trade in general, wages were dropping and the numbers and proportion of children employed were increasing. Married men with their families were said to be leaving for the United States because Montreal wages were too low. Furthermore, most men did not receive a steady wage throughout the year. Wages were regularly reduced in winter. A man had to "work for any price the boss will give him, or else work elsewhere."[30]

The Construction Trades

Carpenters and joiners characterized that branch of the skilled trades that drew on traditional skills and was most vulnerable to seasonal and cyclical fluctuations. In Saint Jacques there was double the proportion of family heads in such construction trades as in Sainte Anne. Men in most construction trades earned slightly more per day than shoemakers. Their wages, like those of labourers, fluctuated over the seasons and with economic cycles rather than showing any general trend across the period. Carpenters and joiners ranked consistently among the three leading occupations of family heads in both wards, representing around one in ten family heads early in the period but becoming less important in Sainte Anne toward the end of the century. Little research has been done into their craft and how it was changing. In Saint Jacques in 1871 fourteen carpentry and joining workshops employed from three to twenty-two employees each. They built houses, built doors and sashes, and performed repairs of all kinds. Sainte Anne had only three such joineries. There, sash and door factories employed from thirteen to eighty men. The largest, James Shearer's establishment, had an estimated fixed capital of $18,000, employed eighty men on all kinds of joining work, and paid out over $24,000 in wages in 1871.[31] Those working in such factories were less likely to face the seasonal unemployment that characterized these trades than were carpenters working on housing construction. For them, winter invariably brought insecurity, with a slowdown or a complete break in the amount of work available. Few earned sufficient to save for this period.

Men working for contractors building houses around the city had the added expense of supplying their own sets of tools at the cost of $100 to $125 and a further estimated $10 to $15 each year for maintenance. The many small, precarious contractors who dominated Montreal's construction industry posed further challenges to those attempting to live on wages in this sector.[32] Contractors sometimes disappeared once a job was done, leaving the workers without their pay and unable to trace them or take legal steps to retrieve it. Other construction workers found they had to wait several days until the master builder turned up with their wages.

Wages varied a lot within the building trades. Carpenters and joiners were among the least well paid after day labourers. During the 1880s, carpenters could earn between $1.50 and $2 a day. In some good years the maximum rose to $2.50.[33] In 1888 one contractor reported that his carpenters received only $1.80 daily, compared to the $3 to $3.50 received by bricklayers.[34] At the end of the 1880s, Montreal carpenters reported that low wages were forcing fathers of families to leave the city to seek work in areas offering better pay. One carpenter argued that there were few Englishmen in the trade in Montreal because "they go west or to the United States."[35]

Other Skilled Workers

Within the working class, men trained as machinists, engineers, and mechanics of all kinds held a privileged position they fought to retain. Dominated initially by the English and Scots, often migrants from the heartland of the industrial revolution, their skills were generally in demand. They could find work not only in the huge workshops of the Grand Trunk, but also in the foundries and factories of Sainte Anne.

These newer skilled trades were minimally important among the male family heads of Saint Jacques, where they were practised by only 2 to 3 per cent of family heads. In Sainte Anne, in contrast, 10 per cent of family heads throughout the period were employed in these trades or in ones demanding older skills, such as moulding and blacksmithing, that were in demand in the foundries, railroad workshops, and other factories of the area. Engineer and blacksmith consistently ranked among that ward's eight leading jobs.

While most of these skilled male workers faced some kinds of major change in the size of their workplaces and some in the kinds of machines they were making or using, most faced no major loss of their control over the work process in this period. They constituted a core of well-paid workers. Organized and often affiliated to international unions, they could dictate the pace and timing of their work to some extent and, in good years, the level of their wages. Existing evidence of wages paid such skilled workers confirms their position near the top of the skill and pay hierarchy. Skilled metal workers could earn from $2 to $2.75 a day in good times, some much more. This was double a day labourer's wage. Winters and times of economic depression, however, especially the Great Depression that began in the United States in 1873 and hit Quebec in 1874, eroded their superior position, pushing wages down to as low as $1.25 a day, even forcing some to seek work as labourers. Even within trades the pattern of seasonal unemployment varied. Among moulders, those working in the fabrication of machines, metal work for bridges, or type founding lost only a few days a year, while those making stoves worked generally for only nine months.[36]

These wage differentials for the leading occupations held by the husbands and fathers of Sainte Anne and Saint Jacques wards reflect those within the larger working class. They suggest a class characterized by major differences in earning ability similar to those described by Peter Shergold for turn-of-the-century Pittsburgh. There, the "inegalitarian income structure was reflected in substantial variations in workers' lifestyle." Differences between the unskilled and the skilled were much more pronounced than in similar English cities.[37] While the evidence used here on wages in different trades is patchy and sporadic, it does suggest two major points. First, what seem to us today to be minuscule differences of 25 cents a day divided up the working class into fractions with the potential for very different standards of living. Thus, a government publication for 1882 reports that labourers were earning between $1 and $1.25; shoemakers from $1.25 to $2; blacksmiths and carpenters from $1.50 to $2; while skilled workers like bricklayers, saddlers, or engineers might earn $2.50 or more.[38] These differences were significant. If men could find six days of work a week for forty weeks a year, these daily wages added up to an annual wage of $240 for a labourer, $300 for a shoemaker, $360 for a blacksmith or carpenter earning $1.50 daily, and $600 for skilled workers able to command $2.50 a day. Second, conjunctural and seasonal fluctuations in wage rates appear to have been more important in most sectors of the economy over this period than any long-term trend toward higher or lower wages. The major exception is in shoemaking, where a growing proportion of workers faced declining salaries over the second half of the nineteenth century.

The Costs of Living: Food, Rents, Fuel, and Clothing

To judge whether families could survive on the wages that men in these trades were able to make requires not only knowing the costs of basic foodstuffs, rents, fuel, and clothing, but also determining a basic diet and grasping what was considered a minimum standard of living. Both normative and quantitative factors are involved. Historians Jerome Clubb, Erik Austin, and Gordon Kirk underline quite rightly that a concept such as standard of living cannot be measured directly. It is an abstract concept, but only empirical data are available to test it.[39] Determining the amount necessary to escape poverty, itself a relative concept, is even more difficult. And, it is too often simply a statistical exercise that ignores the many ways in which men and women stretched, saved, spent, and complemented the wages earned. All such attempts, no matter how scientific their end results might appear, reflect normative judgements about what constitutes an "adequate standard of living."[40] The standard of living expected by people varies over time, between cultures, and for people in different class positions. Even ascertaining what were viewed as the basic necessities of life for specific subgroups in a society is no simple matter. Until late in the nineteenth century few Canadian studies attempted to determine the basic necessities of life. Canadians seldom displayed the fascination for family budgets that characterized the social sciences in Europe, observers of the poor in England, or American bureaus of labour at the time.[41]

A minimum diet can, however, be established by drawing on studies done elsewhere. This can be priced to determine the approximate cost of feeding Montreal families. Adding contemporary evidence on the costs of housing, fuel, and clothing and balancing these against workers' testimonies about their basic expenditures allow an assessment of the cost of the basic necessities of life. Of course, costs, like wages, fluctuated seasonally and conjuncturally. Reconstructing the prices of food and other basic commodities across this period would be a heroic and perhaps misleading task. However, the fact that the federal immigration agent reported on both prices and wages in Montreal in 1882 makes it possible to assess, in an abstract way, how the wage rates outlined for the skilled, injured, and unskilled workers of these wards could have translated into different standards of living at that one point in time. The exercise determines only potential standards of living. In reality, as an American housewife who knew well the complexities of balancing wages against costs tried to explain to the Commissioner of Labor in 1890, the management necessary to maintain "a six dollar house on four dollars" will not conform to statistics. She explained how she substituted some products for others, avoided prepared meats and other extravagances, but could not afford to buy in bulk. "In summer and winter alike I must try to buy the food that will sustain us the greatest number of meals at the lowest price, and I should like to shake hands with the person who can reduce it to figures."[42]

Workers' testimonies about what they expected their wages to cover indicate roughly what their basic expenditures were. They hint, too, at what they considered an acceptable standard of living. When Eli Massy and his fellow cigarmakers sat down in 1888 to estimate their average wages and costs of living for the Royal Commission, they identified only four types of expenses: food, rent, fuel, and schooling for their children. Food, for a family with two to three children, cost them $4 to $5 a week (57 to 71 per cent of their income); rent averaged $1.50 (21 per cent), and fuel around eighty cents (11 per cent). If they spent $5 for food they overspent earnings by 30 cents on basic expenses. At $4 for food, as Jules Helbronner, the Montreal journalist who was hearing the evidence, pointed out, twenty cents were left "for clothing." He then asked about the remaining balance. It is significant that it was he, not the cigarmakers, who mentioned clothing. "For living, we did not calculate," replied Eli Massy, reiterating that he could not live on $7 a week.[43] A Maritime labourer presenting his family budget to the Commission made the same point. Food alone used up all but six cents of his $1.10 a day. This had to go toward rent and fuel. "Do you provide anything for clothes?" asked Mr. Armstrong. "No; nor even for boots, or oil, nor tobacco, nor sugar, nor anything like that," he explained.[44]

In these testimonies, food, rent, and fuel constituted the necessities of life for the unskilled as for poorly paid workers in an injured trade like cigarmaking. In their daily budgets there was seldom money left over for clothing, let alone furniture, other household items, medicine, or drink. Estimates made in 1900 by M. Lacombe, member of the Legislative Assembly for a working-class Montreal constituency, were remarkably similar. He argued that a family of five in Montreal spent $6 monthly on rent (20 per cent of their income), $3 on fuel (10 per cent), and $1.50 on schooling, taxes, and bus tickets (5 per cent), leaving only $19.50 (65 per cent) for food, washing, sickness, and all other small but necessary expenses.[45] The basic budget prepared by the Child Welfare Association in 1912 was similar in the proportions going to food, rent, and fuel. Their insistence that the allowance "does not provide a standard of living which can secure abundant health" should not be forgotten.[46] Budgets produced later in the twentieth century, in contrast, particularly those created by skilled workers, suggest changes in what were seen as the basics of life. Furniture, utensils, clothing, and other goods manufactured at decreasing prices in Canadian factories begin to appear as a right, as part of what men expected their wages to cover.[47]

Bread was the working-class staple food. It was so central to survival that while women were usually the ones who shopped, men like Montreal labourer Thomas Gratorex, when interviewed by the Commission of 1888, knew that a five-pound loaf cost sixteen cents.[48] Bread was also the mainstay of the basic diet developed in 1902 by British capitalist and social investigator B.S. Rowntree. He established a basic diet after examining contemporary literature. It comprised the minimum necessary to keep a man in reasonable working condition and was slightly less generous than that provided for able-bodied paupers in English workhouses who were expected to perform demanding physical labour. Using his diet to estimate minimum food costs for Montreal families seems reasonable. It is so spartan that there is little risk of applying a higher standard of eating than the working class would have expected.[49] The danger is rather the reverse: that by underestimating what was really necessary to eat well enough to remain in reasonably good health, we minimize difficulties of survival in late nineteenth-century Montreal.[50]

Rowntree allowed a grown man about one pound of bread a day. Seven ounces of oatmeal, just over half a pint of milk, half a pound of cheese, nearly five ounces of potatoes, and 1.3 ounces of bacon, as well as "a little" tea, coffee, sugar, treacle, or margarine were the only other victuals allowed.[51] He weighted the food intake of all other family members according to their age and sex. A wife, indeed any woman over sixteen, received only 80 per cent of the male allowance, with no extra allowed for pregnancy or breast-feeding. This weighting, from all available evidence, reflected working-class practice.[52]

With cheap meat replacing the cheese allowance to better reflect local eating habits, the bread, oatmeal, milk, meat, potatoes, and bacon that made up Rowntree's minimal diet would have cost around ninety-one cents weekly in Montreal in 1882 for an adult male. Food for boys over fourteen years old cost seventy-seven cents, women, seventy-three cents, and children aged five to thirteen fifty cents.[53] A couple with no children would have paid out only $85 annually, leaving sufficient cash for rent, fuel, and perhaps some clothing even for a labourer and his wife. A childless couple were at a major advantage for the first fourteen or fifteen years of married life. Costs of food expanded swiftly once a couple had children, varying with the age, the sex, and particularly the number of the offspring. A family with three children under five would have paid $132.08 annually for food alone. For a family with a boy of sixteen and girls aged fourteen and eight, food costs mounted to $182. Any family with five children including two boys in their teens and three girls between nine and sixteen would have had to pay at least $258 for food alone – more than a labourer's annual salary[54] (Figure 3.1).

The rapid escalation of food costs over the family life cycle posed major challenges to those on the low wages characteristic of such jobs as labouring and shoemaking. The growing cost of food could be absorbed on the superior salaries of more skilled workers only when they had fewer than four children (see Table 3.2). The wife of a skilled worker earning $2 a day, who had a boy of sixteen and girls of fourteen and eight, would have spent around two-fifths of his earnings on food. In contrast, the wife of a labourer earning the standard dollar a day would have spent three-quarters of his wages to purchase the same foodstuffs. Had these families had two teenage boys and three girls, the labourer's wife would have needed more than her husband's annual income simply for food, while a saddler's wife would have used up under two-thirds of her husband's annual wage.

Shelter was the second major cost in the working-class budget. Rent was a much less flexible obligation than food purchase, for when food prices rose or wages dropped, women could purchase lower-quality produce, scavenge for food, or buy on credit. Also, some or all family members, usually the wife, could simply eat less.[55] Landlords wanted the rent, however, or they might evict families and garnishee a man's wages.[56] Families might share housing to spread rental payments or take paying boarders, but such strategies should not be built into an assessment of the basic standard of living.

Rent and fuel used up over 30 per cent of wages in the budget prepared in 1888 by Eli Massy and his fellow cigarmakers. All workers giving evidence at the Royal Commission in 1888 stressed that apartment rentals had increased by 12 to 25 per cent since the 1870s.[57] Sherry Olson and David Hanna's study of the city evaluation roles confirms that rentals increased over this period. Furthermore, their findings show a remarkable symmetry between the average rents paid by household heads and the different fractions of the working class.[58] In 1881 the median rent paid by labourers was $33; by shoemakers, $38;

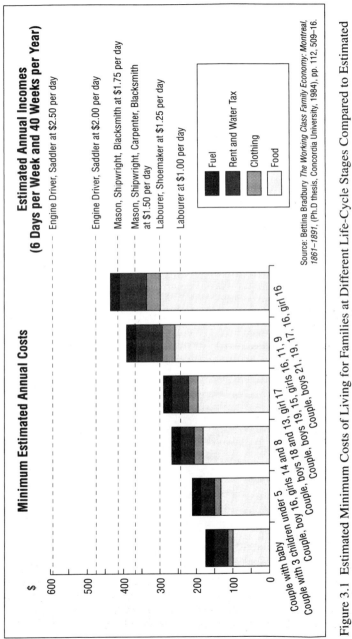
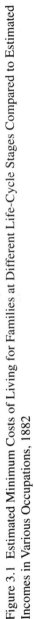

Figure 3.1 Estimated Minimum Costs of Living for Families at Different Life-Cycle Stages Compared to Estimated Incomes in Various Occupations, 1882

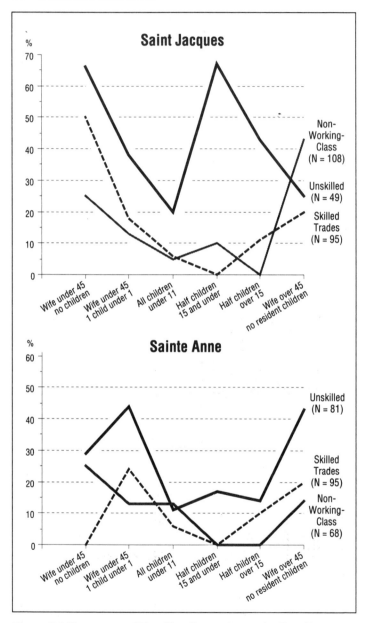

Figure 3.2 Percentage of Families Occupying under Four Rooms at Different Life-Cycle Stages, 1891

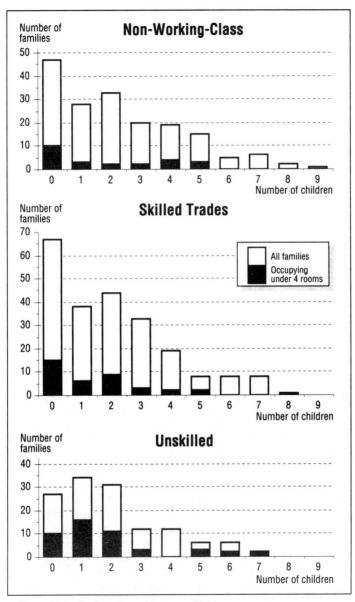

Figure 3.3 Families Occupying under Four Rooms according to the Number of Children Living at Home, Sainte Anne and Saint Jacques Combined, 1891

by carpenters, \$40; at the same time, machinists averaged \$73, and the median was \$55.[59]

The number of rooms occupied is another indicator of housing quality. Dr. Dougless Decrow told the Royal Commission that the poor were obliged to live in the smallest houses and apartments.[60] This is confirmed by census returns. In 1891, the only year in which this indication of standard of living is available, labourers occupied an average of 4.7 rooms, men in the construction trades just over 5, shoemakers 5.2, while skilled workers in the metal trades average 5.7 rooms per family. Less than four rooms would hardly have allowed sufficient space for even the smallest of families. Unskilled workers were much more likely to live in such dwellings at all stages of their life cycle than were the skilled. Before the birth of their first child, two-thirds of the labourers and other unskilled workers in Saint Jacques were living in three rooms or less, compared to half the skilled workers. As children grew and as families expanded, the greater flexibility in the budgets of skilled workers enabled them to avoid overcrowding better than the unskilled. As successive children were born, families attempted to find larger residences. Once skilled workers had over four children, they seldom occupied fewer than four rooms. The unskilled were much more likely to. Once most children had reached working age no families headed by men in skilled trades in the sample populations of either ward were living in two to three rooms. In contrast, around two-thirds of the unskilled in Saint Jacques and one in five in Sainte Anne were (see Figures 3.2 and 3.3). Lower wages, less regular pay, and the greater fall in the earning power of the less skilled as they aged combined with the likelihood that their children would move from home earlier to leave such men and their wives facing old age in tiny apartments like those in which they had started raising a family.

Average rents, even the average number of rooms occupied, do not capture the mobility of working-class families, who changed housing both in response to fluctuations in their income and as family size expanded and contracted.[61] The two-room house that a young couple could occupy alone or with their first child in order to economize on rent simply would not hold large numbers of children. People moved, as family size increased or decreased and when higher earnings allowed them to occupy better housing. Houses with more than seven rooms remained out of reach for most unskilled workers, even when the size of their families meant such housing was not a luxury. Skilled workers in Sainte Anne, especially, were able to afford dwellings of seven rooms or more before their children were born, and again once their offspring began to reach earning age. By the time half or more of their offspring were fifteen or over, more than two-thirds were in such dwellings, suggesting a level of comfort and respectability that was much harder for families headed by unskilled workers to achieve. Once children left home, space needs for all groups diminished, but so, too, did income.

Moving to gain more space meant that rental costs, like those for food, generally increased over the family life cycle, remaining high until children left home. Changing rental needs have been built into the estimates portrayed in Figure 3.1. Like the food estimates, these are on the conservative side. Fully two-thirds of labourers and three-quarters of shoemakers listed in the evaluation roles of Sainte Anne fell into a higher rental category than the $39, $45, or $72 allowed for different-sized families in the estimates.[62]

Once rented, houses had to be kept warm through the long, cold winter. In Montreal, where winter temperatures of minus 20 Celsius are not uncommon. economizing on heating fuel was dangerous. Contracts for the sale of firewood from rural areas to the city created a web of links between town and country, but did not always ensure a sufficient supply of wood at a reasonable price.[63] Riots broke out in 1872 when firewood was scarce in the city. At some such times when supplies were low, prices astronomical, and trouble brewing, the Montreal City Council arranged for the Grand Trunk to transport wood to the city at an agreed cost.[64] Prices for firewood and coal fluctuated both throughout the season and from year to year. In 1887, for example, coal that was delivered cost $4.60 a ton in May, $6 in August, and $7 in November.[65] Few workingmen's families had extra money to buy wood or coal in the summer when it was cheaper. In the autumn any spare cash had to go toward paying the city's water tax. Hence, it was throughout the winter, when wages dropped and fuel prices rose, that most families had to purchase their fuel, probably not by the ton but in small uneconomical amounts.[66]

Labourer Thomas Gratorex argued in 1888 that if great care was taken an average house could be heated in the winter with four tons of coal, at a cost of $24. The organizers of the Child Welfare exhibit in 1912 allowed exactly the same amount in its budget.[67] The $24 allowed for fuel in the estimates illustrated in Figure 3.1 therefore represent a reasonable minimum, but this amount makes no allowance for candles or oil for lighting, for cold winters, or for major price increases.

Clothing was not included in the budget prepared by Montreal's cigarmakers in 1888, nor in that presented by MLA G.-A. Lacombe in 1900. The explanation is clear when the expanding costs of food, shelter, and fuel are compared to the wages men could earn. The incomes of most unskilled or injured trade family heads were used up on these most basic expenses once a couple had several children to feed. Yet, in the harsh winter climate of Montreal, warm clothing and footwear were essential. Charity workers frequently commented on the inadequate clothing of the city's poor. During the Great Depression children ceased attending school because they had no clothing or shoes to wear.[68]

People had to be clothed. Even in the preparation of the most basic of budgets, some allowance for clothing should be made. Following Rowntree's methodology, Figure 3.1 allows an amount equal to around 14 per cent of food costs for clothing. For a couple without children (Stage 1) this represents only $13.52 annually. For a family of seven, at stage six, $40.56 was allowed. Historical evidence suggests that this may be the one generous allowance in the estimates, for the ability to buy clothes varied greatly within the working class. A single man, like printer Walter Smith who emigrated to Montreal in 1874 from England, could afford to outfit himself with $40 worth of winter clothes. Shortly after his arrival, he spent another $26 on clothing for the spring and summer.[69]

Skilled men in 1882 who were earning steadily and supporting a wife and one or two young children had the flexibility in such a budget to buy a new coat at $8 to $10, perhaps one pair of trousers ($3.50), some shoes ($2.50), and one flannel shirt ($2) annually. A labourer's wife more likely sought her husband's clothes in second-hand shops, then mended them and remended them to make them last. She probably made her own clothes and those of her children at home or turned to relatives in the city or the country or to neighbours who made some money sewing. Of course, there were other ways to procure clothes without making or buying them. Hand-me-downs from older siblings, neighbours, and relatives were probably the only clothes that large numbers of Montreal children ever wore. And clothing could be stolen. It was a selective thief who broke into the house of the manager of the Mercantile Agency in 1871 when this Saint Jacques merchant left his house unattended for several months; the thief stole only three or four pocket handkerchiefs worth about thirty cents each and two white shirts valued at $4.[70] The frequent disappearance of clothing from clotheslines in the city suggests the extent to which budgets simply would not stretch to cover wearing apparel.[71]

Costs, Wages, and Poverty

These estimates of the basic cost of living are both crude and approximate, yet they do make clear the problems of survival on all but the most skilled workingman's wage. The amounts allowed are consistently lower than those made by cigarmaker Eli Massy and his colleagues and by others giving evidence at the Royal Commission in

1888. The diet allowed corresponds roughly to workers' evidence about what they ate. It is clearly unhealthy and would have led to illness if followed over a long period. No fruits or vegetables were included. To eat better, workers and their families would have had to use more of their wages for food or procure food in other ways. Even allowing only this minimal diet, the income of most unskilled workers was rapidly consumed. As well, the amounts of money suggested for rent would have sufficed only for some of the worst Montreal housing. No allowance was made for any other purchases – furniture, utensils, cleaning or lighting expenses, medicine or medical care, schooling, church, or transport. Furthermore, the budget assumes that all the money a man earned was used "to live upon," that none went for drink or tobacco – necessary luxuries in the life and culture of many workingmen.

Comparing these most conservative estimates of the costs of living with the wages that men could earn underlines the potential importance of the difference of twenty-five cents a day within the working class, the reality of the need to find as much work as possible,[72] and the necessity of considering costs over the family life cycle. These differences of around twenty-five cents a day set the basis for major variations within the working class. They had the potential to translate into distinctive standards of living and family economies and unequal possibilities of security and comfort. For all workers, the unfolding of the family life cycle carried with it the likelihood of periods of relative ease, followed by economic stringency, even severe poverty, followed again by some comfort once children could earn wages. This cycle was most acute in the families of those workers unable to earn more than $300 a year – the majority of the working class.

Virtually all the families in the largest fraction of the working class, the unskilled, and most in the trades undergoing rapid transformation had to find ways of complementing the wages of the male family head even to achieve the minimum standard of living set out above. Any Montreal worker earning less than $1.50 a day for forty weeks of steady work, six days a week, would not have been able to afford even the spartan Rowntree diet once he had any children in their teens. Only while most children were very young, and only in families with three children or less, would a labourer's wages alone have covered the family's most basic requirements. Even then, he would have had to find steady work, remain healthy, avoid spending any money on alcohol and tobacco, and have had a competent wife who could stretch his wage. And labourers, it should be recalled, made up around one-third of Sainte Anne family heads in 1881 and over one-quarter of those in Saint Jacques.

Those skilled workers in trades that had not been drastically re-organized, *and* with skills in steady demand, *and* with unions able to negotiate higher wage rates had more flexibility in their budgets. A blacksmith earning $1.75 a day or $420 annually could have fed and clothed his family unless he had more than three children over fifteen who were eating like adults and not earning. He could do so, however, only at the minimal standards allowed above and only when he could work steadily.

No allowance was made in the estimates for furniture, utensils, or household equipment. Furnishings appear minimal to us today, even in the homes of some skilled workers. Étienne Féréole-Lagrenade, for example, was a stone-cutter, one of the better-paid construction trades. He had purchased his small, one-storey, brick and wood house on Amherst Street in Saint Jacques ward in 1860 and was still paying it off when his wife died in 1867. The house had two bedrooms. Some of the five children, aged five to fifteen, appear to have slept together in one of these rooms. It was furnished only with one bed and bedding, a washing bowl, an old table, one small child's chair, and a pitcher. In the other bedroom there was one bed, a commode, a leather-covered trunk, six chairs, and a bed cover. The main furniture in the dining room consisted of a brown wooden table, six wooden chairs, and two old sideboards. A mirror, nine framed prints, a spittoon, and a series of small ornaments hint at the respectability of the family. Curtains, an old carpet, and some fabric completed the contents of this room. The kitchen had more furniture. The old brown table was valued at only thirty-seven cents, the three old chairs at ten cents total. There were also a stove, a small, red-painted sideboard, a small washing stand with a mirror, a bench that doubled as a bed, and a clock. Lighting was provided by a coal lamp and candles. Utensils, cutlery, and china included four different kinds of pots, some old knives, forks, and spoons, and some plates and tumblers. A thorough survey of inventories made following people's deaths would be necessary to determine the furniture owned by families in different fractions of the working class and the representivity of this one case. It does suggest the basic furnishings that skilled workers might have had. In his case, belongings may have been sold either during his wife's illness to pay the doctors or afterwards to cover the $40 entailed in funeral costs.[73]

The stark concreteness of the potential earning differences between skilled and unskilled workers oversimplifies the complexity and undependability of Montreal's labour market, as well as the other factors that could effect a man's ability to earn wages. There were structural as well as more individual challenges to balancing budgets. Irregular wage payment and seasonal and cyclical unemployment rapidly eroded differences in earning power. So did illness and the diversion of income to alcohol, gambling, or prostitution.

Irregular Wage Payment and
Seasonal and Cyclical Unemployment

Irregular payment of wages was only too common during this period, when the modalities of wage labour and wage payment were being negotiated and shaped. Some employers continued to pay in kind rather than in cash. Employers went bankrupt regularly. Others simply disappeared without paying their men. Recourse to the courts for rightful wages was a lengthy process.[74] Even men, women, and children with steady work were not always paid regularly. Regular cash payment of wages was a major demand in several strikes during the 1870s. Striking workers on the Lachine Canal in 1877 included both regular fortnightly payment and an end to the truck system in their demands.[75] Longshoremen, joiners, street cleaners, and dry goods employees all testified to the problem of irregular pay in 1888. That irregular payment was still a problem at the end of the century is clear from the Trade and Labour Congress's demand to the Quebec government in 1896 that existing laws regarding wages be amended so that all employees would be paid weekly and in the current money of the Dominion.[76]

Seasonal and cyclical unemployment posed major challenges to balancing family budgets. In the winter many workers were without jobs. The port was open only seven to eight months a year. Its closure slowed the rhythm of business and employment for the whole city. Labourers and carters had to seek other employment, though little was available. Lumberyards closed down between November and May. Carpenters and even shoemakers and moulders expected to lose two to three months during the winter. With little chance of having savings to draw on, they competed for work with general labourers when workshops and factories closed for the winter.[77]

Employers who operated throughout the winter took advantage of these seasonal labour surpluses to cut wages – allegedly "a general habit in this part of the country." Tobacco manufacturer William McDonald had reduced wages in the winter since at least the 1860s. "Labour," he remarked in 1888, with evident satisfaction, "is a remarkable commodity."[78] The proprietor of a Montreal printing office who paid $10 a week in the summer claimed that he could hire as many of the best men that he wanted for $7 in winter because "they were suffering from hunger. They had no work."[79] In such parts of town as Saint Jacques, seasonal unemployment was so widespread that cash was reported to be rare throughout the winter months.[80]

Seasonal joblessness was relatively predictable. Work usually resumed in the spring, and families could arrange short-term credit with their grocer and other merchants to see them through the expensive winter months. Cyclical unemployment was more devastating. The general slowdown in commerce and industry of the late 1850s, and the temporary downswings between 1864 and 1865 and again between 1867 and 1869 were like the tremors that precede a major earthquake, early warnings of the growing gravity of world-wide depressions. When the first "Great Depression" hit Quebec in 1874 employment possibilities shrank. Short time, layoffs, and reduced wages were wide-spread. Factories closed. Housing construction contracted, throwing those in related trades out of work. In many trades work was only available for two to three days week. Employers cut wages by 25 to 60 per cent. Labourers found themselves with occasional jobs, then no jobs at all. Competition among workers intensified, first as Americans thrown out of work flooded the labour market, then as unemployed skilled workers sought work as labourers, leaving "the labouring classes" with "insufficient for themselves."[81]

Numbers relying on charity mushroomed. Peaceful rallies for work or bread in December of 1875 escalated into attacks on police and demands for "bread or blood."[82] Arrests for public drunkenness declined by around 50 per cent, the result of "the stringency in money matters," hypothesized the Mayor.[83] Privation in the early months turned to hunger as family resources and networks of aid were depleted. "The workingmen of Canada are in a terrible condition," wrote one Montreal moulder, whose industry was reported dead by early 1876.

> After months of want and misery, actual starvation drove our people to revolt (the thieves called it a riot) and then they are set to work by thousands at sixty cents per day.
>
> It is hard to see mechanics working on a canal at 60 cents per day, men who have served years in securing a trade, the wages they receive being only a mockery of their misery.[84]

With no flexibility in their budgets to cover any unemployment, the unskilled suffered first. The sheer length of the depression meant that many skilled workers rapidly used up their savings. The apparently neat difference that twenty-five cents a day could make between separate fractions of the working class could easily lose meaning, forging temporarily a more homogeneous working class. Dire poverty, always a possibility for the least skilled, rapidly became a probability for large numbers of skilled workers' families as well.

The central importance of men's wages, the problems facing the unskilled during the depression, and some women's methods of coping when men's wages were insufficient are illustrated in cases where women took their husbands to court for failure to provide. In March,

1878, Marie Cyr pursued her second husband, Israel Beaume, for refusing to provide food and clothing for herself and their child. The case was dismissed five days later for insufficient evidence. However, the evidence presented is revealing.[85] According to his wife, Israel had no trade. He worked by the day. He had been refusing to support her. Had he wanted to he could have given her "something to help me live." At least once, she argued, he had refused to take a job that one of her brothers had offered him. He retorted that it was she who had said the job did not pay enough and had told him not to take it. He had then searched for several weeks all over the city and finally, not finding anything better, had taken the job for two days. Then, discouraged because he had not been able to find any work in Montreal, he had suggested going to Upper Canada to work in the lumber camps. She had replied that if he left he need not come back. Israel's case, then, rested partly on his argument that work was extremely difficult to find. This was undoubtedly true in Montreal in 1877-78. He pointedly asked two of the witnesses whether they were aware that he had ever refused to work when he had a chance to. In such periods of depression labourers certainly did have trouble finding work. They had to take lower-paying jobs and even leave the city to seek jobs elsewhere. Other husbands accused of not providing during the same period were able to turn the problems of insufficient earnings to their advantage and avoid sentencing.[86]

The gradual easing of the depression over the 1880s did not erase the problem of unemployment from workers' lives. As the reality of this characteristic of the industrial-capitalist economy became clear, politicians began to see the importance of having some measurement of its frequency. In 1891, Canadians were asked for the first time in a census whether they were unemployed.[87] The answers of residents of Sainte Anne and Saint Jacques wards appear to underline the different experiences of skilled and unskilled workers: almost one in five unskilled workers in Sainte Anne reported being unemployed compared to only one in twenty skilled workers. In Saint Jacques, where construction dominated the skilled trades, rates were much more similar for the skilled and unskilled, at 11 and 12 per cent.

Drink, Disease, and Debt

The problems of finding work during a period of severe unemployment no doubt aggravated the relationship between Marie Cyr and Israel Beaume. For many other women and their children, money that a husband spent on alcohol or any other form of entertainment made the level of the wage earned irrelevant. The threat was more than economic, for much of the wife-battering that occurred in Montreal during this period was done by drunken husbands. Louis Brisson gave his wife Henriette only $1 of the $7 he had earned one week in July, 1870. She fed him bread and butter for supper. Outraged at this inadequate meal, he struck her violently on the face with his fist, refusing to listen to her explanations.[88] Montreal housewife Mme. Leseige's economic problems were probably compounded when the police court sentenced her husband to two months in gaol because he "was in the habit of spending most of his earnings on drink and not contributing to the support of his wife."[89] Marie Mainville of Saint Jacques ward took her husband to court a year after Marie Cyr had done so, claiming that for the last fifteen days he had neglected her and refused to give her the food necessary to live. A neighbour and relative, Elizabeth Deschenes dit Mainville, supported her argument, testifying that Marie had nothing to eat at her own house and had been going to her for meals. Her husband Edmond was earning a dollar a day but was drinking a lot and wasting his money. Having pleaded guilty, Edmond St. Jean was sentenced to two months' hard labour in the common gaol.[90]

Many a working man desperately needed the relaxation and escape that alcohol offered. Taverns promised distraction, pleasure, and comradeship as well as access to important information about work that might be available in the city.

Drinking could also be a reaction to unemployment. It could precipitate job loss or simply drain family finances. Its impact should not be underestimated. Reformers' rhetoric about the dangers of drink certainly constituted part of a larger movement toward greater control of working-class life. Recognizing this does not eliminate the reality of the misery that drinking caused and the holes that even moderate spending on alcohol could make in budgets already stretched as far as they could go. By the 1880s spokesmen for the workers were beginning actively to promote more sensible drinking.[91] Representatives of the Trades Councils explained to commissioners Lukes and Blakeby in 1882 that a half work day on Saturdays would contribute "greatly to domestic happiness and promote self respect" and have a "great influence in diminishing intemperance. When a workingman had himself washed and dressed and walked out in the afternoon with his wife and family, he was not likely afterwards to go and get drunk."[92] In the 1880s the Knights of Labor newspaper, *Le Trait d'Union*, also encouraged workers to turn away from drink.

> Beside the workshop, you see, there is the bar. Not that we want to argue that the bar is of itself a dangerous institution. No. The customs of the country have created it and the finances of the government grow there. But what we would argue ... is that the bar absorbs

most clearly the salary of the worker. . . . Just think that behind you there is your wife and young children who impatiently await your return from the workshop or shanty. Domestic comfort costs so little however, and drink so much.[93]

Longshoreman Patrick Dalton argued that the frequent but small amounts of pay that he and his fellow workers received increased the "temptation to spend it instead of taking it home to their families." He suggested that weekly payment might keep them out of the grogshops.[94]

For wives who had to scrimp, save, and plot so that the family would eat well even with all of a man's wage to work with, drinking often posed as much of a threat to family survival as did unemployment or low wages. Recurrent illness posed similar problems, preventing some men from earning, or draining money needed for food and shelter. Neither can be measured, nor can their exact impact on family budgets be determined. Yet, they cannot be ignored. Eli Massy tried to explain to the royal commissioners in 1888 that "when health gives way, we must, necessarily contract debts." Octave Delage stressed that a workingman could only save on $9 a week "if he had no misfortune." Yet, when workers emphasized health factors, the commissioners do not seem to have fully grasped their significance.[95]

As we saw in Chapter 2, nineteenth-century Montreal was an extremely unhealthy city. Its rates of mortality were unmatched in North America. Low wages and frequent unemployment accentuated the likelihood of poor nutrition. They combined with damp, unsanitary homes, crowding, and inadequate sewage disposal to create a proletariat only too susceptible to disease. Being ill or having a family member sick was part of the daily life of most working-class Montrealers. Even in years without epidemics Montreal's particularly high rates of disease and death posed constant challenges to family survival. Dr. Philip Carpenter estimated in the late 1850s that for every person dying in the city there were twenty-eight cases of sickness. Even if overall morbidity rates were half this level by the 1870s and 1880s, which is highly unlikely, and if the terrible period of the smallpox epidemic in 1885 is excluded, nearly half the people of Saint Jacques and at least one-third of those of Saint Anne would have fallen sick each year.[96] The potential drain on family budgets can be imagined. Stone-cutter Étienne Féréole-Lagrenade owed two doctors a total of $55 for care given during the final illness of his wife, Zoé.[97]

Sickness and unemployment increased the likelihood of going into debt.[98] Eli Massy and other workers giving evidence in 1888 were adamant about the prevalence of indebtedness. The cigarmakers argued that a small family could not live on $364 a year without going into debt. Joiner Stanislaus Paquette reported that most joiners were more likely to make debts than savings. He had come through the previous winter over $35 in debt. When the foreman of the *Gazette*'s book and job department was asked how much "a good job man, a married man, with a family of three living economically . . . could save at the end of the year" from his wages of $9 to $12 a week, James Connolly replied, "I think he could not save 10 cents. I speak from experience." Men in his trade could earn around $500 annually. Yet that amount seemed only just enough. Fireman James Doolan agreed. He argued that over the years:

> . . . no improvements have been made in the condition of the married men. I would like you gentlemen to put yourselves in the place of the married men – firemen living in a small place at a big rent, with the mother and children living there and the fireman's mother or his wife's mother living there with them. . . . A fireman cannot live on $500.00 a year and pay his honest debts, because I and the others are in debt.[99]

Indebtedness to local storekeepers or to moneylenders at usurious rates permeated the lives of many workers. Debts led some in a vicious cycle from court to wage seizure to loss of job. Non-payment of rent could lead to both eviction and wage seizure. Initially a landlord might simply evict the family. He then proceeded to recover "a sum for damages he sustained by his house being left idle." If this sum was not forthcoming the ex-landlord could take out a writ of possession. All but the most basic of the debtor's belongings would be sold. If any amount of the debt remained uncovered, 50 per cent of wages could be seized. Labourer Thomas Gratorex of Montreal reported in 1888 that he had been evicted for non-payment of three months' rent, worth $22.50. He assumed that his debts had been covered when his furniture, worth an estimated $165, was sold. Six years later, however, a judgement forced him to pay a further $48.[100]

Wage seizure wreaked havoc on budgets that were already too tight. Jules Helbronner described the tragic case of a large family owing $11 on food purchased on credit. They repaid $7, then illness hit. The wife requested a delay on the repayment of the rest but was refused. Judgement was made against them for $15. The husband's salary, which in itself was insufficient to feed the children, was seized. The father, unable to bear the sight of his sick wife and hungry children, and equally unable to pay his debt or to feed his family, gave up hope and committed suicide.[101]

It was only at the turn of the century that the civil law surrounding wage seizure was modified to prevent merchants from directly seizing a worker's wages for debt. M. Lacombe, proponent of the new bill, graphically described how workers became indebted to local merchants, who then raised the prices of the goods being sold, called in their debts when the worker went to shop elsewhere, and then took them to court. Costs on top of a debt of $5 or $6 led invariably in this scenario to wage seizure and dismissal from work. Lacombe argued that his bill would protect the only class that was not protected against the combines and exploiters.[102]

Stretching Family Budgets

Suicides, starvation, indebtedness, and wage seizures paint a grim portrait of working-class family life. It is one that captures elements of the reality but hides moments of fun and periods of ease. It also minimizes both the differentiation within the working class and the ingenuity with which many workers and their wives and children shaped their standards of living. Costs that rapidly outstripped wages, seasonal and cyclical interruptions in earning power, and illness or money spent on alcohol did not lock all working-class Montreal families into a "culture of poverty."[103] Men's wages, after all, were not the only means of survival. Any discussion of standards of living that considers only the wage that a male family head could make, or that considers wages as the exclusive form of income, fails to grasp the complexity of wage dependency in this early formative period of industrial capitalism. Sometimes working together, at other times despite each other, men and their wives constantly sought ways to increase wages, to complement them, and to soften the edges of wage dependency. Men fought for higher wages either sporadically in response to wage cuts or in well-organized struggles. Except in major depressions the skilled stood apart from the rest of the working class. Families went temporarily into debt, hoping that some change in the economy or in their personal situation would give them a chance to recuperate. Additional family members went out to work. Wives and children made and saved money in various ways. By combining the wages men could earn with other strategies, families raised their own standards of living and compensated for low wages.

The wage-earning and residential strategies of two families, the Harringtons and the Cérats, serve to illustrate how families responded to the evolution of costs over the family life cycle, how they modified the balance between earners and consumers and between income and family needs.

Labourer John Harrington came to Canada from County Kerry in western Ireland. When he married Sarah McNutty at Montreal's Notre Dame Church in 1854, he was listed as a labourer, an occupation he appears to have held for the rest of his life. Both his parents were dead when they married, as was Sarah's labourer father. Her mother still lived in Ireland in County Donegal. Sarah bore only two sons who survived – Timothy, born soon after their marriage, and Patrick, born in 1858. A third son, John, had died at the age of four in 1860. When the census-taker enumerated them in Sainte Anne ward in 1861 the boys were aged seven and three. In addition to the nuclear family, the household included a fifty-year-old widower who was a relative of John and an older married couple who appear to have been boarders. The three adult males in the household were all working as labourers. The boarder's wife, Mrs. Lane, had found work as a servant. John's family might have managed to get by on a labourer's wage with just two small children. Taking in a relative and boarders who contributed for their food and lodging gave Sarah and John access to additional money as a hedge against intermittent unemployment. In this way they could raise their standard of living at the most difficult period in the family life cycle.

The Harringtons remained in Sainte Anne ward over the next two decades, moving frequently within the area in response to changes in their economic situation and family needs. A decade later they were cramped into a small rear house on William Street. They had only one additional household member, an Irish widow, aged sixty. In 1861 there had been three adult males earning within the household. In 1871 John was the only wage-earner. Ten years earlier the Rowntree diet for the Harringtons themselves would have cost only $133.12. In 1871, however, with older children and an extra resident with no visible means of support, the cost of food alone would have risen to $171, or 71 per cent of John's potential earnings. Perhaps this explains their moving to a rear tenement, where rents were generally lower.[104] Such rear tenements were "hidden from the public eye" and "rarely well built." Herbert Ames suggested at the end of the century that they were often occupied long after they were "no longer fit for human habitation." This shoe manufacturer and philanthropist suggested that anyone wanting to "find where drunkenness and crime, disease and death, poverty and distress are most in evidence in western Montreal" had only to search out the rear tenements.[105]

By economizing on rental the Harringtons may have sought to improve the lot of their children, for in 1871 both seventeen-year-old Timothy and twelve-year-old Patrick were still in school. The relatively long schooling they received does not appear, however, to have helped their job chances. Ten years later both were working as labourers, as was their father. The difficult years of sharing their living space with boarders and relatives and of renting rear houses were past in 1881. With three adult members of the immediate family earning, the

Harringtons were able to live without relatives or boarders in a section of Young Street peopled by labourers' families.

A different unfolding of the family life cycle is illustrated in the history of the Cérat family. In 1861, twenty-five-year-old Saint Jacques resident Joseph Cérat was listed as the head of a household that included his parents and his brother. The father and the two sons were stone-cutters and both Joseph's wife, Philomène, and his brother Edouard's wife, Sophie, worked as dressmakers. Joseph and Edouard's mother, Sophie, listed her occupation as "économe." With five earning adults and three young children between the two young couples, this extended family could afford to live reasonably well. Linked by kinship and craft they continued to live close to each other, but over subsequent years each brother set up his own household. By 1871 Joseph and Philomène had five children, aged two months to thirteen years. One boarder, a dressmaker, lived with them. Almost next door were Edouard and his family. Food costs for Joseph's family would have increased from approximately $116 for Joseph, Sophie, and the two children in 1861 to about $179. Stone-cutters, however, were among the better-paid workers in the construction trades. Earning at least as much as a mason, at approximately $420 a year, plus whatever board the lodger paid, this couple could probably support their family of five children reasonably well. The two boys, Joseph and Jean-Baptiste, were going to school. Philomène apparently no longer sewed for a living. She would have been fully occupied with housework and the three young children, including a newborn. By 1881 the two oldest boys, now aged twenty-three and eighteen, were in the family trade. With three salaries it was no longer necessary to have a boarder. This family could experience a certain level of comfort despite food costs that had increased to fully $276 a year, even on the spartan Rowntree diet.[106]

The estimated evolution of food costs in the Cérat family, from approximately $116 in 1861 to $276 in 1881, underlines the inadequacy of measures of basic costs that look only at an average family of five – the practice of some historians and most government departments. The fact that in both of these families – one headed by a labourer, the other by a skilled worker – two sons eventually complemented the father's wages highlights the importance of additional wage-earners, and of older boys in particular, in the family economy of all of the working class.

Additional Wage-earners

The simplest solution to the inadequacy of male wages clearly was for other family members to seek paid labour. These extra workers could be children, wives, brothers, or sisters of the couple or even elderly parents. In most families the contributions of older sons and daughters became the crucial complement to the father's wage. Wives worked only sporadically, responding to crises when their husbands were ill, unemployed, or chronically drunk.

The expansion of jobs that accompanied the growth of industry and the population allowed growing numbers of family members to find work in the city. In 1861 families in Sainte Anne and Saint Jacques wards reported an average of 1.3 workers. In 1871 the average had increased to 1.5, where it remained over the subsequent decade. By 1891, however, there were fewer family members at work, an average of 1.4. Behind these averages lie divergent patterns between and within classes, different unfoldings of the family life cycle, and complex negotiations between parents and their children. In a good year like 1871, there was a fairly direct relationship between a father's wage-earning potential and the number of family workers. That year skilled families averaged 1.5 workers while the unskilled had an average of 1.7 members reporting a job (Table 3.3). An examination of changes over the period incorporating the evolution of the family life cycle paints a somewhat more complex picture (see Figure 3.4).

The number of workers reported in the families of Sainte Anne and Saint Jacques fluctuated over the family life cycle, increasing as children reached an employable age, decreasing again as they left home. Wives who had not yet borne children would occasionally report an occupation. Relatives living with a young couple might boost the number of workers in the household. Normally, however, most families had just one worker throughout the long and usually difficult period between marriage and the time when a child reached working age. Once children entered the work force their contributions began to make up for the difficult years. In 1861 families averaged around two workers by the time most children were fifteen or over. In subsequent decades the average increased to nearly three, then declined rapidly as children left home. Couples, widows, and widowers found themselves struggling again in their old age on a single wage, or no wage at all.

Over these years the patterns of family labour commitment of the working-class and non-working-class families diverged. In 1861 the non-working class, particularly in Saint Jacques, included a high proportion of artisans and shopkeepers. Their family economy required not the wages but the work of wives and children. As a result, such families generally had more workers and more of their children at work than other groups. As artisans running their own shops became less common over the following decades, family labour was increasingly limited to such enterprises as small corner groceries. Professionals and

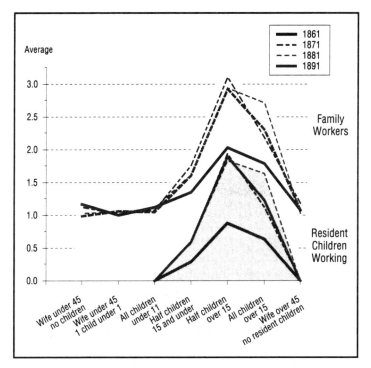

Figure 3.4   Average Number of Family Workers and Resident
Children Working throughout the Family Life Cycle, 1861-91

some white-collar workers became more important among the non-
working-class population. As a result, after 1871, their children were
less likely to contribute to the family economy than those in working-
class families. In 1891 in non-working-class families who had some
children aged eleven and over, an average of under one reported a job
(0.70). This compared to 1.43 among the unskilled and 1.63 in the
injured trades (Table 3.3).

It was within the working-class family economy that the most dramatic changes occurred over this period. The most important was the
growing contribution of children, especially in the period between
1861 and 1881. Although we return to this subject in more detail in the
following chapter, it is important to sketch the overall pattern now. The
average number of children reporting a job in families with at least one
offspring over the age of eleven increased from 0.5 in 1861 to nearly

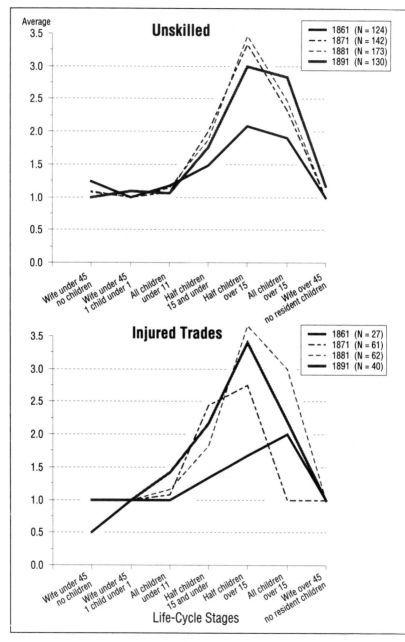

Figure 3.5 Average Number of Workers by Class Positions, 1861-91

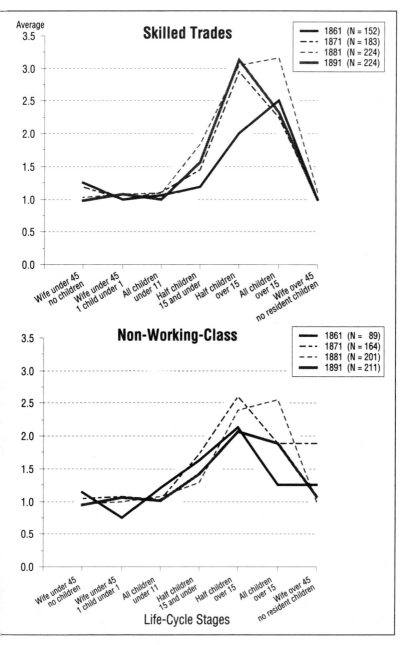

Average

Skilled Trades

——	1861 (N = 152)
- - -	1871 (N = 183)
- - -	1881 (N = 224)
——	1891 (N = 224)

3.5
3.0
2.5
2.0
1.5
1.0
0.5
0.0

Wife under 45 no children
Wife under 45 1 child under 1
All children under 11
Half children 15 and under
Half children over 15
All children over 15
Wife over 45 no resident children

Non-Working-Class

——	1861 (N = 89)
- - -	1871 (N = 164)
- - -	1881 (N = 201)
——	1891 (N = 211)

3.5
3.0
2.5
2.0
1.5
1.0
0.5
0.0

Wife under 45 no children
Wife under 45 1 child under 1
All children under 11
Half children 15 and under
Half children over 15
All children over 15
Wife over 45 no resident children

Life-Cycle Stages

1.2 in 1881, then decreased slightly to 1.07 in 1891, hinting, perhaps, that reliance on several earning children was a temporary response to the particularly low wages and fluctuating economic conditions that characterized the initial phases of industrialization.

There were strikingly different patterns, however, within the working class (Figure 3.5). The inadequacy of the dollar or so a day that a labourer could earn throughout this period meant that unskilled families relied on additional workers whenever they were able to. In 1861 they averaged 1.4 workers, compared to 1.3 among the skilled. The growing number of jobs created in the factories and construction sites of the city combined with relative prosperity to increase the average number of workers in the families of the unskilled over the following decade to over 1.7. Olive Godaire, wife of labourer Pierre, worked as a dressmaker in 1861 when their three children were aged between two and eight. Ten years later, it was her eighteen-year-old daughter who was taking in sewing, while a ten-year-old boy was apprenticed to be a tinsmith.[107] Most of the increase in the average number of workers results from the rapid rise in the number of sons and daughters of unskilled workers who were able to find work in the relatively prosperous early 1870s and who decided to remain living with their parents. Over the subsequent decades unskilled labourers were less and less likely to have additional family members living with them and earning. The average number of workers in such families declined, while the average number of children at work remained steady, rising slightly in 1891, in contrast to all other groups.

Shoemakers and workers in other injured trades responded to deteriorating work conditions and wages by sending growing numbers of family members to seek steady work. In 1861, when masters and capitalists were only beginning to transform the nature of the craft, such families averaged only 1.09 workers – fewer than any other group. By 1891 they averaged 1.75. Most dramatic was the increased importance of the contribution of children resident at home. The average number of children reporting a job in families with children of working age nearly tripled over the three decades, from 0.63 in 1861 to 1.63 in 1891. In their families, like those of labourers, children were expected to work. By the time both shoemakers and labourers of these wards had some children aged fifteen, fully 95 per cent had more than one worker and most had three or four. The family of shoemaker Alexis Larivière and his wife Angeline was fairly typical. In 1881 they reported four workers. Two daughters, twenty-two-year-old Josephine and sixteen-year-old Marie-Louise, worked as general labourers, and twenty-year-old son Charles was a stone-cutter.[108]

The relative superiority of the wages of skilled workers and shoemakers prior to major changes in their trades seems clear in the 1860s and 1870s. In 1871 they averaged 1.5 workers compared to 1.7 among the unskilled. Whereas unskilled families with children of working age had an average of 1.36 at work, the skilled average only 0.92. In 1881, in contrast, after seven years of major depression, their patterns of family labour deployment were much closer to those of the unskilled than in previous decades (Table 3.3). Earning children were as important in their family economies as among the unskilled. Furthermore, their adult sons and daughters appear to have stayed at home longer, perhaps because parents could offer a higher standard of living (Figures 3.4 and 3.5). By 1891 the skilled again had fewer earning children on the average than other working-class groups and a lower average number of workers.

Families clearly attempted to shape their own economies by adjusting the number of wage-earners to meet their expenses when they were able to do so. Additional wage-earners were not only needed but were used by all fractions of the working class, with differences stemming from the economic conjuncture, the nature of the labour market, their own life cycle, and earning power. Wage-earning by children and other family members both enhanced levels of survival and reshaped the city's labour pool. The increasing availability of wage labour in the factories, workshops, and construction sites of Montreal meant that except in times of severe depression more and more sons and daughters could and did find work. The reliance of employers in certain sectors on women and youths resident at home depressed male wages generally, while offering families the opportunity to counter a father's low earnings. Economic transformation thus interacted with family needs to reshape the family economy, the life course of children, and the labour market. The results are clearest in the case of workers in the most injured trades. Not only did these men delay marriage and reduce their family size over these decades, but the importance of children's work increased more steadily than for any other fraction of the working class.

The interaction between the family and the economy is clear in other ways, too. Montreal's proletariat grew over this period not simply by absorbing immigrants from Great Britain and rural Quebec, but also by drawing in growing numbers of children from old and new city families. As a corollary, the importance of secondary family workers in the labour market grew. Between 1861 and 1881 the number of males reporting jobs in Sainte Anne and Saint Jacques who were sons living with their parents increased from one in six to one in three. Labourers were less and less likely to be family heads. In 1861 four-fifths of all labourers were heads of families. The proportions dropped steadily over subsequent decades until in 1891 only two-thirds were family heads. The proportion of labourers who were sons living at home increased from 7 per cent in 1861 to 24 per cent in 1881, then fell back to 11 per cent in 1891 as boarding became more common again. Curiously, the proportion of workers who were living with their parents was even higher in selected skilled metal trades than among labourers in these two parts of town. It rose from one-quarter in the 1860s to two-fifths in the 1870s and 1880s, then fell back to around a quarter in 1891.[109]

By the 1880s nearly one-third of the workers in these two wards lived with their parents. In specific trades the proportion was much higher. Both general wage rates and the possibility of organizing workers must have been affected by the predominance of dependants in the labour force. Certainly male workers in trades undergoing rapid change perceived children as the major cause of depressed wages. Cigarmakers and shoemakers were quite sure that the employment of children was destroying their trade and their living. While shoemakers generally identified machinery rather than children as the reason for lower wages in their trade, they also pointed to the problem caused by young people taken in "only as help in the factory" who took "the place of a mechanic, or even of a man who has a family to work for."[110]

Yet these were precisely the families for whom sending children to work offered a way of improving their standard of living after years of scrimping and getting by. The expansion of wage labour over this period and the creation of a variety of jobs demanding less skill increased the possibility that children would find work, thereby improving standards of living in the short term. In the long term the employment of large numbers of secondary wage-earners helped to keep wages down, maintaining Montreal's reputation as a centre of cheap labour and laying the foundations for the "classic bind" that working-class families continued to face well into the twentieth century.[111]

The employment of young children became a symbol with double significance. For many skilled male workers child labour symbolized the degradation of their craft, the fact that new divisions of labour and updated machinery allowed the hiring of large numbers of unskilled workers. At the same time, for those men whose children had to find employment, their wage-earning was proof of the impossibility of making ends meet on the wages they could earn, a challenge to their role and to their masculinity.

The disparities of twenty-five cents a day that separated diverse Montreal occupations had the potential to cut up the working class into identifiable fractions, each capable of achieving a different standard of living in good times, each vulnerable in diverse ways to the impact of winter, cyclical depressions, and job restructuring. The real differences of purchasing power are clear in the greater ability of the skilled to afford more spacious housing. Yet, in reality, the situation was never so simple. Some men were ill more often than others, some better at finding steady work. Family size varied. So did the configurations of age and sex of the children within families. The major element of flexibility in the family income lay less in the gains that the minority of well-organized workers could make at work than in the ability to call on additional family members to earn wages, to gain or save money in other ways, or to limit the necessity of spending cash.

4

Age, Gender, and the
Roles of Children

"Children aren't pigs you know, for they can't pay the rent," went an old Irish ballad.[1] From the 1860s on the wages that children in working-class families could earn were increasingly likely to help pay the rent. The most striking change in the working-class family economy over this period was the growing number of offspring living with their parents who had some kind of formal remunerated employment. Once sons, in particular, reached an age where they could earn, their pay offered those families who had been struggling for years to balance food and housing costs against inadequate or irregular wages the possibility of escaping poverty or improving a meagre standard of living. The need of a large proportion of working-class families for more income than the family head could generate combined with the increased chance that children would find waged labour to introduce new and different tensions to intergenerational relations and to reshape the life course of sons and daughters.

Among pre-industrial and rural families the types of labour required, the transmission of property, the provision of dowries, and inheritance decisions were all potential points of disagreement. Decisions were liable to expose the unequal positions of sons and daughters or to pit sons against each other.[2] In the expanding working class of cities like Montreal, most parents needed their children's help from an early age. The work they expected of sons and daughters ranged from odd jobs to formal, full-time waged labour. The need for children's contributions was not new. What changed, as industrial capitalism opened up vast sectors of waged work, was the ability of some offspring to contribute cash rather than labour power to the family economy. Children's earning power, which varied significantly with their age and sex, created new possibilities and new sources of conflict. Here was a point of potential co-operation and of strain, a challenge to power

118

relations within the family, for a wage rewarded an individual's labour. Family conflicts could arise only too easily over whether children should remain in school, work for wages, hand over some or all their pay to their parents, or leave home or marry. Such decisions might create friction between children and their parents, between siblings, and also between the different needs of mothers and fathers.

Girls and boys did not play the same role in the gamut of tasks that children were called upon to perform. On farms and in workshops, boys had usually worked beside their fathers, while daughters helped around the house except when extra labour was required in peak periods. To this sexual division of labour were grafted the differential earning power of sons and daughters in the industrial-capitalist labour market and the different nature of housework in an industrial city.

To understand the changing roles of sons and daughters in the working-class family economy and to try to grasp the decision-making processes behind the increase in the numbers of family members reporting work over this period, it is crucial to examine the kinds of work performed by children of different ages and sexes and to see how the jobs their fathers held influenced their working lives. That is the task of this chapter. Because young workers received so much attention, it begins by investigating the patterns of work and schooling of children under fourteen, the age group that would eventually be regulated by the factory acts. The jobs and work patterns of older boys and girls are then examined. Further sections look at the lower labour force participation of girls, the jobs they held, and the importance of their domestic labour at home. The chapter concludes by looking at how the need of parents for their offspring's wages and help with housework combined with general economic depression to keep growing numbers of sons and daughters living longer at home in the initial period of industrial capitalism, and suggests that this was a temporary phenomenon.

Schooling and Work for Children under Fifteen

Until children were old enough to work and to help their mother around the house they represented a drain both on the family income and on the mother's energy and time. Many women must have been relieved when some children reached school age and could be away from under their feet for much of the day. School might serve a babysitting function. The fact that around 3 per cent of children under four were reported to be at school throughout this period suggests that some mothers used schools as alternatives to daycare, or that children attending the city's *salles d'asile,* church-run daycares, were reported as at school.[3] Schooling may have been viewed by some working-class families as an investment in the children's future, potentially giving sons or daughters a chance to improve their position in society and their chances in life.[4] On the other hand, placing a son in a trade or a craft probably seemed more important for many parents.[5] In a period when education was only loosely equated with schooling and when no legislation compelled children to attend school or effectively prevented them from working, patterns of school attendance and work take us to the core of the decision-making process within families.

In the province of Quebec schooling was neither compulsory nor free.[6] And, unlike in the other Canadian provinces, it did not become so over this period. Yet many working-class parents seem to have striven, even sacrificed economic advantages, to give their children some education. Eli Massy and the other cigarmakers who presented their family budgets to the Royal Commission in 1888 had allowed "about fifty cents a week," or 7 per cent of their meagre budget, for school costs.[7] Labourer John Harrington and his wife Sarah appear to have been willing to forgo the advantages of their son's labour to keep Timothy in school until he was seventeen.[8] These workers were not exceptions. Most working-class children in Sainte Anne and Saint Jacques wards attended school for at least a few years, and growing numbers did so as the century advanced.

Formal learning, however, took up a relatively brief part of these working-class children's lives. The numbers of children reported as being at school in Sainte Anne and Saint Jacques wards suggest that for these boys and girls schooling was concentrated between the ages of seven and twelve (Figure 4.1). A few children began school as young as four years old, a practice that appears to have diminished between 1861 and 1881.[9] Not until ages eight to nine were more than half of these girls and boys attending school. Attendance was highest for those aged between eight and eleven, when between three-fifths and three-quarters of all youngsters were reported being in the classroom. After age eleven or so, the pattern for boys and for girls diverges, reflecting the different roles that each held in the family economy. The proportion of girls over eleven years old in school increased steadily, if somewhat slowly, between 1861 and 1881. The pattern for boys was more erratic, as schooling competed with the possibility of wage-earning in good years, such as 1871. By the time children of both sexes reached thirteen or fourteen only a minority attended school. Fewer than one-third of fourteen- to fifteen-year-olds were in school. In these wards they were predominantly the offspring of non-working-class parents. The overall proportion of children receiving some schooling increased between 1861 and 1881, but fairly slowly and more among girls than boys (Figure 4.1).

While a certain number of families took advantage of boom

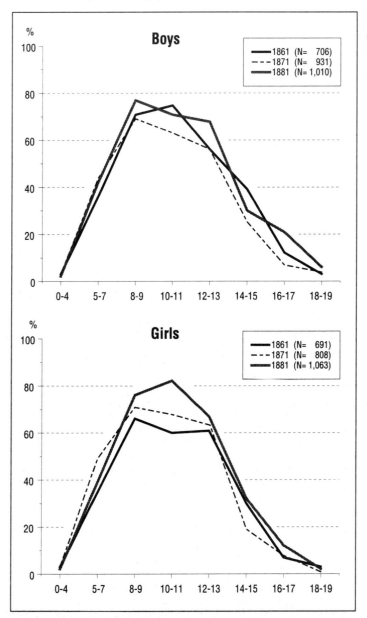

Figure 4.1 Boys and Girls Reported as Attending School, 1861-81, Sainte Anne and Saint Jacques Combined

employment periods to draw their sons out of school, the majority of families appear to have got the best of both worlds. Most of these working-class children went to school for varying lengths of time before they reached thirteen or so. They then left school to work for wages or to help at home.

Although the proportions at school are lower than in Hamilton, Ontario, where schooling was compulsory and free, the number that did attend is an impressive testimony to the desire of parents to educate their children.[10]

Parents seeking schools for their children faced diverse options. Montreal's school system became more complicated over this period as divisions between Catholic and Protestant, English and French, and private and state-subsidized schools proliferated. By 1875 the Catholic and Protestant systems were completely separate. The control and influence of the Catholic Church had expanded in both public and private Catholic schools as in the state structure. Nuns and priests were rapidly outnumbering lay teachers as Bishop Bourget introduced new teaching orders from France and sanctioned the creation of local ones. Various orders ran private and public schools throughout the city. The Protestant School Board ran its own schools, and lay men and women offered education in a variety of private institutions.[11]

For the largely Catholic working-class families of these wards the fact that some orders provided free schooling was a major attraction. The fees of twenty-five cents to two dollars a month demanded in the majority of public schools would have placed inordinate strain on already tight budgets. Both Sainte Anne and Saint Jacques wards had at least ten Catholic schools in 1877. The Sisters of the Congregation of Notre Dame (CND) offered free classes to around 700 girls in each ward that year. The Sisters of Providence ran two free classes for poorer children in their school in Saint Jacques. The size of the classes for non-paying pupils gives some indication of the quality of education these working-class children received. In the Sainte Marie school, located at the corner of Craig and Visitation streets in eastern Saint Jacques, the CND offered six classes to 200 paying pupils. There were an average of thirty-three pupils in each room. The nuns also gave eight classes for the non-fee-paying students in classes averaging eighty-seven girls. Ratios of up to 100 pupils per teacher could be found in such free classes.[12] This practice of educating both fee-paying and "free" students within one school enabled these orders to provide an education for those unable to pay. The fees of wealthy parents subsidized the inferior education of the poor.[13]

Free education did not, however, mean equal education. Not only did paying students enjoy lower teacher-pupil ratios, but they also had better equipment and broader curricula. Even desks were sparse in the free classes. Class differences were thus reflected and perpetuated in the distinctions between fee-paying and non-fee-paying students.[14] So, too, were differences between boys and girls. Education for females, in all but a few expensive academies, covered the most basic subjects and housekeeping-related skills. Boys' schools listed book-keeping and geography. Girls' schools offered music and sewing. The curriculum for girls aimed specifically to prepare them to fulfil their future roles as housekeeper, wife, and mother. Indeed, the Minister of Education found the stress on music and such graces in many state-supported girls' schools superfluous. In 1874 he expressed his concern that many young women were being educated above their station in life. Bookkeeping and domestic economy would better form the basis of female education for such girls, he argued. Most girls learned what would help them at home – elementary literacy and skills suitable to females of their class. Differences in boys' and girls' schooling stretched beyond the subjects taught, as historian Marta Danylewcyz demonstrated. Girls' schools subsidized by the Catholic School Commission received six to ten times less money per student than did boys' schools. Between 1860 and 1877 six new schools were built and financed by the Commission for Montreal school boys. None were constructed for girls.[15]

That children attended these schools does not mean that they turned up regularly, nor necessarily that they learned a lot. Like the Toronto children described by John Bullen, many moved in and out of the classroom as parents kept them home to look after siblings, to run errands, to earn a little money, or simply because they were ashamed to send them to school without adequate clothing or shoes.[16] How many learned the minimum necessary to be defined by their parents as literate can be gauged very roughly from the 1891 census returns. That year no question was asked about school attendance, but respondents were requested to indicate which household members could read and write. Despite their erratic schooling, boys in all groups appear to have been more likely than girls to be able to both read and write. This may be because the greater amount of money invested in male schooling was having an effect. Protestant children were more likely to report they could read and write at most ages than were either French or Irish Catholics (Table 4.1). Protestant children over the age of ten were virtually all able to read and write, whereas among both French and Irish Catholic children, less than nine out of ten boys and closer to eight out of ten girls said they could do so. Class background made more difference than religious and ethnic affiliations. The children of unskilled workers were consistently less likely to say they could read and write than the offspring of skilled workers or the non-working-class. Only 64 per cent of the fourteen- to fifteen-year-old sons and 75 per cent of the daughters of unskilled men could both read and write, compared to 100 per cent of the sons and over 90 per cent of the daughters of skilled workers (Table 4.2).

Schooling and work were not mutually exclusive for nineteenth-century children either in the urban working class or in rural areas. Children often attended school for several months, leaving when required for family or personal reasons. In this, their patterns of schooling resembled those of rural children kept home to help with such seasonal work as planting and harvesting. Children attending pretty well full time could still use the hours after classes to scrounge, beg, or otherwise raise money for themselves or their families. Some of the "little children" selling papers in the streets late at night may well have been working late to combine earning and schooling.[17]

School and work also merged as agents of socialization in nineteenth-century thought. Educators and social observers disagreed about the relative training benefits of each. Many considered labour the best form of education available. Education for the working class, in particular, aimed to serve as a precursor to work. Schools attempted to inculcate just those habits of obedience, punctuality, diligence, and industriousness that would be required in the workplace. Even for young children, work was seen as preferable to idleness or life on the streets. In Ontario, the school acts of the 1870s had provided that every child "from the age of seven to twelve years shall have the right to attend some school, or be otherwise educated for four months in every year." Investigators of the mills and factories were "unable to find any place in which this Act is enforced." They reported that employers would rather "discontinue the employment of such labor than submit to the obligations imposed by the aforesaid Bill." To this suggestion commissioners Lukes and Blackeby commented, "If education be not enforced the question arises whether the children are not better cared for by spending a portion at least of their time at work, rather than wasting it on the public streets."[18]

The census allows a glimpse at the number of early school leavers who spent a reasonable proportion of their time at work. Figures must be treated with caution, for the census undercounted the paid work of young children because it was often irregular and because parents may not have reported that their young were employed. However, given that prior to the 1880s there were no laws against such youngsters holding jobs and no provincial statutes requiring them to stay in school, the census should offer a minimum estimate of the proportions working fairly steadily at ages that would subsequently become illegal.

The number of girls and boys under fifteen who appear to have held jobs are small compared with those found by historians studying cotton mill towns in the United States and England. Few ten- to eleven-year-olds in Sainte Anne and Saint Jacques wards worked between 1861 and 1891. The proportions of twelve- to thirteen-year-old boys and girls reporting a job doubled between 1861 and 1871, but reached only 9 per cent for girls in 1881 and 10 per cent for boys (Figure 4.2). By 1891, as factory legislation began to be applied and a better economic climate rendered their contribution less necessary the percentage of twelve- to thirteen-year-old boys and girls reporting a job had fallen to below 6 per cent.

The father's work and health were the most important factors explaining the employment of young children. Most youngsters under fifteen worked because their father had died, was sick, drank, or earned insufficient wages. In 1861 only 2 per cent of skilled family heads with children aged 10-14 had any at work compared to 14 per cent of the unskilled. A decade later, the growing availability of work meant that more families in all groups could find jobs for small children. Yet, still only 10 per cent of skilled male family heads reported a youngster at work, compared to 18 per cent for those in the injured trades and nearly one-quarter of the unskilled. The effects of the Great Depression were still evident in 1881, when over one in five of all working-class families had at least one child aged 10-14 reporting a job (Table 4.3). Throughout most of the period families living in Sainte Anne, where work opportunities were greater, were more likely to have their sons at work than were those of Saint Jacques. Depression and work restructuring combined to touch the lives of a growing minority of working-class youth, pushing them into the work force at an age that would shortly be made illegal.

By the early 1890s the proportions of families of all class positions, ethnic backgrounds, and life-cycle stages with such child labourers had fallen. New legislation, the changing needs of employers, and a slightly more prosperous economic climate combined in these two Montreal wards, as in other parts of Canada, to reduce the numbers of very young at work.[19] The unskilled continued to be most likely to send their young to work. Yet, whereas nearly one in four families headed by an unskilled worker had had at least one child under fifteen at work in the 1870s and 1880s, only one in eight did in 1891. The proportion of skilled workers' families with such youngsters at work dropped from one in four to under one in ten, as such men regained their relatively privileged position in the labour market (Table 4.3).

This decline in the proportion of children under fifteen listing a job is partially the result of the legislation passed between the 1881 and 1891 censuses. Its origins and impact merit examination. In 1881 "the employment of young children in mills and factories" was considered

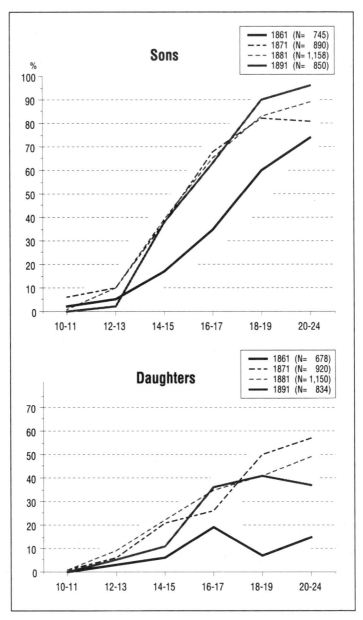

Figure 4.2 Sons and Daughters Resident with Their Parents Who Reported a Job, 1861-91, Sainte Anne and Saint Jacques Combined

to be so widespread as to "warrant the Government in issuing a Commission in relation to the subject." William Lukes and A.H. Blakeby's inquiry into Canada's mills and factories, the report of which was published a year later, confirmed that children aged ten to fourteen and even younger were employed in diverse sectors of the Canadian economy. They suggested with alarm that child labour was both "extensive and on the increase, the supply being unequal to the demand, particularly in some localities."[20]

The publication of their report in 1882, complaints by the Knights of Labor, and political pressure from other reform lobbies led provincial governments in Quebec and Ontario to legislate some control over the work of children in factories. The Quebec Manufacturing Act of 1885 set out a variety of controls over work and safety conditions. They applied only to manufacturing establishments with more than twenty employees. Employers were required to ensure adequate ventilation to counter excessive dust or smells and to provide separate earth or water closets for men and women. Hours of work were officially limited to ten per day for children and women alike. Employment of boys under twelve and girls under fourteen was made illegal without a special work certificate. After 1885 parents seeking factory employment for their offspring were required to produce certificates proving that their sons were over twelve and their daughters over fourteen. Work by children, young girls, and women at home, or in any room or private building where all workers were family members, was explicitly excluded from the provisions.[21]

The loopholes in the Act meant that children in these age groups continued to work in commerce, in the sweatshops, and in other small establishments not covered by the law, as well as in the factories ostensibly covered by the legislation. The government did not appoint any inspectors to apply the legislation until 1888. That year the Act was amended to include all places employing fewer than twenty people and to prevent the employment of boys and girls under fourteen except in private homes. In the eyes of the legislators, childhood appears to have ended at fourteen.[22]

To what extent can the decline in work among children under fourteen be explained by the success of the factory legislation? To attribute the decline totally to the success of the factory acts would be an error. The figures in 1881 had been especially high because many families were still recuperating from years of financial depression and because employers had jobs they considered suitable for such youngsters. As men's chances of steady employment and better wages increased, the need for the minimal wages such youngsters could earn diminished. Furthermore, under-enumeration of working children was much more likely in 1891, the first census taken after the passage of the acts. These factors no doubt combined to reduce both the actual and the reported numbers of child labourers.

Legislation neither reshaped the experience of young people in general nor radically changed the behaviour of that minority of families who sent their young to work. Formal, reported wage-earning by boys and girls under the age of fourteen had been the experience of a minority of working-class children in the years before the passage of the factory acts.[23] Factory work at an early age remained the experience of a smaller minority after the factory acts. Parents who truly needed their youngsters' wages produced false age certificates and employers accepted the children. Inspectors called repeatedly for tests on literacy and for birth certificates and sought other ways of controlling child labour.[24] Employment of these children continued in most cases for the very reason it had existed initially. A certain proportion of families simply could not survive on the wages other family members could make, because of low wages, unemployment, or chronic illness or drunkenness. Controlling legislation had to be accompanied by steady work and better wages before child labour would be curtailed further. For many unskilled and all female family heads this did not occur in nineteenth-century Montreal or early in the twentieth century. In 1912 the *Child Welfare Exhibition Souvenir Handbook* stressed that some young children continued to be "driven out to work by the pressure of a need stronger than all laws, sometimes by the fear of actual starvation for the family."[25]

Such wage labour involved a minority of children, but it was clearly crucial for survival in those families in which it occurred. Employers, knowing well the value of such children's earnings, cleverly used fines as a way of disciplining the youngest children in particular. Deducting money was a particularly effective form of punishment precisely because it implicated the parents. They were likely to be more upset over a child's reduced pay package than about minor forms of corporal punishment. One employer was explicit. Fines were imposed

> in order that the parents may see it marked on the envelope, that it may thus attract the parent's attention. They will see ten cents marked as a fine and they will know about it. They will then find out from the children how it occurred, or they will go to the overseer and speak about it and that generally effects the result we desire.[26]

Fines were an age- and gender-specific form of punishment. They were "only imposed upon females and children, the most helpless class of operatives. Men will not put up with deductions from wages which they have toiled hard to obtain."[27] The practice was most common precisely in those industries employing large numbers of workers under the age of fifteen, particularly in cigarmaking factories and textile mills. Not all parents put up with the arbitrary deduction of much needed money. Some intervened when they considered fines had been unfairly levied, marching in to see the boss and demanding the lost money.[28] Most, no doubt, by exhorting their young to comply with the attempts of employers to make them work harder, to keep silent, or not to fidget and move around, helped the employer get the results he desired: the accommodation of their offspring to industrial labour.

The work conditions of such young children warranted public outrage. So, too, did the conditions under which many adults worked. In the clothing, textile, and tobacco factories or in the dry goods stores and offices where most young workers were employed, not many found jobs that would give them a trade for life. Fewer and fewer signed apprenticeship contracts that promised the teaching of a trade. Instead, the industrial transformation created a variety of age-specific jobs, many of them outside the industrial sector. Children performed them for a while until they became too old or too experienced to be paid such low wages. Then they were let go. In both Sainte Anne and Saint Jacques, boys found work in commerce as office boys and clerks, and in factories as tobacco workers and cigarmakers. In Sainte Anne some also worked as general labourers, nailers, or carpenters. In Saint Jacques many worked as shoemakers, and the young girls were all seamstresses, general unskilled workers, or tobacco workers. Young girls in Sainte Anne found more varied factory work as typecasters, tobacco workers, seamstresses, or in printing establishments and type foundries, or as clerks or domestics.

These young boys and girls were often referred to as apprentices and were paid minimal amounts because they were assumed to be learning cigarmaking, dressmaking, or other trades. Boy cigarmakers, for instance, were paid only $1 weekly during their first year, $2 the second, and $3 in the third. Yet at the end of that time few could make a cigar by hand. Their years of apprenticeship simply gave the employer a source of cheap labour and initiated the boys to the discipline required in factory work.

Physical punishment complemented fines as the most widespread form of punishment. Young children, particularly boys, constituted an exuberant, unruly work force that had to be controlled if production was to proceed in an orderly fashion. Boys were beaten for talking. A cigarmaker reported that when he was fourteen the foreman had "kicked me and struck me with his fist" for talking. One child reported:

> If a child did anything, that is, if he looked on one side or other, or spoke, he would say: I'm going to make you pay 10 cents fine, and if the same were repeated three or four times, he would seize a stick or a plank, and beat him with it.[29]

Employers turned to the local police to enforce attendance and discipline. One boy had been taken by the police after he sneaked away from work on a Saturday afternoon to see the circus. He was "locked up from one o'clock till ten in the evening in a cell at the City Hall." Punishment was most extreme at Fortier's cigar factory. To fines, beatings, and dismissals was added a detention room or "black hole," a "sort of coal box. The coals are stored there, and when the children don't behave they stick them among the coals." Witnesses reported that children remained in this limited space for anything from an hour to a whole afternoon and early evening.[30] Such punishment must surely have had an impact on the adults these children became, their attitudes to employers, and their views on physical violence.

Most young children's jobs involved long and tedious hours, either repeating monotonous tasks or, as in the case of message boys, continually coming and going or sitting around waiting for errands to run. Hours were the same for children and adults – ten hours or more, six days a week. Lukes and Blackeby were shocked to see young children whose appearance and condition by the afternoon of a hot summer's day was "anything but inviting or desirable. . . . They have to be at the mills or factories at 6.30 am. necessitating their being up at from 5.30 to 6 o'clock for their morning meal, some having to walk a distance of half a mile or more to their work."[31] The tobacco of the cigar manufactories and the lead in printing shops exposed them to substances that were health hazards. The commissioners hearing evidence in 1888 were pained to see that working with tobacco had already stunted their growth and "poisoned" the blood of some of the young witnesses. They appeared "undersized, sallow and listless."[32]

The relationship of these young workers, their parents, and the employer was complex. Parents appear to have endowed the employer with the patriarchal and disciplinary powers usually attributed to a father. Indeed, some employers claimed such powers for themselves. M. Fortier justified beatings in his factory by arguing that children had not been beaten "other than what they have deserved for wrongs they have committed, the same as a parent would punish a child." He and his manager claimed that parents asked them to discipline their children, especially in situations where parental control consistently failed. One boy's mother told him to "use any means in my power to chastise the boy as she could not get any good at all out of him." When "apprentices" in his factory failed to turn up on time, he first notified the parents, then "had the child arrested." Employers were apparently using the Act with respect to masters and apprentices against any workers who absented themselves without permission. "We have had parents come to us over and over again," he assured the commissioners, "and threaten to hold us responsible if we did not make the apprentices attend to their work." Other cigar manufacturers also reported having been requested by parents "to correct their children." Still others chose instead to send the children home to their parents when they did wrong.[33]

It is a little too easy to dismiss these employers' assertions as simple rationalizations of their voracious appetite for child labour. Certainly few were willing to relinquish their young workers unless all employers were forced to do so.[34] On the other hand, since most parents whose youngsters were at work were desperately in need of extra cash, they not only wanted their children to work, but also to conform and behave so as to keep their jobs and avoid losing money in fines. Children obviously needed disciplining to conform to factory routine. Adults, too, had to learn the punctuality and application that new work processes demanded.[35] Something more is apparent in the relationship of children, employer, and parents. The latter appear to have assumed that employers performed the same role as masters of apprentices had done in former times. Most factory owners, on the other hand, were concerned only with employing and disciplining a cheap labour force. Neither the child nor the family gained the benefits of a trade well learned in return. They merely earned some much needed money, and this was only too often whittled away by fines.

Fines and beatings aimed explicitly to exact conformity, to break children's independence, and to teach good work habits. The foreman of the shoe department of Canada Rubber Company explained that if a girl did not make the style of shoe that the management had chosen, "and we don't want her to choose for us, and if she insists," fines would "enforce obedience to orders." After several weeks such new hands were trained and had become used to following orders.[36]

Older Sons and Daughters and Their Work

Formal, full-time wage-earning in their early teens was the experience of a shrinking minority of youngsters over the second half of the nineteenth century. For working-class youths over fourteen, in contrast, it was increasingly the norm. The growing availability of jobs for teenaged youth reshaped the family economy, transformed the work lives of working-class youth, and offered a measure of security to many families at later stages of the family life cycle. In the process the contours of youth were reshaped in different ways for boys and girls. The links between the families and the economy were restructured.

Between 1861 and 1881 the proportion of sons and daughters over fourteen who listed a job in the census more than doubled. Most of the expansion of wage-earning possibilities occurred in the first decade of the period under study, for the availability of jobs diminished rapidly after the depression hit in 1874. In Sainte Anne ward the percentage of sons aged fourteen to fifteen reporting a job increased steadily from 23 in 1861 to 50 by 1891. Among boys aged sixteen to seventeen the percentage reporting waged work leaped from 29 in 1861 to 76 in 1871, then remained stable until it dropped somewhat in the 1890s. In Saint Jacques there were generally fewer boys at work, but there, too, the proportions increased for all age groups over the period (Table 4.4). Among boys aged fourteen to fifteen, the proportion increased rapidly from 5 to 46 per cent over the first decade, then decreased in the 1880s and 1890s as boys from the wealthier families in the ward stayed longer in school. By the 1880s over 90 per cent of Sainte Anne boys over the age of eighteen and three-quarters of those of Saint Jacques reported a job. Differences between the patterns of wage labour of boys in the two wards result partly from the nature of local labour markets, partly from the differential impact of the economic depression, but also from the changes in the class structure of Saint Jacques.

For teenage girls as for boys, the chances of finding work increased with the expansion of Montreal industry, but varied between the two wards and with economic fluctuations. There were always fewer girls at work than boys. The proportion of fourteen- to fifteen-year-old girls living at home in Sainte Anne ward and reporting a job shot up from 3 to 25 per cent between 1861 and 1871, then fell slightly to around 20 per cent in the following two decades. In Saint Jacques, in contrast, the percentage of girls at this age with a job increased steadily from 9 in 1861 to 25 in 1881, only to fall off dramatically to 5 per cent by the end of the decade. Girls sixteen and over were increasingly likely to list a job in Sainte Anne ward over the whole period, whereas in Saint Jacques the proportions began to fall after 1881. Daughters were most likely to be involved in wage labour between the ages of eighteen and twenty-four, when up to half of those living with their parents were at work. Until 1891, girls of most ages in Saint Jacques ward were more likely to have found jobs than the girls of Sainte Anne because of the possibility of sewing at home in the neighbourhood (Table 4.4).

The growing likelihood that sons and some daughters in their mid- to late teens and early twenties would find jobs and remain living at home largely explains the increase in the average number of workers in Montreal's working-class families outlined in the previous chapter. Once a family reached the stage of its life cycle when some children were fifteen or older, these teenage and adult offspring became the major additional earners in working-class family wage economies (Table 4.3). In 1861 only 20 per cent of families with an unskilled head and teenaged children reported any at work. By 1891, 80 per cent had at least one fifteen- to nineteen-year-old at work. Increases were similar but not as great for other fractions of the working class, less in need of additional earners. Differences within the working class are clearest in 1881, when unskilled families with at least one child at that age averaged one teenage worker, those in the injured trades averaged 0.90, while the skilled averaged 0.86.

Some teenage boys may have earned almost as much as a labouring father. Sons over twenty were much more likely to do so, potentially making a major contribution to a family's standard of living, but also potentially capable of setting up independently or marrying. While some earning offspring may have left home, establishing themselves in other cities or other parts of Montreal, a growing proportion of families did have children over twenty years old living with them and earning. Just under 60 per cent of unskilled workers in these wards who had children aged twenty and over living with them in 1861 reported offspring that age as working. By 1891 fully 96 per cent did (Table 4.3). The mean number of children that age who were working in these families increased from 0.64 in 1861 to 1.26 in 1891. Young men were twice as likely as their sisters to be the additional worker.

Examination of the average numbers of children working in different families must be treated with some care. When based on census figures, such averages only show us those children residing at home and listing a job. Other children could have worked elsewhere and contributed money. Some may have lived at home and contributed little. The ability of parents to keep earning children at home also varied with the standard of living that they could offer them, so that children of unskilled workers were more likely to leave home to seek work elsewhere. This may well have occurred during the depression that spread into the 1880s, for in 1881 the unskilled had fewer children over twenty reporting a job than any other group.[37]

The Different Work of Sons and Daughters

Children were clearly helping to pay the rent. The lower the family head's wages, the less secure his job, the more likely they were to do so. Sons and daughters were not, however, equally likely to be a family's additional wage-earners. Boys' and girls' experiences stand out as different whether one looks at the proportions involved in wage labour, the patterns of involvement over the life cycle, or the kinds of jobs held and work expected. The proportion of girls aged fifteen and over who reported having a job did increase over the second half of the nineteenth century. Yet their participation rate remained around half that of boys at all ages[38] (Table 4.4). In 1881, 40 per cent of girls aged 16-17 in Saint Jacques were listed as at work. Another 15 per cent were attending school. What the other 45 per cent were doing requires careful consideration. Over half the girls aged fifteen to twenty who lived at home neither reported going to school nor having a formal job throughout this period. The following sections examine the kinds of jobs that girls did hold in the formal waged economy, some of the conditions of that work, and some of the factors explaining their relatively low rate of labour force participation.

Once boys passed their early teens they found work in the wide variety of jobs that existed for males in all sectors and workplaces of Montreal. Boys aged 14-20 in Sainte Anne and Saint Jacques wards listed twenty-eight different jobs in 1861; by 1881 and 1891 they were listing over fifty. Sixty per cent of all boys in this age group had a job in 1861; 70 per cent did at the end of the period. The growth of industry opened up a growing array of jobs for daughters, too, but the variety of jobs, like the numbers involved, remained half of that for boys. Girls aged fourteen to twenty in the sample population for Sainte Anne and Saint Jacques wards listed a limited number of job titles in 1861: dressmaker, milliner, domestic, labourer, teacher, and clerk. By the end of the century, daughters in this age group reported over twenty different kinds of employment and the proportion with a job had increased from 16 to 35 per cent. These were not all industrial jobs. Factory work has too often been assumed to have been women's major occupation during the transformations that accompanied the expansion of industrial capitalism. Certainly the growth of factories and the new divisions of labour opened up new jobs to women. By the 1880s and 1890s daughters in these wards were reporting working in collar factories and shoe factories and as packers, printers, typesetters, pressfeeders, paperbox makers, dressmakers, shoemakers, and cigarmakers. Yet, overall only one-third of the girls living at home reported jobs that were unquestionably located within a factory. Even in Sainte Anne, the industrial heart of Montreal, a relatively small proportion were clearly involved in factory work. Dressmaking, millinery, or sewing for the shoemaking trade involved two-thirds of fourteen- to twenty-year-old girls in 1861 and remained the leading occupation, although the proportion dropped steadily to one-quarter across the period as other work possibilities opened up. It is impossible to tell what proportion of the girls who were sewing worked in factories, what proportion in small workshops, and how many did their sewing at home.

Work as a domestic servant remained important throughout the period, but most girls who were servants lived in with families elsewhere in the city. The advantages and disadvantages of these three different types of workplaces – factories, the family home, and domestic service in the homes of others – need to be examined more closely for us to understand better both the work experiences of young women and the factors that may have influenced choices about whether daughters would work and the kinds of work they might seek.

Factory Work for Girls

For teenage or young adult daughters, factory work offered both advantages and disadvantages over homework, other areas of employment, or staying home. In factories they could meet more people, were usually better paid, and might escape close surveillance by their parents. Yet, parents with the liberty to choose may well have been reluctant to expose their daughters to the danger of accidents, the long hours, continual supervision, exhausting work, and the brutal forms of discipline practised in some factories. As British economic historian Sydney Pollard has argued, the "reasons for the repulsion of factory industry were many and varied and they were not all economic."[39] The unprotected machines and moving parts that revolutionized production levels constituted a potential hazard for all workers. Girls were especially likely to be described by employers as careless when they had accidents. A "careless" seventeen-year-old who was feeding a press in a metal-stamping establishment lost two fingers when she forgot to take them from under the press. Another girl in a factory making playing cards crushed part of her finger under a press. In one Montreal box factory a nineteen-year-old lost part of a finger while gluing by machine. Accidents were common in large cotton and woollen mills where the gearing, hoists, moving parts of looms, and rollers were potential sources of injury. Mésia Gagnier, aged seventeen, injured her left hand when it was caught between rollers. Marie Geoffrion got caught on the gearing of a mule at the Globe Woollen Mills and wounded her hip. Another woman in the same factory severely wounded the flesh on her hip in the same way.[40] Men involved in such accidents turned to the courts and on occasion were awarded "heavy damages." The costs of such judgements predisposed manufacturers to accept the Quebec Workmen's Compensation Act in 1909, as well as to make some more attentive to preventative measures.[41] Women appear, however, to have used the courts much less frequently to obtain redress, perhaps precisely because their work was more temporary.

Accidents were only one factor that might discourage parents from sending their daughters into a factory. When employers and foremen disciplined teenage or adult females, sexual harassment and physical punishment were too easily interwoven. Cigarmaking establishments provided jobs for girls and boys in both Sainte Anne and Saint Jacques, employing one-fifth of the teenage girls in these wards in 1891. While some tobacco manufacturers appear to have been decent men, neither fining nor beating their employees, others, in an apparently desperate attempt to control their youthful work force, resorted to physical violence and heavy fines. M. Fortier's cigarmaking establishment was described by one witness at the Royal Commission hearings of 1888 as "a theatre of lewdness." "There is no such infamous factory as M. Fortier's. . . . nowhere else as bad in Montreal." One cigarmaker described apprentices as being "treated more or less as slaves." The treatment of an eighteen-year-old girl, Georgina Loiselle, shocked the commissioners and the Montreal public. She described how Fortier beat her with a mould cover because she would not make the 100 cigars he gave her to make.

> I was sitting, and he took hold of me by the arm, and tried to throw me on the ground. He did throw me on the ground and beat me with the mould cover.
> Q. Did he beat you when you were down?
> A. Yes, I tried to rise and he kept me down on the floor.

Another witness had seen children beaten "with a piece of hoop that is put around cases" with their pants down. [42]

The publication of such evidence created a sensation at the time. To counteract such bad publicity, Fortier apparently encouraged some mothers of girls working for him to give more favourable evidence. "I am the mother of a family and if I had seen anything improper I would not have stayed there," explained a Mrs. Levoise. "I have my girl working there." [43] Evidence from other factories suggests that what happened in Fortier's represented the extreme on a continuum of work conditions.

In cotton factories, too, there was some evidence of young girls being beaten, and hours were long. Work began at 6:25 in the morning and finished at 6:15 in the evening. When extra work was required, employees had to stay until nine at night, often without time off for supper. There were some advantages to textile work. Nineteen-year-old Adèle Lavoie explained that the girls were accustomed to "take cotton to make our aprons." Apparently this practice was generally allowed. On at least one occasion, however, the foreman accused her of having taken forty to fifty yards of material. He searched her house to no avail, then returned to the factory to insult her sister. When she did not produce the cotton, "he stooped at this time and raising the skirt of my sister's dress, he said she had it under her skirt." [44]

Homework in the Clothing Industry

Knowledge of such forms of sexual harassment and of the work conditions in hot, airless, and dusty factories, as well as the long hours spent away from home, must have made homework particularly attractive for concerned parents who needed whatever money their daughters could earn. Family decisions about suitable workplaces for their daughters interacted with the advantages such production offered to capitalists to entrench homework within the sewing and to a lesser extent shoemaking industries of Montreal. As cutting out and skilled work in the factories became more and more mechanized, increasing the speed at which articles could be prepared for sewing, the number of outworkers multiplied. Employers turned to the growing numbers of women and children willing and even eager to do such work in their homes. "Putting out," "sweating," or "homework" saved on overhead rental or property costs, on machinery, and on the cost of paying and supervising labour. Furthermore, as women worked isolated in their own homes, their was no danger of their organizing or even knowing what other employees earned.

Clothiers, haberdashers, and shoemakers all attested in the 1870s to the widespread existence of homework in their trades. John Young, a Montreal haberdasher, reported in 1874 that his firm had five establishments in Montreal employing "about fifteen hundred people working in-doors and out-doors." He estimated that about one-half of some of their goods were "taken home and made by out-door work-women to be finished. They are all private persons and not small manufacturers." In 1888 wholesale clothiers Hollis Shorley and James O'Brien both testified that almost all their work was done outside. Shoe manufacturer Z. Lapierre explained that in his trade, too, most of the women he employed took "their work home to their families. They have their own machines at home, and they get their work done there." Homework supplied through the putting-out system clearly remained a central feature of the clothing industry and of aspects of the shoemaking trade throughout this period.[45]

Homework also offered parents, mothers in particular, several advantages. First, they could oversee their daughters' work and behaviour, perhaps averting the individualism that working in a factory was seen to encourage and skirting the dangers and moral pitfalls that factory labour was seen by some to pose for young, unmarried women.[46] Second, for those newly arrived in the city and unused to the rhythms and demands of wage labour, work at home seemed to allow them to set their own pace, to avoid "continuous employment . . . one of the most hated aspects of factory work." Perhaps, like their counterparts whom Sydney Pollard describes in the early years of the industrial revolution in Great Britain, they chose to work at home as long as a choice between factory and home existed, hanging on to familiar work settings and relationships, delaying complete submission to the dominating rhythm of factory labour.[47] Equally important, girls doing piecework at home could combine stitching and housework, care for younger children, and run odd errands or carry water as needed. Their mothers would still benefit from some help with domestic labour while the family gained extra cash.

It was not uncommon in Saint Jacques to find three to four sisters, ranging in age from eleven to twenty-eight, all working as sewing girls. This clustering of family members all employed in the clothing trades suggests that this part of town was an important source of labour for Montreal's sewing trades. In the Moisan family of Saint Jacques ward, for instance, four daughters worked as seamstresses in 1871. The father was a labourer, and although the wife reported no occupation, she probably also did some sewing. In 1881, the family of Marie and Michel Guigère had reached a relatively secure stage in the family life cycle. This joiner had nine children at home aged two to twenty-three and reported seven workers. Four of the girls, including a thirteen-year-old, were seamstresses, one son worked as a labourer, and the thirteen-year-old son was an apprentice. The mother no doubt helped sporadically with sewing, while the girls in turn assisted her with housework – caring for the younger children, shopping, cooking, and cleaning, as well as looking after their seventy-year-old grandfather who lived with them.[48]

Working at home, such girls escaped the constraints of factory hours and factory discipline, but they could not avoid the long hours and minimal rates of pay. Nor could they leave their work at the end of the day. In the small homes of Montreal's poorer fractions of the working class, the clothes waiting to be sewn were said to fill up much-needed space in the bedrooms and living rooms. When A.W. Wright examined the sweating system in Canadian cities at the end of the century, he found that women and children sewing at home worked "many more hours daily than would be permitted in shops and factories under the regulation" of the factory acts. Employers who were asked about the conditions of homework in the 1870s and 1880s were conveniently vague about hours worked, wages paid, or even prices paid per piece. Wholesale clothier James O'Brien believed that mothers and daughters "working by the piece" received $1 to $2 for a dozen workingmen's shirts in 1888. A good hand, he thought, might have made two or three shirts in ten hours. At the $2 rate of pay and at three shirts a day, girls could have earned only fifty cents a day, or under $3 a week. And they might not always retain the full amount, for when work was completed it had to be returned to the factory for inspection before payment. If something was wrong the girls had to "take it back and change it." To avoid wasting half a day of valuable work time, many let the inside staff redo the work, but they were forced to accept a deduction from their pay. A.W. Wright found that in these situations the fines usually far exceeded the value of the repairs, further reducing the amount received.[49]

Piecework involved both hand sewing and machine work. Women who invested in sewing machines or buttonholers could make extra money. Yet such investments could prove risky. If regular payments were not made to the sewing machine company the machines were repossessed. "If . . . by sickness or death . . . the poor woman is unable to pay the installment when due," explained a reporter, "she loses all that she has paid upon the machine." Furthermore, while some machines enabled women to make more money initially, prices paid per piece dropped if too many people made the same investment. The money advanced might never be recuperated. Shoe manufacturer Z. Lapierre reported that he had introduced a buttonhole machine into his factory. He stopped using it, however, when large numbers of girls bought similar machines so they could work at home. Within a short time the price per 100 buttonholes had dropped from sixty to sixteen cents. "It paid so well that everybody went into it; and now they are doing it for almost nothing," he explained.[50]

Sewing at terribly low wages appears to have been chosen by the majority of girls or their parents over work in factories or shops where wages, while still low, were higher. Employers had a simple explanation for such choices. One clothing manufacturer explained that most of his employees were French-Canadian "females who can get nothing else to do." Certainly, this was one trade in which women possessed an advantage, usually having at least some experience of sewing. Most schools taught some sewing. Poor women whose sewing skills were disparaged by middle-class charity ladies could learn the most basic sewing abilities in diverse classes run by different Montreal charities.[51]

It would be incorrect, however, to argue that girls and other home-workers had no options outside the sewing industry. Factory jobs were available to a growing number of daughters, as was work as a domestic, in sales, or, at the end of the century, in some areas of clerical work.[52] As the century advanced, fewer and fewer of the girls living in these wards were employed in the clothing trades. Whereas two-thirds of daughters aged 14-20 who were living with their parents in Sainte Anne or Saint Jacques wards were working in some branch of the clothing trades in 1861, only half were by 1881, and a decade later the proportion had dropped to one-fifth. By the end of the century more French-Canadian women had become accustomed to wage labour outside the home and were more militant about their work conditions. New waves of immigrants were arriving. Employers in the clothing trades concentrated their production increasingly in the expanding immigrant corridor surrounding Saint Lawrence Street to the west of Saint Jacques ward so they could draw on this new labour force.[53]

Domestic Service

Domestic service remained among the leading areas of employment for girls living in Montreal over these years despite the growing availability of work related to industrial production.[54] Most, though not all, domestics continued to live with their employers. Their relationship between home and work was very different both from that of girls working in their family home on sewing and from those leaving home daily to work in factories. Live-in domestics left their own families for various lengths of time determined occasionally by formal contracts, more often by the satisfaction of the mistress or the dissatisfaction of the servant. Although contemporary evidence suggests that many of these girls had migrated to the city on their own, either from rural areas of Quebec or from Europe, some were no doubt the daughters and sons of local working-class families. Most of Montreal's servants lived and worked just up the hill from Sainte Anne ward, concentrated in the wealthiest sections of Saint Antoine ward. There, in 1871, lived 1,790 servants, nearly 45 per cent of the city's live-in domestics. Nearly one-half of them were of Irish origin while under one-fifth were French-Canadian.[55] By the end of the century, girls in Saint Jacques could also find employment fairly easily with the growing number of professional and bourgeois families in that ward who hired servants. By 1891 fully 44 per cent of all women in that ward listing a job were domestics.[56]

In the homes of men of commerce, professionals, and manufacturers, these young women worked long hours in return for shelter, for more protection than many appreciated, and for minimal pay. Hiring contracts for the period show that the youngest servants were placed in service quite simply because their own families could not supply their needs.[57] Girls leaving homes where hunger had at times been a fact of life were probably better sheltered, fed, and clothed than before.[58] The wages they received are difficult to determine. One family in 1861 reported paying between $2.50 and $4 monthly to its servants.[59] Claudette Lacelle found that contracts signed in the early 1870s stipulated that girls would receive around £19 or $76 annually, approximately the same amount as the $5 to $6 monthly reported in Snell.[60] In families where the head earned $200 to $300 a year, such an amount would clearly have added much needed flexibility to the family budget. Furthermore, the absence of one dependent female child could save the family around $40 annually in food costs at 1882 prices.

Shreds of evidence in family account books, combined with the growing chorus from middle-class women bemoaning both the lack of servants and the high rate of turnover, suggest that few stayed long enough to earn a full annual wage. Bridget Kearney, the fifteen-year-old daughter of a Sainte Anne widow, received a generous $12 a month when she worked as cook and general maid for Mrs. John T. Molson during the mid-1870s. She worked for the Molsons for half a year, from mid-December, 1876, to June, 1877, and was paid $80. Over subsequent years she came and went for periods of employment that ranged from two to nine months, never more.[61]

Girls working as domestics moved between mistresses, in and out of domestic labour and in and out of waged labour. The testimony of Lina Madore about her experiences as a domestic underlines the complexity of the work histories of many young Quebec women as well as the ways in which their experience of paid labour was influenced by their mothers' own need for help with domestic labour. Her first employment at the age of twelve lasted only two months. Subsequent jobs as a domestic were interspersed with stints picking potatoes in Maine, a job that was much better paid than service, and with periods helping her mother at home.[62]

This movement between earning wages and helping at home was not limited to girls who were servants. A closer examination of the importance of mothers' need for help from their daughters nuances our understanding of the impact of the industrial revolution on women's work and helps us better understand the factors that made girls' experiences in the labour market different from those of their brothers.

The Importance of Girls' Domestic Labour at Home

During Montreal's industrial revolution more girls appear to have worked at home helping their mothers with daily domestic chores than worked in factories, at sewing, or as domestics. While most daughters in the working-class families of Sainte Anne and Saint Jacques wards probably worked for pay for short periods prior to marriage, the relatively low percentages involved each census year suggest that at any one time, up to one-half of unmarried daughters were not doing so. In 1861 three-quarters of the sixteen- to seventeen-year-old girls in Sainte Anne ward were not listed in the census as either at work or at school. The expansion of jobs that accompanied the growth of industrial capitalism reduced this proportion to around one-half by the 1880s.

This low rate of employment among young women demands closer inspection and careful interpretation. It appears to offer a significant caveat to the idea that with industrialization wage labour prior to marriage became a stage of the life cycle for most working-class women.[63] It clearly does not fit Marx's image of the industrial revolution as indiscriminately drawing men and women and boys and girls into wage labour.[64] Interpreting such absence from work and school as "idleness," as Michael Katz and Ian Davy did, simply demonstrates how little thought historians using the census have given to kinds of work that are not clearly listed.[65] To argue that such a major discrepancy is simply a result of the under-enumeration of women's work by census-takers, on the other hand, seems equally inadequate and misleading.[66] Undoubtedly some under-enumeration of the wage labour of daughters, young children, and married women occurred in Montreal at this period. Fathers, ashamed that they could not support their families, may have been reluctant to tell the census-taker that other family members had to work.[67] Others, knowing that a daughter had worked only for a short period, may not have thought it worthy of mention. The phenomenon is not easy to measure. Even if it were, it would not explain away the difference between boys' and girls' rates of labour force involvement because a significant proportion of that difference arose from their specific roles in the family economy and the kinds of jobs they held.

Intermittent patterns of formal work characterized the experience of many daughters. Mothers often needed help at home because of the number of young children they had, illness in the family, the birth of an infant, sheer exhaustion, or so they could earn some money. At these moments those with daughters of an age to assist pulled them out of school or away from their jobs. When girls worked at home on sewing, this happened casually. Among those in factories or working as domestics in the homes of others, this practice contributed to irregular work patterns, which further enhanced the notion that all women workers were secondary wage-earners. This intermittent characteristic of girls' formal waged labour also increased the possibility that they would not be enumerated as having an occupation. Girls who worked a few months or weeks and then stayed home to help their mothers may or may not have been counted. Casual work, such as washing, babysitting for neighbours' children, and making sandwiches to sell to workers, was not likely to be viewed as formal employment.

Most girls who were not reported as having a job were likely to be partially or fully employed helping their mothers around the house.[68] Joan Scott and Louise Tilly have suggested that within the "industrial mode of production . . . single women are best able to work, since they have few other claims on their time."[69] In Montreal, many appear to have had other claims on their time. In particular, the heavy and time-consuming nature of nineteenth-century housework, the prevalence of disease, the wide age spread among children in most families, and the myriad other largely invisible pursuits and strategies necessary to survival for the working-class family meant that many of these girls were needed by their mothers to help with domestic labour.

The role of daughters in the division of labour within the family is highlighted on one census return, where each member's work was explicitly described. Louis Coutur, a carter who was fifty in 1861, reported that his twenty-one-year-old son was a shoemaker, his wife's job was "housework," and the seventeen-year-old daughter's job was "helping with the housework."[70] At home, girls served an apprenticeship in the reproduction of labour power – in babysitting, cleaning, mending, sewing, cooking, and shopping. Transformations in the economy and the passage of time were slow to modify this gender difference in the relationship between girls' and boys' schooling, their work histories, and their roles in the family economy. A study conducted in Quebec in 1942, just before schooling was finally made compulsory in that province, offers an explicit explanation of how the different roles of boys and girls in the family economy continued to influence both their school attendance and the nature of their work. Among children quitting school before the age of sixteen, 61 per cent of girls gave as their reason that "My mother needed me." Half the boys, in contrast, stated that their family needed money, a reason given by only one in ten girls.[71] In turn-of-the-century Toronto potential foster parents were four times more likely to seek girls than boys, specifically because of their usefulness as domestics and nursemaids.[72]

There were other more pragmatic reasons to choose sons rather than daughters to complement a father's wage. In families where there were both sons and daughters it made good sense to have boys earn wages rather than girls. While the youngest workers of each sex might earn a similar wage, once they reached fifteen or sixteen a girl's wage was generally half that of a young man. Girl apprentices in dressmaking, mantlemaking, and millinery sometimes earned nothing for several years until they learned the trade; then they only received around $4 a week. "Girls" in shoe manufactories received $3 to $4 compared to the $7 or $8 per week earned by men. A female bookbinder made between $1.50 and $6 weekly, compared to an average of $11 for male journeymen. Even on piecework, girls and women generally received less than men. In general, wage rates for women were approximately half those of men.[73]

The greater the margin of financial manoeuvre within a family, the less likely daughters appear to have been to work outside the home. In a reasonably good year like 1891, the better earning power of skilled over unskilled workers stands out not only in the numbers of additional family workers, but also in the different rates of involvement of sons and daughters. Skilled workers who had sons and daughters in their teens were almost three times as likely to have a son aged fifteen to twenty at work as they were to have a daughter out working. In the families of unskilled workers, in contrast, slightly more girls these ages were at work than were boys, in part because so many sewed at home, but perhaps also because earning sons left home earlier (Table 4.5).

Even the lowest paid workers appear to have been somewhat

reluctant to send daughters to work outside the home, despite the fact that in all but the smallest of families food costs alone rapidly outstripped a man's incoming wages. Among labourers' families in Sainte Anne in 1881, for example, 66 per cent of those who had boys over ten reported having a son at work, while only 28 per cent of those with girls the same age did so. If older brothers were working, girls generally did not. Girls of twenty or more would stay at home while a teenage son worked. Their respective roles seem clearly defined. Twenty-six-year-old Ellen Mullin, for example, reported no occupation. Two brothers, aged nineteen and twenty-three, worked as carters. Ellen's role was to help her mother with the domestic labour for the three wage-earners and her fourteen-year-old younger brother.[74]

Those labourers' families where daughters were employed appear to have fallen largely into two categories. Half the girls were the oldest child. Either they had no brothers or their brothers were much younger than they were. Nineteen-year-old Sarah Anne Labor, for instance, was the oldest in a family of six children. The closest brother was only seven. She worked as a soapmaker. Her wages and the fact that the family shared the household with several other families must have helped make ends meet.[75] The second group of working daughters came from labourers' families that sent almost all their children to work regardless of gender. They seem to have been the most desperate, perhaps because recurrent illness or the habitual drunkenness of a parent pushed all children out to work.

Families clearly made decisions about the work that different members would perform in the context of their specific needs. The size, age, and gender configurations of the family, the kind of work and level of wages of the family head, and the health of family members all played a role. Strategies were conditioned by the structure of local labour markets, job possibilities, and local wage rates for males and females. And choices were also influenced by what was considered proper for daughters, as well as by a mother's need for help with domestic labour. Duties at home, a relatively limited number of interesting employment opportunities, and low wages combined to create a situation where daughters were much more likely than sons to move back and forth between paid work and housework in response to the family's economic needs and their position in the household.

The Family Economy versus Individual Autonomy: Changing Patterns of Residence

In 1861 living with others was still an important stage in the lives of some young people of both sexes, recalling the pre-industrial custom of young boys and girls spending several years of their youth living "as members of a household other than that of their parents" as domestics or as apprentices learning a trade, or with relatives, helping perhaps with child care and domestic labour[76] (Figure 4.3). Nearly one in three unmarried girls aged fifteen to nineteen who resided in Sainte Anne and Saint Jacques wards in 1861 were boarding with other families, living with relatives, or working and living in as servants. In both 1871 and 1881, in contrast, just over one in ten girls that age were not living with their parents. Boys, too, were less likely to be living with parents in 1861 than in 1881. Four out of ten unmarried men aged twenty to twenty-four were not living with their parents in 1861, compared to under two out of ten two decades later.

The overall decline evident in the proportion of Montreal youth living in what Michael Katz has called a stage of semi-autonomy seems clear for the period up until 1881. It parallels the situation found for youth in other North American communities between the 1850s and 1880s.[77] During the 1870s and 1880s few boys living in Sainte Anne and Saint Jacques wards appear to have been able to take advantage of the wages they earned to leave home prior to marriage. Nor did girls. By 1881 more children of both sexes were living with their parents than had been the case two decades earlier.[78]

By 1891, however, there appears to have been a significant reversal of this pattern. The proportion of boys who were boarding with other families or living with relatives shot back up to levels similar to those of 1861 and were even higher for some age groups. Whereas in 1881 only one out of ten sons aged fifteen to nineteen were not living with their parents, in 1891 two out of ten were not. Only the relatively small number of sons aged thirty or more who had not yet married were more likely to be living with parents than in previous years. Often they were supporting a widowed mother. Girls, too, were less likely to be at home at most ages than in previous decades, although the change was minor compared to that for boys and is largely accounted for by the growing number working as domestics in Saint Jacques ward. Twenty per cent of twenty- to twenty-four-year-old girls in these wards were boarding with unrelated families while a further 10 per cent were with relatives. In contrast, 55 per cent of boys the same age were boarding and 6 per cent were with relatives.

It is difficult to determine who these relatively autonomous boys and girls were, whether they had parents elsewhere in the city or were part of a wave of new immigrants from rural areas or overseas. Almost all those in Saint Jacques were born in Quebec, as were their parents. Most of the youths boarding with Sainte Anne families had also been born in Quebec of Quebec-born parents, although nearly two-fifths were born elsewhere, predominantly in England and Ireland. Some had no doubt made a conscious decision to set out on their own, asserting

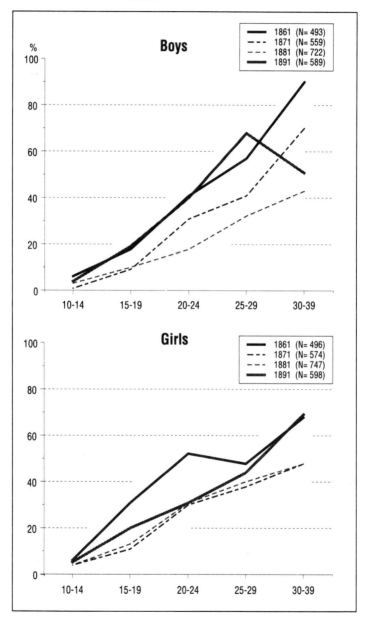

Figure 4.3 Unmarried Males and Females Not Living with Their Parents, 1861-91

perhaps a new kind of independence possible only at a time when higher wages gave them both the bargaining power and the material basis for such freedom.[79]

Once boys reached their late teens, their earning power might rival that of their fathers. Their wages offered their families the possibility of a new prosperity, the chance to pay off debts or to live alone without relatives and boarders. Here was a powerful incentive to parents to keep them at home. Yet wage labour also offered some such children potential freedom from their families in a way that had not been possible in family economies based on shared work and the inheritance of property. Such freedom was less easily achieved by girls unless they found an unusually well-paying job, could board with relatives, or turned to prostitution.

Behind the percentages of children living with their parents or elsewhere, then, lies a complex history of tension between family needs and individual desires, of children balancing the advantages of services offered at home against the relative independence that living with strangers or even with relatives might offer. For families that had passed through at least fifteen years of budget-stretching, house-sharing, and debt accumulation while their children were young, the relative prosperity that several workers could offer was to be jealously guarded. It was precisely "because young adults could find jobs" that it "was in the interest of parents to keep their children at home as long as possible."[80] In the case of daughters it was also because of the help they could offer with younger children and housework. Sons and daughters might well be encouraged to stay home for different reasons.

The potential freedom that wages seemed to offer has led some historians to argue that the spread of wage labour weakened traditional family ties, that finding work outside the home freed working-class youth from earlier and more rigid systems of parental control.[81] Certainly, the separation of home and work that increased with the growth of industry changed the control parents could exercise over their offspring. Mothers and fathers in agricultural or artisanal families had supervised their children's work. Masters and mistresses had closely supervised those learning a trade or working as domestics.

Factory labour was different. This direct control was broken. Elinor Accampo explains in her careful study of family life and class relations in a small French town between 1815 and 1914 how industrialization removed a measure of authority and control over their children from working-class parents and placed it in the hands of manufacturers.[82] There is no question that the fact of earning gave children a different power within the family. Yet offspring were tied to their parents by custom, shared experience, and mutual need. The growth of industry brought new conflicts and untidy resolutions rather than a sudden break and change. As historian Christine Stansell has clearly shown, "the tensions between the meager independence of wage work and the pull of family loyalties defined one dimension of working-class life."[83]

The ways in which wage-earning influenced relations within the family are not easy to discern and are impossible to measure. Whatever struggles went on between parents and children over their work, their wages, and the question of leaving home, they are only occasionally visible in the documents of the period. Hints appear in the comments of contemporaries and more often in court cases. Priests voiced concern about the problems caused by the independence that wage-earning gave youngsters. Bishops' pastoral letters underlined the dangers posed by what they viewed as the premature emancipation of youth and their associated mistrust of parental authority.[84] At times such conflicts spilled over into the streets or into the courts. Parents of younger children, desperately needing their wages and exasperated by unruly, uncontrollable behaviour, turned to employers and to the police when they could not convince their offspring of the importance of steady work. Thus, when employers reported that parents threatened to hold them responsible if apprentices did not "tend to their work" or when boys were sent to reform school on the advice of their mothers, they were not simply justifying their own draconian actions. Some parents, unable to control the actions of youngsters who were able but apparently unwilling to earn a steady wage, turned to employers and the courts hoping to transform their offspring into reliable workers.[85]

No legal structures could help parents convince older sons already earning a reasonable wage that they should remain at home, contributing to the family wage. Yet, the patterns of residence of the youth of these wards suggest that parents generally succeeded in keeping growing numbers of children at home in the early period of industrial capitalism. Not only were more of the youth of these wards remaining longer at home before the 1890s, but more working children were doing so, as the increase in the numbers of employed teenage and adult offspring living in working-class families shows. Loyalty, low wages, and lack of alternatives severely limited the margin of manoeuvre that such children had. When the economy was reasonably good, as in 1871 and then again in 1891, young men in their twenties were better able to leave home and board for several years prior to marriage.

In 1891, however, living independently was clearly important for a significant minority of youths. Nonetheless, the contributions of teenage and adult children remained important for most fractions of the working class. Had there been a widespread decline in parents' ability to retain working children at home, the number of working offspring in families should have dropped more than it did. Figures on the average number of teenage and adult offspring working across the period confirm the continuing differentials within the working class. Unskilled workers who had co-resident children over fourteen reported more teenage and adult working children in 1891 than had such workers in any previous year. In contrast, families headed by men in the skilled trades with unions and more stable employment had slightly fewer teenagers at work by 1891. They could afford to keep their children in school longer (Table 4.3).

The motives behind individual decisions – the relative weight of traditions of family work and of changing economic opportunity – are difficult to grasp in the absence of written records. The factors constraining or encouraging one choice or another are clearer. Most children would have left home once they had a job only if their wages were adequate to pay for lodgings and they felt no commitment to contribute to the family income.[86] More older boys earned enough to pay for room and board than did girls. Unequal wage rates combined with different demands placed on sons and daughters at home to forge distinct life cycles and work and residential histories for boys and girls.

To contribute to the family income, offspring living at home had to agree to hand over some or all their wages to their parents. Shreds of evidence suggest that most children did so. Some mothers went regularly to the factory to collect their children's pay packets.[87] A French-Canadian worker who migrated to the States reported that in her family when they worked "we all gave our pay, except one of my sisters. She gave it at the beginning. Then, when she thought she wanted to get married, she'd give $7.00 and keep the rest."[88] All, even a portion of a teenage son's or daughter's wages, added some flexibility to a family budget.

Finding work for children of all ages appears to have been a family responsibility. Mothers and fathers were frequently cited in 1888 as trying to talk employers into taking on their young. The factory inspectors consistently blamed parents for furnishing their children with false age certificates. Learning where work was available was a somewhat haphazard process for adults and children alike. Men in skilled jobs could find out where work was available through their union. By 1889, however, the Trades and Labour Congress of Canada was requesting that the government "establish offices where the working men out of employment could go and enquire to obtain employment." Some kinds of jobs were more and more likely to be advertised in newspapers over the period. But there was no organized system of getting employer and employee together. Pubs were one place where men might learn about where work was available in the city. Kin were another important source of information.[89] When Walter Smith arrived in Montreal as a teenager from England in the 1870s, for instance, he found work in the following manner.

> We arrived on Tuesday and the next Friday morning before I was up, Uncle knocked at the door; I jumped out of bed and let him in, says he, – offer of a job at printing, right away at J.C. Wilson and Co., come down and start as soon as you have had your breakfast. I did so.[90]

Mothers sought work for their daughters and sons and interceded when problems arose. When Sara Fontaine's two daughters were dismissed from their jobs in a Hochelaga cotton mill she went to the boss to ask why they had been dismissed. "I have need of their assistance to live," she explained. In cotton mills whole families were often hired. Fathers and children could go to work together and sometimes worked side by side. Such family employment was not the norm in most trades outside the textile industry. Nevertheless, several members of the same family and other relatives did often work in the same place. Five siblings were reported as working at M. Fortier's cigar factory. In one Montreal shoe factory at least one girl under the age of fourteen worked alongside her father. One paper box manufacturer reported that seven sisters from the same family had all worked for him before they married.[91]

When whole families worked together the lines between family and work were softened and the tasks of initiation and supervision shared. Fathers maintained more contact, control, and influence than those working apart from their offspring. Families could sometimes influence hiring and other aspects of work.[92] Children working beside their parents were less likely to feel completely independent. Employers, on the other hand, could pay lower wages and expect parents to discipline their children. The whole family could thus be moulded to the demands of industrial work with minimum friction. Furthermore, when most members of a family were earning in one workplace, the ability to withstand a long strike was less than when lost wages could be compensated for by those still earning elsewhere.

In all working families the roles of sons and daughters constituted living apprenticeships for the positions most would later take on if they married. Working-class families in Montreal clearly both needed and used additional family workers to counteract low wages and to improve their standard of living. The number of extra workers varied with the skill of the family head and the worth of that skill in the labour market. Thus, while in good times skilled workers managed with fewer family workers than the unskilled or those in injured trades, economic depression eroded such superiority. The need of families for additional workers was not so great that all children were sent to work at an early age. Most working-class families appear to have had standards pretty close to those set out in the new laws. They seldom sent girls under fourteen or boys under twelve into the factories, although they would keep them home from school on occasion to run errands, earn a few pennies, babysit, or help with chores.[93] Only in the poorest families or those facing some kind of crisis did very young boys or girls report a job. Boys were more likely to be the auxiliary wage-earners than girls and they were generally older children rather than the young ones on whom reformers focused their attention.

Decisions about which children should seek wage labour were made in part in relation to existing wage rates and job opportunities. Such decisions perpetuated and reified the idea that women's work was temporary, performed before marriage or in moments of family crisis. The source of girls' inequality did not lie totally within the formal wage-earning labour market. Mothers' desires and real need for a helper at home were important as well. Domestic labour in the nineteenth century was fundamental to family survival, to the transformation of wages into a reasonable standard of living, and to the reproduction of the working class. Historians and feminist theoreticians have recognized the importance of this job for the working-class wife and mother. They have paid less attention to the role of daughters.[94] For nineteenth-century mothers whose children were widely spaced in age, in whose homes technology had made virtually no inroads to lighten their labour, the help of daughters was invaluable. Wherever possible, once girls reached an age at which they could help their mother they were called on to babysit, to run errands, and to clean, sew, and cook. If housework could be combined with wage-earning activities, as in the case of homework in the sewing industry, then such girls worked more formally. If there were no brothers of an age to earn, daughters might work in factories, offices, or shops or as domestics. But the need of mothers for at least one helper at home meant that the rate of formal labour force participation for girls was generally lower than for boys.

The working out of roles by gender at home influenced the configurations of gender in the workplaces of the city. The structure of industry and the ideas of employers about the best workers in their industry conditioned family decisions. Economic pragmatism and the daily needs of mothers and housewives thus interacted with the structures of the city's labour markets to create a situation in which most girls served an apprenticeship in domestic labour prior to or in conjunction with entering the work force.

5

Managing and Stretching Wages:
The Work of Wives

A "thrifty, economical and thorough good housekeeper who can lay out to advantage [a] . . . fair day's wage, is just as essential to the well-being of the workingman as the fair day's wage itself," wrote a Montreal workman to the editor of the Knights of Labor journal during the 1880s. The editor described the ideal wife for a workingman: "Rosy cheeked and bright eyed," she would know how to "darn a stocking and mend her own dress . . . command a regiment of pots and kettles, and be a lady when required."[1] Such a wife was described with pride and explicitly contrasted with the weak and idle ladies of the "aristocracy of power and money." Not just any wife, but a healthy, hard-working wife was explicitly identified as essential to working-class survival. These men acknowledged the importance of the work of wives in the family economy. It is subsequent generations, through a neat, unnecessary association of wages with work, who have belittled and denigrated the importance of housework and other domestic, non-waged labour.

Men's recognition of the value of the labour that working-class wives performed was tied to pride in their own skill and bound up in their ability to earn sufficient wages to support a wife and children. Their masculinity was constructed in part on their ability to keep their wives dependent.[2] But for women in the working classes, unlike some more bourgeois wives, economic dependence never meant idleness. Work, for nineteenth-century working-class wives, stretched from dawn to after dark. "You complain, my poor husband, of your ten hours of labour. Yet I have been working for fourteen hours and I have not yet finished my day." This caption below the etching of an unknown artist, reproduced in *L'Opinion publique* in 1871 and on the cover of this book, captures the sexual division of labour between husbands and wives, the different rhythms of their work day, and the very different nature of their work. Married women's work day involved an intricate and physically demanding mixture of what today we would call house-work, informal production, casual earning, and wage labour. Such categories intermeshed on a continuum of tasks that, blended together in varying configurations, allowed wives to manage and to stretch the wages earned largely by other family members.

Married women's work among the nineteenth-century urban working classes was crucial in shaping the standard of living and the degree of comfort of family life. Yet wives had little control themselves over the most important element of their work – the wages that they took and transformed into meals, clothing, and daily care. Like men's pride, their work was intricately linked to the earning power of their husbands and other family members. What a wife bought, the health of her family, the conditions of her domestic labour, and the kinds of work she would perform all depended largely on the level and regularity of wages earned largely by others. The differences of twenty-five cents a day that carved up the working class into different fractions combined with the stage of the family life cycle, the number and ages of her children, and the availability of other workers to set the stage for women's domestic labour. These factors, in interaction, framed the material basis of their work as wives and mothers.

We cannot understand that work by using the fixed categories and dichotomies developed to theorize women's work in contemporary capitalist society. Such work extended beyond the child-bearing and child-rearing, cleaning, tension management, washing, cooking, and shopping and budgeting that characterize the late twentieth-century housewife's role.[3] Production, reproduction, consumption, and exchange intermeshed. Bearing and rearing children; producing or buying food and clothing; cleaning, cooking, and caring not only for the young but for the sick and elderly; taking in work, going out to work: all of these were part of a housewife's job of making ends meet.[4] Paid forms of work, only some of which were wage labour, were interwoven with housework and other domestic labour. Revenue-generating and revenue-saving often took place outside the formal labour market. The economy within which these women produced, consumed, and purchased had no clear lines demarcating what economists would today label formal and informal sectors.

Men's wage labour took place increasingly within formal labour markets, away from the home on construction sites and in workshops and factories. The work involved in managing and stretching wages took place in the home, on the streets, in the shops and marketplaces, and more often in the homes of others than in factories. A simplistic or rigidly geographical use of the concepts of separate public and private spheres will not help us to make much sense of these women's lives.[5] Money-saving and revenue-generating, buying and selling, like mutual aid and family quarrels, spilled from crowded dwellings into busy streets and then back again.

What follows briefly examines the rhythms, conditions, and technology of married women's work, then turns to their role in purchasing or producing the basics of life and to ways of stretching and complementing the wages of others.

The Rhythms, Conditions, and Technology of Married Women's Domestic Labour

The rhythms and intensity of married women's work varied over the day and over their lives much more than for workers with paid jobs.[6] Hard physical labour, such as cleaning and carrying coal or water, might be followed by periods of working in extreme heat at the stove to prepare meals or heat water for washing, followed by trips into the freezing cold to shop or to deliver sewing or washing. The seasons made a difference to the conditions of domestic work; so, too, did the progression of the family life cycle. Montreal's working-class wives usually became mothers soon after marrying. Pregnancies, childbirths, and child deaths punctuated the lives of most women for over twenty years, interrupting and reshaping daily housework and changing the ways in which they could make ends meet. The care of young children intensified work at home in the years following marriage. As sons and daughters grew they could run errands or look after younger siblings, relieving a mother of some of her tasks. Yet, as the previous chapters have shown, their aging involved extra expenses for food and clothing, which in most families made stretching or complementing a father's earnings imperative. School attendance deprived mothers of their children's help but relieved them of their care. Once sons were old enough to earn and daughters were able to seek work or help at home, some women re-entered a lighter phase of their work life. If both spouses lived into old age, declining male revenues and the departure of children again posed major challenges to a woman's ability to make ends meet. At any point in time illness, unemployment, or excessive drinking by any family members could change a housewife's work, pushing a minority to find more formal ways of earning money.

Even when married women found paid work, domestic labour did not constitute a second work day separate from a job. The concept of a double day, developed by contemporary feminists to explain women's workload in our society, does not fit well with the way money-earning and domestic labour were articulated in the nineteenth century. Most of the minority of married women reporting employment worked at jobs that could be fitted in between other domestic tasks or that increased such specific domestic tasks as washing, sewing, and even cooking.

Some were performed in the houses of others, many took place at home. Caring for cows, chasing stray pigs, or tending a garden in summer took women and children out of the home. Selling or exchanging extra produce took them into the homes of neighbours and onto the streets, as did the purchases at the basis of most working-class consumption. Working-class women were not isolated in their homes. The home was, however, their major workplace, a space increasingly identified with women and vacated by men and others earning wages during the day.[7]

New machinery and lack of safety regulations in factories proved a dangerous environment for working men. Yet many of Montreal's working-class homes were equally if not more hazardous for the women and children who spent much of their time there. Contemporary doctors identified the city's cheaper housing, with its old and rotten drains, outdoor privies, and minimal sewage facilities as the locus of much disease. In the course of the study he undertook during the autumn and early winter of 1896, Herbert Ames found that "more than half the households" in the area of Sainte Anne that he studied still used the "out-of-door-pit-in-the-ground" privies that he linked to higher death rates in those areas where they prevailed.[8] The outdoor privy was the rule, not the exception, in a city where diarrhea and infectious diseases were rampant. Improved sanitation in the home, argued one Montreal doctor:

> would be a saving to the tenant and to the proprietor. The working-man would be oftener at work, and would be able to prosecute his work better with healthful surroundings at his home. As it was, the law regarding such vital matters as cesspools was such that a coach and four horses could be driven through it.[9]

Wives' daily work in such unhealthy settings, their care of sick family members, repeated pregnancies, and their "forbearance from the necessary quantity of food, that others may have a larger share" rendered them especially susceptible to disease.[10] In all categories of death except violent and unknown causes, women aged 15-40 had somewhat higher rates than men between 1879 and 1882, years chosen to study in detail because of their proximity to the census of 1881.[11] Childbirth accounted for only a small proportion of these deaths. Tuberculosis caused nearly half the deaths of women aged 20-40, contagious diseases a further 14 per cent. More women must have experienced lengthy, debilitating bouts of these infectious sicknesses, rendering daily housework and childcare exhausting, often impossible.

Technological change modified only slightly the nature of working-class women's workplace or the daily tasks they performed within the household. By the end of this period the technology existed to lighten work within the home. Indoor plumbing, better toilets, and gas and electricity for lighting and heating were available in the later decades of the nineteenth century. Fancy stoves, steam heating, and some new household gadgets were making life more comfortable for the mistress of the house in the homes of wealthier Montreal families, while posing new challenges to their servants.[12] Not till well into the twentieth century, however, were gas and electricity installed in most working-class homes. A water connection, a cast-iron cooking stove, and, for the best-paid workers' families, an indoor toilet constituted the major advances for wives in working-class households during the second half of the century.

Water provision did improve. The task of getting water for washing and cleaning was lightened from the mid-century on as piped water gradually replaced trips to the river, purchases from water carriers, and backyard wells. Sanitary reformer Philip Carpenter described women in the late 1850s having to wade on bricks through "liquid manure" to obtain their supply of water from the pipe that served several families. Backyard wells and washrooms were still used in older working-class areas in the 1860s. Historian John Cooper describes backyard washrooms in Pointe Saint Charles during the 1860s. Even in the houses of women married to merchants, inventories show that wash tubs and barrels stored in back sheds continued to be the only means of washing.[13] Women living in houses with outdoor water either had to carry their dirty clothes downstairs and outside to be washed or had to haul the water upstairs to heat. Heavy, wet clothing then had to be carried outside to hang on a clothesline or was dried near the kitchen stove in the house.[14]

By the 1870s and 1880s the city provided piped water to most Montreal dwellings. This suggests that wives' work was not as heavy as in some American communities, where Susan Strasser notes that poor women continued to haul water from urban street hydrants at the end of the century.[15] Usually, however, there was only one tap, which might still be outside, or, for luckier wives, in the kitchen. As late as 1897, the superintendent of the aqueduct reported that around 20,000 Montreal dwellings still had only one tap, which might serve all the households within a duplex or triplex.[16] This represented over half the housing of the city. Water for cooking, washing, and cleaning still had to be carried from the tap to the stove for heating. Nor was the water free. All Montreal citizens paid for the water provided by the municipality in their water tax, a tax levied on occupants, not owners of buildings. When they could not pay, their water supply was cut off, depriving housewives of readily accessible water for cleaning, cooking, and washing. When the Great Depression hit Montreal in 1874, poorer families found it impossible to pay, especially as tax collection occurred just before the winter. As the Mayor acknowledged in 1886:

> the attention of citizens of MODERATE means is being directed to provisions for our long and inclement winter. At the time when the cheapness of fuel renders it important for the working man to be able to lay in a stock of it to outlast the snow, he is called upon to pay in advance for the whole of the water he will consume during the year. It is easy to perceive what a strain this may place upon the resources of men who live upon daily wages, especially if from any casualty, to which they are all liable, they should happen to have been out of employment for any period of the year. [17]

Charity workers soon saw the effects of cutting off water to the poor. In 1880 the Ladies Committee of the YWCA pleaded with the city's Water Committee to turn on the hydrants for one or two hours daily to allow the needy to help themselves. The initial solution was to allow water free to those bringing "a letter from a clergyman testifying to their need." After years of prolonged economic crisis, during which revenues from water taxes dropped dramatically, the city councillors finally resolved to provide water as cheaply as possible, even free, so that "poor people may have the means of attending to their personal cleanliness as well as that of their houses." [18] As late as the end of the 1880s, when times were better, nearly 800 households had their water taxes remitted, reduced, or delayed, 43 per cent for poverty, the others for illness or "sanitary reasons." [19] Women were the ones who protested when their water rates were increased or the water was turned off. Their daily tasks were affected most by lack of water, and they were not tied up all day earning wages. Trips to City Hall to protest were added to the daily round of balancing budgets and keeping their families and households clean. [20]

Cleaning the small, overcrowded houses of the least skilled workers, with insufficient water and deplorable drains, must have been a constant battle. Keeping the inhabitants clean was equally difficult. Few working-class dwellings had baths or the space necessary to install them. As late as 1886 the sanitary officer reported that "in the majority of poor people's lodgings it is rare to see a bath, and they are therefore deprived of the necessary means of securing perfect cleanliness." The numbers using the public baths in the city convinced him that "the labouring classes are aware of the benefits to be derived from such a hygienic establishment." [21] There were, however, only two public baths in Montreal, both for men only. For most of the working class, bathing, like washing, continued to involve heating up water on the stove and filling up a tub in the kitchen or simply sponging oneself down. The minimal equipment involved is clear in the inventory made following the death of Zoé Legault-Deslauriers, the wife of a stone-cutter, in 1867. The only washing or laundry equipment in their four-room dwelling was a red washing bowl in one bedroom, one water pot, a washbowl, and four irons in the kitchen.[22]

Even for those with an indoor water connection, washing continued to be a heavy, hot, and hated task. Some wives soaked clothes overnight before cleaning the worst spots with a washing board. Then they carried water from the tap to a tub to soak the clothes or to the stove to boil them. Hot clothes had to be lifted out of the steaming water, wrung out by hand, rinsed and wrung again, then hung out to dry. The final step was ironing. The dirty water had to be discarded manually as few of the cheap working-class dwellings had drains. Workers built rough wooden slop trunks outside their back doors. Waste water and, according to the sanitary officer, "kitchen refuse and all sorts of filth" could then be easily discharged into the backyards.[23]

Women who could afford to do so put aside money to pay others to do their washing, providing extra employment for poorer wives and widows in the neighbourhood or for the Chinese laundries beginning to flourish in Montreal during this period. By the 1880s some wives must have turned to steam laundries set up by capitalists using the latest machinery for washing and employing up to a hundred women washing, ironing, and folding.[24]

Cast-iron stoves, already widely available in Montreal by the 1850s, had replaced the open fireplace, reducing but not eliminating "most of the hazards and difficulties of fireplace cooking."[25] A stove, argued an English immigrant labourer in 1888, was "the one really essential piece of furniture for a labourer's family." New ranges were said to cost $20 in Montreal in the 1870s, although newspaper advertisements invariably stressed that they could be rented "Cheap! Cheap! Cheap!"[26] By the late 1880s mass production had reduced the cost to around $10, a price apparently fixed by the stove producers.[27] Zoé Legault-Deslauriers, the stone-cutter's wife, had one cooking stove, valued, with its pipes, at $4.50 when she died in 1867. Wives of unskilled workers would probably have cooked on a second-hand one, for these could be had for around $2.50.[28] In the poorest of families "an old cracked stove, some chairs, a couple of cups and a tin plate" made up the cooking and eating area. A "narrow shelf against the wall" served as a table.[29] During the long northern winter the stove was a place of congregation, often the only warm area in quickly constructed, poorly built and poorly maintained houses. On cold nights, weary workers competed for warm space with each other, the children, and the wet washing their wives draped around the stove to dry. City officials complained that this practice was so "widespread among the lower classes" as to constitute one of the major reasons for the very high incidence of fires in the city.[30]

An inside tap eliminated the heaviest water-carrying. A stove was an improvement on earlier methods of cooking over a fireplace. Yet women still had to carry water from the tap to the stove whether it was to be heated for washing or for food preparation. They still had to see that coal or wood was brought in or do it themselves. And stoves required cleaning, blacking, and constant replenishment. While men may have helped chop the wood, carrying the wood or coal, often up one or two flights of stairs, usually fell to the wife or the children when men were absent for most of the day. Furthermore, stoves, like the coal lamps that lit working-class homes, left walls and furniture besmeared with soot, making spring cleaning an annual necessity.

Transforming purchased or even home-produced food into edible meals was also a much heavier and more time-consuming task than it is today. The adulteration of food created extra preparation work for already busy housewives. Flour full of impurities had to be sieved several times, just as oatmeal had to be picked over for inedible extras. Even most unadulterated food required work to turn it into edible meals. Chickens were usually bought unplucked, fish unscaled. Some wives bought bread while others made it themselves. The cheaper cuts of meat that the poorer working-class families could afford had to be cooked for hours. It is little wonder working-class wives were said to buy bread rather than bake it and to feed their labouring husbands on dinners of bread and cheese.[31]

Nursing sick family members added to the work in such homes and, in the case of contagious diseases, increased the risk of illness. In their advice to women on how to control the spread of infectious diseases, doctors recommended isolating the patient, removing "carpets, curtains and other effects" from the sick room, even filling crevices in the floor with wax to prevent "particles of contagion" from getting into them. Even more elaborate procedures were required to disinfect a room after recovery, removal to hospital, or death, including whitewashing the ceilings, removing and burning the wallpaper, and washing the furniture with carbolic soap.[32]

Similar major housecleaning was recommended following the floods that frequently plagued the low-lying areas of Sainte Anne ward in particular. "If the men are careless about the jobs of cleaning up after floods," women were advised not to "rest till all putrid accumulations are removed. Remember, it is the poor little ones who suffer most from the stenches and malaria and with them the question may be of cleanliness or death." Housewives were advised to light large fires to dry and purify the air, clean off all slime, apply quick lime and chloride of lime on all walls, and thoroughly wash floors, woodwork, walls, furniture, and utensils with lye and then with carbolic acid, salicylic acid, or other powerful disinfectants.[33] One can imagine the difficulty faced by a woman with several young children, perhaps sick herself, adding these tasks to her other daily chores.

Managing and Stretching the Workers' Wages

The daily departure of husbands, older offspring, and some young children to work underlined the family's dependence on wages. Their parting resulted from the growing geographical separation of home and work that was accompanying the concentration of production and in the process reshuffling the rhythms of family life and redefining the content and place of women's work. Montreal factories opened as early as 6:30 a.m., six mornings a week. Long before the sun rose on a winter morning, someone, usually the wife, had to ensure that the wage-earners were awake, fed, and ready to go to work. The wages they brought home were the basis for married women's major occupation – the transformation of those wages into daily survival. Yet wives had no control over how often the wage-earners would find work or the frequency or rate of payment, and too often they had little if any control over how much of pay earned would be given to them. One joiner explained at the Royal Commission on the Relations of Labour and Capital that he was usually paid on Saturdays but sometimes had to wait till the following Monday or Tuesday. When asked whether it was a great inconvenience to be without money on a Saturday night, Stanislas Paquette replied, "Naturally, when the wife expects $7 or $8 to live upon and the husband arrives and has not got it it is not convenient."[34]

This man clearly expected to give his wife a reasonable proportion of his wage for the family to live on. Other wives had to argue, cajole, and compete with alternative ways of spending it. When husbands drank, gambled, or spent on other women or prostitutes, the quality of wives' work diminished. They might get by with minimal meals, and by seeking credit, finding other ways of generating the money they needed, or turning to neighbours or kin for help. In these situations conflict and violence erupted only too often.[35] When Louis Brisson gave his wife Henriette only a dollar of the seven dollars he had earned one week in July, 1870, she fed him bread and butter for supper. Outraged at this inadequate meal, he struck her violently on the face with his fist, refusing to listen to her explanations.[36] Marie Mainville's plasterer husband Edmond kept the dollar a day he earned to himself, sometimes paying the rent and a small amount for groceries but spending more on drink. Her initial resolution was to confront his employer, who gave her a dollar. Subsequently, she successfully took Edmond to court for failing to provide.[37]

Getting credit was crucial for wives whose husbands were paid irregularly or were unemployed or sick. One advantage of wives' dependency in the eyes of the law was their right to contract debts associated with basic family needs in their husband's name. When a woman was married in the community of goods regime, her husband was unquestionably liable for any goods she purchased that were considered necessaries for herself or her family.[38] One case in 1861 found that the husband was liable for a promissory note related to "provisions, groceries and necessities," while two years later a couple who had officially separated their property were both found responsible for paying a debt incurred earlier in the marriage, prior to the separation.[39] We know little about how credit was given in nineteenth-century Montreal, although the evidence of workers at the Royal Commission hearings of 1888 certainly suggests that it was widespread, and fragments in the judicial archives underline its importance among the poor of the city. Ulric Charpentier, a carpenter, left his wife and fathered two children with another woman. The children had no shoes, the couple shared a house with her brother, and they lived minimally, buying sometimes with money, sometimes on credit.[40] In the more respectable family of stone-cutter Étienne Féréole-Lagrenade, debts for groceries alone added up to nearly $50 at the moment his wife died.[41] For as long as a couple could retain a good name with the grocer, credit could see them through difficult periods.

Shopping was a daily task for most working-class wives. Some only knew from day to day how much money they would have to work with. Few had the storage space necessary to buy in bulk.[42] And in the hot, humid summer months, perishable items rotted quickly without refrigeration. Even Mary Smith, the wife of a well-paid printer, purchased food and other household items at least once a day except on Sundays. She always bought in small quantities, purchasing even durable items like sugar and oatmeal two to three times a week.[43]

Food, the major item in the family budget, might be purchased in grocery stores for cash or credit or at the market. Trips to the butcher, baker, grocer, or local market could be a major undertaking for women with several small children. Younger children were probably often left at home, sometimes under the eye of an older sibling, sometimes alone.[44] How close housing was to shops made a major difference when public transportation was prohibitively expensive. One immigrant housewife complained in 1879 that on coming to Montreal several years earlier she "was horrified to find I could procure neither beef, fish nor fowl without walking more than a mile to market. It was summer and I found the climate necessitated marketing almost every day. . . . After a walk to market . . . I was always too fatigued for any other work."[45] On the cold winter days, even a short walk was an ordeal for those working-class women unable to afford adequate footwear and clothing.

Milkmen and breadsellers who delivered to the home, street vendors who sold vegetables, fish, meat, fruit, and dairy products, and hucksters selling what they could from door to door relieved women of the need to go out in search of food and bargains as well as of the burden of carrying food home. Street sellers were more than a convenience for women without refrigeration or storage space and with children always under foot.[46] Yet, since the early nineteenth century a growing number of regulations and licensing laws aimed to discourage hawkers of fruits, vegetables, sweets, or biscuits outside the city markets.[47] The $60 licence fee that hawkers and pedlars had to pay by the 1860s not only discouraged women from entering such a trade, but the cutback on the number of itinerant pedlars made it more likely that women would go to shops for their basic needs.[48]

On the other hand, shopping offered the opportunity of casual socializing with other women, of catching up with gossip and exchanging information, even of indulging in a glass of wine, beer, or spirits. Many Montreal groceries doubled as illegal outlets for alcohol. Female traders were arrested frequently throughout the 1870s for selling a vast array of different drinks illegally by the glass.[49] One temperance reformer declared that "at the corner of every street almost, especially where there is a larger population were licensed groceries. . . . People who would not go into saloons would go there, especially women and young people." Those with licences were supposed to sell by the bottle. Many made whisky, brandy, rye, and other drinks available by the glass, converting their shops in the process into places of recreation, a female counterpart to the male taverns.[50]

Some wives, like their husbands, drank to forget their problems. Drinks could be put on the grocery bill along with other household purchases and the problem of making ends meet temporarily delayed. One temperance advocate argued that a man very often found

> that his grocery bill is exceedingly large, and he cannot understand it. He receives a large bill for legitimate groceries while as a matter of fact, a large portion of it is often for liquor sold to his wife.[51]

The money available to a working-class woman for food and other purchases obviously varied with her husband's occupation, wage rate, and work regularity, quite apart from the variations that resulted when men retained different proportions for their own needs or when women spent some on drink. Most diets appear to have been as limited as that Rowntree used for the estimates of the cost of living, discussed in Chapter 2. Bread and potatoes were the staples, complemented by legumes, root crops, lard, and varying amounts of milk, meat, and cheese, depending on the amount of cash on hand.[52] Some variety, but little improvement in nutritional value, was offered by sugar, tea, coffee, molasses, oatmeal, and rice, the major articles that grocers in the 1880s reported selling to working-class women.[53] Wives of skilled workers with a steady income, such as printer's wife Mary Smith, were able to purchase a more balanced diet, including eggs, vegetables, fruit, and a greater variety of meats. In summer, poorer housewives may have been able to buy fresh fruit, especially the apples for which Montreal was famous, as well as vegetables from passing street vendors. In winter, when costs were highest, many a diet must have reverted to a monotonous repetition of starchy, carbohydrate-heavy meals that would have provided few of the vitamins and proteins necessary to resist disease. Doctors were confronted daily with the results of such diets. "Food is so expensive and workers' means so limited," one doctor explained, "that poor families buy inferior or damaged food."[54]

Food purchased in Montreal was only too often not fresh, clean, or pure. Milk might be inadvertently adulterated when cans were washed with "water taken from wells . . . situated too close to stables." "Chalk, starch and even the brains of sheep" were reported to have been deliberately added to increase milk's specific gravity. Evidence throughout the period makes it clear that the milkmen supplying the city with milk were ignorant or did not care about taking even the most minimal of sanitary precautions. The city's chief sanitary officer reported that it was "not a very rare thing to find pus, blood and abnormal cells in milk." In an 1882 examination of dairies supplying the city, not a single milkman's premises were found to be in perfect condition. Drinks of other types were "generally of an inferior quality," being adulterated at times to such an extent as to injure those using them. The water supply in many parts of town was polluted because the sewers and drains were so often inadequate. Meat was frequently infected. Coloured confectionery was said to need careful inspection. Tea, coffee, sugar, mustard, and marinades were also reported to be frequently adulterated. Tea might be "diluted with stalks and teadust," and coffee "largely adulterated with chickory, peas, roasted corn and roasted, damaged wheat."[55]

Home Production

Women could save, even earn some cash, and avoid adulterated or disease-carrying food by keeping a small garden for vegetables and fruit or by keeping animals for milk or meat. Montreal had excellent soil for many crops despite the short growing season. Production of potatoes, corn, barley, and rye flourished within the parish of Montreal in the early nineteenth century. The slopes that led up toward Mount Royal were famous for their strawberries, apples, and plums. Wealthy Montrealers had long kept productive gardens, and their letters and reminiscences confirm the potential for food production.[56] City-based papers such as the *Montreal Daily Witness* included agricultural and gardening columns, which do not appear to have been aimed only at rural subscribers. Seeds for gardeners and farmers alike were advertised during the spring months.[57] From the 1860s to the 1880s, citizens' letters to the editors of different Montreal newspapers complaining of the damage that wandering cows and goats caused among their flowers and vegetables testify to the continued importance of gardens for at least some Montreal citizens.[58]

While growing vegetables or fruit constituted a leisure activity and a means of securing quality food for those able to afford spacious lots, it became increasingly difficult in the years after mid-century for working-class families. Large gardens in the city were concentrated in the hands of the wealthy, not in the hands of those most needing cheap food. In some Canadian cities the nature of land development had allowed workers to build houses in new working-class suburbs on lots with ample space for gardens. In Montreal, in contrast, the development of the duplexes and triplexes that came to dominate working-class housing obliterated most such garden space.[59] The courtyards behind most working-class houses provided neither the space nor the light for a vegetable garden. "Never," wrote a visitor in 1869, had he "been in a Canadian city where among the working classes there was so little appearance of comfortable residences in the outskirts with small gardens."[60]

Pigs and poultry required less space and light than a garden. However, in much of the city, urban development combined with stricter legislation to curtail not only the possibility of gardening but also of raising pigs, goats, and sheep or of keeping cows to save on the costs of milk and meat. A cow, in particular, offered the possibility of a steady supply of cheap, disease-free milk, an important consideration in a city where polluted milk was a major source of intestinal infections and tuberculosis. One Montreal doctor recommended in 1871 that mothers who could not or would not breastfeed should always use milk from the same cow.[61]

In early and even mid-nineteenth-century Montreal, open green spaces that could serve to pasture cows abounded. William Dawson, principal of McGill University, remembered that when he had first seen the campus in 1855 the "grounds were unfenced and pastured at will by herds of cattle, which not only cropped the grass, but browsed on the shrubs." Those owning cows paid for summer pasture. A boy would pass from house to house "until he had a herd," then would drive them home each evening in time for milking.[62] But cows were expensive to keep. They needed summer pasture, space to be stabled, and winter feed. Furthermore, fees had to be paid for "servicing" by a bull if they were to keep producing milk.[63] Thus, while many families may well have hoped to have a cow, access to the capital necessary to buy one and to the greater space and cost requirements for raising it limited the possibility for much of the working class. The 1861 census shows that among families headed by professionals and proprietors, at least 18 per cent in Sainte Anne and 12 per cent in Saint Jacques were keeping cows. In contrast, only 9 per cent of semi-skilled and unskilled workers reported having a cow in Saint Anne and only 4 per cent in Saint Jacques.

Pigs and fowl were cheaper to purchase and to keep than a cow.[64] They cost virtually nothing to raise, as they scavenged for themselves in the courtyards and at the roadside, and they required little space, being kept in yards, basements, or even inside houses. Unlike gardening, keeping animals was not limited to families with plenty of space. In some fairly densely populated streets, families living in rear houses, duplexes, and row houses were keeping both pigs and cows. A walk along George or Catherine Street in Sainte Anne ward, one of the densest areas of pig-keeping, was as likely to involve skirting pigs or cows and their droppings as it was to encounter the unruly, playing children of the neighbourhood. In one exceptional small block on Catherine Street, over twenty families, more than half of them headed by labourers, kept up to nine pigs each. Most enterprising among these labourer's wives was fifty-year-old Elizabeth Martin, a mother of four. On census day she had seven pigs and four cows.[65]

Piglets and chickens could be bought live at market or obtained from relatives in the country. They might also be stolen fairly easily. In the mid-1870s, after pigs were outlawed in the city, farmers reported that their sheep had been stolen when they stopped for refreshment on the way to market.[66] Once mature and fattened, a pig could be slaughtered and salted to provide cheap meat over the winter months or sold to nearby butchers for cash. A pig sold for as much as $12 to $15 in 1874 at a time when labourers were lucky to find work at $1 a day and women involved in wage labour earned as little as $2 a week. A few good laying hens saved a woman the twenty-four or twenty-five cents a dozen that eggs cost at that time. This was the equivalent of two-thirds of the average daily wage for women in the clothing industry.[67] Twenty-five cents, saved weekly, added significant flexibility to the family budget of the lowest-paid workers.

How important pigs, goats, sheep, or fowl were in the budget of working-class wives is hard to determine with any precision. The 1861 census was taken in the depths of winter, when families would have already slaughtered most of their animals for winter consumption. Sheep and goats appear to have been relatively rare. Yet, in Saint Anne and Saint Jacques wards around one in ten of families headed by labourers and other unskilled workers reported having a pig on census day. More would surely have kept them during the summer months. Unlike cows, pigs predominated among the working class. Nearly half the pigs in these wards were kept by the wives of semi-skilled or unskilled men, although they constituted only one-third of the families.

For such families, pigs, poultry, and, when they could afford it, a cow represented not a piece of property but rather a source of food or cash, which could help the working-class wife get closer to balancing the family budget. Both Irish and French-Canadian wives drew on long-standing rural and urban traditions when they turned to raising pigs, chickens, or cows in Montreal. Poultry and pigs were essential supplements to rural and village wage labourers in Quebec as well. The Irish predominated among pig-keepers. In Sainte Anne in 1861 Irish headed about 50 per cent of households but represented nearly 70 per cent of those with pigs. Among the labourers' families of that ward, around 12 per cent of Irish families kept pigs, compared to 7 per cent of the French Canadians. Both groups were continuing a tradition that derived not simply from a farming background but from a history of having to supplement low wages.[68]

Until the mid-1860s it was legal to keep pigs, sheep, cows, and other animals in the city, although a growing number of regulations aimed rather unsuccessfully to control their freedom on the streets. In the late 1860s the newly formed Sanitary Association began a campaign to eliminate "the keeping of pigs in dense and populated cities," which was, they argued, "offensive and prejudicial to public health." In 1868 keeping pigs was made illegal in the most populated central parts of the city. They were allowed only on the periphery – in the western limits of Sainte Anne ward, to the north of Sainte Catherine Street, and in most of Sainte Marie ward to the east. Over the next few years, new by-laws controlled the grazing and browsing of horses, cattle, pigs, goats, and sheep on city streets, lanes, alleys, and public places, set up a system of fines, and made it illegal to keep any "horse, cow, calf, pig, sheep, goat or fowl in a house or tenement."

In 1874 City Council made pigs illegal throughout the city. Only one alderman opposed the outlawing of pigs, arguing that it was hard "if a poor man was to be debarred from keeping a pig or two."[69] Some no doubt continued to keep pigs illegally. Others may have kept poultry instead, for there were no laws against keeping chickens and other types of fowl in nineteenth-century Montreal. When they were first officially counted in 1891 they had replaced all but cows as the leading food animals in the city. Their concentration in working-class areas in

1891 demonstrates the continued importance of some food animals in working-class family economies. Women and men wanting to raise vegetables or keep animals like pigs were increasingly pushed to seek out housing first in the peripheral parts of suburbs where space remained or to cultivate the empty spaces that remained between factories, warehouses, and residential areas, and later to move to developing outer suburbs where there was more space and where animals remained legal.[70]

Raising animals or vegetables at home, or making rather than buying bread, clothing, even cheese, honey, and butter, enabled some women either to minimize the number of commodities purchased or to sell the goods and so earn and control some money themselves. Home production, however, invariably meant an intensification of the housewife's work. Across her life cycle as a wife, a woman might make different choices about what to buy and what to make, depending on the level of incoming wages, the cost of different commodities in the marketplace, and the extra help she had available. Her own skills, interests, background, and proximity to kin would also have been determining factors. When families lived near or with other relatives, gardening or care of pigs or chickens might be shared, or one woman might specialize in sewing, another in baking, another in gardening. For individual women and their families, such decisions made a difference to the standard of living and to the amount of work that had to be done. Their importance, however, stretched further, for similar actions repeated by numerous women across the city influenced the nature of production in the city, local markets, and local demand.

Did most working-class wives buy bread? Bread was certainly produced in fairly large quantities in Montreal throughout the nineteenth century, and qualititative evidence suggests that working-class wives were perhaps more likely to buy commercially produced bread than were the middle classes. In 1848 one cookbook produced in Montreal suggested that most working-class wives bought bread because they seldom had a good stove for making it.[71] Grocers testifying at the Royal Commission hearings forty years later invariably listed bread as one of the major items purchased by the working class.[72] Yet it is interesting that the value of bread produced in Montreal's fifty to sixty bakeries between the 1870s and 1890s did not increase despite the expansion in the population of the city as a whole and of the working class in particular.[73] Families may have been eating less bread. This, however, seems unlikely within most of the working class. Quite probably, a fair proportion of women – as likely middle-class as working-class – were baking their own bread, thus placing limits on the expansion of commercial bakeries.[74]

Sewing clearly did continue to be an important aspect of women's productive labour in the home. Much men's clothing was beginning to be mass-produced during this period. However, the tight, inflexible budgets of the least skilled workers left little space for such purchases despite falling prices. Women's careful scrounging in second-hand shops or at a pawnbroker's might save hours of sewing and turn up the winter overcoat or footware so necessary for a working son or husband.[75] Most kinds of women's clothes, in contrast, continued to be made by housewives sewing at home, making and remaking clothing for themselves and their children, and sometimes producing for neighbours or for general sale. Clothier William Muir testified in 1874 that the vast majority of the wool and cotton imported into Canada was transformed into clothing by the people rather than by wholesale merchants and producers like himself. As late as 1930 clothier R.P. Sparks estimated that apart from coats, "nearly 50% of the total" of women's clothing "consumed is still made at home and is competing with the factory product."[76]

Odd Jobs, Scrounging

When a husband was unemployed, sick, or simply not earning enough to balance the budget, sewing, housecleaning, watching children, and cooking could all be turned into marketable skills and a source of cash. Women made a distinction between work performed for their own family and that done for others. "Working for others" included a variety of ways to fill in the gaps between incoming wages and household expenses. Wives might do other people's washing, ironing, sewing, or mending, babysit for neighbours, relatives, or friends, or seek diverse forms of charwork.[77] Some raised a few cents by making cakes, biscuits, sandwiches, soup, and root beer and other drinks, selling them casually to neighbours, workers, or passersby.

Married women in more desperate straits scrounged themselves or sent their children to seek anything discarded by others that could be used to raise a penny or save one. When seventeen-year-old Felix Vermette dit Lefèbvre was arrested in 1866 for theft he reported his occupation as searching for old rags in the streets.[78] The docks and railway lines were a source of riches for those scavenging for dropped coal, grain, and above all wood that could be sold or used to heat the home. The wharves were such an attractive source of wood that during the Great Depression of the 1870s federal authorities stressed the need to guard the wharves and flour sheds to prevent people from tearing up planking and wood from the wharves and sheds.[79]

Christine Stansell has shown that for young scavengers in mid-nineteenth-century New York this "economy of rubbish," of active recycling, was not always easily distinguished from petty theft.[80] Montreal was similar. Some youths stole to help their parents make ends meet. Others were no doubt tempted by the money to be made for their own purposes. Stolen goods were used, exchanged, and sold to second-hand dealers for ready cash, often linking dealers and thieves in a shady economy of redistribution. Adults, of course, were equally likely to steal. The frequent theft of such items as a coal oil lamp, a turkey, clothing, and firewood underlines the need among Montreal families for food, fuel, and other basic necessities of life.[81]

Such money-raising activities generally took place outside the formal labour market, often outside what economists recognize as the formal economy. They constituted a significant but immeasurable portion of nineteenth-century production and exchange, but must have been a vital element in the day-to-day survival of many working-class families. When Grace Tweedy, wife of a carter, or Sarah Rollestone, wife of a labourer, reported their occupation as "housekeeper," the concept included such productive and reproductive activities.[82] The more that working-class families resorted to home production and informal exchange, the less influence their consumption patterns had on the development of the wider economy. As long as low wages, illness, underemployment, and recurrent depressions meant that a significant proportion of working-class families could not purchase even the most basic commodities new, working-class consumption would play a fluctuating but minor role in the expansion of many sectors of production and exchange. To the extent that people chose or were obliged to devise survival strategies outside the formal marketplace, an additional brake existed to capitalist expansion.

At the same time, the more time and energy that married women expended on the range of tasks that went into making ends meet in the late nineteenth-century city, the less likely it was that they would seek any kind of formal employment. And, when they did, it would invariably be in jobs that allowed them to reconcile their multiple responsibilities as wife, mother, domestic worker, wage-manager, and revenue-stretcher.

Paid Employment

A small minority of wives, impelled by poverty or family illness, worked at some kind of job on a steady enough basis to be acknowledged as at work in the censuses or other documents of the period. Just how many did so is extremely difficult to measure because the different nature of married women's work made consistent enumeration less likely than for husbands and sons or even daughters and widows. There is no question that the paid work of married women, in particular, has been under-enumerated to some extent in the censuses in Canada, as elsewhere.[83] Yet even more than for daughters, the very nature of wives' work contributed to the omission of an occupation. Most earned money sporadically, casually, and only occasionally by working full time. In any given week women might have earned a few pennies in a variety of ways. What, then, was the "special occupation" that enumerators were instructed to report?[84]

The elusive, often informal, and ever-changing nature of married women's work in many communities partially explains why the wage labour of wives has been under-enumerated in most Western countries. Occasionally there are hints at under-enumeration. In the 1861 census, for example, dealer Thomas Davis's wife listed no occupation, yet the city directory of the same year records her as a huckster at Sainte Anne's market. Under-enumeration should not, however, be exaggerated. Most married women did not work formally for pay for long periods during their married life precisely because of their importance as domestic labourers and wage-managers at home. Even allowing for fairly widespread under-counting, the most striking feature of married women's formal wage labour in these areas of Montreal between 1861 and 1891 is its scarcity. Between 1861 and 1891, fewer than one in twenty married women whose husbands were living at home reported a job at the moment the census was taken (Table 5.1). Specific numbers and proportions varied both in time and place, peaking earliest in the period in Saint Jacques, when sewing work was readily available from Montreal tailors and clothiers producing uniforms for the armies in the American Civil War. Throughout the period, wives in Saint Jacques were more likely to report a job than their counterparts in Sainte Anne, largely because of the preponderance of sewing within the putting-out system in the needle and shoemaking trades in that ward.

For wives as for daughters, a combination of structural, ideological, familial, and individual factors explain the relative insignificance of their formal wage labour in Montreal during this period. In English and American mill towns, in particular, early industrialization drew much larger numbers of married women into formal, enumerated, paid employment.[85] This did not occur in Montreal because of a different interaction between the timing and nature of industrial development and local demography. The lack of wage labour among married women reflects the fact that there were invariably more people seeking work than finding it, plus the need of working-class families for a full-time wage-manager and domestic labourer.

Combining household work with most forms of permanent paid work presented such a challenge that married working-class women only appear to have sought relatively formal work when they could find no other way of ensuring their family's survival. They entered and left the work force in response to conditions and needs deriving from within the family, related often, but not exclusively, to the development of the family life cycle. These needs were also shaped by broad changes in the economy and by short- and long-term economic fluctuations. Poverty could be caused or exacerbated by a husband's low and irregular wages, unemployment, illness, or squandering of money. Family expenses increased suddenly when someone fell ill. Married women sought work in these kinds of crisis situations.

Wives reporting employment were clustered in the poorer sections of Sainte Anne and Saint Jacques wards. Virtually all had husbands with unskilled jobs, in the injured trades, or in highly seasonal construction work. Around one-quarter were the wives of labourers. In Saint Jacques in 1871, for example, while only 10 per cent of the ward's male family heads worked in unskilled jobs, 36 per cent of working wives were married to unskilled workers. Only 7 per cent of the ward's family heads were shoemakers, yet 21 per cent of the working wives had shoemaker husbands. Also, 10 per cent of the married men were in construction, but 19 per cent of the working wives had husbands in these trades. A further small percentage of the married working women were the wives of small proprietors, running family enterprises like grocery stores, bakers' shops, taverns, or market stalls. In the Couter family the wife, Mary, worked as the clerk in the family grocery while her husband listed his occupation as both grocer and carter and one son was also involved in the carting side of the business.[86]

In Montreal, married women do not seem to have taken whatever work was available, no matter how desperate the economic needs of their families. While a significant number of Montreal's emerging factories relied largely on female labour, few married women found factory jobs. They turned not to industrial capitalists, except indirectly in the sewing industry, but to individuals seeking someone to clean their houses or to sew or wash their clothes. This was a volatile and changing labour market, but one in which care of children or domestic tasks could be combined with earning money. Until 1891, the overwhelming majority in both wards worked as seamstresses, either on their own account, attempting to get enough custom by building up a clientele or hanging a sign at their door, or within the putting-out system. Taking in washing and doing domestic labour for others were the next most important types of employment (Table 5.1). The availability of these kinds of casual employment fluctuated with seasonal and cyclical ups and downs in the economy. Women were more likely to find work as washerwomen, charwomen, or servants in good years like 1871 than in the more depressed years of the 1860s and early 1880s. Toward the end of the century a few married women could be found in the new types of employment being created as the industrial revolution reshaped the workplaces of factories, offices, and shops. In 1891 some were working as bookkeepers, clerks for the railroad, and in mills and factories. Yet the vast majority who were reported to be working continued to find casual employment sewing, washing, and cleaning for others, earning enough at times to make a major difference in their families' standard of living, rarely if ever enough to manage alone.

For recently married women, steady work in the period between marriage and the birth of a child offered the possibility of saving up for the future, purchasing basic household necessities, and living reasonably well. Once children were born, combining revenue-earning and childcare became more difficult, yet the cost of living increased. Most of the small minority of wives who listed a job in the census were at the most difficult stage of the family life cycle, when their children were all under eleven and too young to get paid employment (Table 5.2). The proportions reporting work dropped off quickly once the oldest offspring was fourteen or fifteen, then rose again as children reached their later teens. In the 1860s and 1870s when sewing was the major form of earning for Saint Jacques married women, they were more likely to continue to work once their children reached sixteen than were wives in Sainte Anne ward, largely because mothers and daughters could work together at home, combining sewing and housework. Once all children had left home married women whose husbands were still alive were unlikely to report a job.

It has been argued by some historians that French-Canadian women, in Canada and in the mill towns of New England, were more likely to work when married than other groups.[87] Tamara Hareven has suggested, for instance, that as working-class immigrants they had not yet absorbed the "middle class ideology that censored the work of wives and mothers outside the home" and that most "couples perceived no conflict" in married women labouring outside the home.[88] Such an interpretation makes several assumptions. First, it assumes all working-class groups had similar ideologies. Second, and this is a fairly commonly held assumption in much of the literature, it implies that the idea that mothers should stay at home was a middle-class ideology that had either to be imposed from above or filter down. Finally, it simplifies the idea of what work meant for married women as well as their desire to earn some money without upsetting their role as both domestic labourers and wage-managers. An interview that Tamara Hareven conducted with a French Canadian in Manchester underlines the complexity of wives' work, as well as a husband's pride in being able to keep a wife at home.

> My father didn't really want her to work. That was the big issue because she always wanted to go in and earn a little money . . . He'd say "no, you're not going to work. You're going to stay home." And that's why she did other things. She'd make clothes for him, take in boarders, rent rooms. She used to rent one or two rooms for $12.00 a week to people who worked in the mills. Sometimes she'd also work little stretches at night, from six to nine, because we lived right in front of the mills. When there were big orders, the mills were always looking for people to work. But my father didn't want to keep the children. That was women's work, his work was outside.[89]

The masculine pride that was bound up in being able to keep a wife at home did not prevent this wife from pursuing a variety of strategies, including a little wage-earning. Except in emergencies, and for the wives of the least well paid workers, it does not seem to have extended to accepting steady wage labour. For other husbands, any attempts by their wives to earn money seemed a threat.[90] When Desneiges Albert, the wife of a French-Canadian woodchopper who arrived in Lowell, Massachussets, in the 1870s, proudly showed her husband a dollar she had earned taking in laundry, he responded angrily: "I have not reached a level here which requires you to work. I think we can get along without that."[91]

Fragmentary as it is, such evidence suggests caution about any idea of a culturally rooted tradition among French Canadians that would have led to a high proportion working for wages across this period. Both French-Canadian and English-speaking wives, particularly those of Irish origin, reported having jobs in Sainte Anne and Saint Jacques wards. In both Sainte Anne and Saint Jacques, French-Canadian wives were disproportionately involved in wage labour, particularly in the sewing trades in 1861. That year around 70 per cent of the female population of Saint Jacques was French Canadian, while nearly 90 per cent of the working wives were.[92] Yet over subsequent decades ethnic differences in rates of job reporting were minimal. Poverty, not cultural tradition, led the majority of married working-class women to seek steady paid labour.

The somewhat higher involvement of French-Canadian women should not be exaggerated. Certainly Suzanne Cross's assertion that these years were characterized by the arrival of French-Canadian mothers in the labour market must be treated with extreme caution. Extrapolating from the existence of *salles d'asiles,* types of daycare run by the Grey Nuns and Sisters of Providence, and the apparent absence of such institutions among the English-speaking population, she concluded that only French-Canadian mothers worked outside the home.[93] There are several problems with this argument. First, sisters, brothers, and other relatives were much more important child-minders in the nineteenth century than were daycares. Second, mothers placing their children were not always working, and certainly not always full-time. Daycares were attractive in part because they offered meals and supervision during the day. Third, Anglophone institutions also took children. By the 1880s the YWCA was running a crèche that opened at seven in the morning and provided for some twenty-five to thirty children daily. Mothers could leave their offspring there for the day for ten cents for one child and fifteen cents for two. Later in the 1880s it was possible to leave children by the week as well, "to enable the parent to earn the necessary means of supporting her family."[94] In the same period over 1,000 children were registered in the *salles d'asile* of the Grey Nuns and several hundred with the Sisters of Providence. They were not all French.[95]

The case histories of several mothers using the YWCA crèche further highlight the fact that women of all origins usually only worked outside the home in times of extreme need. One mother used the crèche for her seven-month-old boy because her husband was dying of consumption. She had become the sole breadwinner. The sick father had been looking after the baby since it was eleven days old, but as he grew weaker he could not manage. Another mother who took in laundry had been leaving her baby with its grandmother, who had been dosing the child with soothing syrup whenever it made a noise "until it was fair in the way to become an idiot."[96]

These two examples, chosen with care by the YWCA women for their poignancy, suggest that mothers turned to institutional care for young children only when family networks and informal arrangements did not work. Mothers were much more likely to turn to older daughters, relatives, neighbours, or other household members.[97] In Saint Jacques in 1861 there were co-resident relatives or boarders who could have helped with childcare in half the households in which a wife with children under eleven reported having some kind of employment. Some had elderly parents or sisters living with them. A few had other female relatives or an additional family where the wife may have been free to help. Still more had female boarders who listed no job. In the Cérat household, already described in Chapter 3, the forty-eight-year-old father worked as a stone-cutter, as did his two married sons. Their wives and children all lived with the grandfather and both mothers worked as seamstresses. Together they could supervise the three children, all aged under five.[98] Additional household members thus served not only to spread the costs of rent and to provide additional household income but also to share the tasks of daily reproduction.

Taking in Boarders

Taking in boarders was another way women could use the space of their homes to make money. Renting out rooms, like taking in washing or sewing, could be reconciled with other housework and childcare. A woman housing several boarders could bring as much cash into the home as she could working for wages. During the early 1880s board and lodging cost between $3 and $4 a week for workingmen.[99] Women's wages varied between $1.50 and $5 a week, and those sewing at home often earned less. Boarders offered a woman a source of income comparable to a wage, a valuable source of cash that was probably paid directly to her. In Carol Groneman's study of Irish women's work in the Sixth Ward of New York in the 1850s, considering women who took in several boarders as working increased fourfold the estimates of the proportions of married women at work.[100] Applying a similar method to the 1891 samples would increase the proportion of married women apparently "working" from 3.3 to 6 per cent in Saint Jacques and from 3 to 11 per cent in Sainte Anne.

Tamara Hareven and John Modell have argued that the "logic of the life cycle" dominated the "economic squeeze" in explaining the phenomenon of lodgers in American cities. In contrast, Michael Katz argues that in Hamilton "the presence of boarders and relatives appears to have been largely accidental."[101] In Sainte Anne and Saint Jacques wards local historical circumstances combined with the economic conjuncture and family needs appear to have determined whether or not people took boarders. The patterns seem accidental, yet they have a certain logic (Figure 5.1). Taking in boarders was most common in 1861 among women whose husbands were skilled workers or outside the working class. Over one-third of the wives of skilled workers took in at least one boarder, compared to only 12 per cent of unskilled workers' wives. This is not surprising, as boarders entailed expenditures for bed, linen, and blankets. Most boarders probably expected a separate room, and they had to be fed well enough for them to want to remain in the household. A boarder thus represented not only extra work for the woman of the house but also additional expenditures and space – resources that were lacking in the poorest families. Thus, advertising "Board and Lodging" or that "A Single Gentleman can be accommodated with a BEDROOM AND BREAKFAST, if required" was offering more than poorer working-class families could offer.

Yet, by 1891, the situation had reversed. The wives of the unskilled and of men in the injured trades were somewhat more likely to take in

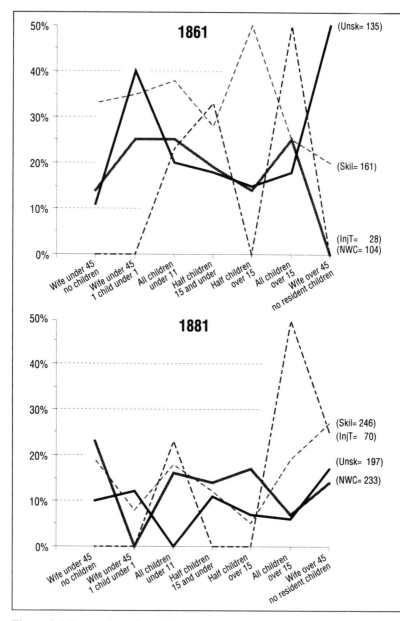

Figure 5.1 Proportion of Families with Boarders at Different Life-Cycle Stages, 1861-91

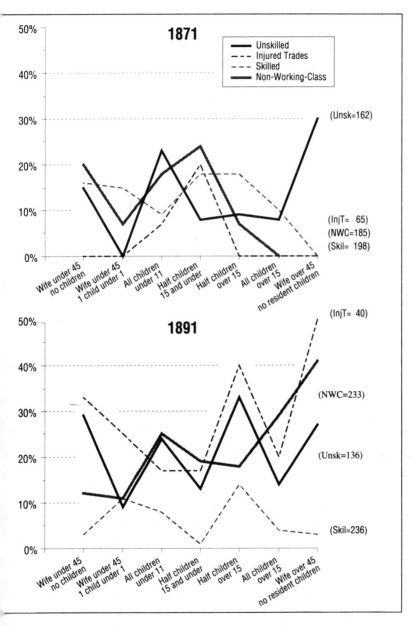

boarders than other women. And the poorest women – those whose husbands were in unskilled or injured trades – were most likely to take in boarders at difficult times in the life cycle, especially before children were old enough to work. In contrast, in non-working-class families boarders were more evenly spread over the life cycle. Thus, in 1871 wives of unskilled workers took in boarders before children were born but avoided them when they were occupied with a newborn. One-quarter of such families had boarders when all the children were too young to work. Women were less likely to take boarders once children reached working age, starting again when their children had all left home. Only among the unskilled does this pattern consistently appear to fit the "social equalization" model suggested by Modell and Hareven, in which economically, if not psychologically, boarders substituted for departed children at the later stages of the family life cycle.[102]

While taking in boarders was more common initially among the best-paid families of the working class, house-sharing, already discussed in Chapter 2, was more common among the poorer classes.[103] In theory, separating the two practices appears simple, but in reality it is virtually impossible to separate them, particularly among the poorer fractions of the working class. Dual-family households were created whether couples were taken in as boarders by other families or they co-rented. The implications were different for family finances and for a married woman's work, but such distinctions are not clear in the censuses. Boarders paid rent. Usually, but not always, they had to be provided with food. When families doubled up, however, arrangements about space and cooking had to be sorted out. How cooking was done was central to the definition of what constituted a family in the census instructions for 1871. Enumerators were instructed to consider whether persons living under one roof had their food "provided together" in determining the boundaries of a family.[104]

The ability to control their own food and cooking appears to have been essential to some women's sense of pride in their own household management. Catherine Farell and her policeman husband had been living with her widowed mother before he packed his trunk and left her in July of 1875 after fourteen years of marriage. When she went to court to attempt to get him to provide for her she explained that prior to his departure she and her mother had each done their cooking independently. Since he had left, however, she had been reduced to eating "at my mother's table."[105]

Those wives who took in boarders or shared space were able to save or make money. At the same time their major workplace – the home – was transformed and their labour intensified and often complicated. For some wives the tension that went with whole families sleeping in one room and several women sharing cooking facilities must at times have been intolerable. In other cases, women co-operated, finding ways to share cooking and other domestic work, relieving each other's poverty and their daily labour. When Marie Cyr's husband left her, the couple she had taken in as boarders contributed not only food and money but also moral support by testifying for her in her court case.[106] Some women sharing their housing with other families clubbed "together, using one stove." Montreal doctor Dougless Decrow testified in 1888 that in the houses of day labourers, where two families might share a house of three or four rooms, each family had "one room for a sleeping room and use the kitchen for a dining room – the kitchen and stove in common with others."[107]

The confrontation between Marie Cyr and her husband in court in 1878 gives us glimpses of the difficulties married women had in piecing together survival strategies when husbands did not provide, and suggests that men and women had a pretty poor understanding of each other's work worlds and labour markets. Marie explained that her husband had no trade and worked by the day. She contended that "had he wanted to work he could have given me something more to help me live" and described him staying at home for three days without working, even though there was work available. Israel Beaume, as we have seen in Chapter 3, attempted to defend himself by explaining that he had sought work for a couple of weeks, but that jobs for day labourers were hard to find in such years of depression. Yet, he also framed his defence on a different argument: that his wife was capable of providing for herself because of her trade. "Is it not true," he asked the boarder giving evidence, "that the plaintiff is a seamstress by trade, that she has a machine at home and could sew instead of seeking jobs by the day elsewhere?" The boarder attempted to point out that Marie could not "make enough sewing at home to live upon." Israel's persistent questioning allows us to glimpse more about the variety of ways in which women sewed in their homes.

> Q. Did she ever put a notice on her door advertising her sewing skills? Or, to the best of your knowledge did she ever try to find work elsewhere as a seamstress?
> A. I don't know, I have never seen an advertisement on the door.
> Q. How can you say then that the plaintiff could not get enough work as a seamstress to support her at home?
> A. I judge by the quantity of clothes which have been brought to her and from what I can see.
> Q. So, the plaintiff does work as a seamstress and thus does have something she can do, even though she does not advertise?
> A. I have seen her often sewing shirts and other things for others.

At this point Israel clearly believed he had made an important point – his wife could support herself but was neglecting to do so – and ceased his questions. The case was dismissed for insufficient evidence.[108]

Some of the mutual incomprehension evident here was no doubt deemed advantageous in court. Behind it, however, lies the fact that increasingly wage labour drew men out of the home for up to twelve hours a day, six days a week, so that women's work was physically separate from that of their husbands to an extent seldom found among either farming or artisanal families. Working-class women were not isolated in a separate sphere, their home. Their shopping, money-stretching, and socializing took them into the streets, shops, and markets of the city. They were, however, less and less likely to be aware of the precise nature of their husbands' work, just as husbands might be ignorant of all that their wives' work entailed. While a skilled worker could well acknowledge the importance of the work of a thrifty, economical housekeeper, he might well not be fully cognizant of the variety of ways in which she made ends meet. Yet, women's domestic labour often made the difference between adequate survival and hunger or discomfort. Steady wages for the major earner, an older son or daughter who could also work for wages, and a wife who could adequately feed and clothe the family certainly comprised the best way to achieve a decent standard of living.[109]

Nineteenth-century housework was both heavy and time-consuming, however, and wage dependency locked wives and children to husband and father in a relationship that was at once mutual and complementary yet hierarchical and dependent for each partner. Wives needed their husbands' wages to perform their work. Men needed their wives' domestic labour and money-stretching activities. This complementarity of roles did not make marriage an equal relationship. Its very equilibrium was embedded in the sexual division of labour within the family and the economy. Women and girls could seldom make as much money as their husbands, brothers, and fathers. Economics, ideology, and practicality mingled inextricably to perpetuate and harden the different roles of men and women.

When the circumstances demanded it, or when women could find work and men could not or were ill, the usual gendered division of labour was re-arranged. That this was rare, and was condemned by middle-class investigators, seems clear in the 1882 report of Lukes and Blakeby on labour employed in the mills and factories of Canada. They reported:

> The number of married women having domestic cares are very few in the mills and factories, although we are sorry to say, we found two or three instances in which the husband reversed the civilized

custom by sending the wife and mother to the factory while he attended to the cares at home. Other instances have come under our observation where the husband and father being delicate, the wife with a moral heroism and courage, has gone to the factory to provide the daily bread for the family. In connection with this it may be mentioned that factory or mill hands can earn better wages than are usually paid for domestic services.[110]

While few married women whose husbands were healthy and in relatively permanent and well-paid jobs sought steady work either in factories or in private service, widows and deserted wives were obliged to. When men like Israel Beaume left their wives, when husbands had to seek work in distant cities and lumbercamps, and when they died, the depth and cost of women's dependence on men's wages were laid bare.

6

Managing without a Spouse:
Women's Inequality Laid Bare

Married, working-class women learned, even expected, to supplement their husband's wages in a variety of ways when low wages, illness, unemployment, accidents, or drunkenness left them without enough money to make ends meet. Skills learned and developed during short- and long-term crises proved invaluable for women whose husbands consistently failed to provide, deserted them, or died. Yet they were seldom sufficient. For while married women's strategies, careful housekeeping, and occasional wage-earning could make a major difference to the standard of living of families with an earning male head, women could rarely earn enough to replace such wages. This chapter focuses on those women who had to manage largely without a man and his wages. It compares, when pertinent, the challenges they faced and the solutions they devised with those faced by men without women and their domestic labour. It highlights how the patriarchal legal system and the discriminatory labour market and wage structure combined to perpetuate women's dependence on men and to render daily survival a constant challenge for women on their own. Yet such women seldom gave up. The chapter also shows how women re-organized their lives and how, limited as their margin of manoeuvre was in the majority of cases, they fought back, organized, and collaborated to survive.

Marriage to a man with a skill and a steady job offered most working-class women their best chance of economic security. There was, however, no guarantee that the husband would provide, that the marriage would be harmonious, or that it would last. Any woman, as Christine Stansell has argued in looking at early nineteenth-century New York, "whether the wife of a prosperous artisan or a day labourers' daughter, was vulnerable to extreme poverty if, for some reason, she lost the support of a man."[1] That all were vulnerable does not mean that poverty and managing alone became the lot of all working-class women. While it is virtually impossible to measure with precision the number of women who either at one point in time or across their lives found themselves without a man's support, some attempt must be made to avoid presenting a view of the working class in which extreme poverty for women seems the norm.

A minority of women and a smaller number of men were left largely or totally responsible for supporting themselves and their families in mid- to late nineteenth-century Montreal. Some women separated informally from cruel and violent husbands. Others separated officially. Some men deserted their wives, disappearing completely. Others simply walked out for short or long periods. Some women kicked their husbands out. Aggressive or drunken wives and husbands could drive the other spouse away. Some men set up house with other women. A few remarried, becoming visible in the court records when charged with bigamy. In many trades men were obliged to leave the city seeking jobs. They might stay away months, even years. Occasionally they kept families in several locations.[2] Wives of men sent to prison could find themselves managing alone for months and even years on end.

Permeable and moving boundaries divided non-support, desertion, and separation, leading to a situation where the boundaries between male- and female-headed households were not always clear.[3] The line between women who would today be seen as single parents and married women was not solid, except when a husband actually died. Widows represented one extreme of this irregular continuum, different from separated or deserted women in their legal status but similar in the challenges they faced.

Separation, Failure to Provide, Desertion, and Death

Exactly how many wives or husbands in nineteenth-century Montreal managed for short or long periods on their own because their spouse had left or they had separated cannot be determined with great accuracy. Widows and widowers, because of their change in recognized marital status, are easier to identify. One way to begin to grasp the extent of lone-parenting is to see who was reported as living with whom when the censuses were taken each ten years. This should reveal the tip of the iceberg, the lowest possible proportions.

Even a minimal estimate of the numbers of widows, widowers, and men and women living without their spouses suggests that lone parenthood was a major nineteenth-century urban phenomenon. In Sainte Anne and Saint Jacques wards between 14 and 16 per cent of families with children present had a lone parent as a head across this period, except in the most prosperous year, 1871, when the percentage fell to 7

(Table 6.1). Widows predominated among such family heads, followed by widowers, with much smaller proportions headed by married men and women whose spouses were absent. In 1891 over 500 families in these two wards, or around 14 per cent of all families with children present, were headed by a lone parent. Had a similar proportion of all the 35,396 families enumerated in Montreal that year been lone-parent families, there would have been well over 4,000 in the city, with 3,000 of them headed by widows or women whose husbands were absent for one reason or another. Such estimates do not fully grasp the impact of desertion, separation, or even death. Any men or women who did not head what census-takers defined as a family are not included in these estimates. If we add the lone parents living with relatives or boarding, the proportion of lone-parent families would be much closer to one in five.[4]

These figures still fail to grasp the full extent of the phenomenon. Census instructions made it likely that many couples who had informally separated would have been enumerated as living together. Nor do the estimates above include any men and women who had separated but had no children living with them. Thus, separations of childless couples are hidden, but so, too, are parents who had placed their children in an orphanage precisely because of their marital problems. Lone-parenting was clearly part of family experience in nineteenth-century Montreal.

Death of a husband was the dominant cause of solo parenthood. Widowhood was not a status limited to a few men and women, nor was it a relatively predictable and final stage of an individual's life cycle as it tends to be today. The 1861 census reveals more than 3,000 widows and nearly 1,000 widowers within the boundaries of Montreal.[5] Three decades later there were over 7,000 widows and over 2,000 widowers. In the city as a whole, as in the working-class wards of Sainte Anne and Saint Jacques, there were generally about three widows for each widower, although the differential diminished somewhat with age. Widowhood and old age were not synonymous in the "city of wealth and death," although the chances of a spouse dying clearly increased with age. By the time women reached their fifties nearly one-quarter were widows, compared to about one in ten men. Once women reached their seventies about two-thirds were widows. Only one-third of men who achieved this age were widowers. These patterns changed little over the second half of the century.[6]

Widows outnumbered widowers largely because men were much more likely to remarry than women.[7] For a man, remarriage quickly re-established equilibrium in the family economy. A new wife took on domestic responsibilities and childcare, leaving him free to pursue his craft, career, or job. Someone had to be free during the day to do the shopping and the washing, to prepare meals, to watch young children, or on occasion to protest raised rents or water rates. Wealthier men could hire a housekeeper, but for the majority of working-class men remarriage must have seemed the best option.

Finding a second wife was easier than finding another husband. The dominance of females over males in the city offered widowers a larger pool of potential wives.[8] For men with children, widows already experienced in motherhood might have appeared to be attractive spouses, yet a woman with young children to support constituted a potential drain on a man's earnings. Widows competed in the marriage market with young, attractive single girls, not yet wearied by child-bearing and domestic labour. Men appear to have been twice as likely to remarry as women, and they chose single women as often as they did widows. Only the youngest widows were likely to remarry, most frequently with a widower.[9]

The family and household structures that can be examined in the censuses give some indication of the numbers and proportions of men and women attempting to run their families on their own, highlighting the predominant cause, death, but pointing also to the presence of a fair proportion of relationships broken because of discord and conflict. Between 1861 and 1881 about 8 per cent of lone-parent families were headed by married men or women whose spouse was not present. The proportion appears to have doubled by 1891. Here again it is important to emphasize that in the censuses we are seeing only a portion of the phenomenon, and the causes of such separations are completely hidden. These have to be sought elsewhere.

Legal Recourse and Legal Rights

Widows and married women attempting to manage without a man's wages faced similar economic problems. Their legal rights and the kinds of recourse they could have to the law were quite different. Built into the Civil Code of Quebec were a series of measures that offered a certain level of protection to widows. In the words of one French jurist, widows' rights formed part of "an ingenious system of protection for women which compensated for her overdependence during marriage."[10] Women whose husbands died were emancipated from most aspects of the legal incapacity imposed with marriage, but not from their exploitation in the wider economy. Yet, during the mid-nineteenth century, many of these civil rights of widows were whittled away, both by legislation and by transformations in the economy that left a diminishing proportion of men with the real property that formed the basis of dower rights.

Women marrying men with real property who had made formal

arrangements within their marriage contracts for or instead of a dower, as well as those married in community of goods whose husband had had the time to accumulate goods and property across his life, might face widowhood with the economic basis for survival.[11] Wives of skilled workers, or of men who had managed to make some provision for their death, might find themselves with a piece of property, a house, or an income that offered some basis for survival. And, unlike their situation during marriage, they had the legal right to manage, sell, and file suits, if necessary.[12]

When a husband died with few goods and no real property, however, his wife faced widowhood with little more than her own resourcefulness and the potential support of her children. When a husband had been so much in debt that her part of the community would have been worthless, she could completely renounce the community, starting her widowhood with nothing rather than with debts to pay. The law offered some minimal protection. Creditors could not simply march in without notice and seize a property for the dead man's debts before a widow and the heirs had claimed to be the inheritors.[13]

In widowhood, then, class divisions and differences of wealth tended to be perpetuated, but always through the prism of the woman's dependence on her husband, his wealth, and the provisions that he had made in a marriage contract or will. It was not only in what they might inherit at the moment of death or receive as dower rights that the wives of more skilled workers and those with property were likely to do better than the unskilled. The possibility of receiving some kind of pension or of having the right to certain benefits was also greater. Mutual benefit societies organized by workers or the churches expanded rapidly during the 1860s. In 1863 there were at least six Catholic mutual benevolent societies with over 2,000 members, as well as several Protestant ones. In addition to paying sick members, they also gave a lump sum for funeral expenses and benefits to widows and orphans. One of the largest, the Union Saint Joseph, was organized in the early 1850s. In 1863 it boasted some 800 members, despite a $5 entry fee, payable over the first five months. Sick members received $3 weekly, while widows were allowed only half that amount, with an additional twenty cents to each orphan of the father who had died. The Union also contributed $20 toward funeral costs.[14]

Benefits offered by the other societies were similar. Irish widows whose husbands had earned enough to pay their dues regularly to the St. Patrick's Benevolent Society received more toward funeral expenses ($30) but the same minuscule $1.50 a week and twenty cents for each orphan under twelve. By 1871 there were at least twelve such societies, some simply covering funeral costs, others offering wider benefits. Some were directly run by the Church, others were independent. The Sulpicians advertised their "Union of Prayer and Good Works" as "papally approved" in the city's 1871 directory. From around 10,000 members in the early 1860s the number had increased to some 23,130 in 1871. For twenty-five cents annually, members were offered the chance to "obtain a happy death and secure a funeral service, the corpse being present in favour of the members, who departs this life without leaving their relatives any means to pay the expenses thereof." Astute businessmen that they were, the Sulpicians quickly accumulated important capital from these memberships and used it for a variety of investments.[15]

Widows' rights to benefits from such associations derived only from their husbands' payments. Not only might payments be limited to the orphans of the deceased man, excluding children from a previous marriage, but they also ceased upon remarriage. And widows relying on such income to help pay the rent might find it reduced if the society had problems. While investment in funeral insurance proved profitable for the Sulpicians, other groups providing wider benefits faced problems. Even before the depression hit in the early 1870s, both the Union St. Joseph and the Union Saint Jacques, two of the largest Catholic benevolent societies, were obliged to engage in rather delicate negotiations with the widows receiving weekly benefits. Both societies turned to the legislature in early 1870, explaining, in exactly the same wording, that the contributions levied on members were too limited and the benefits, "especially those granted to the widows of deceased members," were far too high. Expenses were exceeding receipts because of the benefits paid out. The Union Saint Joseph had been paying benefits to twenty-six widows. Officers claimed they had managed to convince twenty-two of them of the wisdom of accepting to exchange their weekly and life benefits for a lump sum of $200. Four widows resisted the offer. The Union Saint Jacques had a similar problem with two of its four beneficiaries. The legislation, assented to in both cases in early February, allowed the societies to impose this settlement on the defiant women![16]

Employers rarely assumed responsibility for their workers or their families. Widows seeking compensation from employers generally had to argue their right, even in cases where the death was clearly work-related. Numerous widows of former policemen wrote to request help from Montreal's Police Department. Widow Menard, for example, had to write several letters in 1868 until City Council finally agreed to give her $100. Before acceding to her request, the Council verified that her husband had indeed been a good policeman and that the doctor believed that his death was a result of experiencing "cold

and exposure consequent upon his occupation." The Finance Committee further curtailed her flexibility, specifying that the amount be
"invested for the benefit of the children in such manner as the Chairman of the Police Committee may deem most advantageous."[17] By the
mid-1870s, $100 was the standard amount given to policemen's
widows. One hundred dollars, it should be recalled, was well under
half the annual wages of day labourers, men who were seldom capable
of supporting their families on their earnings alone. It was never a right.
Women had to write and request support. Both the policeman's record
and the financial state of the widow were considered before any money
was bequeathed.[18]

The problems resulting from families' absolute dependence on
workers' wages were acknowledged even by the more conservative
minority report of the Royal Commission on the Relations of Labour
and Capital in 1888. The report suggested that employers should pay
compensation to men injured or, if they died, to their heirs "even in
cases where negligence on the part of the employer or his agents, or
defects in machinery, has not caused the accident." This was justified
because the "owners of machinery benefit by its use." The commissioners went further, suggesting that the government should insure
workingmen "by means of a governmental system of payment to the
heirs of persons killed by accident." Like most of the other recommen-
dations of the commissioners, this proposal was not acted on.[19]

By the end of the period insurance companies and pensions in some
workplaces offered protection to that minority of widows whose husbands were eligible.[20] Yet again, the amounts offered were small, even
for the widows of white-collar workers. In 1886 pensions for Quebec
retired civil servants were set at one-fifth of their average earnings in
the three previous years. Men were eligible only if they had worked for
the government for ten years. When a man on a pension died his widow
was eligible for half the amount he had received unless she remarried,
in which case it went to her dead husband's minor children.[21]

Women whose husbands were alive but not providing for them
could not make claims on employers. They had little chance of access
either to the property or to the small sums from benefit schemes or
employers that a minority of widows commanded. They remained
married in the eyes of the law. This meant that their legal incapacity
was unaltered, but so, too, was their right to their husbands' support.
Thus, whereas widows had a rightful claim on their husbands' estates,
benefits, or employers, married women retained their right to their husbands' support. A widow might turn to her notary to untangle what was
hers following a husband's death. The married woman whose husband
was not fulfilling his marital obligations, in contrast, was more likely
to turn to the courts. The most drastic resolution of an intolerable

marriage was for a couple to separate judicially as to bed and board. This was the only official form of separation in Quebec, where divorce was not recognized. Only a small number of women and men appear to have sought this difficult and demanding solution. Women could turn to the criminal courts when their husbands beat them or ceased providing sufficient money. A surprising number of brave women, beaten too many times, accused their husbands of assault during this period,[22] and during the depression of the 1870s a growing number also took their husbands to court for failing to provide.

Formal separations were difficult to obtain. They were similar to divorce in the grounds that were admissible, but different in their results. Divorce, the commissioners reviewing the Civil Code in the 1860s explained, broke "the marriage tie so that it cannot be renewed." Separation of bed and board, in contrast, left "the tie unbroken," allowing "the parties to reunite at will." The grounds for separation paralleled those allowed for divorce under the Napoleonic code in France. A wife's adultery was always sufficient cause. In contrast, a husband had to keep his mistress in their common residence if the wife were to claim adultery. Either party could bring the action in cases of ill treatment and grievous abuse, while only a wife could charge on the grounds that the husband refused "to supply her with the necessaries" according to his position and means. Judges had a lot of leeway. They could easily encourage couples to stay together, even suspending judgement when ill treatment or abuse had been proven "to afford the parties an opportunity for coming to an understanding." Furthermore, if the wife failed to win her case, she was obliged to return to her husband within a specified time, and he was bound to receive her.[23]

Women's dependence on men's revenues, the overriding desire to preserve marriages and male power at all costs, and the double standard surrounding men's and women's adultery are clear in these grounds. Prior to 1865, a wife separate as to bed and board still had to ask her husband's permission if she wished to do anything more than simply administer her own property, rendered separate by the decision. The commissioners deliberating on changes to the Quebec civil law in the mid-1860s realized that this was a "generally useless and always disagreeable" requirement and substituted the permission of a judge. A married women who had separated and who wanted to sell her own land, for example, would therefore still have been obliged to seek a judge's permission.[24] After 1875 such a wife was again obliged to turn first to her estranged spouse for authorization and only to a judge if the husband refused.[25]

What, then, were the advantages of a separation? A wife was legally recognized as having the right to live in a separate dwelling from her husband, a major advantage for those living with violent husbands.

Furthermore, her property, if she possessed any, was separated from his, and she could administer and use it as she saw fit, short of selling real property. It could not be touched for his debts, and he had no right of access to it. She was entitled to "the restitution of her dowry and of what she had brought in marriage (unless declared forfeited for reason of adultery), and also to recover the gifts and advantages resulting from her contract of marriage." She had all the rights of a woman who had originally married and kept her property separate. Furthermore, if she had requested the separation, she might well get care of the children and be awarded a living allowance.[26]

How many of the women or men who appeared in the census as living with their children and separate from their spouses were officially separate as to bed and board could only be determined by matching cases with the censuses, a lengthy and difficult procedure. Nor does the current state of the judicial archives allow an easy count of how many such cases occurred during the nineteenth century.[27] An impressionistic idea of the marriages that led to this kind of formal breakdown and the lot of some women following such agreements can be gained from cases where Montreal women, separate as to bed and board, pursued their husbands for failure to provide.

Angelique Burrel separated officially from Simon Arcand, a grain-seller at the Saint Antoine market, some time in 1876 after thirty years of marriage. He had been beating her before their separation. She had been earning most of the money to run the household. The separation was a nasty affair. The oldest daughter testified against her father. He then began beating her and the other children. Angelique took in sewing before and after the official separation. She was clearly proud of having managed to keep her two young boys in school, but by September, 1878, she had had enough. On September 4, she took Simon to court, claiming he had neglected to provide, but he appears to have been found not guilty. Five days later she returned, this time accompanied by her four children and one of the young women who sewed with her. This time her claim was more specific. She accused Simon of having refused to furnish the necessary clothing and food for her and her children for over a year. Despite their separation, Angelique was struggling to support not only their four children but also her husband's octogenarian father. She had reached the end of her ability to provide. "Mother can no longer earn enough to cover her needs and feed and clothe us," explained her daughter.[28]

Such separations did not absolve men of their responsibility to provide. No viable mechanisms existed, however, to ensure that they did pay maintenance allowances, nor was there any way of making sure women received sufficient amounts to live on. Edwige Handfield had married labourer Octave Dansereau in 1865. They separated in 1876 and the judge ordered Octave to pay her $10 monthly. With six living children, it would have been impossible to get by on less than $2.50 a week had she consistently received the money, for this amount was under half a labourer's salary. Edwige could not manage. In 1879 she went to court, with her six children in tow, claiming that Octave had refused and neglected to furnish her and her children with the necessary food, clothing, and lodging. Octave, who well may not have been able to pay the money, was sentenced to three months' imprisonment with hard labour.[29]

Much more common than these formal procedures for separation were informal estrangements. Few women could afford to free themselves permanently from dependence on their husbands, whatever their character, drinking habits, or earning ability. The apparent advantages of a legal separation fade in the light of the realities of surviving unless an extremely generous allowance was awarded. As previous chapters have shown, few men's wages would have stretched sufficiently to support themselves in one establishment and their wife and perhaps children in another, even though the law only obliged them to provide according to their means.

Informal separations might occur by mutual consent of both spouses as a result of wife-beating, because a man took up with another woman, or when the man simply took off. Less frequently, husbands sought separations because they had been physically abused by their wives. Estrangements might last for days or months, or turn into life-long arrangements. When such separations worked, they are visible to us only to the extent that they appear in the numbers of married women or men living separate from their spouses in the censuses. It was when they did not work that women turned to the courts, where a man's legal responsibility to provide for his family offered some grounds for legal recourse.

In 1869 Canada's criminal legislation was revised to make wilful refusal to provide a wife with the necessary food, clothing, and lodging without lawful excuse a criminal offence. If such neglect led to bodily harm or the endangerment of life, judges could sentence a husband to up to three years' imprisonment.[30] No cases of failure to provide have been found for the period 1869 to 1873. Even in 1874 and 1875 they were relatively rare. They peak between 1876 and 1878, then apparently fall off again.[31] Overall, at least thirty-five women took their husbands to court in Montreal for "not providing" between 1873 and 1879. Cases of failure to provide, like wife-beating, appear to have increased, not so much with the acceleration of industrial transformation and urban growth in the 1860s and early 1870s, but with the impact of the Great Depression in 1874.[32] Economic depression exacerbated the problems inherent both in survival in an industrializing city and in marriages based on a division of labour by sex, which rendered working-class women largely dependent on men's wages.

Women who used the legal system to confront husbands who failed to provide were special in their decision to go to court. Their motivations ranged from desperate economic necessity rooted in the realities of daily survival and economic depression to hate, resentment, and vindictiveness. There is no way of establishing their representivity. People went to court when things were going badly; their histories therefore tend to be extreme rather than representative. Yet, in the accounts of the problems these women were facing, in the descriptions of solutions devised, and in the words and interpretations exchanged between husbands and wives in court, we see echoes of dilemmas, conflicts, and resolutions that were surely more widespread. Such cases need to be read with care, for people's words and evidence were transformed from speech to written affidavit, then filtered through the ritual of court testimony. They are important in part to nuance the image of a complementary division of labour. They also allow us to see some of the human tragedies that occurred when things went wrong.

The evidence in these affidavits and trials has to be read with extreme caution. The very nature of the charge meant that the pleas of husbands and wives follow a pattern. It was in a husband's interest to prove that he had been trying to provide, but could not. If he could also insinuate that his wife had been unfaithful or had driven him away, the chances of being found not guilty appeared greater. It was in the wife's favour to show that she was close to starving and dependent on friends or family, or that working to support her children had broken her health. Both were plausible and real situations. Children brought along for the trial were the woman's major props. Older offspring might testify against their fathers, as did neighbours, usually women, and kin.

Behind these almost scripted pleas, the trial evidence offers the historian much more. We see men and women confronting each other's failures and shortcomings and interpreting the nature of each other's work and role in the family. We see how some of the women managed, their pride and their agonies, and sometimes their independence in the face of their dependence. We enter a murky world of tense, conflictual marriages, rendered visible largely because of their failure. At the same time we see resourceful women struggling to survive and the central importance of neighbours and kin, often on the edge of poverty themselves, who stepped in and helped with food, money, and moral support.

A wife claiming that her husband had not provided for her or their children initially made an affidavit, which usually explained when they had married, how many children they had, and how long it was since her husband had provided money, food, or rent. Kin, workmates, and/or neighbours sometimes also made affidavits, describing what they knew about the defendant or the claimant's situation. A few days later the police magistrate demanded the presence of all the parties involved. The affidavits were read, and the defendant was asked if he had any questions. Thus, a triangular pattern of communication was set up in which the husband and wife confronted each other. The men, or their lawyers, posed questions trying to absolve their guilt, while the women generally answered not to the husband but to the judge or magistrate. Cases might be dismissed for insufficient evidence following this stage. Women could withdraw their claims, or some kind of settlement might be reached. Otherwise, a trial date was set.

Women framed their pleas in two ways. The majority simply professed their dependence and right to support. A significant minority stressed that they were earning what they could but still could not manage. Bridget Terrill's affidavit is typical of the former group.

> I have been lawfully married to the defendent and have lived with him as his wife for the last 29 years. On or about 25 June last past, the defendent who is legally liable as my husband and as parent to my two minor chidren, Edward Higgens ten years of age and Thomas Higgens six years of age, to provide for me necessary food, clothes and lodging did abandon me and my children and did wilfully and without lawful excuse neglect to provide the same.

The questions Higgens posed to his wife capture many of the elements common to men's defence: insinuations of immorality, inability to find work, and the attempt to prove that they had, in fact, provided according to their means.

> Q. How long am I away from that house?
> A. About six weeks. . . .
> Q. Was I your first husband?
> A. Yes.
> Q. Did I give you every cent I earned.
> A. He has never gave me one dollar since last May except one barrel of flour.
> Q. How much have I earned since May last?
> A. I do not know, as he has been working on the harbor with the exceptions of two weeks.
> Q. Had any of your daughters any bastard children?
> A. No. [33]

Other women chose to stress their own ability to earn some money, framing their claim either for the children or on the grounds that their health was breaking down because of the work involved. Emma Gold claimed that she and her children would have been in danger of starving were it not for the help of friends. Yet she would not ask for help for herself. "I want you to support your two children and I will work for myself."[34]

Some men countered their wives' claims by arguing that they had indeed paid the rent, given money, provided clothing or groceries, or simply by explaining that they could not find work. "Is it not true," labourer Edmond St. Jean demanded of his wife, "that 15 days ago Saturday I paid $4.00 for the rent, bought a dollar's worth of groceries, a pair of shoes and a pair of socks and that I paid 50 cents for milk?" Despite her agreement he was sentenced to two months' hard labour.[35] "How does your husband make a living?" Israel Beaume demanded of his wife. "He has no trade," she replied. "He works by the day. It seems to me that had he wished to work he could have given me something more to help me live." Beaume, like other defendants, tried to highlight ways in which his wife had failed to fulfil her wifely role. His case, examined in earlier chapters, rested also on the more complex claim that his wife was ruling the household, had interfered in his job-seeking attempts, and had kicked him out. Do you swear, he asked her in court, that you never told me "to get the hell out of there and that you didn't need me?" This she denied.[36]

Taking a husband to court for failure to provide was no light matter. This was a crime, punished most often by two months' hard labour in jail. There was no guarantee that the wife would receive money while her husband was in prison. Some women turned to the court the minute that a husband ceased providing enough money, evidence indeed of the need of a man's wages. Yet others appear to have gone for years, exhausting their own earning capacity and often their health, before finally demanding their right.

Only a minority of the women who pursued their husbands for some variant of unlawfully neglecting to provide were living with them at the time of the case. In most of the cases, for one reason or another, the marriage had deteriorated to the extent that the couples no longer co-habited. Three-quarters of the women pursuing their husbands lived apart from them. The amount of time they had been apart, like the causes of their separation, were varied. Only two of the couples were officially separated as to *corps et biens*. Of the nineteen couples for whom it is possible to determine residential patterns from their evidence, only five were either living together or the husband appeared to come and go from day to day, week to week or month to month. "Is the defendent living with you?" Philomene Jeannotte-Lachapelle was asked. "Not at present. He hasn't been there for three weeks. Before that we were together for a month, but before that not for 17 months."[37] In these cases, where a tenuous co-habitation was maintained, wives identified gambling or, more often, drinking as the major reason the men had not been able to provide. While the outcome of most of the cases is difficult to determine because of the state of the archives, men who drank and failed to provide for their wives do seem to have been the ones most often sentenced.

When men failed to support their wives or abandoned them, the ridiculous extent of married women's legal incapacity was exposed. In Quebec as in the common-law provinces prior to legislative changes, most such women were left to fend for themselves without the legal capacity or economic power to do so. Worse, a wife's wages were rightfully controlled by the husband except in the case of women married separate as to property. He could return and claim them, or use her earnings to pay his debts. As proletarianization accelerated in the cities, in particular, this problem began to interest male politicians. They were largely middle-class and offended, even affronted, by men who appeared to behave in an unmanly way. From the 1850s on, legislators in the colonies of British North America began to pass laws, first giving women who were deserted the legal power to control their own property and wages, then attempting to force men to do their duty.[38]

Gradually in the Canadian provinces, as in England and the United States slightly earlier, female lobbyists were able to ally with reformers to promote revisions of married women's position in the common law. Bit by bit, women outside Quebec gained the right to keep their property separate from that of their husbands, to administer and control it, and to control their own wages. The dominant motivations behind the resulting married women's property acts often had little to do with a desire for women's equality within marriage. Nonetheless, such legislation meant that outside Quebec, women who had to manage alone had the legal if not the economic means to do so by the end of the century. In Quebec, however, the courts remained the major recourse for those not married separate as to property.

While the state could and eventually did become involved in a limited way, attempting to call men to account for their failure to provide when they deserted their wives and families, no legislation sought to provide women with the economic equality in the labour market that would have allowed both widows and lone mothers to step into the wage-earning shoes of a dead or departed partner.[39] Because of women's exploitation in employment, surviving without a man and his wages posed very different challenges from surviving without a woman and her domestic labour. Each must be examined separately.

Men and the Problem of Domestic Labour

For men left alone by death, disagreement, or desertion, the major challenge was to replace the housekeeping skills of a wife. This was most easily achieved by remarriage.[40] Men who were still legally married could set up house with a mistress, the situation of at least two of the thirty-five husbands taken to court by their wives for failure to provide. A quick perusal of the court records suggests that a fair number of men went further, hoping that in the hustle, bustle, and anonymity of a large city like Montreal, they would get away with taking a second wife while their first was still alive. One bigamist, for example, remarried by representing himself as a widower. Despite the fact that his first marriage had occurred in Saint Esprit forty years earlier he was soon denounced by a merchant who knew his first wife was still living. Further depositions from a priest, who had attended the original wedding, and his new wife confirmed his crime. He pleaded guilty and was sent to jail.[41]

Men who did not remarry or move in with a new woman turned to other females to perform their domestic labour. Professional or bourgeois men solved their problems by hiring housekeepers, nannies, or domestics. Working-class widowers or married men whose wives were absent relied on older daughters, other relatives, or moved in with married sons, occasionally with married daughters, or boarded in households where responsibilities for housework were minimal. Four-fifths of the lone-male parents, widowed or not, who were living in Sainte Anne and Saint Jacques wards in 1891 and who were heading their own households had at least one daughter or other female living with them who was aged ten or older and who did not report having a job when the census was taken. Daughters, sisters, aunts, and sometimes boarders stepped into the wife's shoes, shopping, minding children, and making sure that food was on the table before and after work. Widower Denis Gaham, a street labourer, for example, had five daughters at home with him in 1891. Both twenty-one-year-old Anne and fourteen-year-old Mary Ann were apparently free to do housework as neither was enumerated as having a job. The other daughters were working as a dressmaker, a cigarmaker, and a hoop-skirt maker.[42] Robert Joseph, a fifty-year-old widower, had eight children aged seven to thirty. All reported a job except two little girls, aged seven and ten, and the oldest girl, twenty-two-year-old Euchariste.[43]

A man's ability to run a family and maintain a separate household in the absence of his wife was determined more by the presence or absence of women able to do the housework than by economic constraints. Women faced a different challenge, that of restoring the revenue deficit engendered by the absence of a man while still ensuring that domestic labour and childcare were performed.[44] How they responded to that challenge depended on a variety of factors, some of which were within their control, some of which were not. Their own age, health, and previous work experience, the age and sex of their children, and their marital status were fundamental factors influencing their ability to survive and the strategies they could pursue. Widows who had been provided for in some way might never survive easily, but their position was relatively privileged when compared with widows or deserted wives left completely without resources. Working-class women already used to stretching wages might manage better than the young widows of professionals, left suddenly and unexpectedly without resources.

Women's Survival Strategies

Survival for most working-class widows and other women managing without a husband's wages demanded fashioning a complex and ever-changing blend of strategies. Few would have sufficed on their own. Combined, these strategies offered the possibility of getting by. In the reshuffling and rebalancing of responsibilities that followed a husband's death, some women could draw on experience built up during less enduring crises. Short periods when a spouse had been ill, unemployed, or prone to drinking bouts provided a woman with an apprenticeship in developing some of the skills she would need if she was deserted or her husband died. Wives whose husbands were sick for a lengthy period prior to dying had already learned to make some money, to balance paid labour and domestic labour, and to find ways of having their children cared for. Wives of unskilled labourers, those in the most injured of trades, and others earning irregular wages had already practised a myriad of strategies to augment, complement, or replace those wages in difficult times.

Yet earning a second income and having primary responsibility to earn the needed cash were quite different, given the wages that women could make. Little in the previous work experience of the average working-class woman with several young children prepared her to be the sole supporter of a family. As long as girls were raised primarily as homemakers – the reproducers of labour power – and were seen as secondary earners in the labour market, widows and single women would experience severe difficulty supporting themselves, let alone a young family.

In the web of means that working-class women wove, seven major ways of supporting a family stand out. They merit closer attention.

Businesses, Boarding Houses, and Brothels

In working-class parts of town, some women either took over small businesses or trades from their husbands when they died, or they were able to set up some kind of stall, shop, or business with money received as an inheritance, a pension, or a death benefit. Others turned space in their homes into money-making propositions by taking in boarders, setting up small groceries, running legal saloons and taverns or illegal "sheebeens" where they sold liquor by the glass. Still others took their goods with them, passing door to door to peddle fish, apples, other fruit, and goods. Only some such enterprises were reported to the census-takers. Although widows were quite often brothel-keepers and appeared frequently in court for selling liquor illegally in groceries, their own homes, and brothels, not one widow in Sainte Anne or Saint Jacques wards officially reported that she was either a prostitute or a brothel-keeper, and only one or two each year stated that they ran a saloon or tavern.[45]

Such small businesses, some precarious, some perhaps reasonably profitable, were important among widows. In Sainte Anne ward, nearly one in every five widows who reported their employment in 1861 ran a small shop, traded, or kept boarders. Over the decades the proportion increased, but slowly and unevenly. In the earlier years the majority either turned their homes into boarding houses or moved into dwellings suitable for several boarders. In 1871 trading, with no further clarification, was the leading business occupation, while in 1891, when census-takers were requested to be more precise, keeping a grocery store had become the most common form of business reported among Sainte Anne widows. Those in Saint Jacques were most likely to take in boarders.

With minimal capital, space in houses could be used for boarders or converted into a small shop or an illegal sheebeen. Over the years, from 6 to 16 per cent of widows who listed some form of employment had transformed their dwelling into a boarding house. This strategy, however, meant that space was necessary, some investment had to be made in bedding, and help might be needed with the extra domestic labour. Lone mother Philomène Jeannotte-Lachapelle had only been able to take in boarders when her husband left her because her brother-in-law helped her financially. Her two boarders paid a total of $5.50 a week, helping toward the $9 monthly rent.[46] Sara Nicon's five-room, two-storey dwelling was close to the Grand Trunk Railway shops, an ideal location for finding boarders. She took in four unmarried railroad labourers, fitters, and brakemen in 1891. With four daughters aged fifteen to twenty to help with the necessary shopping, cooking, and cleaning, she could manage the additional domestic labour that boarders entailed fairly easily. On the other hand, she may have worried about the proximity of her teenage daughters and male boarders in a house where nine people lived in only five rooms.[47] Promiscuity was not a worry for Catherine Nagel, another widow keeping a boarding house: her problem was the domestic labour involved in looking after six labouring lodgers in addition to her two working sons. She hired a live-in nineteen-year-old domestic to help, perhaps using some of the money earned by her two sons.[48]

As grocers, saloon and tavern keepers, candy-store keepers, fruit pedlars, or fish sellers, a growing number of widows of these wards traded the daily necessities of life, avoiding isolation in their homes by daily contact and gossip with neighbours and customers in their shops or on the streets. Some continued to run enterprises previously shared with their husbands; others set themselves up following the husband's death, seeing in exchange a way of managing in widowhood.

Wives of small shopkeepers, innkeepers, or independent artisans were more likely to face widowhood with the means and the practical experience of having worked alongside their husbands. Thus when hotelkeeper Antoine Charbonneau of Montreal died in 1869, his wife Victoire Clément continued to operate his hotel. With her assets valued at $2,000 she made a good match for Montreal merchant Touissant Guilbeau, whom she married in 1871. He was quite happy to authorize her to continue as a public merchant and to provide all the money necessary to support her. Her second marriage was cut short by her own death a year later.[49] When Emilie Bélanger's husband, Jean-Baptiste, died suddenly of apoplexy, the fifty-year-old widow continued to supervise the five male workers in his tinsmith shop, paying out the $39 a month in wages to each. Similarly, David Wood's widow continued to run a sawmill on Craig Street in Saint Jacques ward for customers who furnished their own logs and boards for sawing and planing. She reported employing eight men year-round in 1871, with wages totalling $2,600 over the year. Irish widow Hennessy, who lost her husband before she reached thirty, was able to continue his trade as a milkman.[50] As artisanal production became less and less common in Montreal, inheritance of a husband's workshop appears to have diminished. Yet, as late as 1891, fifty-two-year-old widow Philomène Ouellette of Sainte Anne ward was working as a tinsmith, her twenty-one-year-old son as a commercial traveller, while her fifteen-year-old Edmond was apprenticing as a tinsmith.[51]

Among widows who were running their own businesses in Sainte Anne and Saint Jacques wards, most appear to have headed small, precarious enterprises. They might be quite poor, yet they did have a certain amount of autonomy and were not dependent on wages. In most such enterprises home and work did not need to be separate. They could watch their children and even do some forms of housekeeping while tending to business. The reshaping of their family economy would be different from that for wage-earning women. Such women were not younger or older on the average than other employed widows. Nor were they more or less likely to have young children than those earning wages or doing piecework. Rather, luck, prior experience, relative privilege before their widowhood, or extreme distaste for waged labour set them somewhat apart from other widows.

Wage Labour

Setting out alone in their own enterprises, regardless of whether prosperous or marginal, allowed a growing proportion of the widows in these two working-class wards to avoid distasteful, demeaning, or inconvenient facets of wage labour. They sought clients rather than employers, chose the competition of local marketplaces over that of the labour market, and could control their own pace of work, if not their revenues. Yet most widows, and even more of the women left alone, could not choose this option. Some form of wage-earning would be their best chance of security until or unless they had offspring of working age. In 1861, one-fifth of widows reported having some kind of occupation, and four-fifths of these probably earned a wage or payment for services. A decade later nearly one-third of Saint Jacques widows and one-fifth of those in Sainte Anne listed a job, and over three-quarters of them were in waged labour. Proportions remained fairly stable in Saint Jacques and increased only slightly in Sainte Anne over the subsequent two decades. Clearly, more women would have worked sporadically or had such irregular employment that census enumerators did not record it.

The age at which a woman lost her husband and the ages of her children largely determined her income-generating strategy. Those widowed young were most likely to have steadier work. Among older widows the proportions reporting a job dropped dramatically. Thus, in Sainte Anne in 1861, around 40 per cent of those aged twenty to thirty, compared to only 6 per cent of widows over sixty, reported having a job. For all age groups, except the very old, the prosperous early 1870s increased the chances of working, but formal work by widows remained largely the preserve of the younger women, many of whose children had not yet reached earning age.

Widows and other mothers managing alone were seeking work in a labour market overstocked with unskilled labour and were in competition with children, young women, and unskilled males. Unless they possessed a skill that was in demand, they had little option but to take the worst-paying factory jobs or to work in the casual and irregular sphere of private service, shunned by men as "women's work."

Different parts of the city had their own small, local economies and labour markets. Widows living close to bourgeois areas found domestic work more readily available. Those living in Saint Jacques, where so many girls and women sewed at home, responded to the opportunities the sewing trades offered. Around three out of every ten of the widows who reported an occupation to the census-takers in Saint Jacques ward, and at least two out of ten in Sainte Anne, worked at sewing in the clothing or shoemaking industries until the 1870s. By 1891 the proportions in Sainte Anne had fallen further (Table 6.2). The homework that predominated in the clothing trades offered widows, like married women, advantages similar to running a business. They could watch their children and alternate housework with sewing. The pay, as we have seen, was minimal. One woman might bring in $3 a week on piecework in the 1880s, approximately half a male labourer's wage. With several family members pooling the cash earned, combined with cheap housing or income from boarders, such women may have passed over the fuzzy boundary between minimal survival and destitution for varying lengths of time. Widow Adelaide Hébert, for example, had five daughters ranging from sixteen to twenty-two years old in 1871. All reported working at sewing.

Only the occupation of washerwoman or laundress compared with dressmaking as a source of employment. Women could seek washing in wealthier parts of town or from the wives of those well-paid workers who preferred not to do their own. By the 1880s some widows were finding employment in the large steam laundries, where entrepreneurs competed with widows and wives seeking such work. The manager of one Montreal steam laundry reported with pride, "I suppose there is no poorer class of help hired than I hire and I pay them good wages. I hire poor widow women when they come around . . . and I keep a doctor to help any of them when they fall sick, out of my own pocket." What he paid widows he did not say.[52]

Washing, like charring, was particularly vulnerable to seasonal and cyclical fluctuations in the economy. In the relatively good times, captured in the census of 1871, large numbers found this kind of work. That year over one-quarter of the working widows of Sainte Anne and over one-tenth of those of Saint Jacques described themselves as washerwomen or laundresses. In 1891 "washerwoman" again became the leading job category reported by Sainte Anne widows, claimed by one in five of all working widows. Any contraction in the economy, however, eliminated a large proportion of such jobs. "Biddy the washerwoman" would be among the first to feel the pinch.[53]

Washing, cleaning, cooking, and caring for others on a full-time or part-time basis involved nearly half the working widows of Sainte Anne and over a quarter of those of Saint Jacques at a time when unmarried girls were increasingly likely to choose either sewing or factory work. The particularity of this labour market offered specific and different advantages to widows depending on their age, skills, and family responsibilities. Most washerwomen and charwomen were heads of their own households. They were usually either supporting children or living with wage-earning offspring. In contrast, work as a domestic servant was more difficult to reconcile with a family, although the growing importance of day work for servants opened up the possibility of such employment to widows with children.[54] Only one-quarter of the widows who were domestics in Sainte Anne ward in 1891 headed their own households. Another quarter boarded with other families, working as general servants by the day, while at least a third lived in with their employers. Live-in employment offered some benefits to widows or married women with limited resources. Housing was provided and nourishment was ensured, though these might be enjoyed at the expense of giving up children to relatives or an orphanage. Some lived in a comfort they could never have achieved on their own. Compare, for example, the living conditions of one sixty-year-old widow, working for a grocer in his two-storey, six-room brick house with that of a fifty-six-year-old widow living at home with her twenty-five-year-old son in a two-room wooden dwelling. On the other hand, the relative lack of freedom must have irked grown women used to some degree of autonomy and independence.[55]

The expansion of industrial capitalism had little direct influence on the kinds of jobs that widows and married women on their own found for themselves. Like married women with husbands in the home, few appear to have worked in sectors of the economy where factories predominated. Some of those sewing clothing, furs, or shoes definitely worked in factories, but most did not. The rigidity and sheer length of factory hours made balancing domestic and wage labour virtually impossible for those with young families or several other workers to care for. For many of the older widows factory work was too demanding physically. By 1891 a few of Sainte Anne's younger widows were reporting employment as cigarmakers, tobacco cutters, or spinners in a woollen mill. Such jobs remained a minuscule minority in contrast to the importance of private service and the sewing trades.

The likelihood that widows would find relatively formal work fluctuated with swings in the economy, increasing somewhat in the second half of the nineteenth century. Whereas in 1861 around one in five of the widows in both Sainte Anne and Saint Jacques reported some kind of employment, by 1891 one in four in Sainte Anne and slightly more in Saint Jacques did so. Yet they remained concentrated in the lowest-paid sectors of the labour market, characterized by seasonal fluctuations, piecework, and casual employment. In 1891, as in 1861, most were sewing, washing, charring, or working as servants. For women working odd mornings or days as charwomen and washerwomen, the pittances earned clearly had to be combined with other ways of making ends meet. Women's earnings were supplemented by those of other family members and in ways less visible in the documents of the period.

Children's Wages

Around 80 per cent of the widows in these wards were living with off-spring. When they were old enough to work, their contribution to the family economy became crucial and distinguished widows' families from those with two parents. Older widows' need of their children's support was backed up by Quebec's civil law, which made children responsible for the maintenance of "their father, mother and other ascendants who are in want." This obligation extended to the sons and daughters-in-law, but ceased when the mother-in-law remarried.[56]

Rose de Lima Lavoie was the widowed mother of six children, including a boy who had been badly beaten while working at Fortier's cigarmaking factory. When asked whether she needed her son's work for her livelihood she replied simply. "When we are not rich, we need the help of our children's work. I have been a widow these four years."[57] When William Lukes and A.H. Blakeby asked "very young children" in mills and factories in 1881 why they were at work so young, answers included "having no father, had to help mother to get a living."[58] Indeed, the contribution of young children to the family economy of widows was so generally recognized at this time that even some of the reformers who were recommending stricter legislation to control the work of boys and girls suggested that exceptions be made when a widow needed a twelve-year-old to work to live.[59]

Widows and other women managing alone clearly did rely on their children's wages more than other working-class families. On the average there were almost twice as many children at work in female-headed families as in those with a father. In 1881, for example, families headed by the father averaged 0.49 children at work, compared to 0.83 in those headed by a mother. Only 26 per cent of male-headed families with children over eleven had two or more children reporting a job compared to 43 per cent of female-headed families. Reformers focused on the cases that concerned them most: children under twelve who worked. Yet the work of these young children was not particularly widespread among widows' families. Their youngsters were likely to beg, sell newspapers, shine shoes, and take part in other street trades so seldom reported to census-takers. Rather, the continued contribution of teenage and especially adult children most distinguished the family economy of mother-headed families from those with two parents. This was not simply because widows, in particular, were older. In 1881, for example, among male-headed families where the father was over sixty, 25 per cent had co-resident, working adult children compared to 45 per cent of lone mothers at that age.

Mothers who relied on their offspring's wages, support, or company were vulnerable yet powerful in their dependence. Their vulnerability became clear when illness, unemployment, or misconduct placed those wages in jeopardy. Twenty-two-year-old Robert Brownley supported his mother, "an aged woman and incapable of doing any kind of work." During the early 1870s he had worked for a dollar a day at Redpath's sugar factory on the banks of the Lachine Canal. When the depression hit in 1874 he was dismissed. Finding it impossible, like "a great number of day labourers in this city, to find permanent employment during this present winter," he started drinking. Four months later he was arrested after being found "asleep under the influence of drink" the night before he was to start work again. Friends, relatives, and fellow workers from Redpath's banded together to address a petition to Judge Ramsay, requesting clemency. In their plea they not only stressed such structural factors as the difficulty of finding work and his previous good character, but specially emphasized the fact that he was supporting his mother.[60]

Neither the solidarity and concern that these workers and friends expressed for Robert and his mother nor the framing of petitions in such a way as to underline a widow's dependence on her earning offspring was unique. Fellow workers frequently helped workmates' widows and children both individually and collectively.[61] When eighteen-year-old David James Spence, an apprentice moulder, was convicted for shooting with intent to do grievous bodily harm, twenty-six other moulders from the Rogers and King Iron Foundry who had worked with him and his dead father banded together to petition Judge Monk. Central to their claim was the fact that he was "the eldest of his widowed mother's family, whose earnings, though small were of some account in her endeavours to bring up her family respectably."[62]

Widows also used their own dependence to request clemency for earning offspring. Catherine Morgan, a carter's widow, went before Judge Coursol in September, 1873, shortly after her son Michael had been convicted of common assault. She stressed her age and that she looked "to her said son for her support and maintenance, she being very poor and destitute of means." Michael had been in the common gaol for three months prior to his trial because she could not afford bail. She had already "been reduced to extreme hardship and want being deprived of the daily gains of her said son's labour, and having to depend upon the charity of her neighbours and the casual labour that her weak and aged frame could perform for her subsistence and maintenance." The winter season was "now fast approaching," she reminded the judge, and, perhaps with a dose of exaggeration or a clear sense of reality, she suggested that she might "in the meantime for want of proper care be brought to an untimely grave."[63]

The dependence of older widows on their sons' and daughters' wages, housework, or company clearly exerted a powerful influence over the children. Widows' sons and daughters in Montreal, as elsewhere, left the family home much later than most of their peers with two parents.[64] Many married later on the average than those whose parents survived longer. In some cases they did not marry at all. Thus the lives of the children were transformed, not only by the death of their father but also by the mother's need for economic and possibly psychological support.

A strong sense of their mothers' dependence, accompanied in some cases by powerful moral pressure, effectively removed some widows' children from the marriage market. Daughters who never married in order to support their widowed mothers or to keep house for widowed fathers would eventually face old age in a potentially more difficult situation than widows – as single women with no children to help them.

Between 1861 and 1891 the amount of work available for children, adolescents, and adults alike expanded as industry developed and new work opened up for the unskilled. The relatively buoyant period that began with the American Civil War and continued with odd fluctuations until 1874 provided widows and their children with new job opportunities. The average number of workers enumerated in families headed by a woman increased from an average of under one in 1861 to over 1.6 a decade later.[65] Cyclical depressions posed major challenges. The 1881 census, taken while workers were still emerging from years of depression, debt, and unemployment, shows female-headed families with fewer workers per family but a greater proportion of children at work.

The increase in the availability of jobs for boys and girls must have helped widows keep their families together, provided a more stable basis for the family economy, and heightened the incentive to retain older children at home. It also increased the likelihood of conflict between a widow needing her child's support and that child's desire for independence. Widow Angèle Paquet was unable to control her fifteen-year-old daughter, who according to her refused to seek an honest job and lived instead on the fruits of prostitution. Angèle's solution to her struggle with her daughter was to have her committed to the reform school for two years.[66] There she might be "reformed"; she would also be fed. The difficulty of raising children alone and retaining control over them seems clear in the number of widows who took their own children to court for various offences ranging from theft to prostitution. Widow Maria Henry accused her eleven-year-old son of having stolen fifty cents from her. In her deposition she declared that he was a "first class vagrant," would not stay at home, and that "every day he calls me a bitch and a whore."[67] Rebellious, difficult children left their widowed mothers to build their own lives. Overall, however, widows succeeded in keeping a growing number of working children at home. Over this period widows' families with offspring reporting jobs increased from 24 per cent in 1861 to 43 per cent two decades later, then fell somewhat in the last decades of the century. Earlier in the century widows had tended to apprentice their children or send them to work as domestics, but from the 1860s and 1870s on they were more and more likely to keep them at home.[68]

Residential Arrangements and Informal Production or Exchange

Despite the growing importance of children's earnings and the number of widows finding work themselves, around one-third of female-headed families in both 1881 and 1891 reported no workers to the census-taker. In 1871, when the economy was stronger, one-quarter had no formally enumerated workers. Some undoubtedly lived on an inheritance, pension, or other kind of revenue generated by their husbands. Others faced extreme destitution unless they could get help from charity or neighbours and minimize costs.

Re-arranging their households enabled many such women to make or save money. Moving to cheaper premises and taking in boarders were the two most obvious ways of saving or generating revenue from housing space. Moving in with friends or relatives or boarding not only saved money, but sometimes allowed women to rely on siblings or parents for childcare or daily support. Each of these residential options offered both benefits and drawbacks that varied with a woman's age, the number, age, and sex of her children, and her personal relationships with children, relatives, or other housemates.

Maintaining autonomy by continuing to head their own families rather than moving in with others appears to have outweighed the benefits that co-residence offered for the majority of widows and for a smaller proportion of women managing without their husbands. At each census date between 60 and 70 per cent of all widows in the sample populations were enumerated as family heads. Widows living with their offspring were much more likely to head their own families than those without children or whose children had left home. In 1891, for example, around three-quarters of widows aged over sixty and living with children of any age headed their own families, compared with one-third of those not living with offspring.

Few of the widows who headed households in these wards owned their own homes. Yet owning real estate, even a small house, offered some security to those women able to purchase or inherit one. Only 14 per cent of widows on city evaluation rolls in Saint Jacques ward in 1871 owned their place of residence. They were not wealthy women. The homes of the majority were evaluated at well below the median value for the city. Among those renting, 76 per cent fell below the $55 median rental.[69] And while some widows lived in substantial houses with six or more rooms, widows were more likely to dwell in one- to three-room wooden houses than were married couples. Despite the fact that it had long been illegal to construct wooden dwellings in Montreal, nearly one-quarter of the widows heading families in the two wards sampled here lived in wooden houses in 1891, as opposed to 14 per cent of families headed by married men.

Most of those not heading their own households either lived with a married or even a widowed son who was designated as the head of the family, or they boarded. As they aged and their children left home, lone mothers were less and less likely to head a family. In 1871, the best of the census years for widows in terms of their chances of having employment or of living autonomously, 83 per cent of widows in their forties living in Sainte Anne and Saint Jacques wards were designated as family heads. Among women in their fifties only 58 per cent were, and among those sixty and over only 36 per cent were. Widows who lived with married sons were mostly in their sixties and seventies. Census-takers listed them after the son, his spouse, and his children, sometimes as boarders, sometimes as mothers, in what may well have been a literal transcription of their changed status, their dependency in the household.

In 1891, approximately one in ten widows and married women without a spouse present boarded with other families who do not appear to have been relatives. Some may have had no kin in the city, or no kin who could afford to shelter them. Others, unable to afford to rent an apartment, may have proudly preferred lodging over depending on kin. None of these widowed mothers had young children. Most were over fifty and had only one child still living with them. Married women without a husband who boarded were, in contrast, younger and did have children under fifteen. They seldom boarded in houses that offered much comfort. Living mostly with the families of labourers and carpenters resulted in crowding that was at times extreme. Widow Catherine Ducharme and her thirty-five-year-old son Pierre, a trunk-maker, were among eight boarders lodging with a labourer, his wife, and five children in a two-storey, four-room house. Alice Nugent, aged sixty, and her daughter, a tobacco worker, boarded in a three-room house with another labouring couple and their five children.[70]

While some widows turned to their children or other kin when no longer able to maintain their own households, others turned to other widows or women managing without their husbands. Co-residence offered a buffer against poverty as well as a potential support system. When Widow McGrath lost her husband, she was left with three children aged four to nine. In 1861 she took in two other widows, one of whom had an eleven-year-old child. Two of the widows worked as washerwomen, the third had a small stall at the local market. Between them they kept five pigs, probably eating some and raising cash by selling others.[71] Here was an economy of makeshifts and expediency,[72] rendered increasingly difficult for some as pig-keeping was outlawed and space for animals or gardens became less and less accessible.

Producing goods either to eat or to exchange offered widows, like married women, a way of saving or making money. Some raised potatoes, beets, carrots, or other fruits and vegetables on small city lots; some kept pigs, goats, or a cow; others purchased fruit or vegetables at the market and resold them in the neighbourhood.[73] They sent their children to scour the alleys for things to use or sell or for lumps of unburned, reusable coal in other people's discarded cinders. Their children were among those roving the streets selling newspapers, shining shoes, and scavenging to stretch money or make money from other people's discarded garbage.[74] The large number of widows' sons who appear in the registers of the reform school suggests the fine line between making an honest dollar and a dishonest one. Widows, too, broke the law to survive, stealing or turning to prostitution, sometimes alone and quite often in conjunction with their daughters.[75]

Giving Up Children

Placing children with kin or in orphanages or other institutions was another way of re-arranging the balance of consumers and earners within a family and of resolving the conflicts between parenting and paid work. A minority of lone mothers gave up their children temporarily or even permanently to relatives or to orphanages in the city. A growing array of Catholic and Protestant orphanages in the city catered to widows, widowers, and others in need of short- or long-term shelter for their offspring.[76] The Protestant Ladies Benevolent Institution's policy stipulated that true orphans and those with only one-parent were their main focus, although they also took in children who were either

abandoned by their parents or received from parents unable to care for them. Common situations included widowed or deserted mothers who were sick, often in the hospital, and parents who drank too much or had thrown the children into the street.[77]

The Saint Alexis orphanage for girls, run by the Sisters of Providence, was located in Saint Jacques ward. Families of the neighbourhood who were having problems supporting their children because of illness, unemployment, or poverty made up a growing proportion of its clientele over the decades between the 1860s and 1880s.[78] At least one-sixth of the parents placing their children there were widows. Several women's husbands died shortly after they had left their children with the nuns, suggesting that temporary shelter had initially been sought while a sick husband was being nursed or because, without his wages, they could not feed all the children. Yet most of the widows using this orphanage did not relinquish their daughters immediately after the father's death. Of the ten widows whose spouses' death dates are known, only three used the orphanage within a month of his decease, three others did so between one month and a year later, while four turned to the nuns more than a year afterwards. Thus it was not simply the loss of a husband that precipitated such an action. Rather, such women seem to have struggled to survive as best they could for some time following their husbands' deaths, until some additional crisis or the depletion of scanty resources led them to the orphanage. Perhaps like New York's widows, they disliked such institutions, avoiding them unless absolutely necessary, using them for as short a period as possible, and seeing the goal of their survival efforts as being "to keep the home together."[79]

Most widows returned for their daughters. The daughters of widows spent less time in the orphanage than did other girls. Widowers, in contrast, were less likely to return for their daughters than either widows or couples. Here is evidence both of the strong links of affection binding widows and their children and of the need of widows for the wages of their adolescent offspring. Nuns were shocked at the apparently mercenary behaviour of some parents who seemed to neglect their offspring for years, then sought them once they reached working age.[80]

The use of orphanages emphasizes the difficulties women faced when attempting to bring up children alone in nineteenth-century cities like Montreal. Widows and deserted mothers often lacked not only the financial means but also the moral authority associated in the partriarchal legal system and societal norms with a male head of the household. Controlling and supervising young or teenage offspring while working in any way to make ends meet was difficult. Unfortunately, women who were having problems are much more visible in the records than those who were not. The court cases of the period are sprinkled with the histories of widows accusing their daughters of turning to drink or prostitution and seeking asylum and reform for them in the reform school. Sons of widows formed a disproportionate number of the youngsters at the Bon Pasteur Reform School. Of those there for the second time in 1871-72, nearly 40 per cent were the sons of widows.[81] When widow Lucie Paré's fifteen-year-old son was accused of aggravated assault, she made a point of explaining that she was a widow and that her son had been deprived of "the advantage of the advice and surveillance of paternal authority." She requested explicitly that he be placed in the reform school for five years.[82]

Neighbours and Kin

Kin, neighbours, and the workmates of widows' husbands could be vital resources as women set out to restructure their family economies; their help could make the difference between comfort and poverty, or between poverty and starvation. Those living with or near parents, married sons, or daughters might turn to them for money, advice, or babysitting services. In the cases where husbands failed to provide, kin and female neighbours or friends appear to have stepped in again and again, sometimes giving economic support, sometimes the moral courage necessary to kick out a drunken, violent husband.

Most historians examining how families dealt with crises like widowhood or desertion have stressed the important role of kin but have paid less attention to neighbours. Michael Anderson argued that "many, perhaps even a majority, of people" in mid-nineteenth-century Preston, Lancashire, deliberately lived "near one or more kinsmen" because they calculated that at some point they themselves would need help. The frequency of such "critical life situations and the almost complete absence of viable alternatives to the kinship system . . . as sources of help," he argued, "made it well nigh essential for kin to keep in contact." The pragmatic economic calculations that Anderson theorized lay behind such close identification with kin are virtually impossible to verify in most of the kinds of sources available to historians of the nineteenth century.[83] Fleeting indications of the role of relatives in the cases of women whose husbands deserted them suggest compassion and caring more than cold calculation. Furthermore, evidence of the role of female neighbours, friends, and boarders, who were often only recent acquaintances, points to a level of mutual aid, solidarity, and sharing among the poorest fractions of the people that flies in the face of theories of self-interest.

When Bridget Doyle's violent carpenter husband, William Smith, left her without resources, her mother, father, and neighbours supplied the food and firewood necessary to keep her and her two young children alive. Harriette Lindley, a spinster who had only known Bridget for five months, reported that "for two days when I was in the house she and her children were living on bread and water and I gave her money and went out myself and bought provisions for her and her children." At that time there were only "two dust pans full of coal in the house, the double windows were not up at the time, from what I saw Mrs. Smith and her children were in a very miserable state."[84] Mary Barry had only known Winnifred Philbin for three or four months when she went to court to attest to Winnifred's lack of resources since her husband's departure. "Monday last I brought her over bread, and last Monday week I brought her over bread. On Saturday week she had but two spoonfuls of flour and some potatoes." Mary had lent her money "three or four times and I gave her two dollars and fifty cents on Saturday last."[85]

Poverty and Charity

Ingenuity and resourcefulness, even good luck and caring relatives and friends, were not sufficient to keep all widows and lone mothers out of poverty. Some women had none of these resources. At times, charity was the only possible recourse. It was still no guarantee against poverty. Widows were among the major recipients of most of the forms of aid offered to the poor.[86] Indeed, the plight of such poor women had been the impetus behind the founding of several of Montreal's major charitable institutions.[87] Respectable widows were a favoured category for alms givers, appealing because their poverty was quite clearly not their fault, unless they drank or indulged in vulgar behaviour.

Charitable aid took many forms in nineteenth-century Montreal. Visitors for the Saint Vincent de Paul Society, the Sisters of Providence, the Grey Nuns, and a wide array of Protestant charitable groups went into thousands of widows' and other sick and poor families' homes annually. They offered stoves, firewood, clothing, food, and Christmas dinners when those visited proved "respectable" and "deserving."[88] In their work they confronted the worst cases of poverty. A visiting Sister of Providence had tried to help

> a poor woman, a widow, and mother of seven children whose brain had been affected by fever and who was in the direst of poverty. The oldest of her offspring begged for bread from door to door, arriving home utterly frozen with cold.

She had seen nothing more miserable, she added, than this poor home, without furniture and often without heat even in the depths of winter.[89]

A visitor for the Saint Vincent de Paul Society reported finding a mother and her three little children huddled together in a room darkened by frost and snow "an inch thick on the cracked window pane."

The only furniture in their two dirty rooms was a decaying straw mattress. The hungry children had been given breakfast by a kindly neighbour.[90] Such descriptions abound in charity reports, in part because they elicited the public sympathy necessary to encourage donations, in part because of the real impression such cases made on the home visitors.

Going hungry and even starving were realities in nineteenth-century Montreal, although their extent cannot be gauged with any accuracy. Clergymen, priests, charity workers, nuns, and doctors alike reported on cases of extreme deprivation. "Physicians assure us," noted the annual report of the Diet Dispensary run by the YWCA, that "they visit, *constantly,* cases where the want is not of medicine, but of nourishment."[91] Extreme poverty was most likely in families where a male head was sick or unemployed or in female-headed homes.

Those able to leave their homes could go to the soup kitchens for food and to dispensaries for free medicine, or they could send their children. Healthier widows received work, invariably sewing, from several city charities. The Montreal Protestant House of Industry and Refuge, for example, reported in the mid-1870s that it gave out sewing to eighty or ninety women a week, largely "widows with families," who made flour sacks and shirts for wholesale houses in the city.[92] Whether these women considered themselves workers or recipients of charity is unclear.

While most of the old and the sick remained in their homes, alone or with kin, some found refuge in institutions created specifically for homeless, aged, and friendless women. The Grey Nuns took sick and elderly widows and widowers into their General Hospital, the Hospice Saint Charles, and Sainte Bridget's Refuge. The Sisters of Providence cared for many elderly widows and unmarried women in their *asile* in Saint Jacques ward. Poor Protestant women had been able to turn to the Ladies Benevolent Society since the 1830s. By the 1870s they could turn to the Protestant Home of Industry and Refuge or the Home for Friendless Women. "Widows who have sold all they possessed to support the dying husband and father and helpless little ones" were among the major clients of the latter institution.[93] As widows aged, infirmity, poverty, or a need for sustained care led a growing proportion to seek shelter in such institutions. Relatively permanent institutionalization, however, was probably a last resort, possible only for the poorest or those who could pay for care. Elderly widows more often aged and died living with kin or as boarders in other people's homes than in an institution.[94]

For working-class women, desertion and death alike highlighted the dangers of dependence on a male breadwinner and the fragility of family economies based on a sexual division of labour. Some previously middle-class women experienced a precipitous descent to below the lowest fractions of the working classes. For men and women alike, loss of a spouse demanded a re-adjustment of roles for those who remained in a labour market and society that did not reward the sexes equally for their labour. That re-adjustment was, as a result, different for men and women.

Widowers were much more likely to remarry than widows. Those who deserted their wives often set up house with new women or depended on daughters to do their housework. Their own work was not altered dramatically, although that of their daughters' might well be. In contrast, women whose husbands deserted them or died, leaving them without independent means, faced a new work world. They had to reconstruct their family economies. Some intensified practices already used to stretch wages, like taking in sewing, boarders, or keeping pigs or cows. This might be combined with seeking casual jobs or formal employment for the first time. Combining or alternating such strategies appears to have allowed many lone mothers to maintain some level of autonomy, to use charity when needed, but to avoid total dependence. The ingenuity and flexibility of such women contradict the image of the poor helpless widow or the deserted wife portrayed in the literature of those who helped them. Yet few can have lived far from destitution, and their margins of manoeuvre were too often minimal. A change in the economic climate, the departure of an earning child, or illness could suddenly unravel the web of survival, leaving a woman dependent on friends, kin, and charity or in sheer destitution. The working-class widow, once perhaps the "thrifty, economical and thorough good housekeeper who" could "lay out to advantage [a] fair day's wage," idealized by the nineteenth-century Montreal worker,[95] quoted in the previous chapter, stands as a symbol both of the dangers of wage dependence in the absence of any social security and of the oppressive weight and consequences of a division of labour based on sex.

Conclusion

Working-class families in nineteenth-century Montreal were working families. The labour of husbands, wives, and sons and daughters largely determined their standard of living. The work that each member performed, however, was different. So, too, was the impact of the changes caused or precipitated by the development of industrial capitalism in the years between 1860 and the 1890s. To answer the question "What was the impact of industrialization on the family?" involves a much more careful consideration of the different effect of economic change on men, women, and children than sociologists and many historians have given. It involves integrating gender into our understanding of the family and of the economy. And it requires jettisoning the desire to determine whether the family was a dependent or independent variable in this process, an active agent or a passive victim.

The family, or better, families, are complex, contradictory, and ultimately flexible institutions. The families of the working class and their individual members were neither helpless victims totally subjected to inexorable economic transformations, nor were they usually in total control of the direction of their lives. Old traditions and cultural norms were used, reshaped, and transformed, at times strengthened, at other times modified to respond to the contingencies of the present so that new customs and traditions were forged. At any one point in time the amount of leeway, or the margin of manoeuvre, that a particular family had was influenced by a combination of internal and external factors. Family members could control some of these. Others they could not. Internally, the evolution of the family life cycle, the age and sex of family members, and their particular personal or work skills all influenced the degree of control, the standard of living, and the family's interaction with the wider economy. External factors – the structure of local industry, the economic conjuncture, and the sanitary state of the neighbourhood – framed limits to the control they could exercise.

The possibilities opened up by the growth of industry and the new dependencies that were forged, as well as the links to the changing labour markets of the city and the wider economy, were not the same for men as for women, and they varied for different fractions of the emerging working class. The irregular demise of artisanal production, the division and re-division of labour within workshops and factories, and above all the growing dominance of wage labour altered much more than the kinds of work available in the city. Economic change restructured the choices available to people, changed the relationships among individuals, families, and the wider economy, and eventually reshaped the daily rhythms and the material basis of survival for the ordinary people of the city.

How the process of industrialization and the growing dependence on wage labour changed the daily life and the bases of survival for the families that made up Montreal's expanding working class is the major question this book sought to answer. Eight major conclusions can be offered.

(1) Wages became the necessary though seldom sufficient basis for survival for the majority of the urban population. Differential earning power cut up the working class into separate fractions. At the most general level, differences of as little as twenty-five cents a day separated men in skilled trades, those in trades undergoing rapid transformation, and the unskilled. Each fraction was potentially capable of achieving a different standard of living in good times. Each was vulnerable in different ways to the impact of winter, cyclic depressions, and job restructuring. Wage disparities translated into observable differences in standards of living and survival strategies. The unskilled were much more likely to live in apartments of only two or three rooms than the skilled at all stages of the family life cycle. Wives and young children were most likely to work for pay in families headed by labourers, shoemakers, or men in the highly seasonal construction trades.

In addition, poverty and the need for additional wage-earners influenced the education that parents provided for the next generation. In 1891 all non-working-class children aged twelve to thirteen in the sample populations of Sainte Anne and Saint Jacques ward could read, as could 94 per cent of the offspring of the skilled. In contrast, only 75 per cent of the sons of unskilled workers and 88 per cent of the daughters could both read and write. A further 13 per cent of boys could read but not write.

Yet this apparently neat distinction beween fractions of the working class did not translate automatically into different standards of living.

The number of children a couple had, illness, unemployment, drinking problems, the age and sex of the children, and the ability of housewives to stretch and supplement wages were equally important in determining real standards of living.

(2) Had all but the most skilled and steadily employed members of Montreal's working class lived on a family head's wages alone, poverty, even starvation, would have been chronic. Men would not have arrived at work with the strength to labour for ten to eleven hours. Women would not have been sufficiently nourished to produce babies that could survive. The working class would not have reproduced itself. Working-class survival and reproduction can only be understood if the work of all family members, male and female, waged and unwaged, is considered. Families subsisted because men's wages were supplemented by those of other family members and because wives stretched wages by careful shopping and housekeeping and helped devise various other survival strategies. When historians base their analyses of nineteenth-century standards of living only on male wages, they fail to grasp the mixture of means behind daily survival.

(3) Most, though never all, members of society lived in families. The third major argument of the book is that people's roles in the family and their marital status, age, and sex continued to be crucial in determining the rhythms of their daily lives, the unfolding of life courses, and their relationship to the wider economy.

As growing proportions of the population came to depend largely on wages, people's ties to the city and the wider economy were rewoven. However, the growth of industry did not change the broad outlines of the way in which different tasks had been attributed according to gender in pre-industrial and agricultural families. Capitalist industry did not draw all workers regardless of age and sex into workshops and factories, as Karl Marx predicted.[1] Specific industries and sectors did draw very differently on men, women, and children, forging distinctive local labour markets within the larger city. This made a difference in the proportion of sons or daughters that found work. Montreal's diversified industrial structure offered a wide variety of jobs to men and a limited number to women. In this it was very different from single-industry towns, and especially from the textile towns that offered greater work opportunities to girls and even married women than elsewhere. The disproportionate attention that sociologists and historians have paid to such towns has probably led to an exaggeration of the changes that industrialization wrought, especially on women's work, and to a minimization of the differences between the experiences of sons and daughters.[2] Despite the significance of industries employing predominantly women and children in Montreal's economy, the course of children's work lives was framed by gender. Between the

1860s and early 1890s growing proportions of girls and young women did work for money at some point prior to marriage. More did so in parts of town like Saint Jacques, where sewing, chiefly at home, was so important. Yet, their labour force participation rates were never as high as those of their brothers.

The industrial revolution certainly did not liberate women. The growth of industry and the related expansion of wage labour offered the potential of independence, of an alternative to marriage for women. This potential was not realized in part because legal structures and strictures continued to limit women's rights, but more importantly because almost no jobs offered wages to women that would have allowed them to support themselves.

(4) Another major characteristic of Montreal working-class families in these years was the growing importance of wage-earning off-spring and the increasing likelihood that sons and daughters in their teens and twenties would remain living at home. Between 1861 and 1881 the average number of children living with their parents and reporting a job among those families that had children over the age of eleven more than doubled. The average number of workers in families increased proportionately, from 1.33 to 1.55. In families where at least half the children were over the age of fifteen the average number listing a job more than doubled between 1861 and 1871.

The growth of industry created the possibility of jobs for children of all ages. Youngsters under the age of eleven or twelve did work in Montreal's factories and commercial establishments, both before and after the passage of legislation in 1885 aimed at controlling child labour. Yet their numbers never rivalled those found in the textile towns of England and New England. Much more important for working-class families were the wages of children, particularly sons, in their later teens and early twenties. After years of managing largely on one wage and on whatever other ways wives could find to save, stretch, or make money, the wages of one or more children offered the possibility of a major improvement in a family's standard of living. Herein lay major benefits and potential tensions, for a wage rewarded an individual's labour. Conflict could arise only too easily over whether the wage would be handed over, or how much, or whether a child should leave home. The patterns of residence of the youths and young adults in these wards suggest that during the early period of industrial capitalism, parents generally succeeded in keeping growing numbers of their off-spring at home. Loyalty, low wages, and the lack of alternatives kept the majority of daughters and a large proportion of sons with their parents until they married.

By 1891, however, the pattern had begun to shift. More male youths in their twenties were boarding than during the two previous decades, and average numbers of family workers and of children at work had declined slightly. Minor improvements in the economy and wage rates apparently combined with capitalists' needs for a different kind of labour force and new factory legislation to provoke change in the family wage economy. The proportion of families sending children under fifteen out to work fell significantly between 1881 and 1891 among all fractions of the working class. The average number of workers declined. Here was perhaps an initial modification, a first step in a long, uneven process whereby cohorts of parents over the following half-century called less and less upon their children to contribute full-time wage labour to the family wage economy, while still expecting them to perform other tasks and jobs.[3]

(5) Still another argument of the present study concerns the centrality of the work married women performed outside the formal economy. In the mid-twentieth century, wives replaced children as the most important second wage-earners in many families. In the nineteenth century, however, most married women in Montreal and other Canadian cities did not work outside the home for long periods or at jobs that involved them from dawn to dusk. Compared to today, transforming the wages of others into sustenance and shelter was time-consuming and physically demanding. This work started before the wage-earners left in the morning and continued until well after they returned at night. Daily shopping, washing, mending, cleaning, and cooking were only part of a wife's task. The lower the wages earned by other family members and the larger the family, the harder wives had to work to find ways to stretch, supplement, even replace them. Some women kept pigs, cows, other food animals, or poultry. Cows were more common in the better-off fractions of the working class and among non-working-class families because of the costs of sheltering and feeding them. The wives of the unskilled were more likely to keep pigs or poultry. Produce from gardens could be used to supplement purchased food, perhaps even to sell.

However, new municipal restrictions and the growing density of housing minimized the possibility of these strategies within the inner-city core by the 1880s. Those wanting to keep animals or have large gardens moved to newer working-class areas outside the city limits where there was still space and where regulations against keeping animals were not passed until later. Taking in boarders and sharing space with other families were other ways of generating or saving money. The former meant more work for a wife, and possibly an outlay on bedding and food that was beyond the means of the poorest families. The latter meant sharing her major work space with other women. At times such women may have co-operated, sharing cooking and other household tasks. At other times, no doubt, friction resulted from competing needs for space and different habits.

Working-class wives' primary responsibility for reproduction and consumption framed their interaction with the labour market and the wider economy, distinguishing it from that of their husbands, sons, and daughters, carving out particular pockets of the economy and the labour market within which those women who earned wages would work. Both in their daily lives in the home and in the wage labour that some performed before or after marriage, continuities appear to have been greater in the lives of working-class women than in those of their men.

(6) When Montreal's budding industrial capitalists introduced new machinery and new sources of power and restructured the division of labour in their factories, they dramatically altered many of the workplaces of the city. Work and levels of comfort changed in many households, too, as some of Montreal's wealthier families installed hot and cold running water, steam heating, new and fancy stoves, and even electricity. In contrast, only minor changes were made during this period in working-class wives' major workplace, the home. Their houses usually had only one cold water tap. Women had to carry water to the stove for heating and from the tap or stove to fill up baths or washtubs. Fuel for the stove often had to be carted up stairs. And the black soot that stove-cooking and oil lamps produced made cleaning a formidable task. Few working-class homes had baths or indoor toilets. Furnishings were minimal except in the homes of the most skilled workers. And diseases spread only too easily in these homes, with their old and rotten drains, outdoor privies, and minimal sewage facilities, making many homes lethal environments for babies and equally if not more hazardous to women's health than industrial workplaces. Because of the prevalence of disease, the frequency of pregnancies, the large spread in the ages of children, and the heavy nature of housework, most wives needed some help. It made sense to pull their daughters out of school or a job to help at home, initiating divergent work apprenticeships among their sons and daughters. Daughters moved between wage labour and helping with domestic tasks at home, while some never worked outside the home.

During the 1970s and 1980s feminists had to insist that women's domestic labour in the home was work. Over the late nineteenth and twentieth centuries, the separation of home and work, which accompanied the growth of production in factories, made such work less visible, hiding it in the household. First running water and electricity, and then a series of household appliances or "labour-saving devices" made housework lighter. Women produced fewer and fewer commodities either for use or sale. "Work" became equated with remuneration. This devaluation of housework was not yet widespread among Montreal's nineteenth-century working class. Most men and some sons and daughters were certainly absent from their homes for all the daytime hours. But in a situation where there were few cheap alternatives to the meals, clothing, and lodging that women provided, men appear to have acknowledged a wife and mother's work. And, they depended on it, as the much higher rates of remarriage among widowers than widows suggests. A healthy, hard-working wife was indeed essential to working-class survival.

(7) The complementarity of the roles of husbands and wives, sons and daughters, should not blind us to their inequality. Power and rights were not evenly distributed within any families at this time. In working-class families wage dependency locked wives and children to husbands and fathers in a relationship that was at once mutual and complementary, yet hierarchical and dependent. Women were legally incapacitated upon marriage. This meant that most had no right to administer property or even their own wages. Nor could they usually appear in court without the husband's permission. The Civil Code proscribed the wife's submission to her husband, the obligation to live where he wished, and marital fidelity. Husbands were to provide according to their means. Their infidelity was sanctioned as long as a mistress was not brought into the family home. Married women's legal incapacities were reinforced by their unequal earning power in the marketplace and their circumscribed role in the wider economy.

There is little evidence in late nineteenth-century working-class Montreal of the "declining inequality of the sexes" that Ward sees in courtship patterns. Inequalities were recast, not eliminated.[4] By leaving his story at the moment of marriage, Ward does not begin to address the realities of married life for the working class or any other group. For most working-class women with no interest in life in a religious order, marriage remained their best survival strategy. A spouse who was a good provider with a reasonably steady job, who handed over most of his money and did not spend it on drink or gambling, was a better long-term prospect than remaining with aging parents. There clearly were emotional, sexual, and material advantages to marriage over celibacy. Romance may have sparked the relationship for many working-class couples and love and moments of shared laughter no doubt kept many going through difficult times. Tasks were in many ways complementary. But these factors did not render marriage easy, equal, or without tensions and inequalities.

(8) Finally, the nature of women's inequality and dependence was exposed when a husband failed to provide, deserted his family, or died.

The reality of a man's dependence on the domestic labour and child-rearing performed by his wife was rendered equally clear if his wife left or died. A man managed if he had a daughter old enough to perform these tasks. Otherwise he was most likely to solve his problems by remarrying, moving in with another woman, or sometimes moving back to his mother. Widows, in contrast, were much less likely to remarry. Deserted wives and widows with young children struggled to earn enough to survive, drawing on stopgap earning methods that were seldom sufficient on their own. They sought work in the most shaky of labour markets, in private domestic work, and in jobs like washing, sewing, and charring that allowed them to combine work and child-care. Those with older children relied on them for support much more so than did male-headed families. Others turned to neighbours, relatives, and charity. When this did not work, some placed their children temporarily in orphanages. A few gave up and deserted them.

The picture seems grim. It is not uniformly so. Illness, unemployment, desertion, and the death of parents or a spouse undeniably produced their victims in this period of industrial development. Poverty charac-terized the lives of a large but fluctuating proportion of the city's popu-lation during the second half of the nineteenth century, as indeed it would throughout the twentieth century. But poverty and misery did not dominate the lives of all members of the working classes all the time. The history of these families during this period when industrial capitalists reshaped the city is one of struggle and success as much as of poverty and failure. It is one of social networks built up within the wider family, in the neighbourhood as well as in the workplace, and used for recreation and fun as well as for struggle and survival. At times echoes of their laughter have reverberated into the sources historians use. Struggles were most visible when men and women workers went on strike. Other types of struggles took place daily as husbands, wives, and children, sometimes in co-operation, sometimes despite each other, sought out ways to survive and to improve their lives.

Despite the low wages that both commercial and industrial capital-ists paid, despite the high cost of much of the terrible housing that land-lords offered, and despite the unhealthy infrastructure that the city pro-vided, most working-class families survived. They did so because fam-ily members pooled their earnings and ingeniously devised other ways of saving money, generating money, and making ends meet.

The families in these two working-class wards of Montreal experi-enced many changes that were similar to those faced by families in other industrializing cities. Their reactions often paralleled those uncovered by historians studying other cities in Canada, in the United

States, and in parts of Western Europe. Some trends appear to have transcended rural and urban distinctions, even local economic differences and national boundaries, giving us a better idea of large-scale trends and transformations. Others are specific to particular cities and regions. Montreal women who bore fewer children over this period were acting like women in most other Western cities and countries. The proportions and ages of children involved in wage labour varied dramatically in different cities, depending on local customs and the characteristics of the industrial structures created. Yet the growing involvement of children and youths in wage labour was a phenomenon that characterized the early phase of the expansion of industrial capitalism in most Western cities. So, too, did the fact that children were increasingly likely to remain at home with their parents, contributing their earnings to the family wage economy.[5] Sharing housing space to save on rental costs was a common working-class strategy found on both sides of the Atlantic.[6] And families in both rural and urban areas appear, like Montrealers, to have increasingly divested their living space of boarders in roughly the same period.[7]

The similarities of the broad trends occurring in diverse places suggest inevitable patterns and predetermined paths. Yet cities were different and people of diverse cultural traditions made up their populations. Each individual and every family responded to a specific set of historical options, to a particular economic structure. In so doing they drew upon different norms and resources. Montreal's ethnic make-up, its particular industrial structure, and its low wages made it special.

The increase in employment opportunities in Montreal convinced growing numbers of individuals and families from rural Quebec and from Ireland, England, and Scotland to remain and work within the city. French Canadians and the Irish constituted the majority of the working class, as in a growing number of New England towns. In Montreal, however, French Canadians predominated. Divided by language more often than by religion and concentrated in somewhat different sectors of the economy, these groups shared the realities of life on wages. Over this period, their shared class position appears to have become more important in determining much familial behaviour, apparently lessening the influence of norms and traditions drawn from their culture or religion. In 1861 different patterns of marriage, family size, allocation of labour, and residence distinguished French-Canadian Catholics, Irish Catholics, and Anglophone Protestants. French-Canadian males in 1861 married younger than the Irish, who married earlier than most English and Scots. By 1881, after years of depression, all ethnic groups married at roughly the same average age.

Differences among fractions of the working class increased over the period as the effects of economic booms, depressions, and work restructuring combined to alter the age at which most men married. In 1861 French-Canadian women aged 40-44 were more likely to have six or more children living with them than other groups. By 1891 there was little difference between ethnic/religious groups. Similarly, in 1861 French-Canadian working-class families averaged significantly more workers than other groups. Wives and daughters were more likely to work than among those of other origins. By 1881, however, ethnic differences were small. And, in 1861, French-Canadian families had been more likely to take in boarders. Again, differences decreased over the period. This apparent shift in the relative significance of ethnicity and class was not limited to Montreal. Michael Katz and Ian Davey have noted a similar pattern in Hamilton, Ontario. They suggest that during early industrialization "the independent influence of ethnicity had become muted."[8] Obviously differences remained, but increasingly people were modifying old traditions and responding pragmatically to the new realities within which they worked and lived.

Among those realities were the low and intermittent wages that capitalists in many of Montreal's leading industries paid to their workers, the impact of seasonal and cyclical unemployment, and the overstocked labour market. Low wages were not limited to Montreal. Nor were wages in all sectors lower than in other Canadian or American towns. But the wages were significantly low in several key sectors and this combined with Montreal's location at the centre of migration paths from rural Quebec and Europe to create a labour market characterized by heavy competition, especially for unskilled jobs. The wages of sons and daughters and the many ways in which women worked to make ends meet allowed families to survive. However, by allowing employers to continue to pay starvation wages, they perpetuated both the exploitation of workers and the economic structure on which it was based.

Over the twentieth century, workers and reformers have forced the state to assume greater control over the safety of the workplace, housing conditions, education, and social security. Women have fought to eliminate the discrimination and inequality that oppressed them. They face new possibilities, new choices. The hard edges of gender-based role definitions have been softened, but the inequalities remain. Gradually, the contours of the family economy have changed, reshaped in the interaction among the changing needs of a more complex capitalism, the policies of an increasingly interventionist state, and the reformulation of people's beliefs and desires. The lines between childhood and adulthood and the timing of transitions into and out of school have hardened. Wives and mothers have replaced children as the most usual second wage-earners in families, although recently the number of earning youths has again started to rise. Women's domestic labour in the home is lighter, if not shorter, as a result of hot and cold running water, electricity, and a gamut of "labour-saving devices." Single and divorced mothers have replaced widows as the most usual heads of lone-parent families. They, like their nineteenth-century counterparts, continue to be among the poorest citizens, despite (and increasingly because of) the policies of the welfare state.

The sanitized environment of parts of late twentieth-century Montreal, with its skyscrapers, freeways, cars, shopping malls, and tall apartment towers, would seem strange to the men, women, and children who worked there a hundred years ago. So, too, would the consumption of goods and services that fuels much of the economy. Yet they would recognize traces of their city, not only in the houses and old factories that remain but also in the unemployment and poverty that continue to characterize much working-class life. A hundred years later Montreal still has one of the highest rates of unemployment and poverty in the country. The inequalities of class and gender so apparent in the early period of industrial capitalism have not disappeared. They still need to be changed.

Tables

Table 1.1
Sex and Jobs: Men and Women in Selected Leading Occupations,
Sainte Anne and Saint Jacques, 1861-91

Occupations	Sainte Anne				Saint Jacques			
	1861	1871	1881	1891	1861	1871	1881	1891
Women								
Sewing trades	32%	36%	34%	21%	51%	59%	50%	21%
Domestic service	35	9	12	7	25	18	11	32
Labourer	3	4	12	1	4	1	25	2
Cigar, tobacco	–	4	4	15	4	1	–	3
Trader	4	2	2	–	–	1	1	1
Washerwoman	4	1	7	4	–	3	1	4
Charwoman	–	–	–	–	–	3	1	4
% of women in these jobs	78	56	71	48	84	85	89	67
Total reporting jobs	71	114	99	111	92	123	247	179
Number of job titles in sample	18	38	33	46	15	19	24	33

Table 1.1 continued

Occupations	Sainte Anne				Saint Jacques			
	1861	1871	1881	1891	1861	1871	1881	1891
Men								
Labourer	28%	28%	29%	21%	14%	14%	15%	10%
Carter	7	4	10	7	11	5	4	4
Carpenter/joiner	8	6	3	4	10	3	7	10
Clerk	6	4	6	6	7	9	8	8
Trader/merchant	3	3	2	2	7	7	4	4
Shoemaker	3	3	2	1	10	8	10	6
Blacksmith	3	3	3	1	1	1	2	1
Machinist	2	2	3	2	–	–	1	1
% of men in these jobs	60	53	58	44	60	47	51	44
Total reporting jobs	436	521	568	563	287	442	653	593
Number of job titles in sample	53	122	110	140	34	92	108	139

SOURCE: Random samples, Sainte Anne and Saint Jacques, 1861-91.

Table 1.2
The Class Position of Male Family Heads,
Sainte Anne and Saint Jacques, 1861-91

	Sainte Anne				Saint Jacques			
	1861	1871	1881	1891	1861	1871	1881	1891
Non-working-class	19%	22%	21%	25%	26%	35%	34%	39%
Skilled	34	31	28	31	32	29	32	33
Injured trades*	5	7	5	4	7	13	12	13
Semi-skilled/carter, etc.	8	8	11	13	17	6	6	8
Unskilled	35	32	35	27	17	17	16	7
Number of male family heads								
Reporting an occupation	291	344	364	326	190	313	449	425
Not reporting an occupation	4	10	16	8	13	8	23	20
Total	295	354	380	334	203	321	472	445

* Injured trades were those undergoing rapid transformation.
NOTE: Percentages do not always total 100 because of rounding.
SOURCE: Random samples, Sainte Anne and Saint Jacques, 1861-91.

Table 2.1
**Proportions of Men Married at Different Ages
for Selected Class Positions, 1861-91,
Sainte Anne and Saint Jacques Wards Combined**

	1861	*1871*	*1881*	*1891*
Non-working-class				
15-19	4%	0%	0%	3%
20-24	4	28	25	28
25-29	56	47	64	63
30-34	86	90	80	77
35-39	93	90	92	85
Mean age at marriage	28.9	27.8	26.3	26.9
Number of men aged				
15-54 in sample	148	234	300	323
Skilled Workers				
15-19	0%	2%	0%	3%
20-24	28	42	28	32
25-29	62	71	52	61
30-34	78	83	85	90
35-39	90	97	95	90
Mean age at marriage	25.3	24	27.6	24.9
Number of men aged				
15-54 in sample	225	270	357	349

[Table 2.1 continues]

Table 2.1 continued

	1861	1871	1881	1891
Injured trades				
15-19	15%	17%	9%	0%
20-24	27	67	15	40
25-29	67	89	85	57
30-34	100	73	87	90
35-39	100	80	100	100
Mean age at marriage	24.5	23.7	25.8	25.6
Number of men aged 15-54 in sample	50	77	91	56
Unskilled				
15-19	0%	4%	6%	4%
20-24	40	22	24	14
25-29	82	57	70	67
30-34	96	85	78	79
35-39	96	88	96	91
Mean age at marriage	25	27.7	25	26.8
Number of men aged 15-54 in sample	143	186	253	196
Mean age at marriage, all groups:				
Men	26.5	26.5	26.5	26.2
Women	24.2	22.3	25.5	23.9

SOURCE: Random samples, Sainte Anne and Saint Jacques wards combined, 1861-91.

Table 2.2
Children under Five per Thousand Married Women aged 20-49

	1861 Child/woman Ratio	No.	1871 Child/woman Ratio	No.	1881 Child/woman Ratio	No.	1891 Child/woman Ratio	No.	1861-1891 Decline
Religion/Origins									
French-Canadian Catholics	1,040	175	1,030	298	1,030	424	850	351	190
Irish Catholics	1,040	109	1,070	102	990	120	1,000	84	40
English, Irish, and Scottish Protestants	1,280	85	980	104	1,110	94	620	85	660
Wards									
Sainte Anne	1,150	225	1,030	259	1,090	278	860	216	230
Saint Jacques	1,020	145	1,030	237	980	361	820	304	200
Overall	1,100	391	1,030	496	1,030	639	840	520	260

SOURCE: Random samples, Sainte Anne and Saint Jacques, married women only, excluding widows.

Table 2.3
Proportion of Mothers aged 40-44
Who Had Six or More Children at Home,
Sainte Anne and Saint Jacques Wards Combined, 1861-91

	1861	*1871*	*1881*	*1891*
All females	22%	28%	22%	20%
French-Canadian Catholics	27	28	20	21
Irish Catholics	17	26	22	18
English, Irish, and Scottish Protestants	23	28	28	21

SOURCE: Random samples, Sainte Anne and Saint Jacques, ever-married women.

Table 3.1
Male Family Heads in the Leading Working-class Jobs in Sainte Anne and Saint Jacques Wards, 1861-91

	Saint Anne				Saint Jacques			
	1861	1871	1881	1891	1861	1871	1881	1891
Skilled trades	34%	30%	27%	28%	30%	28%	30%	30%
Metal work	9	8	9	9	2	2	2	3
Construction	11	7	5	7	14	16	13	13
Injured trades	5	7	4	3	7	13	11	7
Shoemakers	3	3	2	2	7	10	10	5
Unskilled	34	31	33	24	16	17	15	11
Labourers	33	28	29	21	16	16	14	11
No. of male family heads in these jobs	295	354	380	327	203	321	472	441
% of sample	56%	47%	51%	38%	38%	43%	30%	31%

SOURCE: Random samples, Sainte Anne and Saint Jacques, 1861-91.

Table 3.2

Estimated Income Required To Feed Families on Rowntree's Diet at Different Life-cycle Stages, 1882

		Labourer	Shoemaker	Carpenter	Blacksmith	Saddler
Estimated annual wage for 40 weeks' work		$240	$300	$360	$420	$480
Daily rate		$1.00	$1.25	$1.50	$1.75	$2.00
Family size and children's ages	Estimated annual food costs	Percentage of Income Required for Food				
I Parents; one child under 1 year old	$100.88	42%	34%	28%	24%	21%
II Parents; boys 4, 1; girl, 2	$132.08	55	44	37	31	28
III Parents; boy 16; girls 14, 8	$182.52	76	60	50	43	38
IV Parents; boys 18, 13; girl, 17	$194.48	80	65	54	46	40
V Parents; boys 19, 15; girls 16, 11, 9	$258.44	107	86	72	61	54
VI Parents; boys 21, 19, 17, 16; girl, 16	$297.96	124	99	83	71	61

SOURCES: The calculation of food costs follows the minimum diet set out by B. Rowntree, *Poverty: A Study of Town Life* (London, 1902), but is modified following John Foster, *Class Struggle and the Industrial Revolution: Early Industrial Capitalism in Three English Towns* (London, 1974), pp. 255-56, to include some meat rather than cheese. Prices are those reported by the Montreal immigration agent in 1882. The proportional weightings for males and females of different ages were developed by A. Bowley, *Livelihood and Poverty* (London, 1915), and are also used by Foster. They are as follows:

Weighting		Cost per week in 1882	Weighting		Cost per week in 1882
100	for a man over 18	91 cents	.50	for a child 5 to 13	46 cents
.85	for a boy over 14	77 cents	.33	for a child under 5	30 cents
.80	for a woman over 16	73 cents	.60	for all over 60	42 cents
.70	for a girl 14 to 15	63 cents			

Table 3.3
Average Number of Family Workers and Co-resident Children at Work: Increases and Decreases by Class Position

	1861	1871	+/-	1881	+/-	1891	+/-
Average number of workers							
Non-working-class	1.47	1.41	- 4%	1.42	+ 1%	1.24	-12%
Skilled	1.27	1.50	+18%	1.68	+12%	1.37	-18%
Injured trades	1.09	1.38	+26%	1.56	+13%	1.75	+12%
Unskilled	1.40	1.72	+23%	1.56	- 9%	1.52	- 2%
Number of families	400	628		767		695	
Overall average	1.33	1.54	+16%	1.54	+ 0%	1.41	- 8%
Average number of children at work in families headed by married males who had children 11 or over							
Non-working-class	0.61	0.84	+38%	0.84	+ 0%	0.70	-17%
Skilled	0.50	0.92	+84%	1.40	+52%	1.08	-23%
Injured trades	0.63	0.80	+27%	1.62	+103%	1.63	+ 1%
Unskilled	0.56	1.36	+143%	1.33	- 2%	1.43	+ 8%
Number of families	175	250		282		253	
Overall average	0.51	1.02	+100%	1.15	13%	1.07	- 7%

SOURCE: Random samples, Sainte Anne and Saint Jacques wards: ever-married male family heads and ever-married male family heads with children over the age of eleven at home.

**Table 4.1
Children Reported To Be Able
To Read and Write, 1891**

Ages	Boys		Girls	
	Read + write	Read only	Read + write	Read only
French-Canadian Catholics				
0-4	4%	–	1%	–
5-7	9	5%	11	7%
8-9	48	8	49	17
10-11	80	8	68	16
12-13	92	3	88	5
14-15	79	3	80	6
16-17	87	–	69	6
18-19	83	–	76	2
Total 0-19	470		513	
Irish Catholics				
0-4	5%	–	3%	–
5-7	–	–	8	–
8-9	71	–	50	–
10-11	80	–	55	9
12-13	75	8	100	–
14-15	92	8	67	–
16-17	83	8	100	–
18-19	79	7	93	–
Total 0-19	121		111	
Protestants, All Origins				
0-4	4%	–	8%	–
5-7	13	6	23	8
8-9	71	–	50	–
10-11	100	–	100	–
12-13	100	–	100	–
14-15	100	–	91	–
16-17	100	–	100	–
18-19	100	–	100	–
Total 0-19	220		237	

SOURCE: Random samples: Sainte Anne and Saint Jacques combined, 1891.

Table 4.2
Children Reported To Be Able To Read and Write, 1891,
According to Father's Occupation

	Boys		Girls	
Ages	Read + write	Read only	Read + write	Read only
		Non-working-class		
0-4	5%	–	1%	
5-7	28	5%	14	4%
8-9	61	4	57	17
10-11	91	–	94	6
12-13	95	5	100	
14-15	94	–	85	3
16-17	96	–	79	4
18-19	91	–	89	
Total 0-19	269	–	266	
		Skilled		
0-4	1%	–	4%	–
5-7	6	6%	7	7%
8-9	58	11	44	11
10-11	79	–	71	19
12-13	94	–	94	6
14-15	100	–	94	–
16-17	91	–	94	–
18-19	92	–	81	
Total 0-19	215	–	287	
		Unskilled		
0-4	2%	–	0%	–
5-7	5	–	15	–
8-9	40	–	36	14%
10-11	75	13%	50	–
12-13	75	13	88	–
14-15	64	18	75	–
16-17	57	14	83	–
18-19	67	8	79	–
Total 0-19	120	–	124	

SOURCE: Random samples: Sainte Anne and Saint Jacques combined, 1891.

Table 4.3
Child, Teen, and Adult Workers and Their Families, 1861-91

	With offspring aged 10-14				With offspring aged 15-19				With offspring 20 and over			
	1861	1871	1881	1891	1861	1871	1881	1891	1861	1871	1881	1891
(a) Proportion of those who had children in those age groups that reported one or more working offspring that age, selected class groupings												
Non-working-class	3%	13%	7%	5%	41%	46%	52%	40%	50%	75%	69%	82%
Skilled	2	10	22	8	44	53	67	63	65	60	82	84
Injured trades	50	18	23	9	18	33	70	55	0	100	100	91
Unskilled	14	23	22	12	20	66	78	80	59	76	72	96
(b) Proportion according to the ward lived in												
Sainte Anne	12	17	14	13	40	62	70	57	57	73	76	91
Saint Jacques	2	15	17	4	41	45	59	55	49	70	71	88
(c) Proportion according to religious affiliation/ethnic origin												
French-Canadian Catholic	7	17	16	7	41	55	59	53	52	71	73	88
Irish Catholic	19	12	17	10	33	70	74	75	25	74	77	96
Protestants, all origins	0	18	14	12	24	32	77	54	63	67	71	80

SOURCE: Random samples, families headed by married males with children in each age group.

Table 4.4
Children Aged 10-24 Living with Their Parents
Who Reported Working, 1861-91,
Sainte Anne and Saint Jacques

Ages	Sainte Anne				Saint Jacques			
	1861	1871	1881	1891	1861	1871	1881	1891
Females								
10-11	0%	2%	0%	0%	0%	0%	2%	0%
12-13	3	5	8	8	3	9	9	3
14-15	3	25	18	20	9	16	25	5
16-17	14	30	27	59	27	23	40	13
18-19	0	49	29	48	17	52	48	35
20-24	10	55	38	44	16	58	57	30
Males								
10-11	0	6	0	0	4	6	3	0
12-13	5	18	14	4	5	3	7	0
14-15	23	29	45	50	5	46	34	23
16-17	29	76	76	66	45	59	54	60
18-19	60	79	93	84	59	86	74	96
20-24	73	84	96	98	76	77	82	92

SOURCE: Random samples, Sainte Anne and Saint Jacques wards, offspring living with their parents.

Table 4.5
Average Number of Sons and Daughters Reporting a Job
in Families with at least One Child
in Each Age Group, 1891

	All Children	Age 10-14 Girls	Age 10-14 Boys	Age 15-20 Girls	Age 15-20 Boys	Age 21+ Girls	Age 21+ Boys
Non-working-class	.75	–	–	.22	.79	.20	1.06
Skilled	.97	.09	.10	.36	1.00	.65	1.05
Injured trades	1.64	–	–	.67	1.00	2.00	1.00
Unskilled	1.29	–	.25	.93	.83	.88	.88
Overall average		.03	.12	.51	.91	.65	1.03

SOURCE: All families with children in each age group, random samples, 1891.

Table 5.1
The Leading Types of Jobs Reported by Married Women: Sainte Anne and Saint Jacques, 1861-91

		Sainte Anne				Saint Jacques			
		1861	1871	1881	1891	1861	1871	1881	1891
I	Small shops and trades	8%	14%	21%	13%	10%	4%	8%	14%
II	Trades and factory work								
	Sewing trades	50	53	66	23	75	73	63	29
	Other production	–	–	–	–	–	–	–	14
III	General								
	Labourer	22	4	3	4	7	7	18	7
IV	Private service								
	Servant, housekeeper, etc.	5	8	3	15	3	–	1	–
	Washerwoman	3	15	3	24	1	10	8	36
V	Other	12	6	3	12	4	7	2	–
	Total number	69	78	33*	100	90	75	147	14
	% of married women listing a job	2.2%	2.4%	1%	2.5%	5.3%	2.4%	3.3%	3.3%

* Parts of the 1881 manuscript census for Sainte Anne are impossible to read on the microfilm and the originals have been destroyed. This partly explains the particularly low number that year.

SOURCE: All married women with husbands present listing an occupation in the manuscript censuses for Sainte Anne and Saint Jacques wards, 1861, 1871, 1881, and Sainte Anne, 1891, as a proportion of the total number of married women listed in the published censuses. Sample population Saint Jacques, 1891.

Table 5.2
The Life-cycle Stage of Married Women
Reporting a Job, 1861-81

	Sainte Anne			Saint Jacques		
	1861	1871	1881	1861	1871	1881
Wife under 45, 0 children	28%	27%	21%	13%	17%	20%
Children all 11 and under	33	29	36	35	25	33
Some aged 11-15, none over 16	8	24	12	4	15	12
Some or all over 16	25	19	30	34	43	27
Wife over 45, no children	5	–	–	12	1	8
Total number	60	78	33	147	90	75

SOURCE: All working married women whose husbands were present, Sainte Anne and Saint Jacques, 1861-81.

Table 6.1
Proportion of Families Headed by Men and Women Whose Spouses Were Dead or Absent: A Minimum Estimate

	1861		1871		1881		1891	
	No.	%	No.	%	No.	%	No.	%
Couples								
Two parents, no children	65	12%	103	15%	138	15%	153	19%
Two parents, with children	311	56	460	66	574	63	496	63
Subtotal	*376*	*68*	*563*	*81*	*712*	*78*	*649*	*82*
Lone parents								
Widow with children	48	9	30	4	91	10	54	7
Lone woman								
with children	2	–	2	–	5	–	6	1
Lone female head	*50*	*9*	*32*	*5*	*96*	*10*	*60*	*8*
Widower with children	21	4	12	2	20	2	19	2
Lone man with children	4	1	1	–	5	–	8	1
Lone male head	*25*	*5*	*13*	*2*	*25*	*3*	*27*	*3*
Subtotal	*75*	*14*	*45*	*7*	*121*	*13*	*87*	*11*
Extended families								
Headed by								
married head	88	16	73	10	74	8	53	7
Headed by widow	7	1	8	1	4	–	2	–
Headed by widower	2	–	7	1	4	–	1	–
Headed by								
unmarried person	1	–	0	–	3	–	1	–
Subtotal	*98*	*18*	*88*	*13*	*85*	*9*	*57*	*7*
Total "families"	549		696		918		793	
Lone-parent families as a proportion of all families with children present		16%		8%		16%		14%
Married parents as proportion of all lone parents		8%		6%		8%		16%

NOTE: This table excludes households composed of people alone, non-related individuals, and siblings without children. Lone parents may also be hidden within the extended families.

SOURCE: Random samples, Sainte Anne and Saint Jacques wards, 1861-91.

Table 6.2
The Categories of Employment and Leading Jobs of Widows
Reporting an Occupation, Sainte Anne and Saint Jacques, 1861-91

	Sainte Anne			Saint Jacques		
	1861	1871	1891	1861	1871	1891†
Small Shops and Trades	19%	25%	28%	20%	15%	24%
Boardinghouse keeper	6	7	7	6	–	16
Grocer	–	–	11	–	1	4
Trader	1	7	–	8	9	–
Trades and Factory Work	30	19	19	44	40	28
Sewing trades	27	17	12	42	38	8
General						
Labourer	18	6	1	8	8	0
Private Service	29	47	46	23	26	36
Servant	8	8	14	8	6	8
Washerwoman	22	26	19	8	13	8
Charwoman	–	9	9	–	3	8

[Table 6.2 continues]

| | Sainte Anne | | | Saint Jacques | | |
	1861	1871	1891	1861	1871	1891†
Other						
Teaching	–	2	1	1	3	–
Commerce and sales	–	1	–	6	3	8
Other	2	2	4	2	6	4
Total number of widows	499	670	759	333	565	89
number listing a job	92	134	188	69	174	25
% listing a job	19%	20%	25%	21%	28%‡	28%

† Sample population only.
‡ Excluding the 11 "rentieres."
SOURCE All widows listing an occupation in the manuscript censuses for Sainte Anne and Saint Jacqes wards, 1861, 1871, and Sainte Anne 1891, sample population Saint Jacques, 1891.

Notes

Notes

Introduction

1. Médéric Lanctôt, President de l'Association des ouvriers du Canada, *Association de Capital et du Travail* (Montréal, 1872), p. 1, citing Horace Greeley, *New York Tribune,* 22 January 1872.

2. See, for example, publications of Statistics Canada, including *The Family in Canada: Selected Highlights* (Ottawa, 1989), p. 23.

3. Mss. Census, St. Jacques, 1871, Section B:5, household number 275:329; 1881, Section 17, household number 234:354.

4. This question was posed by contemporaries of the industrial revolution. Men as disparate in their politics as Friedrich Engels and Frédéric Le Play each concluded in different ways that the growth of factories was destroying family life. For reviews of contemporary observations in Europe and recent historiography on the question, see Joan Scott and Louise Tilly, *Women, Work and Family* (New York, 1978), pp. 1-2; Elinor Accampo, *Industrialization, Family Life, and Class Relations: Saint Chamond, 1815-1914* (Berkeley, 1989), pp. 6-16.

5. On the nineteenth century, see Gregory Kealey, *Toronto Workers Respond to Industrial Capitalism 1867-1892* (Toronto, 1980); Bryan Palmer, *A Culture in Conflict: Skilled Workers and Industrial Capitalism in Hamilton, Ontario, 1860-1914* (Montreal, 1979); Gregory S. Kealey and Bryan D. Palmer, *Dreaming of What Might Be: The Knights of Labor in Ontario, 1880-1900* (Toronto, 1982); Ian McKay, "Capital and Labour in the Halifax Baking and Confectionery Industry during the last half of the Nineteenth Century," *Labour/Le Travailleur,* 3 (1978); Joanne Burgess, "L'industrie de la chaussure à Montréal: 1840-1870 – Le passage de l'artisanat à la fabrique," *Revue d'histoire de l'Amérique française* (hereafter *RHAF*), 31 (September, 1977); Peter Bischoff, "La formation des traditions de solidarité ouvrière chez les mouleurs montréalais: la longue marche vers le syndicalisme (1859-1881)," *Labour/Le Travail,* 21 (Spring, 1988).

6. Palmer, *A Culture in Conflict*; Peter DeLottinville, "Joe Beef of Montreal: Working-Class Culture and the Tavern, 1869-1889," *Labour/Le Travailleur,* 8/9 (1981-82).

7. Some recent historiographical and theoretical articles make important steps in this direction. See Bettina Bradbury, "Women's History and Working-Class History," *Labour/Le Travail,* 19 (1987); Craig Heron and Robert Storey, "On the Job in Canada," in Craig Heron and Robert Storey, eds., *On the Job: Confronting the Labour Process in Canada* (Kingston and Montreal, 1986); Jacques Ferland, "In Search of the Unbound Prometheia: A Comparative View of Women's Activism in Two Quebec Industries, 1869-1908," *Labour/Le Travail,* 24 (1989); and especially Mark Rosenfeld, " 'It was a hard life': Class and Gender in the Work and Family Rhythms of a Railway Town 1920-1950," Canadian Historical Association (hereafter CHA), *Historical Papers* (1988). Historical sociologists are contributing to a better understanding of the links between the spheres of production and reproduction. See, in particular, Alicja Muszynski, "Race and gender: structural determinants in the formation of British Columbia's salmon cannery labour force," in Gregory S. Kealey, ed., *Class, Gender, and Region: Essays in Canadian Historical Sociology* (St. John's, 1988); James R. Conley, "More theory, less fact? Social Reproduction and Class Conflict in a Sociological Approach to Working-class History," *ibid.* Joy Parr, *The Gender of Breadwinners: Women, Men and Change in Two Industrial Towns, 1880-1950* (Toronto, 1990), is the only book-length Canadian study in this area. In the United States the pathbreaker in this domain was Tamara K. Hareven, *Family Time and Industrial Time: The Relationship between the Family and Work in a New England Industrial Community* (Cambridge, Mass., 1982). More recent studies have further integrated a feminist analysis. See especially Mary Blewett, *Men, Women, and Work: Class, Gender, and Protest in the New England Shoe Industry, 1780-1910* (Urbana, Ill., 1988); Carole Turbin, "Beyond Conventional Wisdom: Woman's Wage Work, Household Economic Contribution, and Labor Activism in a Mid-nineteenth Century Working Class Community," in Carol Groneman and Mary Beth Norton, eds., *'To Toil the Livelong Day': America's Women at Work, 1790-1980* (Ithaca, N.Y., 1987); Carole Turbin, "Reconceptualizing Family, Work, and Labour Organization: Working Women in Troy, 1860-1880," *Review of Radical Political Economics,* 16 (Spring, 1984); Susan J. Kleinberg, *The Shadow of the Mills: Working-Class Families in Pittsburgh, 1870-1907* (Pittsburgh, 1989).

8. David Gagan and Rosemary Gagan, "Working-Class Standards of Living in Late-Victorian Urban Ontario: A Review of the Miscellaneous Evidence on the Quality of Material Life," *Journal of the Canadian Historical Association,* New Series, 1 (Victoria, 1990), hardly mention the possibility of families having more than one earner or of other ways of getting by.

Note also Michael Piva, *The Condition of the Working Class in Toronto, 1900-1921* (Ottawa, 1979); Terry Copp, *The Anatomy of Poverty: The Condition of the Working Class in Montreal, 1897-1929* (Toronto, 1974); J.G. Snell, "The Cost of Living in Canada in 1870," *Histoire sociale/Social History,* 12 (May, 1979); Edward J. Chambers, "New Evidence on the Living Standards of Toronto Blue Collar Workers in the Pre-1914 Era," *Histoire sociale/Social History,* 19, 38 (November, 1986). Peter Shergold's *Working-Class Life: The "American Standard" in Comparative Perspective, 1899-1913* (Pittsburgh, 1982), a comparison of the differences between the cost of living in Pittsburgh and Birmingham, is a much more successful attempt to assess seriously the importance of the different kinds of work performed by all family members. In this regard, also see Eleanor A. Bartlett, "Real Wages and the Standard of Living in Vancouver, 1901-1929," *B.C. Studies,* 51 (Autumn, 1981). Neil Sutherland's studies of the contribution of children to the family economy in twentieth-century British Columbia represent an important addition to the literature. See especially his "'We always had things to do': The Paid and Unpaid Work of Anglophone Children Between the 1920s and the 1960s," *Labour/Le Travail,* 25 (Spring, 1990). David Frank makes clear the importance of women's role as budget manager in his brief note on "The Miner's Financier: Women in the Cape Breton Coal Towns, 1917," *Atlantis,* 8, 2 (Spring, 1983).

9. Gregory S. Kealey, "The Structure of Canadian Working Class History," in W.J.C. Cherwinski and Gregory S. Kealey, eds., *Lectures in Canadian Working Class History* (St. John's, 1985), p. 23.

10. The simplest analysis of the major approaches within family history remains Michael Anderson, *Approaches to the History of the Western Family, 1500-1914* (Bristol, U.K., 1980). Useful reviews include Martine Ségalen, "Sous les feux croisés de l'histoire et de l'anthropologie: La famille en europe," *RHAF,* 39, 2 (Autumn, 1985); Tamara K. Hareven, "Les grands thèmes de l'histoire de la famille aux états-unis," *ibid*; Laurence Stone, "Family History in the 1980s," *Journal of Interdisciplinary History,* 12 (1981), pp. 51-57; Louise A. Tilly and M. Cohen, "Does the Family have a History? A Review of Theory and Practice in Family History," *Social Science History,* 6 (1982), pp. 181-99; Tamara K. Hareven, "Family History at the Crossroads," *Journal of Family History,* Special Issue on "Family History at the Crossroads: Linking Familial and Historical Change," 12, 1-3 (1987); Louise A. Tilly, "Women's History and Family History: Fruitful Collaboration or Missed Connection?" *ibid.*

11. Peter Laslett with Richard Wall, *Household and Family in Past Time* (Cambridge, U.K., 1972); Sheva Medjuck, "The Importance of Boarding for the Structure of the Household in the Nineteenth Century: Moncton, New Brunswick and Hamilton, Canada West," *Histoire sociale/Social History,* 13 (May, 1980); Michael B. Katz, *The People of Hamilton,*

   Canada West: Family and Class in a Mid-Nineteenth Century City (Cambridge, Mass., 1975).

12. Michael Anderson, *Family Structure in Nineteenth Century Lancashire* (London, 1971), p. 137; Barbara Humphreys, "The Working-Class Family, Women's Liberation, and Class Struggle: The Case of Nineteenth Century British History," *The Review of Radical Political Economics,* 9 (Fall, 1977), p. 248; Hareven, *Family Time and Industrial Time,* pp. 101-14.

13. Among the earlist advocates of this approach was Frédéric Le Play, *Les ouvriers Européens: Études sur les travaux, la vie domestique et la condition morale des populations ouvrières de l'Europe* (Paris, 1855). Disciples applied his method to nineteenth- and early twentieth-century Quebec families. See Charles-Henri Philippe Gauldrée-Boileau, *Paysan de Saint-Irénée de Charlevois en 1861 et 1862* (1862), republished in Pierre Savard, ed., *Paysans et ouvriers d'autrefois* (Québec, 1968); Léon Gérin, *Le Type économique et sociale des canadiens* (Montréal, 1938); and Stanislas Lortie, *Compositeur typographe de Québec en 1903,* republished in Savard, ed., *Paysans et ouvriers.* In England the tradition of investigating how families worked, ate, and lived continued in the major studies of Henry Mayhew, Charles Booth, and B. Seebohm Rowntree. In France careful refinements to the method of determining standards and costs of living were proposed by Maurice Halbwachs, *La class ouvrière et les niveaux de vie: Recherches sur la hiérarchie des besoins dans les sociétés industrielles contemporaines* (Paris, 1913). In the United States the most important such studies were performed by Carroll D. Wright working at the Massachussetts Bureau of Statistics of Labour. Herbert Brown Ames is the only English Canadian to have performed a similar study: *The City Below the Hill* (1897; reprint, Toronto, 1972).

14. Among the most important pioneers were Anderson, *Family Structure*; John O. Foster, *Class Struggle and the Industrial Revolution: Early Industrial Capitalism in Three English Towns* (London, 1974); Richard Sennet, *Families Against the City: Middle Class Homes of Industrial Chicago* (New York, 1970); Stephan Thernstrom, *Poverty and Progress: Social Mobility in a Nineteenth Century City* (Cambridge, Mass., 1974); Hareven, *Family Time and Industrial Time;* and in Canada, Katz, *The People of Hamilton*; Michael B. Katz, Michael J. Doucet, and Mark J. Stern, *The Social Organization of Early Industrial Capitalism* (Cambridge, Mass., 1982); Bettina Bradbury, "The Family Economy and Work in an Industrializing City, Montreal in the 1870's," CHA, *Historical Papers* (1979).

15. Katz, Doucet, and Stern, *The Social Organization of Early Industrial Capitalism,* especially pp. 318, 335, 395; Chad Gaffield, "Canadian Families in Cultural Context: Hypotheses from the Mid-Nineteenth Century," CHA, *Historical Papers* (1979); Gérard Bouchard, "L'étude des structures familiales pré-industrielles: pour un renversement des perspectives,"

Revue d'histoire moderne et contemporain, XIII (October-December, 1981); Jacques Mathieu, "Mobilité et sedentarité; Stratégies familiales en Nouvelle France," *Recherches sociographiques* (1985).

16. Michael Anderson's *Family Structure,* for example, does deal with the different roles of men and women and boys and girls, but this is subsidiary to his interest in the kinds of claims ungendered family members had on each other.

17. Olwen Hufton, "Women and the Family Economy in Eighteenth Century France," *French Historical Studies,* 9 (Spring, 1975); Louise A. Tilly and Joan W. Scott, "Women's Work and the Family in Nineteenth Century Europe," in Charles E. Rosenberg, ed., *The Family in History* (Philadelphia, 1975); Tilly and Scott, *Women, Work and Family*; Accampo, *Industrialization, Family Life*; Christine Stansell, *City of Women: Sex and Class in New York, 1789-1860* (Urbana and Chicago, 1987); Carole Turbin, "Beyond Dichotomies: Interdependence in Mid-Nineteenth Century Working Class Families in the United States," *Gender and History,* 1, 3 (Autumn, 1989).

18. Rayna Rapp, Ellen Ross, and Renate Bridenthal, "Examining Family History," *Feminist Studies,* 5 (March, 1979); Tilly and Scott, *Women, Work and Family*; Accampo, *Industrialization, Family Life;* Ellen Ross, "'Fierce Questions and Taunts': Married Life in Working Class London, 1870-1914," *Feminist Studies,* 8 (1982); Nancy Tomes, "'A Torrent of Abuse': Crimes of Violence Between Working Class Men and Women in London, 1840-1875," *Journal of Social History,* 11 (1978); Kathryn Harvey, "'To Love, Honour and Obey': Wife-battering in Working-Class Montreal, 1869-1879," *Urban History Review,* X, 2 (October, 1990); Marjorie Cohen, *Women's Work, Markets, and Economic Development in Nineteenth-Century Ontario* (Toronto, 1988).

19. On married women's changing legal rights in England and the United States, see especially Norma Basch, *In the Eyes of the Law: Women, Marriage and Property in Nineteenth Century New York* (Ithaca, N.Y., 1982); Suzanne Lebsock, *The Free Women of Petersburg: Status and Culture in a Southern Town, 1784-1860* (New York, 1984); Mary Lyndon Shanley, *Feminism, Marriage, and the Law in Victorian England, 1850-1895* (Princeton, N.J., 1989); Lee Holcombe, *Wives and Property: Reform of the Married Women's Property Law in Nineteenth-Century England* (Toronto, 1983); Susan Staves, *Married Women's Separate Property in England, 1660-1833* (Cambridge and London, 1990); and, for Canada, Constance B. Backhouse, "Married Women's Property Law in Nineteenth Century Canada," *History of Law Review* (1988); Constance Backhouse, *Petticoats and Prejudice: Women and Law in Nineteenth-Century Canada* (Toronto, 1991); Cohen, *Women's Work,* p. 47; Jennifer Stoddart, "The Dorion Commission: 1929-1931: Quebec's Legal Elites Look at Women's Rights," in David H. Hamilton, ed., *Essays in the History of Canadian*

Law (Toronto, 1981); Parr, *The Gender of Breadwinners.*; Veronica Strong-Boag, *The New Day Recalled: Lives of Girls and Women in English Canada, 1919-1939* (Toronto, 1988).

20. Carole Turbin stresses the idea that interdependence modified the degree of domination and subordination of women within working-class families in "Beyond Dichotomies." I am not convinced. Men's dependence on women may equally have made them more authoritarian. Kathryn Harvey provides a thoughtful analysis of the different kinds of dependence of men and women in " 'To Love, Honour and Obey', Wife-battering in Working-class Montreal, 1869-1879" (M.A. thesis, Université de Montréal, 1991), especially p. 100. A useful review of different North American, British, and French feminist theories, most of which stress the relationship of wives and husbands, is given by Danielle Juteau and Nicole Laurin, "L'évolution des formes de l'appropriation des femmes: des religieuses aux mères porteuses'," *Revue canadienne de sociologie et anthropologie/ Canadian Review of Sociology and Anthropology,* 25, 2 (1988).

21. Unfortunately, the manuscript forms that give personal information on each family in the city in 1851 were destroyed.

22. Considering women taking in boarders as employed led Carol Groneman to increase her assessment of the proportions of married women working by anything from four to ten times, depending on the age group. See " 'She Earns as a Child; She Pays as a Man': Women Workers in a Mid-Nineteenth-Century New York City Community," in Richard Ehrlich, ed., *Immigrants in Industrial Society* (Charlottesville, Va., 1977). Determining patterns of household sharing in the Canadian censuses is not as easy as it seemed at first glance to historians and sociologists, including myself. Gilles Lauzon has carefully examined the census-takers' use of the term "household" in St. Henri, an outer suburb of Montreal, between 1861 and 1871 and concludes that duplexes and triplexes were being listed as one "household." Gilles Lauzon, *Habitat Ouvrier et revolution industrielle: Le Cas du village St-Augustin* (Montréal, 1989). Obviously this inflates dramatically the proportion of families actually sharing space and renders questionable the conclusions of articles dealing with the subject, including Bradbury, "The Family and Work in an Industrializing City"; Gordon Darroch and Michael D. Ornstein, "Family and Household in Nineteenth Century Canada: Regional Patterns and Regional Economies," *Journal of Family History,* 9 (Summer, 1984); Gordon A. Darroch and Michael D. Ornstein, "Family Co-residence and Networks of Mutual Aid," CHA, *Historical Papers* (1983). But see also Chapter 2 of this book.

23. Compare with Gordon Darroch, who argues this is not possible, then treats all people listing a craft as artisans. Darroch, "Class in nineteenth-century, central Ontario: a reassessment of the crisis and demise of small producers during early industrialization, 1861-1871," in Kealey, ed., *Class, Gender, and Region,* pp. 49-72.

24. Tamara Hareven, "The Dynamics of Kin in Industrial Communities: The Historical Perspective," in John Demos and Sarane Spence Boocock, eds., *Turning Points: Historical and Sociological Essays on the Family,* Supplement to the *American Journal of Sociology,* 84 (Winter, 1978); Hareven, "Family History at the Crossroads," pp. xi-xii.

25. The sophisticated SOREP project directed by Gérard Bouchard aims to do precisely this. At a smaller scale and focusing on the region of Montreal, see Alan Stewart, "Settling an 18th-Century *Faubourg*: Property and Family in the Saint-Laurent Suburb, 1735-1810" (M.A. thesis, McGill University, 1988); Joanne Burgess, "Work, Family and Community: Montreal Leather Craftsmen, 1790-1831" (Ph.D. thesis, Université de Québec à Montréal, 1986). In both of these works diverse documents drawn from notarial archives are used to recreate patterns of property transmission over individual and family life cycles. These are complemented by analysis of parish registers and other types of listings made at the time.

26. Anderson, *Family Structure*; Katz, *The People of Hamilton*; Hareven, *Family Time and Industrial Time*; Scott and Tilly, *Women, Work and Family*; David Gagan, *Hopeful Travellers: Families, Land and Social Change in Mid-Victorian Peel County, Canada West* (Toronto, 1981); Gérard Bouchard and Yolande Lavoie, "Le projet d'histoire social de la population du Saguenay – l'appareil méthodologique," *RHAF,* 32 (June, 1978); Christian Pouyez *et al.*, *Les Saguenayens: Introduction à l'histoire des populations du Saguenay, XVIe-XXe siècles* (Montréal, 1983).

27. Samples of 10 per cent of households were randomly chosen for 1861, 1871, and 1881, while a random sample of 7.5 per cent was taken for 1891. The number of individuals and families in the samples and reported in each published census were:

Sainte Anne	Individuals		Families	
	Sample	Total	Sample	Total
1861	1,672	16,200	338	3,419
1871	1,898	18,639	374	3,703
1881	2,006	20,443	442	4,368
1891	1,688	23,003	363	4,405

Saint Jacques	Individuals		Families	
	Sample	Total	Sample	Total
1861	1,212	13,104	241	3,854*
1871	1,648	17,680	348	3,519
1881	2,531	25,398	531	5,207
1891	2,186	32,398	502	6,781

* How those aggregating the census returns for 1861 reached this figure is unclear. There is no evidence in the manuscript returns of this many families.

28. R.S. Scholfield, "Sampling in Historical Research," in E.A. Wrigley, ed., *Nineteenth Century Society: Essays in the Use of Quantitative Methods for the Study of Social Data* (Cambridge, U.K., 1972). Similar 10 per cent samples were used by Anderson, *Family Structure;* Foster, *Class Struggle and the Industrial Revolution;* Lynn H. Lees, *Exiles of Erin: Irish Migrants in Victorian London* (New York, 1979); and Theodore Hershberg, ed., *Philadelphia: Work, Space, Family and Group Experience in the 19th Century* (New York, 1981). The only other Canadian city for which manuscript censuses have been used as a major source is Hamilton, Ontario. Between 1851 and 1871, the period covered by Michael Katz and his colleagues, it grew from around 14,000 people to 26,000. These historians were able to study the total population because it was relatively small and they had a large team of workers and access to unprecedented funding.

Chapter 1   The Economic, Geographic, and Social Context

1. William Chambers, *Things as they are in America* (London and Edinburgh, 1854), p. 63.
2. William J. Patterson, *Annual Report of the Trade and Commerce of the City of Montreal* (Montreal, 1863), p. 3.
3. Isabella Lucy Bird, *The Englishwoman in America* (London, 1856), pp. 251, 255.
4. The inventory of visitors to Montreal produced by the Groupe de recherche sur la société montréalaise au 19e siècle in "Rapport et travaux, 1973-1975" (Department of History, Université du Québec à Montréal, 1975) is extremely useful. My thanks to Jean-Claude Robert and Joanne Burgess for allowing me to consult their photocopies of these accounts. I draw on the following accounts: Christophe Allard, *Promenade au Canada et aux États Unis* (Paris, 1878), p. 37; Dominique Bonnaud, *D'Océan à Océan: Impressions d'Amérique* (Paris, 1897), pp. 411-19; Bird, *The Englishwoman,* pp. 251-55; Chambers, *Things as they are,* pp. 63-70; Edmond Cotteau, *Promenade dans les deux Amériques, 1876-77* (Paris, 1886), pp. 30-32; L. De Cotton, *À travers le Dominion et la Californie* (Paris, 1889), p. 71; Baron Étienne Hulot, *De l'Atlantique au Pacifique à travers le Canada et le nord des États Unis* (Paris, 1888), pp. 158-62.
5. *The Montreal Post,* 19 June 1882, cited by D. Suzanne Cross, "The Irish in Montreal, 1867-1896" (M.A. thesis, McGill University, 1969), p. 239. Montreal Railroad Celebration Committee, *Montreal in 1856* (Montreal, 1856), pp. 35-39; Chambers, *Things as they are,* p. 65.
6. The most obvious example is the Molson family, whose brewery business began in the 1780s. Alfred Dubuc and Robert Tremblay, "John Molson," *Dictionary of Canadian Biography,* Vol. VIII.
7. Jean-Paul Bernard, Paul-André Linteau, and Jean-Claude Robert estimate

that producers made up about one-quarter of the listed occupations of Montrealers in 1825: "La structure professionelle de Montréal en 1825," *RHAF,* 30, 3 (December, 1976), pp. 409-11; Burgess, "Work, Family and Community."

8. For dissenting views on when and how this process occurred, compare the arguments of Burgess, "Work, Family and Community"; J.-P. Hardy et D.-T. Ruddel, *Les Apprentis artisans à Québec, 1660-1815* (Montréal, 1977); Robert Tremblay, "La formation materielle de la classe ouvrière à Montréal entre 1790 et 1830," *RHAF,* 33, 1 (June, 1979).

9. Gerald Tulchinsky, *The River Barons: Montreal Businessmen and the Growth of Industry and Transportation, 1837-1853* (Toronto, 1977), pp. 211-12.

10. Ben Forster, *A Conjunction of Interests: Business, Politics, and Tariffs, 1825-1879* (Toronto, 1986), p. 11.

11. On accumulation and the economy in the early decades of the nineteenth century, see Robert Sweeny, "Internal Dynamics and the International Cycle: Questions of the Transition in Montreal, 1821-1828" (Ph.D. thesis, McGill University, 1985).

12. Burgess, "Work, Family and Community."

13. *Ibid.*, pp. 89, 192-93.

14. Archives Nationale du Québec à Montréal (hereafter ANQM), Notary R. O'Keefe, No. 304, 21 February 1826, cited in Burgess, "Work, Family and Community," p. 75.

15. Apprentice dressmakers, unlike apprentices in any other trade, often paid for the privilege of learning the art of dressmaking. See Mary Anne Poutanen, "For the Benefit of the Master: The Montreal Needle Trades during the Transition, 1820-1842" (M.A. thesis, McGill University, 1985). On transformations in diverse trades and the emergence of early worker organizations, see Charles Lipton, *The Trade Union Movement of Canada, 1827-1959* (Montreal, 1973), pp. 4-6; Joanne Burgess, "L'industrie de la chaussure à Montréal: 1840-1870," *RHAF.* 31, 2 (September, 1977); Jacques Rouillard, *Histoire du Syndicalisme au Québec: Des origines à nos jours* (Montréal, 1989), pp. 11-20; Bryan Palmer, *Working-Class Experience: Rethinking the History of Canadian Labour, 1800-1991* (Toronto, 1992), pp. 87-95; Craig Heron, *The Canadian Labour Movement: A Short History* (Toronto, 1989), pp. 2-4.

16. William Kilbourn, *The Elements Combined: A History of the Steel Company of Canada* (Toronto, 1960), p. 9.

17. "Plan of the City of Montreal from a Survey made by order of the Mayor and Common Council in 1835 with the new Improvements to 1839," republished in Newton Bosworth, *Hochelaga Depicta* (Montreal, 1839); S.P. Day, *English America: or Pictures of Canadian Places and People* (London, 1864), p. 192. The importance of this area in the 1850s is made

clear in the much cited Montreal General Railroad Celebrations Committee's publication, *Montreal in 1856* (Montreal, 1856), pp. 39-44. John
Willis looks specifically at the water power of the Lachine in his broader
study, *The Lachine Canal, 1840-1900: Preliminary Report* (Quebec,
1983), 79-91.

18. Tulchinsky, *The River Barons,* pp. 221-27.

19. Mss. Census, 1861, Ste. Anne; *Montreal Gazette,* 19 July 1864, p. 4.

20. Little work has been done on specific trades in Montreal, with the excep-
tion of shoemakers and moulders. Burgess, "L'industrie de la chaussure";
Peter Bischoff, "La formation des traditions"; Peter Bischoff, "Tensions et
solidarité: la formation des traditions syndicales chez les mouleurs de
Montréal, Hamilton et Toronto, 1851 à 1893" (Ph.D. thesis, Université de
Montréal, 1992).

21. Canada, *Census of 1891,* Vol. II, p. iv; Vol. III, p. vi.

22. Mss. Census, Industrial Schedules, 1871, Subdistricts b-6 and b-10.

23. It was therefore very different from towns where one industry dominated,
as described by Thomas Dublin, *Women at Work: The Transformation of
Work and Community in Lowell, Massachusetts, 1826-1860* (New York,
1979); Hareven, *Family Time and Industrial Time*; Daniel Walkowitz,
*Worker City, Company Town: Iron and Cotton Worker Protest in Troy and
Cohoes, New York, 1855-1884* (Urbana, Ill., 1978); Katz, Doucet, and
Stern, *The Social Organization of Industrial Capitalism;* Katz, *The People
of Hamilton.* A better parallel with Montreal would be Philadelphia. See
Hershberg, ed., *Philadelphia.*

24. Kealey, *Toronto Workers Respond to Industrial Capitalism.*

25. In 1863, for example, Patterson estimated that around half of the city's production of flour was absorbed by local demand. His reports offer the possibility of assessing the importance of Montreal as a market in various economic sectors. William J. Patterson, Secretary of the Board of Trade and
Corn Exchange, *Statistical Contributions relating to the Trade, Commerce
and Navigation of the Dominion of Canada: Including Annual Reports of
the Trade and Commerce for the City of Montreal* (Montreal, 1863), p. 44.

26. *Ibid.*, p. 59; *ibid.* (Montreal, 1873).

27. Suzanne Cross, combining figures for Hochelaga and Montreal, found an
increase in the number of working women, although it was minimal compared to that among men. She concluded that new jobs were opening more
slowly for women than for men. This argument ignores the other sectors
that began to open up for women during this period – office work in particular. Suzanne Cross, "The Neglected Majority," in Susan Mann Trofimenkoff and Alison Prentice, eds., *The Neglected Majority: Essays in
Canadian Women's History* (Toronto, 1977), pp. 73-74, 86.

28. Walkowitz, *Worker City, Company Town*; Hareven, *Family Time and
Industrial Time*; Dublin, *Women at Work*; Blewett, *Men, Women, and
Work.*

29. Michelle Payette-Daoust, "The Montreal Garment Industry, 1871-1901" (M.A. thesis, McGill University, 1987), pp. 71-74.

30. Ferland, "In Search of the Unbound Prometheia"; Jacques Ferland, "Syndicalisme 'parcellaire' et syndicalisme 'collectif': Une Interprétation socio-technique des conflits ouvriers dans deux industries québécoises (1880-1914)," *Labour/Le Travail*, 19 (Spring, 1987), pp. 49-88. On women's place in the sexual division of labour in the New England shoemaking sector, see Blewitt's excellent study, *Men, Women, and Work*.

31. Canada, *Census of 1891*, Vol. III, Table I, Industrial establishments. These average wages represent the total wages paid by employers in those trades divided by the number of workers in that industry. They are, therefore, only an approximate guide to what individual workers would have received.

32. Montreal General Railroad Celebration Committee, *Montreal in 1856*, p. 37.

33. Ferland, "In Search of the Unbound Prometheia"; Bischoff, "La formation des traditions de solidarité ouvrière."

34. Canada, *Journals*, 1876, Appendix 3, "Report of the Select Committee on the Causes of the Present Depression of the Manufacturing, Mining, Commercial, Shipping, Lumber and Fishing Interests," pp. 93-98, 133; Canada, Royal Commission on the Relations of Labour and Capital, Vol. III, *Quebec Evidence*, p. 446. (Hereafter RCRLC unless otherwise indicated.)

35. Canada, *Journals*, 1874, Appendix 3, "Report of the Select Committee on the Manufacturing Interests of the Dominion," p. 38, Chair A.T. Wood; "Report on the Causes of the Present Depression," p. 108.

36. "Report on the Manufacturing Interests," 1874; "Report on the Causes of the Present Depression," pp. 93, 108, 133; Canada, *Sessional Papers*, 1885, "Report on the State of the Manufacturing Industries of Ontario and Quebec," Chair A.H. Blakeby.

37. "Report on the Manufacturing Interests," 1874, p. 38.

38. *Montreal Gazette*, 19 July 1864, p. 4; *Montreal Business Sketches . . . with a description of the City of Montreal, its Public Buildings and Places of Interest* (Montreal, 1865), pp. 18-19, 13.

39. "Report on the Manufacturing Interests," 1874, p. 22.

40. Christina Burr argues that male workers in the printing trades in Toronto succeeded in keeping women out of the most skilled trades: "Class and Gender in the Toronto Printing Trades, 1870-1914" (Ph.D. thesis, Memorial University of Newfoundland, 1991).

41. RCRLC, evidence of Henry Morton, stationer, bookbinder, and printer, pp. 296-98; J. Finn, foreman, *Gazette* news room, pp. 321-24; Hugh Graham, proprietor, *The Star*, p. 327; John Lovell, printer and publisher, pp. 328-30; F. Stanley, foreman, *The Star* composing room, pp. 331-32; James Conolly, foreman, *The Gazette*, book and job department, pp. 332-33; John Beatty, foreman, *The Witness* composing room, pp. 355-60;

Lewis Z. Boudreau, president, Montreal Typographical Union, pp. 419-25.

42. Marilyn Barber, "The Women Ontario Welcomed: Immigrant Domestics for Ontario Homes, 1870-1930," *Ontario History,* 62, 3 (September, 1980), shows how eager this class was to procure good domestic workers by any means. See also Claudette Lacelle, *Urban Domestic Servants in 19th-Century Canada* (Hull, 1987); Canada, *Census of 1861, Census of 1871, Census of 1881.*

43. The published 1891 census does not list people's occupations within different cities. In these two wards the percentage of girls in the sample populations employed in commerce, including clerical work, in a shop, or for the government generally increased from 4 per cent in 1861 to 11 per cent in 1891.

44. ANQM, Judicial Archives, pre-archives, The Queen vs. Israel Beaume, 1878, Box 497.

45. Paul-André Linteau, *The Promoters' City: Building the Industrial Town of Maisonneuve, 1883-1918,* trans. Robert Chodos (Toronto, 1985), p. 14.

46. E.P. Thompson, "Time, Work-Discipline and Industrial Capitalism," *Past and Present,* 38 (1967).

47. RCRLC, evidence of Alexander McGregor, pp. 102-03; Eli Massy, p. 21; anonymous machinist, Hudon Cotton Factory, p. 276; Benjamin Antoine Testard de Montigny, Recorder of the City of Montreal, pp. 389-90; John S. Hall, advocate, p. 388; Charles J. Doherty, advocate, p. 212. On the Masters and Servants Acts in Ontario, see Paul Craven, "The Law of Master and Servant in Mid-Nineteenth-Century Ontario," in David Flaherty, ed., *Essays in the History of Canadian Law,* I (Toronto, 1981), pp. 175-211; Kealey, *Toronto Workers Respond,* pp. 150-53; Eric Tucker, "'That Indefinite Area of Toleration': Criminal Conspiracy and Trade Unions in Ontario, 1837-77," *Labour/Le Travail,* 27 (Spring, 1991), pp. 50-51.

48. Complaints about the condition of streets and sidewalks are frequent in the minutes of the meetings of the Montreal City Council. See also Day, *English America,* p. 164.

49. Stansell, *City of Women.*

50. Christopher Armstrong and H.V. Nelles, *Monopoly's Moment: The Organization and Regulaton of Canadian Utilities, 1830-1930* (Philadelphia, 1986), pp. 38-49, 88-89.

51. Day, *English America,* p. 160.

52. *Ibid.*

53. Patterson, *Annual Reports of the Trade and Commerce,* 1863, p. 3.

54. Jean-Claude Robert estimates that 83 per cent of the total growth of Montreal between 1852 and 1861 resulted from the increase in the number of French Canadians. "Urbanisation et population. Le cas de Montréal en 1861," *RHAF,* 35 (March, 1982), p. 527.

55. Bruno Ramirez, *On the Move: French-Canadian and Italian Migrants in the North Atlantic Economy, 1860-1914* (Toronto, 1991), pp. 21-49, 86-92.

56. Robert, "Urbanisation et population"; France Gagnon, "Parenté et migration: le cas des Canadiens français à Montréal entre 1845 et 1875," CHA, *Historical Papers* (1988); Joanne Burgess, "The Growth of a Craft Labour Force: Montreal Leather Artisans, 1815-1831," *ibid.*; Peter Bischoff, "Des forges du Saint-Maurice aux fonderies de Montréal: mobilité géographique, solidarité communautaire et action syndicale des mouleurs, 1829-1881," *RHAF,* 43,1 (Summer, 1989); "Report of the Montreal Immigration Agent," Canada, *Sessional Papers,* 1876, Paper No. 8, p. 11; *ibid.*, Paper No. 8, 1877; *ibid.*, Paper No. 9, 1878.

57. Current historiography stresses that many Irish became rural, farming folk and that the early waves of migration were predominantly Protestant. Donald Harmon Akenson, *The Irish in Ontario: A Study in Rural History* (Toronto, 1984); Cecil J. Houston and William J. Smyth, *Irish Emigration and Canadian Settlement: Patterns, Links, and Letters* (Toronto, 1990); Bruce S. Eliot, *Irish Migrants in the Canadas: A New Approach* (Kingston, 1988); D. Suzanne Cross, "The Irish in Montreal, 1867-1896" (M.A. thesis, McGill University, 1969). While Montreal had a sizeable component of Protestant Irish, the vast majority were Catholic. Among couples marrying in the Catholic Montreal parish between 1842 and 1845, for example, around one-third were Irish. Many, of course, may have been en route for rural areas.

58. Changes in the questions asked about people's origins make it difficult to compare the ethnic origins of Canadians over this period. Whereas in 1871 and 1881 people were asked to list their "origin," in 1861 and 1891 they were simply asked where they had been born. In the latter census there were also questions on where each of their parents were born, and French Canadians were identified in a special column. Unfortunately, in at least some parts of Montreal this column was rather arbitrarily filled out, and instructions about its meaning were non-existent. As a result, in predominantly French parts of town, those with an Irish father and French-Canadian mother tended to be identified as French Canadians, while in Sainte Anne they were not.

59. *Golden Jubilee Number, Redemptorist Fathers at St. Ann's* (Montreal, 1934), p. 18.

60. H. Clare Pentland, "The Development of a Capitalistic Labour Market in Canada," *Canadian Journal of Economics and Political Science,* 25 (November, 1959).

61. Burgess, "The Growth of a Craft Labour Force"; Bishchoff, "La formation des traditions"; Jean Paul Bernard, Paul-André Linteau, et Jean-Claude Robert, "La structure professionelle de Montréal en 1825," *RHAF,* 30, 3 (1976).

62. Marcel Bellevance et Jean-Daniel Gronoff, "Les structures de l'espace Montréalais à l'époque de la confédération," *Cahiers de géographie de Québec,* 24 (December, 1980); Raoul Blanchard, *L'Ouest du Canada Français* (Montréal, 1953), pp. 263-64.

63. Stephen Hertzog and Robert D. Lewis, "A City of Tenants: Homeownership and Social Class in Montreal, 1847-1881," *The Canadian Geographer,* 30 (1986), pp. 316-23.

64. Bischoff, "Des forges du Saint-Maurice."

65. Lucia Ferretti, *Entre voisins: La Société paroissiale en milieu urbain: Saint-Pierre-Apôtre de Montréal, 1843-1930* (Montréal, 1992); Brian Young, *In its Corporate Capacity: The Seminary of Montreal as a Business Institution, 1816-1876* (Montreal, 1986).

66. See Ferretti, *Entre voisins,* for an important analysis of the Oblates and parish life in the southwestern part of Saint Jacques ward. On Catholic charities, see Huguette Lapointe-Roy, *Charité bien ordonnée: Le premier reseau de lutte contre la pauvreté à Montréal au 19e siècle* (Montréal, 1987); L.A. Huget-Latour, *Annuaire de Ville Marie: Origine, utilité et progrès des institutions catholiques de Montréal* (Montréal, 1869).

67. There is no complete overview of Protestant institutions. Good listings can be found in the city directories and many did publish detailed annual reports. On some of these Protestant institutions, see Janice Harvey, "Upper Class Reaction to Poverty in Mid-Nineteenth Century Montreal: A Protestant example" (M.A. thesis, McGill University, 1978).

68. L'Institut de la Providence, *Histoire des Filles de la Charité, Servantes des pauvres soeurs dit de la Providence,* Vol. VI (Montréal, 1940), p. 191; Lettre Pastoral, 1866, in *Mandements, Lettres Pastorales, Circulaires et autres documents publiés dans le Diocèse de Montréal depuis son érection,* Vol. V (Montréal, 1887), p. 143.

69. ANQM, Judicial Archives, pre-archives, General Sessions of the Peace, 2 May 1871, Box 461.

70. Cited by Palmer, *Working-Class Experience,* p. 92. See also Jacques Rouillard et Judith Burt, "Le mouvement ouvrier," Noël Bélanger *et al.,* *Les Travailleurs Québécois, 1851-1896* (Montréal, 1973).

71. Médéric Lanctôt, *Association de Capital et du Travail* (Montréal, 1872), pp. 4-11; Denise Julien, "Médéric Lanctot, le mouvement ouvrier québécois et les influences américaines et européens" (M.A. thesis, Université de Montréal, 1974), pp. 133-38; *L'Union Nationale,* 12 juin 1867, cited in Julien, "Médéric Lanctot," p. 147; Paul-André Linteau, Jean-Claude Robert, et Réné Durocher, *L'histoire du Québec contemporain* (Montréal, 1979), Vol. I, p. 212.

72. Bischoff, "La formation des traditions," pp. 25-27, gives a good account of the involvement of Montreal moulders in this movement. On the nine-hour movement in general, see J. Battye, "The Nine Hour Pioneers: the Genesis

of the Canadian Labour Movement," *Labour/Le Travailleur,* 4 (1980); Palmer, *Working-Class Experience,* pp. 106-08; Heron, *The Canadian Labour Movement,* pp. 14-18; Rouillard, *Histoire du Syndicalisme,* pp. 25-29.

73. Palmer, *Working-Class Experience,* p. 115.

74. Rouillard, *Histoire du Syndicalisme,* p. 41; Richard J. Kerrigan, "The Dynamic Year of 1886," *One Big Union Monthly,* 23 September 1927, cited in Palmer, *Working-Class Experience,* pp. 130-31.

75. Cited in Kealey and Palmer, *Dreaming of What Might Be,* p. 14.

76. "Report of the Select Committee To Investigate and Report Upon Alleged Combinations in Manufactures, Trade and Insurance in Canada," Canada, House of Commons, *Journals,* 1888, Appendix 3, p. 370.

77. Michael Bliss, *A Living Profit: Studies in the Social History of Canadian Business, 1883-1911* (Toronto, 1974).

78. Forster, *A Conjunction of Interests,* pp. 140, 183-87.

79. Ideas of this street life are drawn partially from the testimony surrounding the murder of George Menden. ANQM, Judicial Archives, pre-archives, 1869, The Queen vs. George Gratton. Yvan Lamonde begins to categorize the nature of nineteenth-century Montreal sociability in "La sociabilité et l'histoire socio-culturelle: le cas de Montréal, 1760-1880," CHA, *Historical Papers* (1987).

80. See, for example, De Cotton, *À Travers le Dominion et la Californie,* p. 71; Bonnaud, *D'Océan à océan,* pp. 412-13.

81. Scott and Tilly, *Women, Work and Family*; Louise A. Tilly, "The Family Wage Economy of a French Textile City: Roubaix, 1872-1906," *Journal of Family History,* 4 (Winter, 1979), p. 381.

Chapter 2 Marriage, Families, and Households

1. *Montreal Daily Witness,* 5 December 1879.

2. Edmond Lareau, *Le Code Civil du Bas-Canada* (Montréal, 1885), Article 175. Francois Olivier-Martin, in commenting on the equivalent sections of the French *coutume,* argues that women's incapacity stemmed from marriage itself and not the regime. He is categorical: "La femme est frappée d'incapacité par l'effet même du mariage et non seulement comme conséquence du régime de communauté; un régime exclusif de communauté ne la soumettrait pas moins à la puissance maritale et le mari lui-même ne pourrait l'affranchir que dans une faible mésure d'une dépendance d'ordre public; il pourrait tout au plus lui donner le pouvoir d'administrer ses biens." *Histoire de la Coutume de la Prevoté et Vicomte de Paris,* vol. 2 (1879; reprint, Paris, 1972), p. 257.

3. ANQM, Notary McIntosh, Marriage Contract, #2416, 1861.

4. Modifications to this provision in 1888 made little difference. A wife could

not testify against her husband except when "one of the consorts separate as to property, administers as agent the property of the other." Quebec, *Revised Statutes,* vol. II, 1888, "Amendments to the Civil Code, 5.5808," article 1231, p. 660..

5. The most important articles setting out the legal incapacity of married women are 175 to 179.

6. Jennifer Stoddart, "The Dorion Commission, 1929-1931: Quebec's Legal Elites Look at Women's Rights," in David H. Flaherty, ed., *Essays in the History of Canadian Law* (Toronto, 1981).

7. Yves-F. Zoltvany, "Esquisse de la Coutume de Paris," *RHAF,* 25, 3 (décembre, 1971), pp. 365-84; Bettina Bradbury, Peter Gossage, Evelyn Kolish, and Alan Stewart "Property and Marriage: The Law and the Practice in early Nineteenth Century Montréal," *Histoire sociale/Social History* 26 (May, 1993).

8. Little has been written by historians about the position of women in the Quebec legal system. Useful are Stoddart, "The Dorion Commission"; and Micheline Dumont, "History of the Status of Women in the Province of Quebec," in *Cultural Tradition and Political History of Women in Canada,* Study No. 8, prepared for the Royal Commission on the Status of Women in Canada (Ottawa, 1971). However, by talking little about *séparation de biens* and by focusing only on the law rather than on practice, both paint an overly simple picture of women's rights and their legal incapacity.

9. Louis J. Loranger, *De l'Incapacité légale de la femme mariée* (Montréal, 1901), pp. 3, 34. This role of the man is different in its fundamental assumptions from that of a husband under common law, where the very existence of the woman was seen as subsumed in his.

10. Nicolas Benjamin Doucet, *Fundamental Principles of the Laws of Canada* (Montreal, 1841), Vol. 2, p. 206, articles 234-35. Brian Young hints at the limits to the independence that operating as a trader appeared to offer married women in "Getting around Legal Incapacity: The Legal Status of Married Women in Trade in Mid-Nineteenth Century Lower Canada," in Peter Baskerville, ed., *Canadian Papers in Business History,* 1 (1989), pp. 1-16.

11. A detailed list of those situations in which a woman could act without a husband's authorization at the turn of the century is given in Loranger, *De l'Incapacité légale,* pp. 12-14. On women traders, see Young, "Getting around Legal Incapacity."

12. In the 1820s only 23 per cent of couples marrying in Notre Dame parish, Montreal's Catholic parish, made a marriage contract; by the 1840s this had fallen to 10 per cent. See Bradbury *et al.,* "Property and Marriage." I am especially indebted to Alan Stewart and Evelyn Kolish for helping me to inch toward an understanding of legal terms and concepts.

13. Doucet, *Fundamental Principles,* Vol. 2, pp. 202-04 (Articles 220, 225, 223, and 224). This book sets out the English and French versions of the *coutume* as used in Quebec in the early nineteenth century.

14. Married women in Quebec were given the right to their own wages following the Dorion Commission in 1931. Stoddart, "The Dorion Commission."

15. By 1887 two-thirds of American states had passed earning laws protecting women's rights to their own wages. Amy Dru Stanley, "Conjugal Bonds and Wage Labor: Rights of Contract in the Age of Emancipation," *Journal of American History,* 75 (September, 1988), p. 482. Stanley's is the best examination of this question in the States. I know of no Canadian article that parallels this study. For a tantalizing hint on France, where women got the right to their own salaries only in 1907, see Colette Guillaumin, "Pratique du pouvoir et idée de nature," *Questions féministes,* 2 (1978), p. 20. The English Married Women's Property Act of 1870 specified that the "wages and earnings of any married women ... acquired or gained by her after the passing of the act should be considered her separate property." Holcombe, *Wives and Property,* p. 179. Backhouse, "Married Women's Property Law in Nineteenth Century Canada"; Cohen, *Women's Work,* p. 47.

16. Stanley, "Conjugal Bonds and Wage Labor," p. 473. On the revision of married women's property rights, see Backhouse, "Married Women's Property Law"; Basch, *In the Eyes of the Law*; Holcombe, *Wives and Property.*

17. According to Loranger this was one of the situations where the wife could act without her husband's permission. "Quand la femme achète des choses nécessaires à sa vie, et à celle de ses enfants, le mari est responsable des dettes qu'elle contracte dans ce but, car l'obligation qu'elle contracte est faite pour et au nom du mari, qui y est tenu par la loi, et qui néglige ses devoirs." *De l'Incapacité légale,* p. 13. The question of whether women married separate as to property could themselves be held responsible for such expenses led to some disagreement, but judgements generally held that they could. *The Lower Canada Jurist, Collection des Decisions du Bas-Canada,* Vol. VII, Paquette vs. Limoges, pp. 30-32.

18. Kathryn Harvey gives details of wife-beaters who also insisted on helping themselves to money their wives had earned. "'To Love, Honour and Obey,'" pp. 82-83.

19. *Montreal Star,* 2 June 1876, cited by Harvey, "'To Love, Honour and Obey,'" p. 82.

20. ANQM, Judicial Archives, pre-archives, GSOP, Box 483, 30 May 1876 and 2 June 1876. How women used the courts to attempt to force husbands to provide for them will be examined in the final chapter.

21. John Hajnal, "European Marriage Patterns in Perspective," in D.V. Glass and D.E.C. Eversley, eds., *Population in History: Essays in Historical Demography* (London, 1965); Leslie Page Moch, "Marriage, Migration and Urban Demographic Structure: A Case from France in the Belle Epoque," *Journal of Family History,* 6 (Spring, 1981), p. 71; Cohen, *Women, Work, Markets,* p. 165. Criticisms and support for Hajnal's

arguments, and specifically for their Malthusian component, can be found in the Special Issue of the *Journal of Family History* on "New Perspectives on European Marriage in the Nineteenth Century," 16, 1 (1991).

22. On single women in France, see Arlette Farge et Christiane Klapisch-Zuber, eds., *Madame ou Mademoiselle? Itinéraires de la solitude féminine XVIIIe-XXe siècle* (Paris, 1984); on England, Martha Vicinus, *Independent Women: Work and Community for Single Women, 1850-1920* (Chicago, 1985); Sheila Jeffreys, *The Spinster and her Enemies: Feminism and sexuality, 1880-1930* (London, 1985); on the United States, Lee Virginia Chambers-Schiller, *Liberty A Better Husband. Single Women in America: The Generations of 1780-1840* (New York, 1984).

23. Marta Danylewycz, *Taking the Veil: An Alternative to Marriage, Motherhood, and Spinsterhood in Quebec, 1840-1920* (Toronto, 1987).

24. For an introduction to changes in courtship among the middle class in nineteenth-century English Canada, see Peter Ward, "Courtship and Social Space in Nineteenth Century English Canada," *Canadian Historical Review*, LXVIII, 1 (1987), pp. 35-62; Ward, *Courtship, Love, and Marriage in Nineteenth Century English Canada* (Montreal and Kingston, 1990), pp. 9-14, 64-89; Lucia Ferretti, "Mariage et cadre de vie familiale dans une paroisse ouvrière Montréalaise: Sainte-Brigide, 1900-1914," *RHAF*, 39, 2 (Autumn, 1985); Denise Lemieux et Lucie Mercier, *Les Femmes au tournant du siècle, 1880-1940: Ages de la vie, maternité et quotidien* (Montréal, 1989), pp. 141-72.

25. ANQM, Marriage Registers, 1842-45.

26. Gagnon, "Parenté et migration," p. 24.

27. This is true of the couples in the random samples and remains true later in the century. See Ferretti, "Mariage et cadre de vie."

28. Their birthplaces are listed as Ireland in the census, while they have children born in England.

29. Ferretti, "Mariage et cadre de vie." Lemieux et Mercier, *Les Femmes au tournant du siècle,* pp. 159-61, speak of marriage ceremonies. However, their failure to distinguish changes over time or the class of the people involved, or to make much distinction between rural and urban practices, makes it hard to have more than a general impression. Suzanne Morton shows how working-class weddings became public, commercialized, scripted affairs in the North End of Halifax during the 1920s. "The June Bride as The Working-Class Bride: Getting Married in a Halifax Working-Class Neighbourhood in the 1920's," in Bettina Bradbury, ed., *Canadian Family History: Selected Readings* (Toronto, 1992).

30. Gagnon, "Parenté et migration," p. 24.

31. ANQM, Marriage Register, 1861. This observation is based on a perusal of the register, not on a systematic analysis. Furthermore, analysis of marriage contracts and the numbers of witnesses signing them suggests that this was a more important moment for witnesses than the marriage itself.

32. Accampo, *Industrialization, Family Life, and Class Relations,* p. 113.
33. Ward, *Courtship, Love, and Marriage,* pp. 53-56, summarizes much of the literature on the subject, concluding, rather too quickly, that marriage age "can be quite insensitive to immediate population and economic trends." He focuses on national-level data but does not consider either occupation or wealth when dealing with more detailed, local sources.
34. Jacques Henripin, *La Population Canadienne au début du XVIIIe siècle* (Paris, 1954); Jacques Henripin, *Trends and Factors of Fertility in Canada* (Ottawa, 1972).
35. Lynn Lees, *Exiles of Erin: Irish Migrants in Victorian England* (New York, 1979), p. 142.
36. The mean ages at marriage and the proportions married in the following sections are based on analysis of the behaviour of the sample populations of Sainte Anne and Saint Jacques wards. The mean singulate age at marriage was calculated following the formula set out by J. Hajnal in "Age at Marriage and Proportions Marrying," *Population Studies,* 7 (November, 1953).
37. Chad Gaffield, "Canadian Families in Cultural Context: Hypotheses from the Mid-Nineteenth Century," CHA, *Historical Papers* (1979), pp. 58-61; Jerry Wilcox and Hilda H. Golden, "Prolific Immigrants and Dwindling Natives?: Fertility Patterns in Western Massachussetts, 1850 and 1880," *Journal of Family History,* 7 (1982); Bengt Ankarloo, "Marriage and Family Formation," in Tamara K. Hareven ed., *Transitions: The Family and the Life Course in Historical Perspective* (New York, 1978), p. 122; John Modell and Lynn Lees, "The Irish Countryman Urbanized: A Comparative Perspective on the Famine Migration," in Hershberg, ed., *Philadelphia,* pp. 352-53; Lees, *Exiles of Erin,* p. 260.
38. Peter Ward found a similar pattern among recent Scottish immigrants in different Ontario communities. *Courtship, Love, and Marriage,* pp. 52-53.
39. Hareven, *Family Time and Industrial Time.*
40. Henripin, *Trends and Factors,* pp. 71, 80.
41. Michael Haines, *Fertility in Occupation: Population Patterns in Industrialization* (New York, 1979); Gagan, *Hopeful Travellers,* p. 73.
42. Tamara K. Hareven and Maris Vinovskis, *Family and Population in Nineteenth Century America* (Princeton, N.J., 1978), p. 100.
43. Some caution is necessary here, particularly regarding the Protestant women, as the numbers are not very large.
44. Jacques Henripin, "From Acceptance of Nature to Control: the Demography of the French Canadians since the Seventeenth Century," in Michiel Horn and Ronald Sabourin, *Studies in Canadian Social History* (Toronto, 1974), pp. 79-80.
45. Peter Gossage, "Absorbing Junior: Patent Medicines as Abortifacients in Nineteenth Century Montreal," graduate paper, McGill University History Dept., 1980. The *Montreal Transcript,* 2 May 1862, for example,

advertised several remedies that promised to be peculiarly suited to married ladies as they would bring on the monthly period with regularity. They could be obtained at a cost of a dollar by mail or were said to be on sale at respectable Montreal druggists. Angus McLaren, "Birth Control and Abortion in Canada, 1870-1920," *Canadian Historical Review,* LIX (September, 1978), pp. 319-40; Angus McLaren and Arlene Tigar McLaren, *The Bedroom and the State: The Changing Practices and Politics of Contraception and Abortion in Canada, 1880-1980* (Toronto, 1986), pp. 18-20. Marie-Aimée Cliche, "L'infanticide dans la région de Québec (1660-1969)," *RHAF,* 44, 1 (Summer, 1990), uncovers only 392 cases that came before the coroner in the region surrounding Quebec City in the whole period she studied. Peter Gossage, "Les enfants abondonnés à Montréal au 19e siècle: la Crèche d'Youville des Soeurs Grises, 1820-1871," *RHAF* (Spring, 1987), pp. 537-60. Patricia Thornton and Sherry Olson suggest that breastfeeding was widespread among all groups in this period, but may have been practised for a shorter time by French Canadians. "Family Contexts of Fertility and Infant Survival in Nineteenth-Century Montreal," *Journal of Family History,* 16, 4 (1991), pp. 409, 413.

46. Jean-Claude Robert, "The City of Wealth and Death: Urban Mortality in Montreal, 1821-1871," in Wendy Mitchinson and Janice Dickin McGinnis, eds., *Essays in the History of Canadian Medicine* (Toronto, 1988); Thornton and Olson, "Family Contexts."

47. This somewhat controversial argument was advanced by Rose Frisch in "Nutrition, Fatness and Fertility: The Effect of Food Intake on Reproductive Ability," in W. Henry Mosley, ed., *Nutrition and Human Reproduction* (New York, 1978), cited in Peter T. Marcy, "Factors Affecting Fecundity and Fertility of Historical Populations: A Review," *Journal of Family History,* 6 (1981), pp. 313-17.

48. Andrée Lévesque examines the norm and ways in which women controlled the numbers of children born during the 1920s and 1930s in *La Norme et les déviantes: Des femmes au Québec pendant l'entre deux guerres* (Montréal, 1989). The pressure placed on women to perform their duty and the anguish that breaking Church regulations caused some of them is beautifully captured in Denyse Baillargeon, *Ménagères au temps de la crise* (Montréal, 1992). On the period preceding this book, see Serge Gagnon, *Plaisir d'amour et crainte de Dieu: Sexualité et confession au Bas-Canada* (Sainte-Foy, 1990).

49. The fact that until 1891 this group was marrying younger, yet still having fewer children, lends support to this hypothesis.

50. Robert, "City of Wealth and Death."

51. See Anderson, *Family Structure,* pp. 125-27, for a very careful analysis of which sons left home under what conditions.

52. For the industrial period, the assertion that rural/urban differences are most

important captures only one element of demographic reality and leads to ignoring important variations within a city. On differential fertility in New France, see Lorraine Gadoury, Yves Landry, et Hubert Charbonneau, "Démographie differentielle en Nouvelle France: villes et campagnes," *RHAF,* 38, 3 (Winter, 1985), pp. 357-58.

53. RCRLC, evidence of Elie Ricard, shoemaker, p. 369.

54. Accampo, *Industrialization, Family Life,* p. 112.

55. Katz *et al.*, *Social Organization,* p. 303.

56. Hareven, *Family Time and Industrial Time,* p. 101.

57. Anderson, *Family Structure,* ch. 10; Hareven, *Family Time and Industrial Time,* pp. 101-13.

58. Mss. Census, St. Jacques, 1861, fo. 7429; 1871, B:5; 1881, Section 12, 203: 228. John Lovell, *Montreal City Directory,* (Montreal, 1859-60, 1860/61); ANQM, Notre Dame Parish, Parish Registers, Marriage 26 November 1856, fo. 95 and 20 October 1888, fo. 64; Birth, 11 May 1867, fo. 131.

59. Mss. Census, St. Jacques, 1881, 13:248:344; *Montreal City Directory,* 1880-81, 1881-82.

60. Gagnon, "Parenté et migration."

61. Olivier Marrault, *Marges d'histoire* (Montréal, 1929), pp. 215-19; Raoul Blanchard, *L'Ouest du Canada français: Province de Québec* (Montréal, 1953), pp. 262-63; David Hanna, "Montreal: A City Built by Small Builders: 1866-1880" (Ph.D. thesis, McGill University, 1986); Hertzog and Lewis, "A City of Tenants."

62. Hanna, "Montreal: A City Built by Small Builders"; Gilles Lauzon, *Habitat ouvrier et revolution industrielle: Le cas du village St-Augustin* (Montréal, 1989); Jean-Claude Marsan, *Montreal in Evolution: Historical Analysis of the Development of Montreal's Architecture and Urban Environment* (Montreal, 1981).

63. Hanna, "Montreal: A City Built by Small Builders," p. 111; Herbert Brown Ames, *The City Below the Hill* (Montreal, 1897; reprint Toronto, 1972).

64. Hanna, "Montreal: A City Built by Small Builders," pp. 117-25.

65. *Ibid.*, pp. 54-58, 121-22.

66. Hertzog and Lewis, "A City of Tenants," pp. 316-19. No one has studied Montreal coopers. On Toronto, see Kealey, *Toronto Workers Respond.*

67. Hertzog and Lewis, "A City of Tenants," p. 318; Lauzon, *Habitat ouvrier,* pp. 139-47. Yet even in Saint Henri access to land declined over the 1870s as the accessible land area was built over and the depression ate up people's income and savings. *Ibid.*, pp. 116, 151.

68. John Cooper, "The Social Structure of Montreal in the 1850s," *Canadian Historical Association Annual Report* (1956), p. 68.

69. Hanna, "Montreal: A City Built by Small Builders"; *Montreal Annual Reports* (hereafter *MAR*), Report of the Building Inspector, 1867-81.

70. David Hanna et Sherry Olson, "Métier, loyer et bouts de rue; L'armature de la société montréalaise, 1881-1901," *Cahiers de géographie du Québec*, 27 (1983).

71. *MAR*, Report of the Building Inspector, 1866-91.

72. Robert, "The City of Wealth and Death," pp. 18-19.

73. Philip P. Carpenter, *On the Relative Value of Human Life in Different Parts of Canada* (Montreal, 1859), pp. 7, 9, republished from *The Canadian Naturalist and Geologist* (1859); Robert, "The City of Wealth and Death"; Copp, *The Anatomy of Poverty.*

74. *MAR*, Report of the Building Inspector, 1866-82; *ibid.*, Report of the Medical Health Officer, 1876; Jacques Bernier, "La condition des travailleurs, 1851-1896," in Noel Bélanger *et al.*, *Les Travailleurs Québécois, 1851-1896* (Montréal, 1975), p. 47.

75. Carpenter, *On the Relative Value*, p. 15.

76. Philip Carpenter, "On Some of the Causes of the Excessive Mortality of Young Children in the City of Montreal," *The Canadian Naturalist and Quarterly Journal of Science*, 4 (June, 1869), pp. 195-96; "A Chronicle of the Montreal Diet Dispensary, 1879-1957," Montreal Diet Dispensary Records, McGill Rare Books Room, "Box," p. 14.

77. I return to mothers in Chapter 5. For examples of this kind of literature, see William Mondelet, "La ventilation," *L'Union Medicale du Canada*, II, 7 (juillet, 1873), p. 300; Dr. T. McGrath, *Lectures on Health* (Quebec, 1877), pp. 29-30; Dr. Jean-Philippe Rottot, *L'Union Medicale*, 1 (avril, 1872), p. 146, all cited in Martin Tetrault, "L'État de santé des Montréalais, de 1880 à 1914" (Ph.D. thesis, Université de Montréal, 1979), p. 10.

78. See especially *MAR*, Report Upon the Sanitary State, 1889, p. 97.

79. RCRLC, evidence of Arthur W. Short, editor of *The Canadian Workman*, pp. 547-49.

80. *MAR*, Report Upon the Sanitary State, 1885, p. 26.

81. Ames, *The City Below the Hill*, p. 45.

82. Mondelet, "La ventilation," p. 300, cited in Tetrault, "L'État de santé," p.12.

83. RCRLC, pp. 606-09.

84. *Montreal Daily Star*, 24 December 1883; Anon., *Montreal By Gaslight* (Montreal, 1889), p. 17.

85. Gareth Stedman Jones's *Outcast London: A Study in the Relationship between Classes in Victorian Society* (Harmondsworth, 1971), is one of the classic studies of such groups, people immortalized in Hogarth's sketches of London. Judith Fingard studies those people in what she calls the underclass who persistently ran afoul of the law, landing repeatedly in court for stealing, fighting, insulting, prostitution, etc., in nineteenth-century Halifax in *The Dark Side of Life in Victorian Halifax* (Halifax, 1989).

86. RCRLC, evidence of John W. Grose, Chairman of the Board of Assessors

of the City of Montreal, p. 266; evidence of Pierre Hubert Morin, Assessor, p. 552.

87. That it can be done with care for a limited number of houses and by combining as many sources as possible is clear in Gilles Lauzon's careful reconstruction of housing strategies. See Lauzon, *Habitat ouvrier,* pp. 77-107.

88. Canada, *Sessional Papers,* 1872, Paper No. 64, Report of the Department of Agriculture, "Instructions to Officers," p. 133.

89. Lauzon, *Habitat ouvrier.*

90. This question was first addressed in my "The Family Economy and Work in an Industrializing City: Montreal in the 1870's," CHA, *Historical Papers* (1979), where I simplistically assumed that the census definition of household and reality coincided. The problem of this position was acknowledged in my later works, "Pigs, Cows and Boarders" and "The Working-Class Family Economy," although no alternative explanation was ventured.

91. Gordon Darroch and Michael D. Ornstein do not even raise the issue of problems with the application of the census definition in their "Family Co-residence in Canada in 1871: Family Life-Cycles, Occupations and Networks of Mutual Aid," CHA, *Historical Papers* (1983), pp. 30-56; Gordon Darroch and Michael D. Ornstein, "Family and Household in Nineteenth Century Canada, Regional Patterns and Regional Economies," *Journal of Family History,* 9, 2 (Summer, 1984), pp. 158-77. Gilles Lauzon has made the major and most cogent critique of this uncritical use of census categories in his *Habitat ouvrier.* See also Robert Sweeny, "Un passé en mutation: Bilan et perspectives pour une histoire socio-économique de Montréal au XIXe siècle," in Jean-Rémi Brault, ed., *Montréal au XIXe siècle. Des gens, des idées, des arts, une ville* (Montréal, 1990), pp. 28-29.

92. Lauzon, *Habitat ouvrier,* p. 100.

93. His hypothesis that in 1871 and 1881 street numbers usually indicate census households is largely correct. Thus a household number could refer to three apartments within one building, or to two houses, one on the front and one on the back of the lot.

94. This section is based on matching the material found in the 1871 census with the evaluation role and "feuille de route" produced by the city assessors, the city directories of 1870-71 and 1871-72, and the 1881 Good's atlas, which shows the shape of buildings as well as the building materials. Lauzon also used rental agreements. These are difficult to seek out in a city the size of Montreal. Furthermore, I doubt if more than a minority of subletting arrangements would have been made with a notary.

95. This whole question requires further detailed study, as Lauzon concludes. Gagnon, "Parenté et migration," p. 79.

Chapter 3   Men's Wages and the Cost of Living

1. Québec, *Second Rapport des Commissaires chargés de codifier les lois du Bas Canada en matières civiles* (Québec, 1865), p. 193. A husband, in contrast, could request separation of bed and board if his wife was guilty of adultery anywhere.

2. Kathryn Harvey examines these cases in "'To Love Honour and Obey', Wife-battering in Working-Class Montréal, 1869-1879" (M.A. thesis, Université de Montréal, 1991). I use some in Chapter 6. ANQM, Judicial Archives, pre-archives, 1871-79, Failure to Provide cases. The number of cases appears to increase as the depression of the 1870s deepened, although it could be that women were becoming more aware of the rights given them by the 1869 statute that made failure to provide a criminal offence.

3. *Ibid.*, 22 March 1878, The Queen vs. Israel Beaume, Box 497.

4. To my knowledge nothing like the detailed accounts of wages and days worked collected by the Ontario Bureau of Industries exists for Quebec during the nineteenth century. Rosemary and David Gagan use this material to show how central the number of days' work that men could find was in "Working-Class Standards of Living in Late-Victorian Urban Ontario."

5. Clyde Griffin, "Occupational Mobility in Nineteenth Century America: Problems and Possibilities," *Journal of Social History,* 5 (Spring, 1972).

6. Sweeny, "Financing the Transition"; Poutanen, "For the Benefit of the Master"; Burgess, "Work, Family and Community."

7. Notary McIntosh seems to have specialized in inserting this clause in contracts written in 1870. See ANQM, McIntosh, #12519 Indenture of M. Severe Latour as journeyman and foreman shoemaker, to Mssrs. William and David McLean, 13 December 1870; #12526 M. Edmond Mainville as journeyman cooper to Joseph Cadieux.

8. Peter Bischoff, "La formation des traditions," p. 15.

9. Jacques Ferland, "Les Chevaliers de Saint-Crépin du Québec, 1869-1871: Une étude en trois tableaux," *Canadian Historical Review,* LXXII, 1 (1991), pp. 11-25.

10. Montreal painter Joseph Arel, for instance, bound himself in January, 1861, to "paint, varnish all and every wheeled vehicle of any kind, and shape done made and executed by the . . . Messieurs Cusack." They, in turn, agreed to provide all necessary supplies of varnish and paint, not to bother him in his work, and to pay specified amounts for various kinds of wagons and buggies as the work progressed, with the balance payable by the end of the contract time. ANQM, Notary Edward McIntosh, Deed #2413.

11. Paul Craven and Tom Traves, "Dimensions of Paternalism: Discipline and Culture in Canadian Railway Operations in the 1850s," in Heron and Storey, eds., *On the Job,* p. 55. A few labourers who mistakenly reported

their own monthly wages on their census schedule in 1861 reported monthly wages of between $18 and $21.66 or between seventy-five and ninety-one cents a day; *L'Union Nationale,* 14 mars 1867, 23 mars 1867, cited by Denise Julien, "Médéric Lanctôt," p. 129; F. Braun to Public Works Canada, 19 December 1877, National Archives of Canada (hereafter NAC), RG 11 B1 (a), Jean de Bonville, *Jean-Baptiste Gagnepetit: les travailleurs Montréalais à la fin du XIXe siècle* (Montréal, 1975), p. 87; Canada, *Sessional Papers,* No. 14, 1883, "Annual Report of the Montreal Immigrant Agent," p. 105; *ibid.* 1882, pp. 110-11.

12. Palmer, *Working-Class Experience,* p. 92.

13. "Petition from labourers upon the Government works upon the Lachine Canal Enlargement to the Ministry of Public Works," 18 January 1878, NAC, Dept. of Public Works, RG 11, B1(a), Vol. 473, pp. 2514-20.

14. *Ibid.*

15. *Ibid.,* p. 2517; Mss. Census, Ste. Anne, 1881, District 5, 330:373.

16. "Petition," 1878, p. 002518.

17. *Montreal Witness,* 26 December 1877, cited by DeLottinville, "Joe Beef," p. 23.

18. Jacques Ferland describes the changes in the organization of work, the kinds of technology introduced, the perceptions of the workers, and the oppressive role of the Church in "Les Chevaliers de Saint-Crépin." The earlier work of Joanne Burgess, "L'industrie de la chaussure à Montréal: 1840-1870 − Le passage de parlisonat à la fabrique," *RHAF,* 31 (September, 1977), is useful for the description of some conflicts in the 1860s. On the kinds of transformations that preceded the introduction of machinery, see her doctoral thesis, "Work, Family and Community." The testimonies taken at the Royal Commission on the Relations of Labour and Capital in 1888 give a detailed idea of many aspects of the nature of the trade at that point in time. The reports of other government commissions during the 1870s and 1880s do so, too, as do the reports Patterson made for the Montreal Board of Trade.

19. RCRLC, evidence of Samuel Wells, superintendent, pp. 554-55.

20. Ferland, "Les Chevaliers de Saint-Crépin," pp. 5-9.

21. RCRLC, evidence of Alfre Patrie, pp. 239-43.

22. Mss. Industrial Census, Montreal, 1861-71.

23. RCRLC, evidence of Z. Lapierre, shoe manufacturer, pp. 437-39; evidence of M.C. Mullarky, shoe manufacturer, pp. 445-47; evidence of James McCready, boot and shoe manufacturer, pp. 491-93.

24. RCRLC, evidence of Olivier David Benoit, shoemaker, p. 364; evidence of a leather cutter, p. 238.

25. Ferland, "Syndicalisme 'parcellaire' et syndicalisme 'collectif'," pp. 55-59; de Bonville, *Jean-Baptiste Gagnepetit,* p. 87.

26. Burgess, "L'industrie de la chaussure à Montréal"; *Mandements, Lettres Pastorales, Circulaires et Autres Documents Publiés dans le diocèse de*

Montréal depuis son érection, Vol. V, pp. 458-59; *La Minerve,* 10 septembre 1869.

27. RCRLC, evidence of Elie Ricard, Olivier David Benoit, Alfred Viger, shoemakers or leather cutters, pp. 369, 364, 373.

28. RCRLC, evidence of Elie Ricard, p. 369; evidence of Olivier David Benoit, p. 364. An earlier hint of this is to be found in the evidence of Mr. Mullarky, "Select Committee on the Manufacturing Interests," 1874, p. 63.

29. RCRLC, evidence of George S. Warren, p. 55.

30. RCRLC, evidence of George Robley, cigarmaker, pp. 47-51; evidence of George S. Warren, cigarmaker, pp. 55-59.

31. Mss. Census, 1871, Industrial Schedules, Ste. Anne and St. Jacques. James Shearer, Ste. Anne, a. 9, p. 5.

32. David Hanna, "Montreal: A City Built by Small Builders."

33. Bernier, "La condition des travailleurs," p. 40.

34. RCRLC, evidence of Ludger Cousineau, contractor, p. 581.

35. RCRLC, evidence of S. Paquette, joiner, p. 650; evidence of Douglas Rutherford, builder, pp. 534, 542; anonymous evidence, pp. 641-42; evidence of A. Short, pp. 550-51.

36. Evidence on wages in the skilled trades is drawn from the following sources: Craven and Traves, "Dimensions of Paternalism," p. 55; earnings reported in error on the manuscript census, 1861; Proceedings, Iron Moulders of America, 7th Congress, New York, January 1866, p. 47, cited in Peter Bischoff, "Les ouvriers mouleurs à Montréal, 1859-1881" (M.A. thesis, UQAM, 1986), p. 58; "Report on the Manufacturing Interests of the Dominion," p. 151; "Report on the Causes of the Depression," pp. 148-49. It was against such cuts that the engine drivers of the Grand Trunk struck in December, 1875, paralysing train service across Canada. Desmond Morton, "Taking on the Grand Trunk: The Locomotive Engineers' Strike of 1876-7," *Labour/Le Travailleur* (1977).

37. Shergold, *Working-Class Life,* p. 225.

38. The first list of a reasonable number of wage rates along with an indication of prices that I have found for Montreal is that of the immigration agent in 1882. The figures in this paragraph are all based on the wages he cites in Canada, *Sessional Papers,* No. 14, "Annual Report of the Montreal Immigration Agent," 1882, pp. 110-11.

39. Jerome M. Clubb *et al.*, *The Process of Historical Inquiry: Everyday Lives of Working Americans* (New York, 1989), p. 102.

40. Michael R. Haines, "Poverty, Economic Stress, and the Family in a Late Nineteenth Century American City: Whites in Philadelphia, 1880," in Hershberg, ed., *Philadephia.* For other attempts to critique and to assess the standard of living historically, see Steven Dubnoff, "A Method for Estimating the Economic Welfare of American Families of Any Composition: 1860-1909," *Historical Methods Newsletter,* 13 (1980); Foster, *Class*

Struggle, Appendix I; Anderson, *Family Structure,* pp. 29-32; Lees, *Exiles of Erin,* pp. 100-06; Copp, *The Anatomy of Poverty,* pp. 30-43; Piva, *The Condition of the Working Class in Toronto, 1900-1921,* pp. 36-39; Shergold, *Working-Class Life*; Clubb *et al.*, *The Process of Historical Inquiry,* pp. 20-21, 102.

41. The Ontario Bureau of Industries did begin to attempt systematic evaluations of wages earned and the cost of living from 1884 on. See Gagan and Gagan, "Working-Class Standards"; Herbert Brown Ames's 1897 study of part of Sainte Anne ward, *The City Below the Hill,* examines incomes but makes no estimates of what people spent. Only Henri-Phillipe Gauldrée-Boileau's study of Saint-Irénée Parish in 1861 and Stanislas Lortie's study of a Quebec City typographer's family explicitly apply Le Play's approach to Canadian families, although Léon Gérin's work is also heavily influenced by Le Play's methodology. On his influence in Canada, see Pierre Trépanier, "Les influences leplaysiennes au Canada français, 1855-1888," *Journal of Canadian Studies,* 22, 1 (Spring, 1987). It was not until 1910 that the Canadian Department of Labour first attempted to estimate a basic budget for the working class.

42. Letter reproduced in the *Sixth Annual Report of the Commissioner of Labour, 1890* (Washington, D.C., 1891), pp. 688-90, cited in Clubb *et al.*, *The Process of Historical Inquiry,* pp. 17-18.

43. RCRLC, pp. 250-51; on Helbronner, see de Bonville, *Jean-Baptiste Gagnepetit.*

44. RCRLC, *Maritime Evidence,* evidence of Patrick Kennedy, labourer, p. 264.

45. Québec, *Débats de l'Assemblée législative,* 8 March 1900.

46. Child Welfare Exhibition, *Souvenir Handbook* (Montreal, 1912), pp. 32-33.

47. See the budgets reproduced in Copp, *The Anatomy of Poverty,* pp. 149-63.

48. RCRLC, pp. 86-87; evidence of Edmond Chaput, baker, p. 566. So did other men. See, for example, RCRLC, *Maritime Evidence,* p. 265.

49. Dubnoff, "A Method for Estimating the Economic Welfare of American Families," is a good introduction to many of the different methods that historians and economists have used to measure the standard of living. Shergold, *Working-Class Life,* includes valuable comparisons between the standard of living of American and English workers that modify the accepted wisdom of all American workers enjoying a substantially better real wage.

50. American and British historians have been able to develop fairly sophisticated ways of measuring the adequacy of wages and to determine the actual goods purchased by working-class families. Until the twentieth century this appears difficult to do in Canada because little consistent material on wages, prices, and purchasing habits exists. I have therefore opted for a simple estimate based on what it was possible for men in

different occupations to earn, contrasted with the costs of a minimum diet, at Montreal prices, and rental and fuel costs in one year, 1881. Cf. Eudice Glassberg, "Work, Wages, and the Cost of Living: Ethnic Differences in the Poverty Line, Philadelphia, 1880," *Pennsylvania History,* 66 (January, 1979), pp. 17-58; Haines, "Poverty, Economic Stress, and the Family," pp. 240-76.

51. Since English, Irish, and French-Canadian workers alike appear to have eaten meat in preference to cheese, the diet used for Montreal workers replaces the cheese allowance with the same amount of cheap meat. Foster, *Class Struggle,* does the same, pp. 255-56. For further indications of Montreal workers' eating habits, see the testimony of Thomas Gratorex, labourer, RCRLC, p. 86; "Cash Book," Walter H. Smith Collection, McGill University, Rare Book Room.

52. Rowntree, *Poverty.* Canadian prison diets were apparently similar, although more bread and potatoes and fewer extras seem to have been allowed. S.P. Day reported that in 1864 prisoners received 1 pint of oatmeal and gruel and 8 oz. of bread for breakfast; 1 pint of soup, 8 oz. of bread, and 6 oz. of meat twice a week, with bread and potatoes or gruel on other days for dinner and supper the same as breakfast. S.P. Day, *English America: or Pictures of Canadian Places and People* (London, 1864), pp. 124-25. Following Rowntree, boys aged fourteen and over received 0.85 of a male allowance; women, 0.80; girls 14-15, 0.70; children 5-13, 0.50; a child under five, 0.33; and all people over sixty, 0.60.

53. Lacombe's estimate of fourteen cents a day or ninety-eight cents weekly as the basic food cost in Montreal in 1900 suggests that this figure is not far from reality. Québec, *Débats,* 8 March 1900.

54. Dubnoff, "A Method for Estimating the Economic Welfare of American Families," p. 172, shows the same phenomenon. In the United States the food share of the budget had apparently, on the average, declined from 58 per cent in 1874 to about 20 per cent in 1970. *Ibid.*, p. 173.

55. Laura Oren, "The Welfare of Women in Labouring Families: England 1860-1950," *Feminist Studies,* 3-4 (Winter-Spring, 1973).

56. RCRLC, evidence of Charles Doherty, advocate, p. 215; evidence of Christopher B. Carter, advocate, p. 718; evidence of Thomas Gratorex, labourer, p. 86.

57. RCRLC, evidence of Lewis Z. Boudreau, printer, p. 243; Thomas Gratorex, labourer, pp. 85-87; William Keys, machinist, p. 517; William T. Costigan, Artizans' Dwelling House Company, p. 732; Dr. Dougless Decrow, p. 609.

58. Sherry Olson, "The Tip of the Iceberg: Strategy for research on Nineteenth-century Montreal," *Shared Spaces/Partage de l'espace,* no. 5 (June, 1986), p. 7.

59. David Hanna et Sherry Olson, "Métiers, loyers et bouts de rue: L'armature

de la société montréalaise de 1881 à 1901," *Cahiers de géographie* (1983), p. 260.

60. RCRLC, evidence of Dr. Dougless Decrow, p. 609.

61. Lauzon, *Habitat ouvrier.* See the discussion of housing in Chapter 2 above.

62. Families of five have been allowed the labourer's average of $39 until their children passed the age of eleven. The average for a shoemaker ($45) was allowed thereafter. Families with five children, nearly all in their teens, were attributed an annual rent of $72.

63. On the importance of firewood in Montreal earlier in the century and a critique of the staples thesis, see Robert Sweeney with Richard Rice and Grace Laing Hogg, *Les relations ville/campagne. Le cas du bois de chauffage* (Montréal, 1988).

64. *MAR,* Mayor's Inaugural Address, 1871.

65. Canada, House of Commons, *Journals,* 1888, Appendix 3, p. 243. A decade earlier the winter price was similar. The 12 December 1879 issue of the *Montreal Daily Witness* advertised high-grade coal at $7 to $7.50 delivered; coke could be had for $4.50 a ton. Wood was between $3.50 and $6 a cord. November appears to have been the peak month for the number of cords of wood landed in Montreal harbour. That year 6,530 of the 42,741 cords reported to be landed at Montreal came in November, compared to 3,452 in April.

66. Canada, House of Commons, *Journals,* 1886, p. 8. Whether coal and firewood could be purchased on credit needs examination.

67. A less generous two tons of coal and two cords of wood were allowed by Montreal MLA Mr. G.-A. Lacombe in his estimates of the cost of living in Montreal in 1900. Quebec, *Debates,* 8 March 1900; *Child Welfare Exhibit,* 1912, p. 32.

68. "Notes pour les chroniques de L'Asile St. Vincent," handwritten chronicles, 1877-78, p. 41, Archives of the Sisters of Providence (hereafter ASP), Montreal; Montreal Young Women's Christian Association, Annual Report, 1887, p. 15, PAC, MG 28 I 240, Vol. 38.

69. Rare Book Room, McGill University, Walter H. Smith Collection (748-9), "Box"; "Diary."

70. ANQM, Judicial Archives, pre-archives, GSOP, 1871, #12 Queen vs. Gustave Beriau.

71. Clubb *et al.* suggest in their study of American working-class budgets in 1890 that "for a large but not precisely known portion of the families, clothing was not adequate in terms of a reasonable standard." *The Process of Historical Inquiry,* p. 131.

72. Thus, they support the Gagans' argument about the importance of the number of days men could work, while going against their suggestion that skill was a negligible factor. Gagan and Gagan, "Working-Class Standards of Living."

73. ANQM, Notary Amable Archambault, act no. 3213.

74. Grace Laing-Hogg, "The Legal Rights of Masters, Mistresses and Domestic Servants in Montreal, 1816-1829" (M.A. thesis, McGill University, 1989).

75. Jean Hamelin *et al.*, *Repertoire des grèves dans la province de Québec aux XIXe siècle* (Montréal, 1971); DeLottinville, "Joe Beef," p. 21.

76. "Petition to the Honorable Ministers and Members of the Provincial Assembly of the Province of Quebec," Resolution of the Annual Meeting, September, 1896, ANQ, Quebec, Travaux Publique, Box E-0025, 09724.

77. RCRLC, diverse evidence.

78. RCRLC, pp. 530-31. This practice pre-dates industrial work, as Judith Fingard makes clear in "The Winter's Tale: The Seasonal Contours of Pre-Industrial Poverty in British North America, 1815-1860," CHA, *Historical Papers* (1974), pp. 66-68.

79. RCRLC, evidence of E. Globensky, p. 455.

80. "Notes pour les chroniques de L'Asile St. Vincent," p. 21.

81. Hamelin et Roby, *Histoire Économique,* p. 90; Bernier, "La condition des travailleurs," p. 31; *MAR,* Mayor's Inaugural Address, 1875, p. 6; Canada, "Select Committee on the Causes of the Present Depression," 1876, p. 111; Bischoff, "Solidarité ouvrière," pp. 28-29; Morton, "Taking on the Grand Trunk," p. 12; Patterson report, 1874, p. 100; Canada, *Sessional Papers,* 1882-83, "Annual Report of the Immigration Agent."

82. Bryan D. Palmer, "Labour in Nineteenth-Century Canada," in W.J.C. Cherwinski and Gregory S. Kealey, eds., *Lectures in Canadian Labour and Working-Class History* (St. John's, 1985), p. 55.

83. *MAR,* Mayor's Valedictory Address, 1876, p. 10.

84. *Iron Moulders Journal,* February, 1875, p. 235, cited in Bischoff, "La formation des traditions," p. 30.

85. ANQM, Judicial Archives, pre-archives, The Queen vs. Israel Beaume, 22 March 1878.

86. See, for example, ANQM, Judicial Archives, pre-archives, Julie Belec vs. Ulric Lamoureux, Court of the Queen's Bench, 1878, Box #495, 20 December 1877. Most cases brought against husbands appear to have been brought by women who had either separated legally from their husbands and had some kind of agreement about support payments, or whose husbands were living with a "concubine." See, for example, Edwige Handfield vs. Octave Dansereau, *ibid.*, Box #503, where this labourer was meant to provide $10 per month to support her and her children. He was sentenced to three months' hard labour for not paying. Also, Mathilda Leveille vs. Joseph Amesse, Queen's Bench, 1879, Box #503, 20 January 1879, where he was supporting his concubine but not his wife and children.

87. Eric Sager and Peter Baskerville, "The First National Unemployment

Survey: Unemployment and the Canadian Census of 1891," *Labour/Le Travail,* 23 (Spring, 1989).

88. *Montreal Star,* 15 July 1870.

89. *Montreal Daily Witness,* 9 December 1879.

90. ANQM, Judicial Archives, pre-archives, Queen's Bench, 9 August 1879, Box 503.

91. DeLottinville, "Joe Beef"; Kathryn Harvey, "'To Love, Honour and Obey,' Wife-battering in Working-Class Montreal, 1869-79," *Urban History Review,* XIX, 2 (October, 1990).

92. "Report of the Commissioners Appointed to enquire into the Working of the Mills and Factories of the Dominion and the Labour employed therein," Canada, *Sessional Papers,* No. 42, 1882, p. 17.

93. *Le Trait d'Union,* Montréal, 1 February 1887 (my translation).

94. RCRLC, p. 186.

95. See RCRLC, evidence of Eli Massy, pp. 150-51; evidence of Octave Delage, p. 1496, cited in Fernand Harvey, *Révolution industrielle et travailleurs: Une enquête sur les rapports entre le capital et le travail au Québec à la fin du 19e siècle* (Montréal, 1978), p. 307.

96. Carpenter, *On the Relative Value of Human Life,* p. 12. These proportions were calculated on the basis of only fifteen cases of illness for each death, excluding those caused by smallpox, a very conservative measure compared with that of Carpenter.

97. ANQM, Notary Amable Archambault, *Inventaire des biens,* no. 3203, 30 July 1867.

98. "Could we use a year's earnings as I have divided them we might get through," wrote an American woman to the Commissioner of Labor in 1890, "but bills that were made when the children were sick or the husband out of employment the year previous press heavily sometimes, and cut into the present year's earnings." Cited in Clubb *et al., The Process of Historical Inquiry,* p. 19.

99. RCRLC, pp. 651, 332-33, 697.

100. *Ibid.*, evidence of Charles Doherty, advocate, p. 215; evidence of Christopher B. Carter, advocate, p. 718; evidence of Thomas Gratorex, p. 86. In 1881 new legislation limited the seizable proportion of wage-earners' income to half. Quebec, *Statutes,* Cap. XVIII, assented to June, 1881.

101. RCRLC, *First Report,* cited in de Bonville, *Jean-Baptiste Gagnepetit,* p. 109.

102. Quebec, *Debates,* 8 March 1900.

103. Cf. Copp, *The Anatomy of Poverty,* p. 43.

104. ANQM, Notre Dame Parish, Marriage, 9 January 1854; births, 27 June 1858; deaths, 14 December 1860; Mss. Census, Ste. Anne 1861, fo. 2497; 1871, A:7, 141:212; 1881, 9, 87:89. Note that this exercise is also hypothetical. It involves the extrapolation backward of 1881 prices and wages.

All evidence suggests that wages did not change much, nor did the price of the most basic foodstuffs. Rents, however, were much higher by the 1880s.

105. Ames, *The City Below the Hill,* pp. 44-45.

106. Mss. St. Jacques, 1861, fo. 7429; 1871, B.5 at 310 Jacques Cartier St.; 1881, 12, 203: 228.

107. Mss. Census, St. Jacques, 1861, fo.7888; 1871, B-2, 129.

108. Mss. Census, St. Jacques, 1881, Section 17, 110:140.

109. This trend was not limited to these two parts of town. Peter Bischoff reports that among the moulders of Montreal the percentage who were sons still living with their parents rose from 25% in 1861 to nearly 40% in 1881. Bischoff, "Les mouleurs," p. 108.

110. RCRLC, evidence of George Warren, p. 56; evidence of Olivier David Benoit, boot and shoemaker, pp. 364-65.

111. Copp, *The Anatomy of Poverty,* p. 44.

Chapter 4 Gender, Age, and the Roles of Children

1. Cited in Lees, *Exiles of Erin,* p. 22.

2. Gérard Bouchard and Jeannette Larouche, "Paramètres sociaux de la reproduction familiale au Saguenay (1842-1911)," *Sociologie et sociétés,* 19, 1 (avril, 1987), pp. 133-44; Gagan, *Hopeful Travellers,* pp. 40-60; Allan Greer, *Peasant, Lord and Merchant,* pp. 48-88.

3. Micheline Dumont Johnson, "Des garderies au XIXe siècle: les salles d'asiles des Soeurs Grises à Montréal," *RHAF,* 34 (June, 1980).

4. Many historical studies suggest that most working-class children received minimal education in school. Furthermore, Harvey Graff's examination of the differences in the social position and mobility of illiterates and literates suggests literacy was not a major element of economic success at this period. Harvey J. Graff, *The Literacy Myth: Literacy and Social Structure in the Nineteenth-Century City* (New York, 1979); John Bullen, "Hidden Workers: Child Labour and the Family Economy in Late Nineteenth-Century Urban Ontario," *Labour/Le Travail,* 18 (Fall, 1986), pp. 163-87.

5. Carl F. Kaestle and Maris A. Vinovskis, "From Fireside to Factory: School Entry and School Leaving in Nineteenth Century Massachussetts," in Tamara K. Hareven, ed., *Transitions: The Family Life Course in Historical Perspective* (New York, 1978); Chad Gaffield and David Levine, "Dependency and Adolescence on the Canadian Frontier: Orillia, Ontario, in the Nineteenth Century," *History of Education Quarterly,* 18 (Spring, 1978); Michael B. Katz and Ian Davey, "Youth and Early Industrialization in a Canadian City," in John Demos and Sarane Spence Boocock, eds., *Turning Points: Historical and Sociological Essays on the Family* (Chicago, 1978).

6. Schooling was made compulsory for six- to fourteen-year-olds in Quebec in 1943, and fees in public primary schools were abolished at the same

time. For an excellent description of the relations between families and the state over these policies and of the ways in which schooling had been encouraged despite the absence of legislation, see Dominique Jean, "Familles québécoises et politiques sociales touchant les enfants, de 1940 à 1950: obligation scolaire, allocations familiales, travail juvenile" (Ph.D. thesis, Université de Montréal, 1989).

7. RCRLC, evidence of Eli Massy, cigarmaker, pp. 150-51.

8. See previous chapter.

9. It is not possible to determine the numbers of children in school in 1891 as no question concerning school attendance was asked that year.

10. In 1871, for example, 23 per cent of boys aged 13-16 were listed at school in Sainte Anne and Saint Jacques wards combined, compared with 43 per cent in Hamilton. For girls the figures were 29 and 49 respectively. Katz and Davey, "Youth and Early Industrialization," p. S93.

11. Louis Phillipe Audet, *Le Système scolaire de la Province de Québec* (Montréal, 1950), pp. 56-59.

12. L.A. Huguet-Latour, *L'Annuaire de Ville Marie: Origine, utilité et progrès des institutions catholiques de Montréal* (Montréal, 1877), pp. 142, 165-70; L'Institut de la Providence, *Histoire des Filles de la Charité, Servantes des Pauvres dites Soeurs de la Providence*, IV (Montréal, 1930), pp. 205-06.

13. Marie-Paule Malouin, "Les rapports entre l'école privée et l'école publique: l'Académie Marie-Rose au 19e siècle," in Nadia Fahmy-Eid et Michelene Dumont, eds., *Maîtresses de Maison, maîtresses d'école* (Montréal, 1983), p. 89.

14. *Ibid.*

15. *Ibid.*, p. 90; Québec, *Documents de la Session,* 1874, "Rapport du Ministre de l'instruction publique," p. vii; Marta Danylewycz, "Sexes et classes sociales dans l'enseignement: Le cas de Montréal à la fin du 19e siècle," in Fahmy-Eid et Dumont, eds., *Maîtresses de maison,* p. 102.

16. Bullen, "Hidden Workers."

17. NAC, MG28 I 129, Society for the Protection of Women and Children, Minutes, 11 June 1889.

18. "The Working of the Mills and Factories," p. 3; Bullen, "Hidden Workers," pp. 182-85.

19. A similar pattern is clear in Ontario. See Lorna Hurl, "Overcoming the Inevitable: Restricting Child Factory Labour in Late Nineteenth Century Ontario," *Labour/Le Travail,* 21 (Spring, 1988), p. 119.

20. "The Working of the Mills and Factories," p. 8.

21. Québec, Cap. XXXII, 48 Vict. 1885, pp. 57-71.

22. Québec, Cap. XLIX, 51-52 Vict. 1888, p. 151; John A. Dickinson, "La législation et les travailleurs québécois, 1894-1914," *Relations Industrielles,* 41, 2 (1986), pp. 357-80.

23. Even the figures collected by Lukes and Blackeby confirm that the labour

of such young children was limited to specific sectors and to a small proportion of children. Overall, in the 465 factories they visited in Ontario, the Maritimes, and Quebec, under 5 per cent of workers were below fifteen and well under 1 per cent were under ten. "The Working of the Mills and Factories," pp. 10-13.

24. "Report of Louis Guyon, Inspector of factories, Western District, Montreal," Quebec, *Sessional Papers,* No. 7, 1893, pp. 100-01.

25. *Child Welfare Exhibition Souvenir Handbook* (Montreal, 1912), p. 32. Terry Copp describes the continued presence of young wage-earners between 1896 and 1930. See Copp, *The Anatomy of Poverty.* As late as the 1940s Quebec children would continue to miss school or leave school early in order to contribute to the family income despite the passage of compulsory schooling legislation in 1943 and the Family Allowances available after 1945. See Jean, "Familles québécoises."

26. RCRLC, evidence of R.W. Eaton, manager, Merchants Cotton Manufacturing Co., p. 392.

27. RCRLC, "Appendices to Armstrong Report," cited in Gregory S. Kealey, *Canada Investigates Industrialism* (Toronto, 1973), p. 47.

28. RCRLC, evidence of Ferdinand Brisette, cigarmaker, p. 28.

29. RCRLC, anonymous evidence, p. 42.

30. RCRLC, evidence of Edouard Miron, cigarmaker, p. 30; anonymous evidence, p. 42; evidence of cigarmakers: George Robley, p. 48; Achille Dagnais, p. 26; Theophile Charron, p. 26.

31. "The Working of the Mills and Factories," p. 3.

32. RCRLC, "Appendices to the Freed Report," cited in Kealey, *Canada Investigates Industrialism,* p. 22.

33. RCRLC, evidence of J.M. Fortier, pp. 124-25; evidence of Charles J. Doherty, advocate, pp. 212-14; evidence of Alexander McGregor, foreman, Fortier's factory, pp. 98-99, 103; evidence of cigar manufacturers: A.H. Wood, p. 140; Ovide Grothe, p. 145.

34. "The Working of the Mills and Factories," p. 3.

35. David Russell, "Fines, Piece Work, Factory Morality, and Blackholes: Factory Discipline in Nineteenth Century Montreal," *The Register,* 3, 1 (March, 1982); E.P. Thompson, "Time, Work, Discipline, and Industrial Capitalism," *Past and Present,* 38 (1967).

36. RCRLC, evidence of William Gallagher, p. 685.

37. John C. Holley, "The Two Family Economies of Industrialism: Factory Workers in Victorian Scotland," *Journal of Family History,* 6 (Spring, 1981).

38. Caution has to be exercised when using reported jobs for women and children. There is a tendency now in some of the literature on the subject to suggest that gender differentials in work-force participation are largely a result of women's work not being enumerated. While I am sure that some

under-enumeration of women's work occurred in Montreal, as elsewhere, I don't think that under-enumeration can explain away the differential. Nor is the phenomenon easy to measure. More important, I think, was the nature of women's work, which, because of its lack of regularity and its more informal nature, was less likely to be reported. On the problem of under-reporting, see, in particular, Sally Alexander, "Women's Work in Nineteenth Century London: A Study of the Years 1820-1850," in Juliet Mitchell and Ann Oakley, eds., *The Rights and Wrongs of Women* (London, 1976), pp. 63-66; Karen Oppenheim Mason, Maris Vinovskis, and Tamara K. Hareven, "Women's Work and the Life Course in Essex County, Massachussetts, 1880," in Hareven, ed., *Transitions: The Family and the Life Course in Historical Perspective.* (New York, 1979), p. 191; Margo A. Conk, "Accuracy, efficiency and bias: The interpretation of women's work in the U.S. Census of Occupations, 1890-1940," *Historical Methods,* 14, 2 (Spring, 1981), pp. 65-72; Edward Higgs, "Women, Occupations and Work in the Nineteenth Century Censuses," *History Workshop,* 23 (Spring, 1987).

39. Sydney Pollard, *The Genesis of Modern Management: A Study of the Industrial Revolution in Great Britain* (London, 1965), p. 162.
40. "Report of the Montreal and District Factory Inspector," Quebec, *Sessional Papers,* 1893, No. 7, p. 107; "Report of the Commissioner of Agriculture," *ibid.*, 1891, pp. 128-29.
41. "Report of the Montreal and District Factory Inspector," 1893, no. 7, p. 100; Dennis Guest, *The Emergence of Social Security in Canada* (Vancouver, 1981), p. 42.
42. RCRLC, *Quebec evidence,* pp. 44-47; evidence of Georgina Loiselle, p. 91; evidence of George Robley, cigarmaker, p. 48.
43. RCRLC, evidence of Mrs. Levoise.
44. RCRLC, evidence of machinist, Hudon factory, Hochelaga, pp. 273-74; evidence of Adèle Lavoie, pp. 280-82.
45. "Select Committee on the Manufacturing Interests," pp. 61-63; RCRLC, *Quebec Evidence,* pp. 294, 439.
46. On the commissioners' concerns about this, see Susan Mann Trofimenkoff, "One Hundred and Two Muffled Voices: Canada's Industrial Women in the 1880's," *Atlantis,* 3, 1 (Fall, 1977). How the working class viewed these morality issues requires examination.
47. Pollard, *The Genesis of Modern Management,* pp. 162-66.
48. Mss. Census, St. Jacques, 1871, 6:137; St. Jacques, 1881, 12:101.
49. Canada, Parliament, *Sessional Papers,* 1896, Paper no. 61, "Report Upon the Sweating System in Canada," pp. 7-8; RCRLC, pp. 294-95; evidence of Hollis Shorley, clothier, p. 287.
50. RCRLC, evidence of *Montreal Daily Witness* journalist, pp. 603-04; evidence of Z. Lapierre, p. 439.

51. See, for example, "Select Committee on the Manufacturing Interests," 1874, p. 8; YWCA, "Annual Reports," 1880-84; Montreal House of Industry, "Annual Reports."

52. Girls placed by the YWCA in the early 1880s remained overwhelmingly in service jobs, but a few each year were placed as copyists or saleswomen. "Annual Reports," 1880-85.

53. Mercedes Steedman, "Skill and Gender in the Canadian Clothing Industry, 1890-1940," in Heron and Storey, eds., *On the Job,* pp. 153-76.

54. In 1871 domestic service was, after general day labouring, the second most important form of employment and accounted for around one-third of all female workers. Canada, *Census of 1871,* Table XIII, "Occupations of the People."

55. Claudette Lacelle, "Les domestiques dans les villes canadiennes au XIXe siècle: effectifs et conditions de vie," *Histoire sociale/Social History,* XV (May, 1982), pp. 185, 199.

56. Census instructions were sufficiently ambiguous to make it unclear whether parents or employers should report domestics on their schedule. "Instructions to Census Enumerators," pp. 127-28. Although girls from these families certainly did go and work elsewhere in the city as servants, it is impossible to measure this phenomenon accurately. It should not be forgotten that boys, too, went and worked elsewhere, in lumber camps and on railroad construction, for example, so that for children of both sexes what we see in these figures are those who remained at home with their parents. Had there been a massively unequal exodus of girls over boys, sex structures should have been distorted among the 15-20 age group. To the extent that they are, it is by female, not male, dominance.

Men and Women aged 15-20, Sainte Anne and Saint Jacques, 1861-1871

	Sainte Anne		Saint Jacques	
	Male	Female	Male	Female
1861	769	801	828	820
1871	815	934	815	934

Census of Canada, 1861, 1871.

57. Lacelle, "Les domestiques."

58. Lacelle, *Urban Domestic Servants* (Ottawa, 1987), p. 103.

59. Mss. Census, St. Jacques, 1861, fo. 8765.

60. Lacelle, "Les domestiques," p. 201. Conversion to dollars made from Hamelin and Roby, *Histoire Économique,* Appendix I; J.G. Snell, "The Cost of Living in Canada in 1870," *Histoire sociale/Social History,* 12 (May, 1979), pp. 189, 191.

61. Account Book, 1875-92, John T. Molson, McCord Museum, Molson Collection, "Flat Box."

62. Lina Madore, *Petit coin perdu,* 2nd edition (Rivière-du-Loup, 1979), pp.

80-81, cited in Denise Lemieux and Lucie Mercier, *Les Femmes au tournant du siècle, 1880-1940* (Ville Saint Laurent, 1989), p. 93.

63. Scott and Tilly, *Women, Work and Family*; Lynn Y. Weiner, *From Working Girl to Working Mother: The Female Labor Force in the United States, 1820-1980* (Chapel Hill and London, 1985).

64. Karl Marx, *Capital: A Critical Analysis of Capitalist Production* Vol. 1 (Moscow, 1956), p. 372.

65. Katz and Davey, "Youth and Early Industrialization," p. S94.

66. See note 47 above.

67. Frances Early cites the reaction of a French Canadian in Lowell, Massachusetts, whose pride was piqued whenever his wife earned money taking in laundry. "My wife had always been cared for by me and had never had to work for others," he explained. Early, "The French Canadian Family Economy and Standard of Living in Lowell, Massachusetts, 1870," *Journal of Family History,* 7 (1982), p. 183.

68. In Lynn Jamieson's study of working-class mothers and daughters in Scotland, which is based on interviews, she makes it clear that mothers made different demands upon boys and girls in terms of the contributions they should make to the family economy. Mothers "pre-occupied with their housekeeping responsibilities" were much more likely to keep girls home from school to help with housework than to encourage boys to go out and earn. If a father died, for example, daughters or sons might enter full-time paid employment, but if a mother died "only daughters left school early to become full-time housekeepers." Jamieson, "Working Class Mothers and Daughters in Scotland," in Jane Lewis, ed., *Labour and Love: Women's Experience of Home and Family, 1850-1940* (Oxford, 1986), pp. 54, 65.

69. Scott and Tilly, *Women, Work and Family,* p. 231.

70. Mss. Census, 1861, St. Jacques, 11:7750.

71. "Le problème des jeunes qui ne fréquentent plus l'école," *École Sociale Populaire,* 351 (avril, 1942), p. 26, cited by Jean, "Familles québécoises."

72. "First Report of Work Under the Children's Protection Act," p. 26; "Third Report of Work Under the Children's Protection Act," p. 10, cited in John Bullen, "J.J. Kelso and the 'New' Child-Savers: The Genesis of the Children's Aid Movement in Ontario," paper presented to the CHA annual meeting, Windsor, Ontario, June, 1988, pp. 35-38. See also Joy Parr, *Labouring Children: British Immigrant Apprentices to Canada, 1869-1924* (London, 1980), pp. 82-96.

73. RCRLC, evidence of Patrick Ryan, cigarmaker, p. 37; machinist, Hudon Mills, p. 271; Samuel Carsley, dry goods merchant, p. 15; Olivier David Benoit, boot and shoemaker, p. 365; Henry Morton, printer, p. 297; F. Stanley, foreman at the *Star,* p. 331.

74. Mss. Census, Ste. Anne, 1881, 5:1.

75. Mss. Census, Ste. Anne, 1881, 9:208.

76. Katz, *The People of Hamilton,* pp. 257-61.

77. Katz and Davey, "Youth and Early Industrialization," pp. 87-92. This pattern duplicates that found in such diverse parts of North America as Oneida County, New York, Hamilton, Orillia, and Peel County, Ontario, in fact, in virtually all areas where the issue has been addressed by historians. It was not simply economic, for it appears to transcend class boundaries. Mary P. Ryan, *The Cradle of the Middle Class: The Family in Oneida County, New York, 1790-1865* (New York, 1981), pp. 168-69; Gaffield and Levine, "Dependency and Adolescence on the Canadian Frontier," p. 44; Richard Wall, "The Age at Leaving Home," *Journal of Family History,* 8 (1983), p. 238; Harvey J. Graff, "Remaking Growing Up: Nineteenth-Century America," *Histoire sociale/Social History,* XXIV, 47 (May, 1991).

78. Here I am referring to the percentage of children at home as opposed to boarding, living with relatives, or living in someone else's house as a servant. The samples taken in each census do not allow me to follow children over time and identify those who actually left home.

79. Gary Cross and Peter Shergold discuss this trend among girls in the mid-1890s in "The Family Economy and the Market: Wages and Residence of Pennsylvania Women in the 1890's," *Journal of Family History,* 11, 3 (1986), pp. 248-49.

80. Paul Spagnoli, "Industrialization, Proletarianization and Marriage," *Journal of Family History,* 8 (Fall, 1983), p. 238.

81. Edward Shorter, *The Making of the Modern Family* (New York, 1975), pp. 259-60; Michael Mitterauer and Reinhard Seider, *The European Family: Patriarchy to Partnership from the Middle Ages to the Present* (Oxford, 1982), pp. 110-11.

82. Accampo, *Industrialization, Family Life,* pp. 109, 214.

83. Stansell, *City of Women,* p. 53.

84. "Lettre pastorale des Pères du Quatrième Concile Provincial de Québec," *Mandements, lettres pastorales, circulaires et autres documents publiques dans le Diocèse de Montréal depuis son éréction* (Montréal, 1887), Tome V, p. 326, for example.

85. ANQM, Judicial Archives, pre-archives, General Sessions of the Peace, 1871, Box 461. Alexander McGregor, manager of Mr. Fortier's cigar factory, argued that parents came "over and over again and threaten to hold us responsible if we did not make the apprentices tend to their work." RCRLC, pp. 103, 106. On these kind of struggles in New York in the early nineteenth century, see Stansell, *City of Women,* p. 54. Tensions are clearest in court cases and in the cases of parents sending their children to reform school. Yet read alone, in the absence of sources showing families resolving their problems in other ways, such sources lead to an over-conflictual view of family life. They err in the opposite direction of family historians who assume complementarity from census listings.

86. Michael Anderson's careful analysis of which children left home shows

that boys in Preston, Lancashire, were more likely to do so than girls. He believes children made "a conscious calculation of the advantages and disadvantages, in terms of the standard of living which they could enjoy," based on the wages they could make, their father's wage, and the amount they were required to hand over to their parents. Anderson, *Family Structure,* pp. 67, 127-29.

87. RCRLC, evidence of Mrs. Sarah Hardy, mother of cigarmakers, p. 208.

88. Tamara K. Hareven and Randolph Langenbach, *Amoskeag: Life and Work in an American Factory City* (New York, 1978), p. 239. There is no good reason to suppose that such a practice would have either increased with immigration to the States or increased over time. Indeed, the opposite is more likely. See also Hareven, *Family Time and Industrial Time,* p. 214.

89. RCRLC, *Quebec Evidence*; Udo Sautter, "The Origins of the Employment Service of Canada, 1900-1920," *Labour/Le Travailleur,* 6 (1980), p. 95; DeLottinville, "Joe Beef."

90. Draft letter in notebook, "Box," Walter H. Smith Collection, Rare Book Room, McGill University.

91. RCRLC, *Quebec Evidence,* pp. 380, 394, 128, 438, 407.

92. Hareven, *Family Time and Industrial Time,* pp. 90-101, 128-30.

93. Bullen, "Hidden Workers."

94. Some of the problems faced by feminist theoreticians grappling with the relationship of women's oppression by males within marriage, their subordination in the labour market, and the wider forces of patriarchy stem from the assumption that only wives perform domestic labour. This seems to me a profoundly ahistorical view that downplays the importance of the family as a place of socialization and training. See, for example, Sylvia Walby, who argues that the patriarchal mode of production includes "a producing class . . . composed of housewives . . . [and] a non-producing and exploiting class . . . composed of husbands." Walby, *Patriarchy at Work* (Minneapolis, 1986), pp. 52-53.

Chapter 5 Managing and Stretching Wages

1. Cited in Kealey and Palmer, *Dreaming of What Might Be,* pp. 318-20.

2. These men are articulating what appears to have been a common ideology among skilled working-class males in Canada, England, and the United States, who aimed to keep their wives at home in a ladylike manner. See Angela V. John, ed., *Unequal Opportunities: Women's Employment in England 1800-1918* (Oxford, 1986), p. 3; Jane Humphries, "The Working-Class Family, Women's Liberation and Class Struggle: The Case of Nineteenth-century British History," *Review of Radical Political Economics,* 9 (Fall, 1977), pp. 25-42; and especially Martha May, "Bread before Roses: American workingmen, labor unions and the family wage," in Ruth Milkman, ed., *Women, Work and Protest* (Boston, 1985), pp. 3-8.

3. Meg Luxton, *More than a Labour of Love: Three Generations of Women's Work in the Home* (Toronto, 1980), pp. 18-19; Pat and Hugh Armstrong, *The Double Ghetto* (Toronto, 1984), p. 67.

4. While for theoretical purposes it makes sense to divide up the components of domestic labour, many of the categories devised overlap so much in practice that it is difficult to treat them as distinct. A more useful definition for historians is suggested by Veronica Strong-Boag, "Keeping House in God's Country: Canadian Women at Work in the Home," in Heron and Storey, eds., *On the Job*, pp. 126-27.

5. Critiques of an overly simplistic use of these concepts have been growing over recent years. Among the most useful have been Susan Strasser, *Never Done: A History of American Housework* (New York, 1982); Linda K. Kerber, "Separate Spheres, Female Worlds, Woman's Place: The Rhetoric of Women's History," *Journal of American History*, 75 (June, 1988), pp. 28-36; and Mary P. Ryan, *Women in Public: Between Banners and Ballots, 1825-1880* (Baltimore and London, 1990).

6. Ellen Ross, "Labour and Love: Rediscovering London's Working-Class Mothers, 1870-1918," in Lewis, ed., *Labour and Love,* p. 78; Strong-Boag, "Keeping House," p. 129.

7. Ruth Schwartz Cowan, *More Work for Mother: The Ironies of Household Technology from the Open Hearth to the Microwave* (New York, 1983), pp. 63-68.

8. Ames, *The City Below the Hill,* pp. 7, 45, 85.

9. RCRLC, evidence of Dr. Dougless Decrow, p. 607.

10. Anon., *The Skilful Housewife's Guide: A Book of Domestic Cookery, compiled from the best Authors* (Montreal, 1848), p. 112; Lauren Oren, "The Welfare of Women in Labouring Families: England, 1860-1950," in Mary S. Hartman and Lois Banner, eds., *Clio's Consciousness Raised: New Perspectives on the History of Women* (New York, 1974), pp. 229-31.

11. Analysis of age, sex, and disease specific mortality rates in Montreal, 1879-82, based on the "Report Upon the Sanitary State," *MAR,* 1879-82; 1881 *Census of Canada.* I calculated the rates for these years so I could use the details on the age and sex of the population published in the census of 1881. For further details, see Bettina Bradbury, "The Working Class Family Economy: Montreal, 1861-1881" (Ph.D. thesis, Concordia University, 1984), p. 303.

12. The question of technological change in the home and its impact on the work of domestics is hardly considered in Lacelle's *Urban Domestic Servants.* However, see the cartoons on pages 101-02 for hints at mistresses' perception of their servants' ability to deal with "new fanglings."

13. Cooper, "The Social Structure"; ANQM, Notary Hugh Brody, *Inventaire après décès,* nos. 1067, 1136, 11 May 1868, 27 July 1868.

14. Carpenter, *On the Relative Value of Human Life,* p. 13.

15. *MAR,* 1867-91; Strasser, *Never Done,* pp. 86-87; cf. Cowan, *More Work*

for Mother, p. 86, who argues that in the cities even the poor had been provided with a water tap in the courtyard by the end of the century. This contrasts with the situation described by Susan J. Kleinberg, "Technology and Women's Work: The Lives of Working Class Women in Pittsburgh, 1870-1900," *Labor History,* 17 (Winter, 1976).

16. *MAR,* Annual Report of the Superintendent of the Aqueduct, 1897, p. xxii. The census of 1901 listed 36,503 dwellings in the city and 38,768 families. Table VII, pp. 114-16.

17. *MAR,* Mayor's Farewell Address, 1886, p. 8.

18. YWCA, *Annual Report,* 1880, p. 13; *MAR,* Report Upon the Sanitary State, 1886, p. 15.

19. *MAR,* Report Upon the Sanitary State, 1889.

20. RCRLC, evidence of George E. Muir, Assessor, City of Montreal, p. 262; *Montreal Daily Witness,* 8 December 1879, reports that twenty-one applications were submitted to the Water Committee that Saturday afternoon "on behalf of afflicted and indigent families in the East End for free water."

21. *MAR,* Report Upon the Sanitary State, 1890, p. 21; *ibid.*, 1886, p. 41.

22. ANQM, Notary Amable Archambault, *Inventaire des biens,* Act no. 3203, 30 July 1867.

23. On the process of washing, see Strasser, *Never Done,* pp. 104-09; Cowan, *More Work for Mother,* pp. 65, 85-89; *MAR,* Report Upon the Sanitary State, 1886, p. 13.

24. On sending out laundry, see S.A. Lortie, "Compositeur typographe de Québec en 1903," in Savard, ed., *Paysans et ouvriers Québécois d'autrefois,* p. 106; and on laundries: Denise Helly, "La promotion d'un secteur de service à Montréal: Les buandaries chinoises (1877-1923)," Rapport de recherche, Federal Ministry of Education, 1981; RCRLC, evidence of Thomas Henry Love, manager of the Montreal Steam Laundry, pp. 688-90.

25. Strasser, *Never Done,* p. 29. Such stoves were readily available in Montreal, as numerous local foundries produced them. They seem to have been adopted rapidly by women of all classes.

26. See, for example, *Montreal Daily Witness,* 15 December 1879; *Montreal Transcript,* 2 May 1862.

27. RCRLC, evidence of Thomas Gratorex, labourer, p. 87; Cross, "The Irish in Montreal," p. 202; "Report of the Select Committee to Investigate and Report Upon Alleged Combinations in Manufactures, Trade and Insurance in Canada," Canada, House of Commons, *Journals,* 1888, Appendix 3, p. 370, evidence of Thomas Workman.

28. Cross, "The Irish in Montreal," p. 202.

29. *Montreal Daily Star,* 24 December 1883, p. 4.

30. Cited in Huguette Lapointe-Roy, "Paupérisme et assistance sociale à Montréal, 1832-1865" (M.A. thesis, McGill University, 1972), p. 30.

31. See the complaint of C. Baillairge about a supper at a friend's place where

"the poultry did not arrive and finally Madame informed us that the poor girl had put the whole bird in to cook, that is without eviscerating it." C. Baillargé to the Reverent Sisters of the Ursuline Order at Quebec City, 29 March 1897, cited in Lacelle, *Urban Domestic Servants*, p. 160. On this domestic labour in the United States, see Strasser, *Never Done*, p. 29. Also see Anon., *The Skilful Housewife's Guide*, p. 112.

32. *MAR*, Report Upon the Sanitary State, 1883, pp. 49-50.

33. *Montreal Daily Witness*, April, 1873; *MAR*, Report of the Montreal Officer of Health, 1886, pp. 42-43.

34. RCRLC, evidence of Robert McCoy, p. 632; evidence of Stanislaus Paquette, joiner, p. 652.

35. Harvey, "'To Love, Honour and Obey.'"

36. *Montreal Star*, 15 July 1870.

37. ANQM, Judicial Archives, pre-archives, Box 503, 1879.

38. Loranger, *L'Incapacité légale*, pp. 13-14.

39. See, for example, Cholet vs. Duplessis *et vir.*, Superior Court, 28 February 1861, *The Lower Canada Jurist*, Vol. VI, p. 80 and Vol. VII, 1863, pp. 30-31.

40. ANQM, Judicial Archives, pre-archives, Box 495, 1878.

41. ANQM, Notary Amable Archambault, *Inventaire des biens*, Act. no. 3203, 30 July 1867.

42. On this type of buying in England, see Maud Pember Reeves, *Round About a Pound a Week* (1913; reprint, London, 1979), p. 104.

43. Walter H. Smith Collection. Rare Book Room, McGill University, "Cash-book."

44. English wives observed by Maud Pember Reeves reported doing their shopping "when the baby is asleep." *Round About a Pound*, pp. 108-09.

45. Letter to the editor, *Montreal Daily Witness*, 15 December 1879.

46. For a lively description of the noise such street deliverers made in late nineteenth-century Montreal, see Edgar Andrew Collard's column in *The Gazette*, 16 June 1988, p. B-2. The whole subject of retail trade in nineteenth-century Montreal, and of food in particular, requires studying. The late 1870s saw a battle between market-based butchers and those wishing to set up shops elsewhere in town. See the *Montreal Daily Witness*, December, 1879, for a running discussion of this issue. For a preliminary study of hawking and peddling in this period, see John Benson, "Hawking and Peddling in Canada, 1867-1914," *Histoire sociale/Social History*, XVIII, 35 (May, 1985), pp. 75-83. Peter Shergold reports that in Pittsburgh in 1913, 1,500 hucksters' wagons distributed and sold 30 per cent of the city's consumption of fruit and vegetables. *Working-Class Life: The "American Standard" in Comparative Perspective, 1899-1913*, p. 127.

47. Montreal City Archives, Committee of Markets, 1840-42, "By-Law of the Council of the City of Montreal," 22 May 1841. The question of pedlars

within and beyond the boundaries of Montreal continued to spark debate throughout the nineteenth century. See, for example, *Montreal Daily Witness*, 12 December 1879, on attempts by the municipal council of Saint Henri to deal with pedlars.

48. Benson, "Hawking and Peddling in Canada," p. 77; Bliss, *A Living Profit,* pp. 33-35.

49. Such cases abound in the judicial archives. See, for instance, Widow Julia Weir, commercante, charged with selling "by retail, beer to wit, one bottle of beer." ANQM, Judicial Archives, 1874, Box 572; Euladie Bourdeau, commerçante, widow of Louis Laroche, charged with selling "whiskey, savoir une chopine de whisky," 1874, Box 129.

50. RCRLC, evidence of F.E. Grafton, p. 234; ANQM, Judicial Archives, pre-archives, Box 466, General Sessions of the Peace, "Selling Alcohol Without a License." Each year numerous cases were heard against merchants, traders, grocers, and private citizens, men and women alike, who sold alcohol in small amounts without a licence.

51. RCRLC, evidence of Stedman A. Lebourreau, Law and Order League, pp. 299-301.

52. Anon, *The Skilful Housewife's Guide;* Anon., "La vaccination à Montréal," *L'Union medicale du Canada,* Vol. 3, 9 (September, 1874), p. 419, cited in Martin Tetreault, "L'Etat de santé des Montréalais de 1880-1914" (M.A. thesis, Université de Montréal, 1979), p. 116.

53. RCRLC, evidence of Charles Lacaille, grocer, p. 87; Lapointe-Roy, "Paupérisme et assistance sociale," pp. 37-44.

54. J.I. Desroches, *Traité élémentaire d'hygiène privée* (Montréal, 1888), p. 132, cited in Tetreault, "L'Etat de santé," p. 116.

55. *MAR,* Report Upon the Sanitary State, 1882 in *MAR,* 1883, p. 62; 1879, p. 19; RCRLC, evidence of John Baker Edwards, pp. 664-66.

56. On early nineteenth-century agriculture in the parish of Montreal, see Jean-Claude Robert, "Activités agricoles et urbanisation dans la paroisse de Montréal, 1820-1840," in Francois Lebrun et Normand Seguin, *Sociétés villageoises et rapports villes-campagnes au Québec et dans la France de l'Ouest, XVIIe-XXe siècles* (Actes du colloque Franco-Québécois de Québec, 1985), pp. 91-100. On the importance of gardening for the wealthy, see, for instance, the correspondence between Bernie Harrington and Anna Dawson, 1877 (MG 1022, McGill Archives).

57. See, for instance, *Montreal Daily Witness,* 8 December 1879, p. 6; and advertisements of seeds for sale in the spring months.

58. *Montreal Daily Witness,* 16 September 1868; *Post,* 13 August 1881.

59. Cooper, "The Social Structure of Montreal in the 1850's," p. 68.

60. *Montreal Daily Witness,* letter to the editor, 4 January 1869.

61. Georges Grenier, *Quelques considerations sur les causes de la mortalité des enfants contenant des conseils aux mères sur les soins à donner aux enfants* (Montréal, 1871), pp. 32-47.

62. Cited by Edgar Andrew Collard in his column in *The Gazette*, 27 February 1988.

63. For more details on the keeping of cows, pigs, and other animals, as well as of the laws curtailing it, see Bettina Bradbury, "Pigs, Cows and Boarders: Non-wage forms of survival, Montreal, 1861-1891," *Labour/Le Travail*, 14 (Fall, 1984). See, for example, the advertisement in the *Montreal Transcript*, 3 May 1862: "Two bulls, Ayshire and Devonshire breed – for the Service of Cows, $1.00 each."

64. Poultry were not counted until 1891, when over 8,000 fowl were listed for Montreal.

65. Mss. Census, Ste. Anne, 1861, fo. 2076.

66. *Le Courier de Montréal,* 16 December 1874.

67. Retail prices are taken from *Le Courier de Montréal,* 11 November 1874; and Hamelin et Roby, *Histoire Économique,* Appendix 20. Wages are from "Select Committee on the Manufacturing Interests," Appendix 3.

68. Great Britain, Parliamentary Papers (Commons), "First Report . . . [on] the Condition of the Poorer Classes in Ireland," Appendix D, pp. 89-90, 108-11, cited in Lees, *Exiles of Erin,* p. 107; Gauldrée-Boileau, "Paysan de Saint-Irénée en 1861 et 1862," pp. 31-32.

69. Montreal City By-Laws, Nos. 43, 77, 223, 105; *Montreal Daily Witness,* 22 September 1874.

70. Residents in Saint Henri, for example, were much more likely to keep pigs than Montrealers. See Lauzon, *Habitat ouvrier,* p. 124. In the municipality of Saint Louis du Mile-End, to the north of Montreal, a 1907 by-law explicitly allowed people to raise not more than two pigs for their own use or that of their family as long the premises were cleaned at least twice a week. Ville de St. Louis, Comté d'Hochelaga, Reglement No. 14. My thanks to Sylvie Taschereau for this reference.

71. Anon., *The Skilful Housewife's Guide.*

72. RCRLC, *Quebec Evidence,* pp. 710.

73. The published censuses list the following details:

	Bakeries	Workers	*Value of* *bread produced*
1871	56	339	$1,162,656
1881	57	397	$1,265,358
1891	51	379	$1,057,896

74. RCRLC, 1889, evidence of Edward Pole, pp. 597-99. For more detail on the transformation of production in the baking trade, see Ian McKay, "Capital and Labour," *Labour/Le Travailleur,* 3 (1978).

75. See, for example, advertisements in the *Montreal Daily Witness,* 8 December 1879, p. 5, by pawnbrokers listing sales of unredeemed pledges that include jewellery, clothes, furs, robes, overcoats, new and second-hand clothing, etc.

76. "Report on the Manufacturing Interests," p. 35; R.P. Sparks, "The Garment and Clothing Industries, History and Organization," *Manual of the Textile Industry of Canada,* 1930, cited in Michèle Payette-Daoust, "The Montreal Garment Industry, 1871-1901" (M.A. thesis, McGill University, 1987), p. 55.

77. Women appearing in court claiming that their husbands had failed to provide frequently used this term to describe this kind of casual employment. ANQM, Judicial Archives, pre-archives, 1878, Box 497; 1876, Box 487.

78. Register, École Mt. St. Antoine, 1866.

79. G.G. Baillarge to Braun, Secretary of Public Works, 11 February 1878, NAC, RG 11 B1(a), Vol. 573, pp. 2581-82.

80. Christine Stansell, "Women, Children and the Uses of the Streets: Class and Gender Conflict in New York City, 1850-1860," *Feminist Studies,* 8, 2 (Summer, 1982), p. 316.

81. *Montreal Transcript,* 27 May 1862; *La Minerve,* 18 mars 1879; *Montreal Daily Witness,* 6 December 1879, 27 December 1879.

82. Mss. Census, Ste. Anne, 1861, fo. 1248, fo. 2402.

83. On the question of under-enumeration, see Sally Alexander, "Women's Work in Nineteenth Century London: A Study of the Years 1820-1850," in Juliet Mitchell and Ann Oakley, eds., *The Rights and Wrongs of Women* (Harmondsworth, 1976), pp. 63-66; Mason, Vinovskis, and Hareven, "Women's Work," p. 191; Edward Higgs, "Women, Occupations and Work in the Nineteenth Century Censuses," *History Workshop,* 23 (Spring, 1987), pp. 59-80.

84. "Instructions to Officers," Canada, *Sessional Papers,* 1872, p. 134.

85. Here the situation is very different from that found in the mill towns of New England, for example, where finding enough workers was a constant problem and, as a result, rates of employment for married women appear to have been around 12 per cent among French Canadians. Judith A. McGaw, "'A Good Place to Work'. Industrial Workers and Occupational Choice: The Case of Berkshire Women," *Journal of Interdisciplinary History,* 10 (Autumn, 1979), p. 240; Hareven, *Family Time and Industrial Time,* p. 198; Mason, Vinovskis, and Hareven, "Women's Work," p. 197. English cotton and knitting towns were different, too, especially the latter, where opportunities for home-based labour continued to be important during this period. See Sonya Rose, "Proto-Industry, Women's Work and the Household Economy in the Transition to Industrial Capitalism," *Journal of Family History,* 13, 2 (1988), pp. 181-94.

86. Mss. Census, 1891, Ste. Anne, c:13, No. 42.

87. Tamara Hareven, in *Family Time and Industrial Time,* makes this argument in discussing the families of Manchester, New Hampshire, in 1900. In different towns with similar economic structures, on the other hand, historians report particularly low rates of involvement among French-Canadian wives. Frances Early, "The French-Canadian Family Economy and

Standard of Living in Lowell, Massachusetts," *Journal of Family History,* 7 (Summer, 1982), p. 183; McGaw, "'A Good Place to Work,'" p. 240. Hareven, writing with Mason and Vinovskis, reports in another study that economic rather than cultural factors seem to explain any high rates of employment of married women. "Women's Work," p. 209. Clearly the structure of work available in the neighbourhood is of crucial importance here.

88. Hareven, *Family Time and Industrial Time,* p. 202.

89. Hareven and Langenbach, *Amoskeag,* p. 255.

90. Men's attitudes toward their wives working outside the home were not homogeneous. Ambiguities and personal differences are clear in the interviews Denyse Baillargeon conducted with women living in working-class areas of Montreal during the 1930s. "Travail domestique et crise économique: les ménagères montréalaises durant la crise des années trente" (Ph.D. thesis, Université de Montréal, 1990), pp. 266-86.

91. Early, "The French-Canadian Family Economy," p. 183. Pat Ayers and Jan Lambertz examine interesting aspects of how women avoided letting their husbands know that their wages needed to be supplemented in early twentieth-century Liverpool in "Marriage Relations, Money, and Domestic Violence in Working-Class Liverpool, 1919-39," in Lewis, ed., *Labour and Love,* pp. 195-219.

92. Bradbury, "The Working Class Family Economy," p. 331.

93. Cross, "The Neglected Majority," pp. 74-75.

94. YMCA, Montreal, *Annual Report,* 1886, p. 26; 1888, p. 25.

95. Micheline Dumont describes the *salles d'asile* run by the Grey Nuns, focusing on the period between 1859 and 1869, in "Des garderies au 19e siècle: les salles d'asile des soeurs Grises à Montréal," in Fahmy-Eid et Dumont, *Maîtresses de maison,* pp. 261-85; Cross, "The Neglected Majority," p. 76; ASP, "Notes pour les chroniques de l'Asile Saint Vincent," pp. 79-80.

96. YMCA, Montreal, *Annual Report,* 1886, pp. 26-27.

97. "Les premières salles d'asiles et les premières crêches au Canada," in *Journal de l'Instruction publique,* 11, 10 (octobre, 1858), pp. 184-85, cited in Dumont, "Des garderies," p. 264.

98. Mss. Census, St. Jacques, 1861, fo. 7429.

99. "Annual Report of the Montreal Immigrant Agent," Canada, *Sessional Papers,* 1882, paper no. 14, Appendix 3.

100. Groneman, "'She Earns as a Child; She Pays as a Man'" p. 89.

101. John Modell and Tamara Hareven, "Urbanization and the Malleable Household: An Examination of Boarding and Lodging in American Families," *Journal of Marriage and the Family,* 35 (August, 1973), p. 476; Katz, *The People of Hamilton,* p. 244.

102. Modell and Hareven, "Urbanization," p. 476.

103. RCRLC, evidence of Dr. Dougless Decrow, pp. 606-09.
104. "Instructions," Canada, *Sessional Papers,* no. 64, 1871, p. 122.
105. ANQM, Judicial Archives, pre-archives, Court of Special Sessions, Box 477, 8 July 1875, Catherine Farrell vs. Michael Hughes.
106. ANQM, Judicial Archives, pre-archives, 1878, Box 497.
107. RCRLC, *Quebec Evidence,* p. 606.
108. ANQM, Judicial Archives, pre-archives, 1878, Box 497. My translation of the evidence, all of which was given in French, except that of Janvier's wife.
109. Jane Humphreys, "Class Struggle and the Persistence of the Working-Class Family," *Cambridge Journal of Economics,* 1, 3 (1977); Jane Humphreys, "The Working Class Family, Women's Liberation, and Class Struggle: The Case of Nineteenth Century British History," *Review of Radical Political Economics,* 9 (Autumn, 1977). This argument has been much criticized. Its great advantage is that it recognizes the mutual dependency of working-class men and women.
110. "The Working of the Mills and Factories," 1882, p. 4.

Chapter 6 Managing without a Spouse

1. Stansell, *City of Women,* p. 44.
2. Bischoff, "La formation des traditions," and "Tensions et solidarité."
3. Linda Gordon, *Heroes of their Own Lives: The Politics and History of Family Violence* (New York, 1988), p. 91.
4. Random samples, Ste. Anne and St. Jacques, 1891, all widows and widowers with co-resident children of any age, and all men and women listed as married with children of any age living with them. These are gross estimates only.
5. These figures are based on the transcription of all widows and widowers from the manuscript censuses. The figures in the published census are lower: 2,674 widows and 974 widowers.
6. See Bettina Bradbury, "Surviving as a Widow in 19th-Century Montreal," *Urban History Review,* XVII, 3 (February, 1989), p. 150.
7. The possibility that large numbers of widows migrated to the city seeking the advantages that the labour market and large numbers of charitable institutions offered also requires further examination. Differential death rates explain no more than a third of the difference after age forty and none before.
8. See Suzanne Cross's classic on this, "The Neglected Majority," p. 69.
9. Bradbury, "Surviving as a Widow," p. 150.
10. Francois Olivier-Martin, *Histoire de la Coutume,* pp. 275-76.
11. For a general reflection on the kinds of constraints operating on a widow's

freedom surrounding her dower in France, see Michele Bordeaux, "Droit et femmes seules. Les pièges de la discrimination," in Farge et Klapisch-Zuber, eds., *Madame ou Mademoiselle?*, pp. 31-41.

12. Article 247, Civil Code, cited in Doucet, *Fundamental Principles.*

13. *Ibid.*, Article 168.

14. L.A. Huguet-Latour, *L'Annuaire de Ville Marie* (Montréal, 1863), pp. 105-07, 113-14.

15. *Montreal Directory for 1870-71* (Montreal, 1871), p. 510; Young, *In Its Corporate Capacity*, pp. 24, 121, 157.

16. Quebec, *Statutes,* 33 Vict. 1870, Cap. LVII, Cap. LVIII.

17. Montreal Minutes, 3 October 1868.

18. Montreal Minutes, 26 October 1875, 13 January 1876, 7 March 1873. See also *MAR,* Annual Report of the Chief of Police, 1888, p. 6, on the later organization of an insurance scheme.

19. RCRLC, Freed Report, cited in Kealey, *Canada Investigates,* p. 17.

20. Research is needed on who used insurance companies in their early years, how much they paid, and what the benefits were.

21. Quebec, *Statutes,* 49-50 Vict. 1886, Cap. XCVIII, p. 372.

22. Harvey, "'To Love, Honour and Obey.'"

23. A useful comparison of Quebec's civil law on this question prior to the codification of 1865 and after, as well as to the sections drawn from the Napoleonic code, may be found in the *Deuxième rapport des commissaires chargés de codifier les lois du Bas Canada en matières civiles* (Québec, 1865), pp. 189-97.

24. *Ibid.*, pp.193-95.

25. Quebec, *Statutes,* 39 Vict. Cap. XXIV, assented to 24 December 1875.

26. *Deuxième rapport des commissaires,* pp. 191-95.

27. Later, in the first decade of the twentieth century, historian James Snell has found that there were only 117 cases of separation of bed and board for the whole province of Quebec. Furthermore, they diminished over subsequent decades. What is most interesting about his findings is that in contrast to divorce proceedings in other provinces, women in Quebec were ten times more likely than men to sue for such separations. Personal communication, James Snell.

28. ANQM, Judicial Archives, pre-archives, Queen's Bench, 4 September 1878, Box 499; *ibid.*, 9 September 1878, Box 498.

29. ANQM, Box 503, 1879.

30. Canada, *Statutes,* 32-33 Vict. Cap XX, 1869, #25.

31. The thirty-five cases reported here were found by searching the boxes of all criminal court cases, located in the pre-archiving section of the ANQM. It is quite possible that other cases were mixed up in boxes misfiled elsewhere, and some cases that began in or passed to other courts could be located elsewhere. As the state of the Archives makes this difficult to

determine at the moment, I have opted for a largely impressionistic reading of the cases found. My thanks to Kathryn Harvey for locating them and making them available to me.

32. Harvey, "'To Love, Honour and Obey,'" M.A. thesis, pp. 85-87

33. ANQM, Judicial Archives, pre-archives, Box 503, 7 September 1879.

34. *Ibid,* Box 497, 15 April 1878.

35. *Ibid.*, Box 503, 9 August 1879. See also Box 497, 15 April 1878.

36. *Ibid.*, 21-22 March 1878. Dismissed 26 March for insufficient proof.

37. *Ibid.*, Box 497, 8 April 1878, Queen vs. Pierre Beaudoin.

38. Constance Backhouse, "Married Women's Property Law in Nineteenth-Century Canada," in Bradbury, ed., *Canadian Family History,* pp. 325-29.

39. James Snell reports that in Ontario – but in no other provinces – a Deserted Wives' Maintenance Act was first passed in 1888. "'The White Life for Two': The Defence of Marriage and Sexual Morality in Canada, 1890-1914," *Histoire sociale/Social History,* XVI, 31 (May, 1983), pp. 122-23. The cases discussed above suggest that before this was written explicitly into criminal legislation, some men were being forced to provide in Quebec, even when the life or safety of spouse and offspring were not clearly in danger. Certainly the Civil Code obliged them to do so.

40. In rural areas, where the possibility of finding alternatives to a wife may have been fewer, male and female remarriage rates appear to have been much more equal. See Daniel Gauvreau and Mario Bourque, "Jusqu'à ce que la mort nous sépare: Le destin des femmes et des hommes mariés au Saguenay avant 1930," *Canadian Historical Review,* LXXI, 4 (December, 1990), pp. 441-61.

41. I have not systematically sought bigamy cases in the judicial records. A careful search of the cases for 1870 and 1871 revealed three cases, two where the man had remarried, one where it was the woman. Box 461, Queen vs. Francois Dandurand; Queen vs. Philomène Dery; Recognisance for Amedée Fontaine dit Bienvenue, 16 January 1871.

42. Mss. Census, 1891, Ste. Anne, c:7, #86.

43. *Ibid.*, c:19, #108.

44. Olwen Hufton argues that in the eighteenth century the "critical question was whether her efforts, reinforced by those of her children, her family and his family, could be extended to make good the labour occasioned by his death." Hufton, "Women without Men: Widows and Spinsters in Britain and France in the Eighteenth Century," *Journal of Family History,* 9 (Winter, 1984), pp. 364-65. In nineteenth-century cities, in contrast, money was the crucial factor.

45. ANQM, Jucidicial Archives, pre-archives, boxes for 1870-75.

46. *Ibid.*, Box 497, 8 April 1878.

47. Mss. Census, 1891, Ste. Anne, c:17, #73.

48. Mss. Census, 1891, Ste. Anne, c:18, #48.

49. ANQM, Notary Edward McInstosh, marriage contract between Touissant Guilbeaut and Victoire Clement, 7 January 1871, #12553, birth, death, and marriage registers.

50. Mss. Census, 1861, Ste. Anne, fo. 1446, fo. 1662.

51. *Ibid.*, 1891, Ste. Anne, c:10, #285.

52. RCRLC, evidence of Thomas Henry Love, manager, Montreal Steam Laundry, p. 690.

53. "Joe's Advice to Biddy, the Washerwoman," *La Minerve,* 7 November 1873, cited in DeLottinville, "Joe Beef," p. 17.

54. Claudette Lacelle gives the proportion of domestics in 1871 who lived in for Halifax (78 per cent), Quebec City (69 per cent), Toronto (60 per cent), but does not give a figure for Montreal. Of those living in Saint Antoine ward, 3.7 per cent were widows. It seems likely that widows would have been much more important among day servants, which unfortunately she does not discuss. Lacelle, *Urban Domestic Servants,* pp. 73-74

55. On the conditions of live-in servants, see *ibid.*, pp. 105-24.

56. Henry des Rivières Beaubien, *Traité sur les Lois Civiles du Bas-Canada* (Montréal, 1832), pp. 38-39; *Deuxième des commissaires,* p. 294.

57. RCRLC, *Quebec Evidence,* p.74.

58. "The Working of the Mills and Factories," p. 2.

59. RCRLC, evidence of S. Carsley, dry goods merchant, p. 18.

60. ANQM, Judicial Archives, pre-archives, The Queen vs. Robert Brownley, Court of Queen's Bench, Montreal, Box 472, 1874.

61. Mary E. Richmond and Fred S. Hall, *A Study of Nine Hundred and Eighty-Five Widows Known to Certain Charity Organization Societies in 1910* (1913; reprint, New York, 1974), gives many descriptions of men raising money for their workmates' widows.

62. ANQM, Judicial Archives, pre-archives, The Queen vs. David James Spence, Court of Queen's Bench, March, 1878, petition.

63. *Ibid.*, The Queen vs. Michael Hoey, Court of Quarter Sessions, September, 1873, petition of Catherine Morgan. See also petition of Widow Lyons, 1872, Box 465.

64. Hufton, "Women without Men"; Tamara K. Hareven and Louise A. Tilly, "Solitary Women and Family Mediation in American and French Textile Cities," *Annales de démographie historique* (1981).

65. It is possible that this increase simply reflects better reporting in the later censuses. I don't think so. It corresponds too neatly to the expansion of industry in Montreal and to a decline in newspaper comments about roving gangs of young adults. Furthermore, the fact that the proportions remain fairly stable, even fall in the 1881 census, a period of relative depression, suggests that even allowing for under-enumeration, especially of girls' work, the census figures are capturing a reality – the formalization of children's work and of the labour market itself.

66. ANQM, Judicial Archives, pre-archives, GSOP, Box 461, 26 January 1871.
67. ANQM, Judicial Archives, pre-archives, Box, 469, 3 January 1873.
68. The apprenticeship contracts signed before Montreal notaries in the 1820s, filed at the Montreal History Group, McGill University, bear witness to the importance of this strategy for widows. Joanne Burgess reports that around one-quarter of the boys who were apprenticed in the leather trades in Montreal beween 1790 and 1829 were the offspring of widows or abandoned mothers. Burgess, "Work, Family and Community," p. 64.
69. Raw data collected by Sherry Olson and David Hanna, Geography Department, McGill University. For a discussion of this data, see Sherry Olson, "The tip of the iceberg: scope and progress of research on the sharing of social space in nineteenth-century Montreal with Bibliography," *Shared Spaces/Partage de l'espace,* McGill University, No. 5 (June, 1986).
70. Mss. Census, 1891, Ste. Anne, c:4, #122; c:9, #407.
71. *Ibid.*, 1861, fo. 3160.
72. Hufton, "Women without Men," p. 360.
73. See Bradbury, "Pigs, Cows and Boarders."
74. On similar strategies in New York, see Stansell, "Women, Children, and the Uses of the Streets."
75. "Register," École Mont Saint Antoine, École des métiers de Montréal; ANQM, Judicial Archives, pre-archives, 1869-79.
76. The most important Catholic institutions are described in Huguet-Latour, *L'Annuaire de Ville Marie.* The Hôpital Général took in an average of twenty-nine Irish and forty-two French-Canadian boys and girls a year between 1831 and 1871.
77. Janice Harvey, "Upper Class Reaction to Poverty in Mid-Nineteenth Century Montreal: A Protestant Example" (M.A. thesis, McGill University, 1978), pp. 141, 96.
78. Bettina Bradbury, "The Fragmented Family: Family Strategies in the Face of Death, Illness, and Poverty, Montreal, 1860-1885," in Joy Parr, ed., *Childhood and Family in Canadian History* (Toronto, 1982).
79. Katharine Anthony, *Mothers Who Must Earn* (New York, 1914), p. 153, and Richmond and Hall, *A Study of Nine Hundred and Eighty-Five Widows,* p. 45, cited in Joyce D. Goodfriend, "The Struggle for Survival: Widows in Denver, 1880-1912," in Arlene Scadron, ed., *On Their Own: Widows and Widowhood in the American Southwest, 1848-1939* (Urbana and Chicago, 1988), p. 192.
80. Huguette Lapointe-Roy interprets the fact that the Grey Nuns made parents sign a paper renouncing their rights to their children so that such abuses could be avoided as evidence of the Nuns acting to protect unhappy children long before legislation existed in this domain. Such an interpretation seems to gloss rather too quickly over the economic

challenges that many families faced. Lapointe-Roy, *Charité bien ordonnée,* p. 157.

81. "Rapport des années 1871-72, Ecole du Bon Pasteur," Quebec, *Documents de la Session,* no. 23, 1875.

82. ANQM, Judicial Archives, pre-archives, Court of Queen's Bench, 1874, Box 472, petition.

83. Anderson, *Family Structure.*

84. ANQM, Judicial Archives, pre-archives, General Sessions of the Peace, 3 June 1879, Box 501; 19 May 1879, Box 464.

85. *Ibid.,* Queen vs. Richard Jaap, Box 484, 6 November 1876; Box 485, 31 January 1878.

86. Lapointe-Roy, *Charité bien ordonnée,* p. 265. This is suggested in the discourse on poverty. Often, elderly unmarried women were even more in need of most forms of charity because they did not have children to care for them. Certainly there were disproportionate numbers in the hospices and *asiles* of the city. Bradbury, "Mourir chretiennement. La vie et la mort dans les établissements Catholiques pour personnes âgées à Montréal au XIXe siècle," *RHAF,* 46, 1 (Summer, 1992), pp. 154-55.

87. The Bureau de Charité run by the Sulpicians was aimed at lone women and women heading families, widows in particular. Care of elderly and sick women was the initial focus of Émilie Gamelin even before the foundation of the Sisters of Providence. They continued to help widows across the nineteenth century, in their *asile* and by visiting them in their homes. The Grey Nuns also received large numbers of widows at the Hôpital Général. After the re-establishment of the Ladies Benevolent Society in 1832 widows with small children and others who because of age or infirmity could not procure their subsistence were the targeted clients. For descriptions of the Catholic charities, see Lapointe-Roy, *Charité bien ordonnée,* pp. 248-68. On Protestant charities, see Harvey, "Upper Class Reaction."

88. During the 1880s the Sisters of Providence visited anywhere between 3,839 and 22,400 sick people in their homes annually and distributed between 2,409 and 4,587 meals. The nurse from the Montreal Diet Dispensary visited 2,000-3,000 sick families in the same period. The diet dispensary of the YWCA gave out over 400 free orders of food in 1881. By 1885 they were providing over 1,713 free orders. YWCA, *Annual Reports,* 1881-85. Thousands more received aid from the Grey Nuns, the Saint Vincent de Paul society, and other charitable organizations within the city.

89. "Chroniques de l'Asile St. Vincent," 1879, ASP; my translation.

90. *Montreal Daily Witness,* 22 December 1879.

91. YWCA, Montreal Branch, *Annual Report,* 1880, pp. 14-15; 1881, p. 15.

92. Protestant House of Industry, *Annual Reports,* 1872-75.

93. Protestant Home for Friendless Women, *Second Annual Report* (Montreal, 1877), p. 6.

94. Bradbury, "Mourir chrétiennement."
95. Cited in Kealey and Palmer, *Dreaming of What Might Be*, p. 319.

Conclusion

1. Karl Marx, *Capital: A Critical Analysis of Capitalist Production*, Vol. I (Moscow, 1956), p. 372.
2. Neil Smelser, *Social Change in the Industrial Revolution: An Application of Theory to the Lancashire Cotton Industry, 1770-1840* (London, 1959); Anderson, *Family Structure*; Thomas Dublin, *Women at Work: The Transformation of Work and Community in Lowell, Massachusetts, 1826-1860* (New York, 1979); Hareven, *Family Time and Industrial Time.*
3. Lorna Hurl, "Overcoming the Inevitable: Restricting Child Factory Labour in Late Nineteenth Century Ontario," *Labour/Le Travail*, 21 (Spring, 1988); Jean, "Familles Québécoises et politiques sociales"; Neil Sutherland, "'We always had things to do': The Paid and Unpaid Work of Anglophone Children Between the 1920s and the 1960s," *Labour/Le Travail*, 25 (Spring, 1990).
4. Ward, *Courtship, Love, and Marriage*, p. 176.
5. Tilly, "The Family Wage Economy," pp. 383, 389-90; Anderson, *Family Structure*; Katz, *The People of Hamilton*, pp. 297-303.
6. Anderson, *Family Structure*, p. 49; Foster, *Class Struggle*, p. 97.
7. Gagan, *Hopeful Travellers*, p. 63; Modell and Hareven, "Urbanization and the Malleable Household."
8. Katz and Davey, "Youth and Early Industrialization," p. S107.

Index

302

THE CANADIAN SOCIAL HISTORY SERIES

Terry Copp,
*The Anatomy of Poverty: The Condition
of the Working Class in Montreal
1897-1929,* 1974.

Alison Prentice,
*The School Promoters: Education and
Social Class in Mid-Nineteenth Century
Upper Canada,* 1977.

John Herd Thompson,
*The Harvests of War: The Prairie West,
1914-1918,* 1978.

Joy Parr, Editor,
*Childhood and Family in Canadian
History,* 1982.

**Alison Prentice and Susan Mann
Trofimenkoff, Editors,**
*The Neglected Majority: Essays in
Canadian Women's History, Volume 2,*
1985.

Ruth Roach Pierson,
*"They're Still Women After All": The
Second World War and Canadian
Womanhood,* 1986.

Bryan D. Palmer,
*The Character of Class Struggle: Essays
in Canadian Working Class History,
1850-1985,* 1986.

Alan Metcalfe,
*Canada Learns to Play: The Emergence
of Organized Sport, 1807-1914,* 1987.

Marta Danylewycz,
*Taking the Veil: An Alternative to
Marriage, Motherhood, and
Spinsterhood in Quebec, 1840-1920,*
1987.

Craig Heron,
*Working in Steel: The Early Years in
Canada, 1883-1935,* 1988.

**Wendy Mitchinson and Janice Dickin
McGinnis, Editors,**
*Essays in the History of Canadian
Medicine,* 1988.

Joan Sangster,
*Dreams of Equality: Women on the
Canadian Left, 1920-1950,* 1989.

Angus McLaren,
*Our Own Master Race: Eugenics in
Canada, 1885-1945,* 1990.

Bruno Ramirez,
*On the Move: French-Canadian and
Italian Migrants in the North Atlantic
Economy, 1860-1914,* 1991.

Mariana Valverde,
*"The Age of Light, Soap, and Water":
Moral Reform in English Canada,
1885-1925,* 1991.

Bettina Bradbury
*Working Families: Age, Gender, and
Daily Survival in Industrializing
Montreal,* 1993.

Andrée Lévesque
*Making and Breaking the Rules: Women
in Quebec, 1919-1939,* 1994.

Cecilia Danysk
*Hired Hands: Labour and the
Development of Prairie Agriculture,
1880-1930,* 1995.